NEVER TELL OUR BUSINESS
TO STRANGERS

Villard Books
New York

NEVER TELL OUR BUSINESS

TO STRANGERS

. . .

a memoir

. . .

JENNIFER MASCIA

To Eleanor and Johnny,
for refusing to live a normal life

Lady Bracknell: Are your parents living?

Jack Worthing: I have lost both my parents.

Lady Bracknell: To lose one parent, Mr. Worthing,
may be regarded as a misfortune;
to lose both looks like carelessness.

—*Oscar Wilde,*
THE IMPORTANCE OF BEING EARNEST

NEVER TELL OUR BUSINESS TO STRANGERS

I F I HAD MY WAY, THIS IS HOW MY LIFE WOULD BE:

I'd sleep in, as usual, because my workday starts at 4:30 P.M. When I finally stirred, around noon, I'd check my phone and see that I've already missed two calls from the same number. I'd call my mother, and make plans for Sunday dinner with my parents at their apartment, just over the Verrazano Bridge in Staten Island, starring The Sauce: a cooperative effort involving tomato paste, meatballs, sausage, and a large sheet of pork fat for flavoring. Accompanying The Sauce would be a tomato, onion, garlic, and olive oil salad (no lettuce) in one of their good blue Arabia ware pasta bowls from Finland. I detested this tomato and onion salad (no lettuce!), but I'd make use of it anyway, as the tomato-and-onion-infused olive oil was especially good for dipping the soft, warm Italian bread they'd heated up in the oven.

As I sipped my wine I'd be force-fed a curious cocktail of my mother's kvetching over every inch of my life, her concern regarding my admittedly shady paramours, her contention that I am not nearly ambitious enough (true), and, as a confusing chaser, beaming pride that her only child lives in "the city," has a good job, has been published in the Newspaper of Record, and supports herself (as I probably wouldn't have bothered them for money).

My father would attempt to rein in my mother's nagging with wisecracks and behind-her-back smirks as he emptied the steaming spaghetti into a colander in the sink. Then, to show he was just kidding, he'd make a funny face and flash his gap-toothed grin, even though he was deeply ashamed of his missing teeth. I'd listen to the two of them fiddling in the kitchen and, sensing dinner was imminent, reluctantly tear myself away from *60 Minutes* to set the table with the requisite paper napkin, fork, knife, butter, bread, and glasses, times three. We wouldn't need a knife to cut the bread, because my father would use the "Italian knife"—his thick, stubby hands. In a few minutes his nose would be running from the liberal dusting of red pepper flakes with which he'd coated his pasta. (He wasn't really enjoying a red sauce unless it made him cry.) My mother would sit down last, martyr that she is, and finish eating first.

"*Oy,* I'm gonna bust," she'd say after the last bite and relax into her chair while my father scooped up seconds. After dinner we'd have "cawfee," and my dad would nibble on a sfogliatella—a crispy layered Italian pastry stuffed with ricotta cheese—and, while my mother would feign disinterest—"Stop it, Johnny, I have no room!"—a piece somehow always ended up in her mouth.

At the end of the night one of my parents would drive me up the hill to the X1 express bus, which would take me back to Manhattan. They'd let me wait in the car, which was convenient if it was very hot or very cold, until I saw the bright yellow lights of the bus in the rearview mirror. We'd restrict ourselves to small talk—"You got everything? Whaddya doing tomorrow?"—because we knew the bus's arrival would quickly yank us apart. But before the bus reached the Brooklyn side of the Verrazano, my phone would vibrate and the familiar number would show up on the caller ID and I'd already be deep in conversation with my mother, gabbing about everything and nothing all at once.

"Thank you for coming," my mother would say.

"Thank you for having me," I'd say.

"I love you so, so much," she'd say.

"I love you, too, Mama," I'd reply, gazing out the window at the sparkling Manhattan skyline, beckoning to me as I made my way through Brooklyn. And then, just when I was about to hang up:

"And, Jenny, you may love him, but your boyfriend *is* a loser."

"Ma!" I'd shout into the phone, startling the slumbering weekend commuters on the darkened bus. She always had to have the last word.

The next day my week would begin again, and another after that, until my life changed: marriage, career progression, a family of my own. My parents would have made superb grandparents: my father, so good with kids, so lovable and engaging, and my mother, who gained the trust of children by speaking to them like they were adults. But all of that will never be. I haven't actually uttered the words "Mama" or "Daddy" in several years, the syllables vanishing from my vocabulary when I wasn't looking. My parents don't know where I work; last either of them knew I was waiting tables in a restaurant. I haven't actually set the table with a napkin, knife, and fork in several years, choosing instead to sit with a plate in front of the television on the rare occasion I prepare a meal at home. My mother didn't live to see me dye out my grays for the first time, my father didn't live to see me go to graduate school, or even graduate from college—he missed it by a month. Dad was also spared 9/11, and the Iraq war, and my mother didn't live long enough to see America elect an African American president, something she would have savored, since she'd traveled down to Washington to hear Martin Luther King, Jr., deliver his "I Have a Dream" speech forty-five years earlier. When (or if) I ever marry, when I have a child, when I finally pay off my student loan debt, all of these things will go unreported to the two people who mattered to me the most. There is no family home to visit on the other side of the Verrazano, no simmering Sauce to be stirred.

I could choke to death on what might have been.

My father died at sixty-four, my mother at seventy-one. They were too young, though I suppose I should be grateful I had them at all. I never imagined I'd live most of my life without parents, but unless I die especially young, that will be my reality. And in a way I hope it is: If there is one thing I have learned to fear, it is death, which has run roughshod over me, robbing me of my family, as I sat helpless to stop it.

But this wasn't always the case. I had a family, however imperfect, and not that long ago. I had a life, albeit one that doesn't remotely resemble the one I'm living now. Where there was once a house full of laughter and argument and cooking smells there is now nothing, just a furnished reverie that exists only in my memory. Sometimes I wonder if my time with them was real. I could say I conjured it from the ether and no one would be the wiser, because there is no one left to corroborate my past. As a journalist I have been trained to find two sides to each story, and often more. But now I only have mine.

CHAPTER 1

150 Rockview
Irvine, California
May 1983

. . .

I WAS FIVE WHEN THE FBI CAME FOR MY FATHER. TWICE. THE FIRST time, I was alone with him in our two-story condo in Turtle Rock, a new development in Irvine, California, when two agents knocked on our door one sunny afternoon just before Christmas. They wanted to arrest him right then but couldn't, as I would be left home alone, so he called my mother, who sped to the house with her boss. When they arrived, agents cuffed my father and took him away. I turned to my mom's boss, also a family friend of ours, and asked him, "Jesse, are they arresting my daddy?"

"No, honey," Jesse replied, kneeling down next to me. "It's not real. They're making a movie." Of course I didn't know it was the FBI who had come to take my father, nor do I remember my father being led away in cuffs or my exchange with Jesse—my mother told me about it years later. But that episode represents the final blind spot in my memory, as I remember everything after that.

Christmas was kind of a bust without Dad, so my mother and I decamped for our next door neighbors'. Virginia and Al had two teenagers, Monica and Albert, Jr., whom I adored. Albert chased me around the house as I squealed with delight and taught me his fool-proof Rubik's Cube strategies: either remove the stickers or take the thing apart piece by piece and reassemble. Monica, sixteen, gorgeous, and popular, tried to give me makeovers with her scary metal eyelash curler—I refused—and took me along when she and her brother "borrowed" a neighbor's car from the supermarket parking lot. My mother fetched my presents and placed them under their tree, and on Christmas Eve I curled up with Monica in her bed while my mother slept in solitude next door. But when I awoke Christmas morning, to my surprise, my father bounded through the front door wearing his bathrobe and carrying a cup of coffee, nonchalant as the cloudless sky.

"Hey, kids!" he called out in his cigarette-scarred Brooklyn sing-song. At the sound of his voice I shot up and bolted downstairs into his waiting arms, and he scooped me up and threw me onto his shoulders. I was in heaven.

Until they came again, some months later. My cousin Kara was visiting from Miami at the time. She was sixteen and improbably blond, since my mother's family was populated with raven-haired Russian Jews. Kara was involved with a Colombian dealer on the lower rung of one of Miami's drug cartels, and their relationship was so toxic that her mother, Rita—my mother's youngest sister—had shipped her west and enrolled her in University High School just to separate them. The distance didn't help, as Kara and Miguel burned up our phone line for so many consecutive hours that she wore a hole in the seat of one of our rattan chairs. But when my parents were at work she let me eat all the grape jelly sandwiches I wanted, so she was fine in my book.

My father was a carpet cleaner with his own business, C&C Carpets—which stood for Cassese and Cassese, our last name—and my mother stayed at home with me until my first day of school, when she handed me off to my preschool teacher, who held me on her lap while she addressed the class because I was crying so hard. I was an only child and begged my mother for more siblings, but she patiently explained why she couldn't have any more. "I had a cesarean," she said, nudging her pants down and pointing out the horizontal white scar situated in one of the folds of her burgeoning middle-aged belly. Because she had spent every day of the past five years with me she was more like my sister, and we developed quite a bit of friction: I'd egg her on with my petulant mouth, which could whip her into a frenzy, and she would retaliate by whacking my backside with her hand, her hairbrush, or whatever was available, until her long brown hair frizzed and her almond eyes burned with fury. Once she broke one of her wooden spatulas on my ass. We laughed about that when I was older.

My mother had appointed herself the disciplinarian, the "no" person, leaving my father the role of yes man. Where my mother sought to curb my calorie intake, my father left Twix and Skor bars under my pillow and pretended not to notice when I crawled into his nightstand and raided his stash of Baby Ruths and Red Vines. After dinner he'd let me dip my finger in his scotch, and even though its fiery malt burned my mouth, I appreciated the gesture. After my mother tucked me in at night, my father would tiptoe up the stairs and rouse me from sleep by playing King of the Mountain, wrestling me for dominance of the bed. "Don't stimulate her!" my mother would shout from the bottom of the stairs. We'd then lie flat on our backs, face each other, and join the soles of our feet in a reciprocal bicycle motion and he would sing to me, encouraging me to join in:

Daisy, Daisy,
Give me your answer, do!
I'm half crazy
All for the love of you!
It won't be a stylish marriage,
I can't afford a carriage,
But you'll look sweet upon the seat
Of a bicycle built for two.

Then he'd hurl me heavenward and hoist me up onto his shoulders, and even though I was afraid of heights I always lost my fear around him. When I had nightmares it was my father who rescued me from the bogeymen, bounding up the stairs like a bunny rabbit to save me from the dancing clown who popped up in my dreamscape and frightened me so. He would drive me to kindergarten every morning and we'd make up silly songs, usually riffs on pop and musical theater classics, with slight alterations. Like my father's signature "How Are Things in Guacamole?"—an homage to the more traditional "How Are Things in Glocca Morra?" from *Finian's Rainbow,* which he'd warble in his gravelly baritone. (I was raised in the 1980s by parents who grew up in the 1930s and '40s, and it showed.) My father brought home colored pencils and tried in vain to pass on his talent and enthusiasm for drawing, and even though it was apparent that I hadn't inherited his substantial gift he plugged away with me anyway, buying me how-to books on the craft that spoke to young children. When I had chicken pox at three, strep throat that made me vomit all over him at four, or that nasty bout of diarrhea that sent me home from school at five, he came home from work with armfuls of stuffed animals, coloring books, or candy. When I was a little older, my mother informed me with a hint of chagrin that my first word had been "Da." Apparently my father had indoctrinated me while my

My father and me, 1978. Note the gun rack on the wall.

mother took a short solo trip and she returned to find him triumphant over my newly acquired verbal skills.

Daddy took me trick-or-treating; Daddy bought me Slurpees that gave me brain freeze; Daddy told me that the oceans were formed by dinosaur pee, and I believed him. Daddy heroically caught a little boy before he could crack his head open as he fell off the carousel in South Coast Plaza, cementing his status as my savior. Daddy also nearly lost me to an undertow in Laguna Beach, giving me root beer to chase the salt water out of my nose, and even though I could have died I didn't hold it against him. My day wasn't complete until I heard the keys jangling from his belt as he approached our front door after work every night; as soon as it opened I'd jump up as if on a spring and run to greet him. "Daddy's home!" I'd scream, loud enough for the whole block to hear. My adoration of my father was such that I turned to my mother one day and announced, "I like Daddy better." Her face crumpled; it must have been a parenting nightmare come true.

One night after dinner there was a knock at the door. I was sitting on the stairs when it happened, gazing upon Kara and my parents as they cleared the dining room table. Before I knew what was happening, Kara ushered me into my bedroom and closed the door. "Let's play, Jenny," she said, and tried to engage me in a coloring book or a board game or my wooden blocks. I really can't remember what tricks she used to try to pull my focus, because I was so intent on opening that door. Whenever her back was turned for the slightest window of time I took it, bum-rushing the door and prying it open. "Daddy!" I yelled, until Kara pulled me back into the bedroom by my shirttails. When her back was turned I ran for it again, and this time she pulled me back by my hair. I tried again and again; we replayed this scene until we were both breathless and sweaty. Finally my mother came upstairs and opened the door, freeing me. But when I got downstairs my father was gone. He never said goodbye.

My parents probably wanted to avoid the scene of his previous arrest—they couldn't exactly say that he was filming another movie—but as a result I was left with only my imagination to explain his absence. Kara flew home soon after that and my mother left me in the care of the family of one of my classmates, a girl I couldn't stand. Her mother, Rifka, kept kosher, which I was not used to, as I'd been raised largely without my mother's Jewish influence. My classmate, whose name eludes me now, treated me like an interloper, a second-class citizen. One night I complained that I was hungry and she ran into the kitchen and came back with a cracker crumb. "Here," she said sarcastically, extending the crumb on her fingertip. "Thanks anyway," I said, and threw the covers over my head. She teased me because I ate the skin on my chicken—it was my favorite part!—and her mother didn't discourage her, instead warning me that swallowing the skin would make me throw up. (Certainly not more than the egg noodles and ketchup she called "pasta.") After three days I pleaded with Rifka to let me call my mother. Through tears, I begged her to pick me up, and she did, even though it was very late at night. On the way home we got a flat tire—it seemed nothing could go right for us. As the car sagged and thumped its way back to Irvine, I told my mother I didn't want her to ever leave me again. "Please, Mommy," I begged her.

"I promise, baby," she said, a promise just ready-made to break.

Some days later my mother took me to a building in downtown Santa Ana where, after walking through a metal detector, I found myself staring at my father through a thick plate of glass. My mother had explained on the ride up that he was in a "correctional facility," which I could refer to either as "corrections" or "the facility." I was so happy to see his gentle, familiar face, but I screamed like a banshee when he couldn't come home with us. Talking to him through a telephone that hung off the wall seemed preposterous when he was right there in front of me. Why couldn't I sit on his lap? "Be a good girl for Mommy," he said before my mother carried me out, his voice sounding hollow and tinny over the phone. "I'll be home soon, I promise."

It was the spring of 1983 and I was due to finish kindergarten. When my mother brought me home from my last day of school I found our apartment empty, our furniture and possessions having been put in storage. "Mommy, why?" I asked, sad to leave our house, the only one I'd ever remembered living in. She told me we were going to New York, a place I'd never been, where she and my father had grown up. Because my mother was afraid to fly we had to take a train, and Phil, my father's partner at C&C, drove us to the Amtrak station. I understood that my father was also headed to New York and we were going there to join him, but he apparently had another way of getting there.

For four days we rumbled eastward, sleeping and eating and playing so many hands of War that our cards bent and softened from all the shuffling. I annoyed my mother by making silly faces in the mirror. "Stop it!" my mother scolded, annoyed by all that she could not control. And then: "Oy, I need a Valium."

We got stuck in a snowstorm around Denver and my mother took me outside and pointed out the snow, the first time I'd ever seen the stuff. To lull me to sleep each night, my mother, though harried and chain-smoking and shedding pounds by the day, was an oasis of calm as she sang "Dona Dona," her signature lullaby in her fragile soprano—first in English, then in Hebrew—and stroked my butt-length brown hair:

How the winds are laughing,
they laugh with all their might.

"I like the donut song," I murmured before I fell asleep.

We disembarked into a New York I can't quite pull into focus save for the lights on the Verrazano Bridge, a glittering necklace suspended in the night sky that dazzled my young, unsophisticated eyes. We didn't have bridges in Orange County; Irvine still had tumbleweed rolling down the street. (I'm not kidding—the day we moved to 150 Rockview, a big round piece of brush blew past my mother's front fender. "I don't believe this," she gasped, horrified.) Instead of tumbleweeds New York had litter, even in Staten Island, which is where my father's brother Frankie and his family lived and where my mother and I were going to stay. For how long, I didn't know. But I cringed as I stepped over a broken bottle on a sidewalk in Annadale. My mother laughed: "My daughter has never seen glass in the street, can you believe it?" she reported to Frankie's family. But California's surfaces had been pristine, honeysuckle and hibiscus blooming even in a planned development like Turtle Rock, where their fragrance beckoned from every traffic island.

One day my mother and I took a trip back over the Verrazano, ending up in a neighborhood lined with cobblestoned streets, which I had also never seen, and which fascinated me. She led me into a building, and after we passed through various layers of security, there he was.

Still tan and healthy, with his prematurely gray comb-over and strapping lean muscle mass, my father greeted us once again with "Hey, kids!" like everything was hunky-dory.

"Daddy!" I squealed, and ran into his arms. He wasn't behind glass in this facility; this time we sat with him in the open at a long table with other people wearing the same color uniform. I got to see him, smell him, peck him on the cheek; I was thrilled. He bounced me up and down on his lap for a while as he talked to my mother, but I wasn't paying any mind to their conversation. At the end of the hour I got yanked away, and I cried and reached for him as my mother carried me out of the facility. She appeased me with Hostess cupcakes purchased from a snack truck outside, and I stopped crying as soon as my mouth was stuffed with chocolate.

Before the weather got really hot my mother and I were on Amtrak again, this time headed to North Miami Beach to stay with Aunt Rita. Thirty-seven and leggy, Rita had grown up with my mother and their sister, Arline, in the Brooklyn neighborhood of Manhattan Beach. While my mother's almond eyes made her appear Asian, by some twist of genetic fate Rita resembled a Spanish goddess. Her olive skin and curly brown hair, christened with golden-

*My mother (left) and Rita clad in their
beloved St. John Knits, 1983.*

flecked highlights, attracted male attention all over Miami, usually of the damaged variety. Already twice divorced, Rita lived in a sixth-floor apartment on the Intracoastal Waterway with Kara, who was now engaged to Miguel.

"Will Daddy be there, too, Mommy?" I asked on the train.

"Maybe," she said, "Daddy might come later."

"Mommy, do you know everything?" I asked, wanting to be sure before I continued with my line of questioning.

"Yes," she said, without missing a beat.

"Then why can't he come now?" I asked, frustrated.

"Shhhh, my little peanut-face, take a nap." She stroked my hair and stared out the window as the orange groves flew past and softly sang another lullaby from her repertoire:

And even though we ain't got money
I'm so in love with ya honey,
And everything will bring a chain of love.
And in the morning when I rise
You bring a tear of joy to my eyes,
And tell me everything is gonna be all right.

It was a song she sometimes sang to soothe me when we took long car rides. It took on new meaning as we journeyed south into the unknown, into a part of the world populated with questions that yielded few answers—for her or for me.

CHAPTER 2

North Bay Road
North Miami Beach, Florida
July 1983

. . .

MY MOTHER AND I HAD ONLY BEEN IN FLORIDA A FEW DAYS when she had to leave. As she waved goodbye from the window of her northbound train, Rita held me close and tried to dam the flow of my tears. "Maaaaaaa," I wailed, unable to conceive of another separation from another parent. Rita, helpless, could think of only one thing that might cheer me up.

"Hey, Jenbo," she said, using her newly coined nickname for me. "You want some ice cream?" Rita gave everyone nicknames: My mother was Swellenor, because her tiny frame had become uncharacteristically bloated when she was pregnant with me; my father was Yonny, because Rita dropped the *J* from everyone's name, and by that same principle, Kara became Yisa and I was also sometimes Yenny; and Rita was Retard, and sometimes Tardy, because, as she liked to joke, "I'm manually retarded." This stemmed from her inability to operate even the most basic electronics.

"Ice cream?" I asked, abandoning my sorrow as quickly as it came. "Yes! I want chocolate ice cream!" And with that, Rita had cemented her status as Favorite Aunt.

In my mother's absence I woke with Rita just before eight and we headed down to the pool, where I shimmied into my yellow tube and floated all afternoon, bronzing my skin until the Mexican family down the hall assumed I was one of them. (They were Mexican Jews, so they were half right.) When we came back to the air-conditioned apartment around lunch, Rita would grab the bag of Milky Way bars out of the freezer and we'd chase them with Coca-Cola. Then she'd rub some Banana Boat on my skin and we'd go back down for more. When the sun set we'd fix fresh bagels and lox for dinner and watch reruns of *Love, American Style* and *Bewitched*. Later in the evening Rita would give me her lingerie to play dress-up, and I'd walk out in her four-inch Ferragamos and a negligée so big that it trailed behind me. She'd laugh until she snorted, and hand me more of her designer duds to model: bikinis, slip dresses, her prized St. John Knits. She'd paint my lips with Saint, her favorite shade of red lipstick (and my mother's). Before bed I'd get to stretch out in her long bathtub and she'd fill it up with warm water mixed with Spring Green Vitabath, a treat I'd never before enjoyed. I was in the lap of luxury, and I loved it.

But some days when I'd wander into Rita's bedroom and take a nap on the little mattress she'd placed near the ocean-facing window for me, I'd gaze out onto the Intracoastal and try to conjure my father through sheer mental force. "Daddy, please appear, right now," I'd say into the air. Then I'd turn toward the bedroom door and repeat in my head, "Daddy, walk through this door right this second. Please, Daddy, if you can hear me, please come back for me." But he didn't hear me, and the door stayed shut.

"How long have I been here?" I asked Rita one day as I dressed and undressed my Barbie dolls.

"A month," she said from the couch, where she was reclining and watching TV.

"How long is a month?" I asked.

"Thirty days," she said. She was sucking on sour balls from Winn-Dixie. I crawled up and grabbed some. She kept them around the apartment in glass jars and they were quickly becoming my favorites.

"How much longer will I be here?" I asked. "When is Daddy coming home?"

"I don't know, Jenbo," she said, concerned. "Soon."

Sometimes I annoyed Rita, too, and since Kara and Miguel were off doing their own thing, our relationship became tense, like the one my mother and I had shared in solitude in Irvine. One night we had an argument over what to eat for dinner—"I want Cheerios!" I insisted; "You can't have Cheerios for dinner, Jenny!"—and she smacked me across the face and split my lip with one of her long nails.

"I want Mommy!" I wailed; but my mother would have done the

same thing. I stared out the window at the orange and purple sky and fantasized about Cheerios until Rita came back in and apologized. She looked pained. I guess we all were.

My mother did come back, though we knew she would have to leave again. Not that Rita's life didn't have its share of excitement. When my mother wasn't around, Rita had all kinds of interesting friends over, often into the wee hours, and they'd camp out in her bedroom. Whenever the door opened I got a whiff of cigarette smoke, except it didn't smell like her usual cigarettes. One night I finally got to see the source of those funny-smelling cigarettes up close. Rita was lying on her bed watching TV next to a small orange contraption that looked like a mini paper towel holder lying on its side. In it she put a thin piece of paper from a package marked "Zig Zag," which looked like the tracing paper I'd used to copy Daddy's drawings, and sprinkled some stuff on it that looked like dried bits of grass. It went through the roller and came out looking like a cigarette.

"Rita, what's that?" I asked, mesmerized by the process.

"This?" she asked, holding up her homemade creation. "This is a Turkish cigarette. Your aunt Rita smokes a lot of Turkish cigarettes." My aunt Rita also liked smoking a lot of regular cigarettes, and often fell asleep with a lit one dangling between her elegantly manicured fingers.

My mother went up and down the coast all summer, though I don't know how long she stayed in each place. Time to me then was like lava, somehow creeping and bubbling its way forward without my consent. When my mother was finally in Florida to stay, I took it to mean that my father was here, too.

"When do I get to see Daddy?" I asked, excited, after her train pulled in.

She sighed. "Honey, we can't," she replied.

"Why not? Isn't he here, too?"

"He is," she said. "He's in another facility. But this facility is different." As long as my father was in corrections in Florida, I didn't get to visit him. Which was probably better; I was tired of feeling so frustrated when he couldn't come home with us.

"Mama, I have one more question," I said.

"What?" she said, exasperated.

"Why would somebody smoke the grass?"

She stopped and clenched her jaw. "Where did you hear that?"

"Well, I heard Aunt Rita talking about grass. Why would somebody want to smoke the lawn?" Perhaps it was an odd delicacy, like Rita's Turkish cigarettes?

"They're not smoking the lawn, Jenny," she said, stifling a laugh.

One day my mother took me to an apartment in Miami and introduced the shy twenty-three-year-old inside. "Jenny," she said, "this is your sister, Angela. Angela, this is the brat, my little peanut-face, Jenny."

"I'm Jennifer Cassese Mascia," I said, pronouncing each syllable of our other last name with pride: MASS-see-ya. "But you can call me Jenbo." My mother smiled at Angie and turned to me.

"Jenny, we don't have to say 'Cassese' anymore," she said. "And your Daddy isn't Frank anymore, either. People are going to call him John now. No more Frank." I was confused. She called my father "Frank" in public but "Johnny" around the house.

"But aren't Frank and John the same name?" I asked. Like William and Bill, or Richard and Dick. One was a nickname for the other. Wasn't it? Suddenly we had new names and I was finally meeting one of my siblings.

"JENNY, DID I EVER TELL you that you have two sisters and a brother?" my father had asked as he tried to teach me to draw at our big round glass dining room table in Irvine.

"I have brothers and sisters?" I'd replied, overjoyed at the prospect. "Where are they?"

"They live in Miami, which is where you were born," he said.

"Are they coming to visit, too?" My grandpa Frank and grandma Helen—my father's parents—had already been to Irvine to visit, as had Aunt Rita, though I barely remembered her visits.

"No, not yet, Jenny Penny," he said, using his nickname for me. "They can't come visit us here yet. But—"

"Why not?" I asked. "I want to meet them!"

"I'll show you pictures," he promised, and went upstairs. He came back down with a manila folder filled with drawings on yellowing paper. There was a bold pencil rendering of Sid Caesar and Imogene Coca, a comic book character named Captain Comet, Mickey Mouse and Daffy Duck, the dresser in someone's house, a Camel ad come to life, a '59 Ford, shaded powder blue, and a list of "Old Songs to

Remember"—"The Still of the Night" by the Five Satins, "Tears on My Pillow" by the Imperials, "I Only Have Eyes for You" by the Flamingos. He pulled out a piece of paper dated "Dec. 11, 1958," and on it a smiling girl younger than me with a pageboy haircut pulled a blanket around her little body; she looked off to the right and smiled slightly.

"This is Tina, she's your half-sister," he said. Then he pulled out another sheet of paper, a smaller square, dated "11-14-59." It was a woman with dark lips and upswept hair accented with light pink. She wore a pink wrap and had pearls dangling from her ears.

"This girl right here, her name is Marie," he explained. "When I was very young, Marie and I were married. I loved Marie very much, but I was bad and dated all her friends when she went away to summer camp."

"You didn't!" I said. "Daddy!"

He laughed and pulled up his right sleeve and flexed his considerable biceps. There he had a blue bird with the name "Marie" etched in cursive underneath it. "I got this in Coney Island when I was nineteen," he said. "They colored it in with needles."

"Needles?" I asked, flinching instinctively. I was so scared of needles, and medicine in general, that when I scratched my cornea with a piece of plastic my father had to bribe me with a Snoopy Sno-Cone machine before I let him put the drops in my eye.

"You think that's bad, kiddo, look at this," he said, and rolled up his other sleeve. On his left arm was another blue bird, this time with "Johnny" written there.

"Daddy!" I said. Then: "I want a tattoo!"

"No," he said, sternly.

"Why not?" I asked.

"Please, Jenny," he said, exasperated, like I was already a rebellious sixteen-year-old. "What if you marry a doctor one day?" I imagined myself a doctor's wife, clad in a nurse's uniform.

"So you got the tattoo because you were married?" I asked, wondering even at that tender age whether my mother had a problem with it.

"Yes," he said.

"But you're married to Mommy," I pointed out.

"I'm married to Mommy *now*," he said. "But Marie and I were married when we were very young. I was nineteen and she was fifteen, and that was when we had your half-sister, Christina," he said, pointing to his drawing. "Tina."

"Tina," I said, trying it out. "How old is Tina, Daddy?"

"Tina is, uh, let me see," he said, doing the arithmetic in his head but theatrically counting on his stubby sausage fingers for my benefit. "If she was born in 'fifty-six, that would make her twenty-six now," he said. "She will be twenty-seven in September."

"I was born in November," I said.

"That's right," he said, still shading in his characters. He could have been an illustrator for Disney, he was that good. "You were born November 22, and your motha and I were married on the nineteenth. Three days before you were born."

"Nooooooo!" I said, laughing. He frequently made this joke, and it annoyed my mother no end. "Don't tell her that, Johnny!" my mother would protest. "She'll tell all her friends one day and they'll think I was *schwangered* when we got married. Jenny, your father and I were married in 1976; you were born in 'seventy-seven." Knowing my mother as well as I do now, I can't believe something like that ever mattered to her, when so much about her life was so utterly unconventional.

"Your other sister," my father continued, "is named Angela. She lives in Florida, too, with Tony, who is your brother. Tony is, *madonn'*, how old is Tony now, El?" he shouted into the kitchen.

"Uhhhhh . . . Tony is . . . he must be nineteen now, Johnny? Twenty?" my mother called back.

And now here was Angela, the sister closest to my age, standing before me in the city where I was born. I took her in: brown hair and brown eyes, like me, and a grin so infectious and sincere it gave her chipmunk cheeks. She bent down and hugged me, then leaned in for a much longer hug with my mom.

"How have you been, Ange?" my mother said into her neck as she patted her back.

"Good, good. Eleanor, god, it's been so long," she said. My mother left me for the day with Angela, who let me stand on her coffee table and sing my favorite song on her karaoke machine, "What a Feeling" from *Flashdance*. I was so obsessed with that movie that my mother came back from Nordstrom one afternoon with an off-the-shoulder pink sweatshirt with a cut-out neck, just like Jennifer Beals. Never mind that I was five.

Next I got to meet my other sister, Tina. "Well, how are you, Miss Jennifer?" Tina said after my mother introduced us. "It's very nice to meet you, but we've met before. I was your first babysitter." She looked at my mother and beamed, then turned to me, awaiting my response.

"I need a Valium," I replied. Tina suppressed laughter while my mother slowly shook her head and sighed.

Tina was married to a man named Bill, who was closer to my mom's age. They lived in Indian River Estates and had a dog I fell head-over-heels in love with, a golden retriever named Bridget. I ran around Tina's property with Bridget in tow, waging duels with tree branches and composing musical theater. My mother sometimes left me with Tina for weekends, probably figuring I needed a change of scenery. I liked her immediately; she reminded me of my father. Plus, she gifted me with my first Cabbage Patch Kid, procured from a friend who was on the waiting list at the toy store.

That September my mother enrolled me in first grade at Bay Harbor Elementary, which signaled that she wasn't sure when my father was going to be able to leave the facility. I hated school there; I found myself lost in my classes, which had many more students than I was used to. Lessons rushed right past me, and while everyone else copied down notes from the overhead projector I doodled absentmindedly in my notebook, or reread the letters my father had sent me from the facility, adorned with Mickey Mouse and characters from the *Peanuts* gang. I got punished for talking during class and spent most recesses picking trash off the carpet, which suited me just fine, as socializing in a school this large overwhelmed me. One day, my frustrated teacher opened the door to the classroom, which faced the street, and instructed me to keep watch for my father.

"You just stand there and wait for your daddy to come and get you so he can punish you," she told me. I searched the traffic for his red Oldsmobile, wishing it were that easy to bring him back to me.

IN OCTOBER, I FINALLY got my wish. My mother had been gone all day, and when she waltzed through Rita's front door my father was standing behind her, wearing his familiar beige cable-knit sweater.

"Hey, kiddo!" he called to me. I ran into his arms like a cheetah, colliding with him with such force that I could have broken my neck. He scooped me up and threw me onto his shoulders, and I was home again. It was my mother's birthday, October 12, and she called it "the best birthday present I ever got in my life." I have a photograph that was taken later that night, in which I am sitting on his lap and he is holding out his cheek for me to kiss. I'm tan and topless—I was still young enough to pull that off—and my hair is long and brown. He looks thinner than I remember him being, and his arms are wrapped firmly around me. We were whole again.

The night my father was released from jail, Miami, October 1983.

We didn't leave Florida right away, as we were out of money. I gathered as much when my father was installed as the new line cook at Bagels and Donuts, where Rita was the manager. I celebrated the last day of 1983 at the counter watching my father flip burgers and fry eggs, and at the end of the night I got my first sip of champagne.

I don't remember saying our goodbyes, but by spring we were on the road again, this time in a car. My mother, amused by our plight, sang "On the Road Again" incessantly as we spent a week traversing the dusty Southwest. We got caught in a sandstorm near the Arizona-California border, and since there were no rest stops as far as the eye could see, I got out and peed right there on the road as the sand stung my ears and eyes. To pass the time as we inched toward Orange

County, my mother and I crafted a shopping list for when we finally got our own place. "Ivory soap," she recited as she stroked my hair, "Cheerios, maple syrup, balsamic vinegar, extra virgin olive oil, Gold's horseradish, the purple kind; heavy cream for my coffee and half & half for Daddy's coffee; Yuban coffee; Dijon mustard; Uncle Ben's; shampoo; capers, nonpareil—"

"Mommy, what does 'nonpareil' mean?" I'd ask.

"You know, I'm actually not sure," she admitted.

"But Mommy, I thought you knew everything," I said. It had to be true; she'd said it.

"Well, I know everything but this, all right?" she snapped, then continued with her inventory in more soporific tones: "Valencia oranges, grapefruit, romaine lettuce, Baker's chocolate squares, so we can make brownies"—her brownies were deliciously decadent and dusted with a thin coating of powdered sugar, which she dumped into a sieve and gently shook over the plate.

"Mommy, do you remember when you made zeppoles?" I asked. Another of her powdered sugar delicacies.

"Yes," she said. "Those were good, huh?"

"And that stuff you made that night with Daddy, I loved it, it was brown and burned a little, those dry fish pieces. Mommy, what was it?" I couldn't erase the flavor from my mind, nor the scene, at our condo in Turtle Rock, of her and my father laughing as they dabbed the sluglike pieces of fish on paper towels to absorb the oil.

"Calamari," she said, but pronounced it "calamah." "And it wasn't supposed to be burnt," she added, tightening her lips into a firm pout, as if someone had pulled a drawstring on either side of her mouth. It was her signature scowl and she employed it until the end of her life.

"Mommy, can we make it again?" I asked. "And zeppoles, can we make those, too, just you, me, and Daddy?" I wanted to have our life back, just the three of us. So did she.

"Soon," she said. "Very soon."

CHAPTER 3

Rio Verde Street
Lake Forest, California
May 1986

. . .

Aﬀer two years spent in a tiny two-bedroom apartment so cramped that when you sat down on the toilet your knee hit the tub, we moved into a spacious one-story spread located in a tract housing development that had just been carved out of a hillside in Lake Forest. Though the scenery changed, my mother's "I need a Valium" refrain echoed for years, transcending the crisis we'd narrowly averted. Her little blue pills made her irritable and her temper was shorter than usual when they wore off, and the only thing that centered her somewhat was her epic phone conversations with David, her ex-husband, whom my mother anointed my uncle. I grew accustomed to picking up the phone and hearing David's friendly, effeminate drawl, and he seemed to be equally fond of me, sending me rings with small, brightly colored stones from his antique jewelry business in the diamond center in New York.

"Hello, Jennifah," David would say in greeting when he called every other afternoon.

"Hi, Uncle David!" I'd say, twirling myself into the long, metallic blue cord from the kitchen phone until I was wrapped up like a mummy. "Whaddya doin'?"

"Nothing much, Jenny, how are you?" he replied. "How is your motha?"

"She's mad at me, Uncle David," I said. "Today she took the skin on my arm and pinched it and twisted it around! It hurt so bad!"

"Hey!" a voice barked from behind me. *"Gimme that phone!"* If this had been a cartoon, steam would have been escaping from her nostrils.

"Dammit, Mom!"

"Shit, Jenny, I told you to use 'darn it'!" my mother snapped, whipping the phone out of my hand.

Yet another dance recital, Laguna Beach, 1987.

Perhaps employment as my personal chauffeur was grating on her—between school, acting classes, Girl Scouts, tap, jazz, and ballet, we were single-handedly keeping Chevron in business—but she got her revenge by dragging me to South Coast Plaza every weekend. The three of us had gone there many Sundays when we lived in Irvine, which was five miles from the mall's Costa Mesa locale. But now my mother was taking me for shopping excursions without my father, and instead of a leisurely stroll through the May Company and I. Magnin, followed by a ride on the carousel, she would make a beeline for Bullocks and Nordstrom as I blithely trailed behind her. At first I enjoyed visiting the upscale mall because I was guaranteed hot chocolate and a croissant at Vie de France, and the occasional trinket from Sanrio Gift Gate, home of Hello Kitty. We knew the saleslady at Brass Plum by name, and soon I was outfitted in the same clothing I saw draped over the young characters on my favorite TV shows. Esprit, Guess, Benetton, Reebok, Z Cavaricci, DKNY, L.A. Gear, Jessica McClintock, Gucci watches—I had it all, but not because

I wanted it. I wanted Garbage Pail Kids and Keroppi stationery, but my mother wanted a child dressed in the latest fashions. She even bought me a pair of Keds that were mismatched on purpose—the left foot was yellow and the right was red—and I was teased mercilessly at school for it. "I don't understand," she said, dismayed, when I cried to her. "This is what's 'in.'"

But she was cultivating a sophisticated sense of style in her daughter, even if she was boring her to death. Our mouths would water as we passed Escada and gaped at the smart suits; we'd amble past Caché and she'd target her next fantasy acquisition in the window; she already had two St. John Knits and she hungrily eyed the latest designs, fingering the tight stitching even as she balked at the price tag. Joan & David shoes were her favorite extravagance; honorable mentions included her Gucci keychain topped with its signature gold-plated interlocking G's, three Louis Vuitton purses with a matching wallet, and a Vuitton checkbook holder, which I inherited. On the rare occasion I need to write a check, my friends gasp and admire it with that same glazed-over look my mother sported for years. The shiny amber brick floors of the sprawling hundred-acre mall became as familiar to me as my own bedroom carpet, while traversing the passageway to FAO Schwarz, in a semisecluded wing of the mall, was like an adventure. I was as enamored with the mall as my mother was, until I wasn't.

The honeymoon ended with Williams-Sonoma. Children and cookware generally do not mix, and my mother was determined to fill her free time with all aspects of the culinary arts; she even went through a phase where she baked her own bread and made her own mayonnaise. She bought two oven bricks so she could make pizza, a feat which took just eight short hours but produced a thin-crusted margherita that wasn't half bad. Nothing we ate ever came from a bottle. She made her own pasta sauce and even her own vinaigrette— there was no Hidden Valley at my house. She bought a wok so we could stir-fry our dinner if we wanted, a pressure cooker to make risotto, a double boiler, a Donvier ice cream maker—which did churn out some pretty good ice cream, the one time she made it—and a food processor, which I used to crush ice that I ate like snow. We had a juicer so we could have fresh-squeezed orange juice every morning, a purchase that spoiled me for life, and a deep fryer we used to crisp French fries. We owned the entire set of Le Creuset pots and pans, which were orange and blue and incredibly heavy; we got silverware from Italy with stems that looked like bamboo, except it was stainless steel. She bought the entire set of Henckels knives and a wooden block in which to keep them; we had blenders, corkscrews, cheese graters, ladles, pasta spoons, zesters, cutting boards, strainers in three different sizes, different knives for cheese and grapefruit, ice cream scoopers, pie servers, plates just for artichokes, a gravy pourer in the shape of a rooster, colanders, stainless steel spoons and cups just for measuring, an espresso machine that I am pretty certain she never used, wineglasses, champagne flutes, juice glasses, coffee mugs, tea-kettles she simply returned when they wore out, and beer steins we kept in the freezer so my father's beer could stay colder longer—so cold, in fact, that ice crystals formed in his Coors. She bought Dansk dishware for our more casual meals and began to store the expensive Arabia ware set of dishes, cups, and saucers from Finland that couldn't be replaced. Not only did she have enough cookware to open a small restaurant, but she collected cookbooks that represented every imagin-able cuisine: Cuban, Mexican, soup, bread and soup, spa cuisine, pizza, Italian, French, *Joy of Cooking,* Asian, 20-Minute Menus, Cuisine Rapide. Julia Child, James Beard, Paul Prudhomme, and Maida Heat-ter were all represented, as were Craig Claiborne, Marcella Hazan, and Pierre Franey.

In addition to Williams-Sonoma, we visited the bedding depart-ments of Saks, Neiman Marcus, and Robinson's, and my patience was rewarded with goose down pillows and Laura Ashley comforters. Fre-quent visits to makeup counters meant she had the latest in Shiseido, Chanel, and Fendi, and later, MAC and Bobbi Brown. She always had a fresh bottle of Opium or Joy on her dresser, her favorite fragrances, and when the levels were low my father and I always knew what to get her for Christmas. She had a hairstylist she visited once a month in West Hollywood who dyed out her grays, and under his advisement she went through every brand in the hair care pantheon: Sebastian, Phyto, Matrix, Biolage, Nexxus, Aveda, Joico, Bain de Terre, Sorbie—every time we got into the shower there was a different brand staring back at us, supposedly better than the last because it was more expensive. (Not that my father cared: The only shampoo he ever used was Selsun Blue for his dandruff, and he eschewed conditioner altogether.) I grew so disenchanted with shopping that to this day it makes me so anxious that I start sweating and my legs turn to Jell-O if I have to spend more than twenty minutes in a department store. That list she had created on the road had a secret counterpart, and she spent a decade making sure we procured everything on it.

For a spell my mother caught a break when the bills came, because they didn't—her credit card company was sending her bills to Lake Forest, Illinois, because our California town was so new. But when they finally arrived they were paid with my parents' earnings from a lucrative two-summer-long custodial contract they'd secured from Chapman College, money that was never put into a bank. My parents' idea of a checking account was to cut a hole in the padding underneath the carpet in the master bedroom, where my father stored his cash; if times were flush, my father cut another hole, then another. Money came into my parents' lives in big, unaccounted-for bundles and flowed between their cigarette-stained fingers like fine Long Island sand. Nothing was official—my father's carpet business was off the books and taxes were a rumor. My parents did put my birthday checks into a savings account and called it my "college fund," but it never went north of $2,000 and didn't pay for a single textbook. Except for a car here and there we never owned anything, ever, including the house on Rio Verde.

Almost as soon as we moved in, everyone from "Back East" came to visit—my father's sister, Rosalie; her daughter, Helen, with her husband and kids, twice; my half-sister Angie, with her husband, Frankie, and their newborn, Nicole, my father's first granddaughter; my half-brother, Tony, and my father's Aunt Katie, who taught me how to play solitaire. I thought we were the coolest family in town because everyone wanted to visit us, and I only realized years later that our popularity stemmed from the fact that we lived in immaculate, sunny Southern California, which is apparently every New Yorker's idea of paradise.

But best of all, there was Rita. Rita visited a few times a year and her trips were Special Occasions. "Jenbo!" she'd yelp as I ran into her arms at the airport and buried myself in her Opium-scented hair. Rita was bronzed to perfection, with perfectly lined lips and freshly manicured nails. She always adorned herself with expensive sweaters and pantsuits that my mother often borrowed, then bought for herself as soon as Rita left. Rita was my mother's material idol, I could tell—all those trips to South Coast had a focal point, a dream to work toward, and that dream was Rita, seven years younger than my mother, who was nearing fifty.

Rita always flew in from Florida armed with a catalog of wild stories about her crazy friends, some of whom I'd met that summer in Florida. Like her ex-boyfriend Steve—nicknamed "Steve-Steve"— a creepy stalker type who had tried to curry favor with Rita by reading me bedtime stories during my tenure in Miami, whispering the words into my neck with breath so hot it glued my hair to my skin. In a particularly boneheaded move, Steve was arrested in Ecuador for attempting to smuggle cocaine in the sole of his tennis shoe. Or her friend Betty, who owned a sweets store next to Bagels and Donuts (that my father and Rita had routinely pillaged, much to my delight)—who had irrigated her eye with what she thought was Visine, only to discover when she couldn't open it again that it was really nail glue. At first I had no idea what my parents and Rita were gabbing about, but they were uncensored in their speech and I picked up quick. But the fact that I was privy to such adult subject matter wasn't exactly a departure from the way I was already being raised. There was no Disney in our house; instead of *Mary Poppins* and *Dumbo* I was reared on Woody Allen. I could recite the jingles and snappier lines from *Radio Days,* a favorite of mine because it depicted the world in which my parents grew up, but I had no idea what songs the Little Mermaid sang. When, at the age of seven, I started memorizing dialogue from *The Breakfast Club,* my father gave me a lecture about watching movies that were beyond my maturity level. But it was too late; he couldn't expect me to curb my viewing habits when I had influences like HBO, Cinemax, MTV—and, of course, Rita.

Her zaniness was not dampened by the passing of time; on the contrary, it seemed to grow in proportion to her years. Rita, who preferred to park in the fire lane when we went to the supermarket, was the playmate who lit matches with me, a nine-year-old budding pyromaniac, in the bathroom of a fancy restaurant in Coronado. I had recently fallen in love with the smell of phosphorus, and I swiped a matchbook from the host stand. Rita, game for anything, suggested we sneak into the bathroom, where her eyes lit up with each spark. My mother later told me that our waiter approached the table and politely informed her, "Ma'am, your daughter and another woman are lighting matches in the bathroom." My parents knocked on the door and rescued the two of us from a lawsuit waiting to happen, and after we resumed our dinner and strolled along the island's streets in the summer heat, Rita assured me, "If *I* was your mother, I'd let you play with your friends whenever you wanted, as late as you wanted." Being the stool pigeon I was—my father's character assessment, as I spilled every secret I ever possessed to my mother, including his Friday night candy donations—I informed on Rita not ten minutes later,

My mother and her sister Rita were the best of friends. December 31, 1982.

and my mother pulled her aside right there in the street and set her straight: "She is *not* your daughter," she admonished. "She is *my* daughter, and she will live by *my* rules. Do you understand me?" But there were moments, before I knew what mature love was, when I wished Rita had been my mother. She was magnetic. I noticed that she and my father had a special bond, laughing and joking together like they were the married couple, and in a strange mix of fantasy and confusion, I began to wonder if I was really their child and not my mother's. They just seemed so perfectly matched that if I was casting the movie, they would be the romantic leads. Rita and my father mirrored each other's energy, while my mother's tended to lag.

But my mother didn't seem to notice—if anything, Rita's presence gave my mother an excuse to shop. The four of us would take off for long weekends to San Diego on Rita's dime, staying at Le Meridien in Coronado and ordering niçoise salad as we lounged by the pool. Sometimes just my mother, Rita, and I would drive up to Beverly Hills and spend a weekend at the Bel Age enjoying room service while my father stayed behind to work. Rita led the three of us into the lap of luxury, and it was a hard habit to break when she left. She provided a brief respite from the drudgery of dirty carpets/unfulfilling homemaking/third grade, and gave us an excuse to laugh, which came in handy when we lost the Chapman contract. After two years the college decided to use an in-house crew and it was a big financial loss. The pile under the carpet dwindled and our reliance on plastic grew. We had just purchased a powder-blue Ford Econoline work van for my Dad and a cream-colored Taurus for my mom, a lemon that constantly leaked coolant. But because we'd lost Chapman we couldn't replace the Taurus, so we stuck it out through the syrup smell and the unending repairs.

Our decreased spending ability was something even I picked up on, as I found myself home more often instead of at the mall. I also grew more conscious of the fact that my father performed tedious, back-breaking work for a living, while my friend Heather's father owned a hardware store; Tori's father worked in an office and even had a home computer—a Wang!—and Kara's father . . . well, I'm not sure what Kara's father did, but he didn't come home with bulging biceps covered in sweat and rough, callused hands. By the time my father had put in ten years of carpet cleaning he had to stop wearing his wedding ring because, he said, his hands had become so swollen. Every day when he came home I'd ask, almost like a doting wife, "How was your day?" to which he'd respond, "Tiring." We ran through this routine every evening for years and he always answered the same way.

Since my mother wasn't crazy about outdoor activities, it was my father who spent an hour in bumper-to-bumper traffic on winding Laguna Canyon Road every summer Sunday so we could spend a few blessed hours at the beach. He was the one who took me to Wild Rivers, either alone or with one of my friends, and sat around watching me career down one water slide after another without even the benefit of beer. Once I hid an inflamed throat from my mother so she couldn't prohibit us from one of our weekend jaunts; I'd already had pneumonia twice, in addition to numerous bouts with bronchitis and strep throat, and she would have locked me in my room with a humidifier if she'd known I was ill.

"See, Eleanor?" my father would say over dinner, which we had together at the same time every night with few exceptions. "We're bonding!" And here he'd hold his wrist up to his forehead and keep it there as he sipped his wine and passed the bread, like it was Krazy Glued to his skin. Get it? Bonding. My father's lame humor never ceased to tickle me, and I always laughed at his silly jokes. Another one of his dinnertime gags was his contention that he wasn't John Mascia, but Bruce Springboard—a play on the reigning prince of rock, Bruce

My father and me right before my tenth birthday party, November 1987.

Springsteen—a guest in our house who swung by for my mother's sautéed escarole and oven-baked chicken. I must have been a great audience, cascading giggles as I accompanied him to weekend home measuring appointments and trips to the upholstery warehouse where he picked up books of carpet samples. As soon as we got home I'd press my nose against the swatches and breathe in the new floor smell; to this day I can't pass a carpet store without staring at the multicolored patches and suppressing a desire to walk up to them and sniff.

At the same time, my social life on Rio Verde was vastly improving, though friends one day could turn out to be bullies the next. The little devils who lived across the street, a pair of prepubescent brothers, were behind one of the scariest and most exciting hoaxes of my young life up till that point: a chain letter. It had arrived in my mailbox on a Saturday morning, precipitated by a prank call and a hangup, and luckily Heather, my friend from school, was there when I opened it. "Come here!" I shrieked, and read the sinister contents aloud. It said something like, "We know what you did, and if you don't pass this letter on, everyone will know." It may or may not have mentioned the government, but either way, I soon became convinced that the government had sent the letter. I looked at Heather with wide, terrified eyes: How did they know about what had happened to Daddy? I mean, it *must* have been about that. It was just too accurate a guess for it to involve anything other than the fact that my father had been in jail.

"Heather," I said grimly, "there's something I have to tell you." I told her about how the police had come for my father in Irvine and how we had to follow him back to New York and Florida, where he was kept in various facilities. "I don't know how they found us here," I said, hysterical, "but please, *please* don't tell anyone!"

"I promise, Jenny," she said, clearly not sharing my sense of urgency.

"Cross your heart?" I said. "Because if the government is after us again I can't tell my mommy. It would kill her." But I told my mommy anyway, showing her the letter the next morning when Heather was still asleep.

"Jenny, get over here," she said sternly, dragging me into the garage and locking the door. She wagged her finger in my face. "Listen to me," she said. "You are *never* to tell anyone about what happened with Daddy and the facility. Do you understand me?"

"But Mommy," I explained, "it could be the government! They could be after us again! They could take Daddy away again!" If I found out before she did, I reasoned, then maybe I could stop it this time. I could rewrite history.

She opened the letter, mockingly read the first few lines aloud, and laughed. "Jenny, if the government is coming for us, it won't be in the form of a chain letter," she said. I whimpered for a few minutes, unable to weed out the real from the imagined, but I came to understand her way of thinking. Chain letters, newly discovered by my peers, were fast becoming the rage in my class. I should have been able to differentiate a low-tech viral hoax from the very real events that had transpired three years before. "Now," she said, folding up the letter and handing it back to me, "you go in there and tell Heather that your father was arrested and let go immediately afterward—because he got a traffic ticket. It was a mistake, that's all. Your father was *mistakenly* arrested." I nodded. But I had one more question:

"Is that really why Daddy was sent to the facility?" I asked. "That's not why, right?" I'd never really gotten an explanation and I wasn't going to ask him. She sized me up and probably realized that she couldn't explain away two separate arrests and five months in jail with a misunderstanding at a routine traffic stop.

"No," she admitted. "Do you want to know why Daddy was arrested and sent to the facility?"

"Yes, please!" I exclaimed.

"Shhh," she said, "calm down. Okay. Your father was arrested because there is another man with his name who did something bad, something very bad. This man is also John Mascia. It was a simple case of mistaken identity. But you are *not* to tell Heather that. Do you hear me?"

"Yes, Mommy," I said obediently.

"You must never tell our business to strangers," she said. "They are not your family. They are not your blood. Do you understand?"

I nodded again.

"Now go tell her the truth—he was arrested because of a ticket, and let go *right away*."

"Yes, Mommy."

But I didn't have to worry too much about Heather holding our skeletons over my head, as my parents decided a few months later to send me to Catholic school, which boasted a superior education. The only hitch was the forty-five-minute morning commute. My parents alternated driving days; if my father had a job that took him north he would be the one to take me, though this only happened once or twice a week. My father would let me listen to all the pop music I wanted, whereas my mother insisted on the news and smoked with the windows closed; in the space of a year the cream velour seats became pockmarked with cigarette burns. But after commuting an hour and a half each day for two years the news became tiresome, and before long she turned off KFWB 980 and began to tell stories in her mannered, animated way: about the gods on Mount Olympus and their lusty, hubris-infused adventures; Scheherazade weaving her yarns for King Shahryar; Robert Kennedy and all the promise lost when he was killed ("He would have kept us out of the war!" she railed); and in the same vein, the tragedy of Vietnam ("You've *got* to read a book called *The March of Folly* by Barbara Tuchman—well, maybe when you're a little older"); the glory of Elizabeth I; great dancers like Suzanne Farrell and Isadora Duncan ("Poor Isadora died a horrible death—her scarf got caught in the car wheels and rear axle, strangling her!") and their Svengalis, like Balanchine; great actresses like Sarah Bernhardt, who played Hamlet and performed long after her right leg was amputated, and Meryl Streep, who we both believed to be the Greatest Actress of Our Time (I'd even decided to be an actress after seeing her in *Heartburn*) and who, my mother told me, was a graduate of the Yale School of Drama (where I therefore decided I must go); even James Irvine, onetime owner of a third of Orange County, after whom Irvine was named.

"When James Irvine arrived, the only people living here were Spanish settlers and Serrano Indians," my mother, who had just finished reading *Bury My Heart at Wounded Knee*, told me, "and the hills were covered with row after row of orange California poppies as far as the eye could see. It must have looked like the hills were on fire! Well, Irvine took one look at those golden hills and declared, 'All this is mine.'" Here she would stretch out her arms and her voice would get deep, mimicking the zealous entitlement of Donald Trump. No topic was off-limits, as she could pontificate about pretty much anything, lecturing as if she stood before a class of twenty-five. "You have such big gaps in your history," she would lament, and proceeded to do her best to fill them in, talking long after we'd pulled in to the school parking lot. Even the prospect of my tardiness couldn't slow her down; I often had my hand on the door handle for a good ten minutes before she was finished with her story for that day.

As we sailed down long stretches of freeway with little to gaze upon other than the glorious snow-capped mountains we quickly took for granted, her recitations of history turned into tales of her life before me. It would always begin, "Did I ever tell you about . . ." and from there I was launched into April 1945, when FDR died, something she said she vaguely remembered. "My mother ran outside and everyone on the block was standing around the radio crying," she recalled. "This is when we lived on Ocean Avenue. I was only five or six at the time, so I didn't really know what was happening." That same year my mother nearly died from double pneumococcal pneumonia, the unintended side effect of tonsil removal surgery, which everyone had in those days even if they didn't need it. "I inhaled the ether," she said, "and I got so sick afterward, they thought I might die. They weren't sure for a while. My parents were very wealthy so they got private round-the-clock nurses who came to the house and kept me sequestered from everyone. The pneumonia was in both lungs and I was in bed for weeks."

"And you *still* smoked after that?" I asked. I had already begun ribbing my parents for smoking so much, and for so many years—they'd both started in their early teens.

"Yeah, I know," she conceded. "Stupid, huh?" She told me that her father had made a fortune in the garment industry only to lose it all because of bad business decisions. "He was an alcoholic," she said, "and as he drank more he began to lose his judgment." He also terrorized my mother and her sisters, threatening with a sneer in his voice that he'd flatten them into the wall if they made too much noise. "He always called us morons," she said, "which was funny, because we were all so smart." Arline was the one with the genius IQ and my grandmother agreed to let her skip two grades, which my mother insisted was a mistake because she was already short for her age. My mother graduated from Brooklyn College with honors, "so for my father to call us morons was ridiculous," she spat.

"So what did you do when your dad called you that?" I asked, my voice full of concern. I couldn't imagine being treated that way by my parents. Even if we fought, I knew they loved me. I couldn't imagine doubting it.

"I told him to shut up," she said. "But that was later on. At first, when he yelled at me that way, I'd get such a lump in my throat, you know, where you feel like you're swallowing your tongue, d'ya evah get that?" I nodded; I knew it well. Arline and Rita both left home as soon as they were old enough to marry. At seventeen, Arline hitched herself to the construction worker who was building the house across the street and went to live with him in Connecticut; my mother had helped Arline carry her suitcase out to the car and their father locked her out of the house in retaliation. Rita met Kara's father during a family vacation to Miami when she was also seventeen, but my mother didn't leave until she married David at twenty-four. "Did I ever tell you what my father did when I got my fellowship to Columbia for Russian studies?" she asked me. I shook my head. "We went out to dinner one night: me, David, my mother and father, and Rita. My father was drunk, *nokhamol,* and I said to my mother, 'We don't have to go celebrate, it's okay,' but she insisted we go. A fellowship to Columbia is a big deal. I ended up in class with all of these CIA agents who were cramming for the cold war," she said, laughing. "Too bad I didn't finish my degree—I was three credits shy, all I had to do was finish my master's thesis, but David and I were going through a divorce, so I stayed in bed and didn't get up."

"You never finished?" I asked.

"Yeah. Boy, was I stupid. Anyway, when I was accepted we went to this restaurant, and we were sitting at the table, and out of nowhere, my father announces, 'You all think she's so smart? She's not fit to lick Arline's boots!'"

"What?" I asked, horrified.

"Well, David was livid. Rita started crying. I didn't know what to say, I was just stunned, so David says, in front of everyone, 'Why don't you throw your drink in his fucking face?'"

"Did you?" I asked.

"Nah," she said.

"Still," I said, "that was so cool of David!"

"I know," she said, nodding. David and my mother both taught English literature for several years at Thomas Jefferson High School in East New York, Brooklyn. In the mid-seventies they opened a live-in drug-rehabilitation center for high school students called Alpha School. It went without saying that David was gay; it's not something she ever had to explain to me. "Sex is the glue that binds people together," she once mused, "and when that's gone, everything else follows." That didn't stop my mother from remarrying him four years after they divorced the first time. "We were best friends, Jenny, what can I say? Besides, the Mexican divorce I got for us after the first marriage probably wasn't legal anyway." All told, they were married for twelve years, finally divorcing in 1975, the year she met my father.

David's being gay meant that he could still be friends with my mother without incurring any jealousy from my father, not that my father seemed like the jealous type. In fact, my mother was set to visit David soon because he was sick. She said it was some type of blood cancer but she wasn't sure if it could be treated.

"My father called David a *fagalah* behind his back all the time," my mother said. "When he walked me down the aisle when we got married—we had this big tent wedding in our backyard in Manhattan Beach—he handed me to David and said, 'Here. Now *you* can deal with her.'"

"Oh, Mommy," I said, feeling genuinely sorry for her.

"Not everyone has a good daddy like you do," she said. "Just remember that. You're very lucky." I nodded obediently. "He was awful to my mother, too," she added.

"How?" I asked. "What did he do?"

"Well, he came home drunk all the time, and I know for a fact he cheated on her, too," she revealed. "And my mother knew it. In fact, she once begged me to follow him around and report back."

"Did you?" I asked from the edge of my seat.

"No, I refused," she said. My grandmother never left him, even after he forced her to sell her share in a brownstone on Fifth Avenue because he needed the money to pay off his debts. He also forced her to sell their mansion in Manhattan Beach for much less than it was worth, something like $75,000. "Today, my god, it could probably go for at least three-quarters of a million, maybe more," my mother told me. "The day he died, I'll never forget, she called me up in Miami, and I answered the phone, and I couldn't even understand what she was saying—she was wailing, crying, 'My husband is dead! My husband died!' Even today, if you ask her about Sam Sacks, he's Saint Sam, who never drank, never cheated on her, ugh, please," she said, waving her hand in disgust.

"I'm sorry, Mommy," I said.

"What are you sorry for?" she asked. "I just learned that there is no such thing as unconditional love."

I studied her face; surely she couldn't mean that. "But I love you unconditionally," I said.

"And I love you unconditionally, too," she said. "But that's never guaranteed. And that's what the wonderful Sam Sacks taught me."

"Mommy, Daddy never cheated on you, right?" I asked, believing such a thing to be impossible but asking anyway.

"Oh, no," she said, shaking her head. "Never." Sam had started drinking not long after my grandma Vivian's mental breakdown. "My mother was so beautiful, Jenny," she told me. "You have to understand, she came here from the Ukraine before the Depression, and even when everyone else was starving she looked like a movie star." My mother was right—we had black-and-white thirties-era portrait photographs of both sets of my grandparents displayed prominently throughout the house, and my grandmother Helen could have passed an MGM screen test as well. Vivian was raised by her grandparents in a tiny Ukrainian town called Mogilev-Podolskiy but came to the States when she was a teenager, fleeing the post–World War I pogroms that engulfed her corner of the Soviet Union. In one particularly harrowing incident, Vivian and her extended family were forced to hide in a closet to avoid capture and six-year-old Vivian began to cry. Her uncle held a knife to her throat, ready to end her life if she made enough noise to arouse their attackers. "After the Holocaust my mother said, 'I will never set foot in Europe again as long as I live,' and she didn't." One night when Vivian and Sam went to see *The Best Years of Our Lives,* a postwar MGM weepie, she suddenly turned to Sam in the darkened movie theater and said she didn't feel well and had to leave immediately. She appeared to be in the throes of a massive panic attack. Sam ushered them into the car and a doctor was called, then a psychiatrist. After that night a revolving door of doctors treated Vivian at the house, and the three Sacks girls soon found themselves reared by nurses and housekeepers for the next several years as Vivian struggled to function. The most loyal staffer they had, a young black housekeeper named Clotie, became their surrogate mother.

"Clotie would bring me a hot lunch to school every day," my mother recalled, "steamed fish, fresh vegetables. Of course, I was mortified, because I was the only kid who had her lunch brought to her on a silver platter—literally."

Vivian was found to be suffering a nervous breakdown in addition to agoraphobia, and the only effective treatment in 1946 was electroshock therapy, which was administered to Vivian for a year. In the house. When the children were home.

My mother shrugged. "They were rich," she explained. "They could afford to keep her out of the asylum." But they couldn't find a way to muffle Vivian's screams before the electricity coursed through her body, and once or twice a week, when Vivian was getting treatment in the bedroom, my mother and Arline would sit on the staircase in silence and listen.

"I could hear her screaming. *Oy*, Jenny, it was awful," she said. "After that, my mother had housekeepers come in six days a week, and on the seventh day she would make us get on our hands and knees and scrub the floor."

"Like *Mommie Dearest*?" I asked. Because of its high camp factor it was one of my favorite films. My mother joked about it with me for years, occasionally popping into my room with a hanger in her hand and cryptically reciting its signature line, "No more wire hangers!"

"Not quite that bad," she said. "But she was so obsessed with cleanliness that she once threatened to throw all my books into the incinerator if I didn't put them away. And then she did it."

"Books?" I asked, alarmed. That must have cut my mother deeply. She read at least five books a week, all procured from the Orange County Public Library, some of which went unreturned.

"But that's nothing. My mother once told me how she tried to abort each of us," she said quietly, staring straight ahead as we circled the El Toro marine base. "She said she took hot baths to try to force a miscarriage each time. What can I say? She was not a well woman."

"Wow," I said, not knowing what else to say. However much my mother told me about her own life, there was little she said about my father's. Even the smallest inquiries yielded vague results.

"Hey, Ma?" I asked one day.

"Ye-*es*?" she replied.

"How did you and Daddy meet?"

"Through friends," she said blithely.

"Oh," I said.

"Well, we were good friends first," she added. "And then one night we went to dinner at a friend's house and started playing footsie under the table. After that we went home and the rest, my dear, is history."

"Mom! Ew!" I exclaimed, pantomiming retching.

"Well, you *asked*," she said.

"Hey, Ma?" I asked a few seconds later.

"Ye-*es*?"

"Where did Daddy grow up?" I asked.

"Daddy grew up in Red Hook, in Brooklyn," she said, "but they moved to Bay Ridge when he was still a kid."

"Was that close to Manhattan Beach?" I asked.

A haughty chuckle escaped her lips. "No, my dear," she said, "that is nowhere near Manhattan Beach."

"Because you guys could have passed each other on the street, like, a thousand times! And you were strangers. And now you're married!" The thought delighted me to no end.

"I doubt we ever passed each other on the street," she said.

"How come? You never know," I said.

"I just have a feeling," she replied.

"If you both grew up in Brooklyn, how come you moved to California?"

"Well, we were living in Miami when you were born, and after a little while we decided we wanted a change," she said. "We'd moved there because his kids were there, but things didn't really work out with them as he'd hoped, but that's a story for another time. We went to Houston but I got sick of it after about a year and a half, so I said to your father, 'What about California?' David and I had been to Southern California once before, and I remembered really liking it. I also really liked San Francisco, but San Francisco gets cold in the winter, so we decided to try Orange County. I told your father that the weather there is like the Mediterranean, always sunny and never really humid. So we went to California and ended up in this little cottage in Laguna Beach. That was where you choked on the tortilla chip and Grandma Helen gave you the Heimlich, remember?" I nodded. "We loved Laguna, but it was expensive, even in 1980. So we had to move, and we found the place in Turtle Rock. It's funny, a friend once told me, 'Never move anywhere for the weather.'"

"But you did," I pointed out.

She shrugged. "What do they know?"

THAT SPRING RITA came for a visit. She'd already spent Christmas with us, and four months later she returned because my mother was spending a few weeks in New York to see David and someone needed to drive me to school and tap, jazz, and ballet. Of course, my mother was taking Amtrak, which extended the trip by at least a week. When she returned she found her only daughter had grown a double chin, thanks to all the junk food my favorite aunt was feeding me. "Jenny?" she said when we picked her up at the train station, as if she didn't recognize me. "We're putting you on a diet, kiddo."

The day after she returned was my father's birthday. The four of us planned an informal dinner of bagels and lox; any kind of celebration seemed inappropriate because of David's illness. Apparently he was in the hospital when my mother had boarded her train at Penn Station, so she was understandably blue. Sometime in the afternoon my father took me to my favorite stationery store to get a new pencil box, even though I already owned half a dozen, but I think my father just wanted to get out of the house for an hour. When we returned we were confronted by Rita at the garage door.

"David died," she said quietly. I ran to my parents' bedroom to find my mother lying on her side of the bed with a phone in her hand. Even though her cheeks were wet with tears she was laughing.

"Why is she laughing?" I asked Rita. "Shouldn't she be sad?" Maybe it wasn't true, a false alarm, and she'd just discovered the truth and her laughter signified relief.

"She is sad, Jenbo," Rita said. "But sometimes we laugh to feel better. We're different like that." By "we" I knew she meant the Sacks side of the family.

"Mommy? Are you okay?" I called from the doorway. "Why are you laughing?"

"I'm on the phone with Donald," she whispered. Donald was David's best friend, a former high school classmate of theirs who was raised a few streets away in Manhattan Beach. I had spoken to him on the phone a few times since David had been sick and I noticed that they employed the same effeminate drawl. I had asked my mother if David and Donald were boyfriends, but she said no, they were more like brothers. "Well, maybe more like cousins," she said, correcting herself.

She never told me that David had AIDS, but a few months later an HBO special about the AIDS quilt came on and I turned to my mother, who was watching from the kitchen doorway, and said, "Mommy,

David died of AIDS, didn't he?" It didn't take a genius—I'd seen Randy Shilts's *And the Band Played On* lying around the house, and she seemed especially interested in news reports about the disease.

"Yes, Jenny, he did," she said. "Do you want to know how AIDS is transmitted?" Leave it to her to turn this episode into a lesson plan.

"I already know," I said. It was all over the news. Despite the tragedy, my mother sat down with us for dinner that April 10, my father's fifty-first birthday. As she dished out the bagels she recited snarkily, "April is the cruelest month, breeding lilacs out of the dead land. . . ." I didn't get the T. S. Eliot reference, as my attention was focused on the clock, which I was watching intently; my father had been born at 5:05 and my goal was to stick a candle in his bagel in lieu of a cake, which we didn't have.

"Um, Daddy?" I asked with faux ignorance.

"What?" he asked, sounding agitated and passing the plate of lox to Rita.

"What time is it?" My candle was poised . . .

"There's a clock right in front of you," he snapped, clearly annoyed. I broke into tears and ran to my room. My mother followed suit, returning to her bedroom, and Rita followed, calling after her, "El? El!" Our house was in turmoil. It wouldn't be the last time, either—in the months after David's death my parents fought into the night about one thing or another. I couldn't make out their sharp yelps and retorts, but a few times my father left and I feared he wouldn't come back. Whenever the front door slammed I'd tiptoe out of my bedroom and knock on her door. "Did he leave?" I'd ask my mother. "I don't know," she'd respond. But he always came back, until he didn't.

CHAPTER 4

THE CALL CAME EARLY THE NEXT SPRING: THE OWNER OF THE house on Rio Verde was moving back and we had to leave. Such are the perils of perpetually renting. My parents found us a three-bedroom, two-story house off Jeronimo Road with a brown-carpeted conversation pit, that 1970s-era relic, two living rooms, a bar, a dining room, and three fireplaces. The backyard was tiny, just big enough for a few tomato plants, which we never tended. It set us back $1,300 a month, and I occasionally heard grumblings from my father about "cash advances." The house turned out to be too big for the three of us, and too dark—the west-facing windows let in little light and the setup of the place left vast areas shrouded in darkness. The Rio Verde house had been bright and sun-kissed; at Peacock we were vampires. We never, ever sat in the conversation pit, and we never burned a single log in any of the fireplaces.

Soon after we moved into the Peacock house my mother took me to the Capezio store to get ballet clothes. "Mom, nooooooo," I complained. I'd had enough superfluous shopping for a lifetime.

"But you need new ballet shoes," she argued.

"No, please, I'm fine," I said.

"But Jenny, it's okay, we're right here," she said, pulling into the lot.

"Mom," I said, in a "Let me level with you" tone. I waited until she turned off the engine before presenting my case. "You don't need to spend money on me. I hear you and Daddy fighting, I know how bad we're doing with money. You don't have to do this, I'm fine with the ballet shoes I have." It was all an act. I just couldn't stomach another shopping trip, but what I'd said about their fighting was true.

She looked stricken and leaned back in her seat. "Jenny," she finally said, "there's something I should tell you."

"What is it?" I asked.

"Your father and I are busting out all the credit cards," she said gravely.

"What does that mean?" I asked.

"It means that we're going to go bankrupt, and since we're not going to pay our bills—because we're eventually gonna declare bankruptcy anyway, so, you know, what's the point—we can spend all the cards to the limit. Do you understand? So, we *can* get you those ballet shoes. You don't have to feel bad, because we're not going to pay the bill."

Damn! She'd found a way to take me shopping despite my efforts to resist. "What does that mean, you're going bankrupt? Isn't that bad?"

"Well, it can be," she said, "but we've been using fake Social Security numbers. Your father used his father's for a time, and I've been using someone else's, don't ask me why. Long story. And after we declare bankruptcy, we're gonna go back to using our real ones."

"Oh," I said. A more mature person might have called it fraud, but my parents weren't capable of something as ugly-sounding as fraud. This was Yonny and Swellenor! They were too cool to be criminals. No, there was a special name for what they were doing: "busting out the cards." Their bust netted all we could have asked for: another set of couches for the front living room; the train set my father had always wanted; a surprise twelfth birthday party at Medieval Times; several months of cash advances for tuition and rent; dinners in Newport; braces, now that I had finally stopped sucking my thumb; Chanel and Ann Taylor for my mother; countless cartons of cigarettes; and new tools for my father. What he should have gotten was a set of dentures, because his teeth had started to fall out. But this was the same man who still wore his brown leisure suits from the seventies. Wore them well, don't get me wrong, but he just wasn't the type to splurge on appearances.

One of the reasons my parents fought so much was the disparity in their incomes. My father earned north of $50,000 a year, tax-free, while my mother earned, well, nothing. Ironically, it was my father who had talked her into early retirement right before they married, when she got sick of dragging herself out of bed every morning to teach junior high and realized she was burned out. She took the California teaching test a few times in an effort to restore her license, but she kept failing the math section by a few points. So she started her own carpet sales outfit, an offshoot of my father's business she dubbed Gold Coast Carpets. Soon I was joining her on appointments to carpet warehouses as I had with my father. Still, she didn't work as much as he did, and I found myself riveted by their arguments, which mainly dwelled on her inability to "contribute."

"You don't *contribute,* Eleanor, dammit! I'm killing myself here!" my father would shout, spit flying, before he slammed the front door. One night I overheard my parents screaming at each other in the living room next to the empty conversation pit:

"Eleanor, shut the fuck up!"

"Oh, go fuck yourself, Johnny!"

"Go fuck myself? *Fuck you!*"

I felt so helpless, doing nothing as my world was imploding. I decided I had to act or I'd never forgive myself, so I stomped halfway down the stairs and watched as they fought over a white cardboard box of bills, which was caught in a game of tug-of-war between them. As soon as I saw this I screamed, "Will you two . . . stop . . . acting . . . like . . . *children!*" My throat was pained and my voice came out in tight little huffs, that's how scared I was to raise my voice to my father.

They froze. My father had just hurled the box skyward and the ceiling's cottage-cheese-textured coating fluttered down around him like snow; credit card bills, gas bills, electric and water bills drifted down to their feet.

"Okay, okay," my mother said, nodding, appearing to come to her senses. My father's face was still contorted into a grimace; he took the half-empty box and ducked into the other living room, the one without the conversation pit. I could tell he was going to leave again, and I had a feeling it wasn't going to be for just a few hours this time.

The next morning I awoke to find a note to my mother on the dining room table with thirty-six dollars folded inside. It was all the money he left us with.

"He's gone, isn't he," I said to my mother, who joined me at the dining room table. Her arm circled my waist.

"Yep," she said. "Looks like it." The two of us spent the day driving around, halfheartedly keeping an afternoon carpet sales appointment but mainly staying away from our empty house, which was now much too big for us. It was just the two of us again, and we steeled ourselves to face each day without him.

My father's absence hardened my mother; soon she confided the real reason behind his departure, an admission prompted by the sight of her twelve-year-old daughter standing at the refrigerator pouring a drop of white wine into her water.

"What are you doing?" she asked.

"What? Nothing, just taking a drop of—"

"You're too young to drink that," she said. "Let me see." I held up my four-ounce juice glass for her to inspect.

"Mom, you and Daddy always let me have wine and water with dinner," I argued. "I like the taste." She'd gotten a particularly tart Sauvignon Blanc just when I was becoming obsessed with everything sour: Granny Smith apples, salads dressed in nothing but balsamic vinegar, Sour Patch Kids.

"Let's talk for a second," she said, and led me into the living room. She told me that my father had left because his drinking had spiraled out of control, and until he fixed it he couldn't live with us. This was a surprise to me—I'd never once seen him drunk. He must have been drinking after I went to bed. "I've been going to something called Al-Anon," she went on. "It's a support group for codependents, which are people married to alcoholics. If you want, you can come with me—or, better yet, there's a group called Alateen, if you want you could go to that."

"Um, no, it's okay," I said. I didn't really find it necessary, since his alcoholism didn't directly affect me. My father didn't seem to be in any hurry to fix his problem, either, renting an apartment in Dana Point. It was much smaller than any place we'd ever lived, and it reeked of bachelor. The dishes he served our lunch on were cheap, probably from Kmart, as was the silverware, which was not nearly as nice as our stainless steel bamboo. The place was also stocked with bottles of scotch, vodka, and gin. If a bone of contention with my mother had been his alcohol consumption, he was flaunting it now. I visited a couple of times, took lonely jaunts with him along the beach, and we even went fishing once, but all he could talk about was how every sappy pop song on the radio reminded him of my mother. And in 1989, that was every song but "Funky Cold Medina."

Several weeks later my parents decided they would attempt a recon-ciliation. The plan was to meet at Peppino's, our favorite Italian restau-rant. It was close to the house, so if all went well Daddy would maybe possibly come back home with us. At least that was what I hoped.

It didn't pan out that way. My parents met in the parking lot and put their names in for a table. While they waited outside they smoked their brains out and began to argue. It became so fierce that my father sped off in his big blue truck and my mother and I followed after him in the Taurus. We passed each other on the road and my parents slowed down just enough to flick each other off. Repeatedly.

"Fuck you, Eleanor!" my father shouted out his window.

"Ma, please, I don't want to crash!" I yelled, clicking my seat belt into place.

"Go fuck yourself, Johnny!" she screamed, and we accelerated ahead of him. When my father gave up his pursuit and headed toward the coast we continued home at a saner speed. When we got back to Pea-cock Street I ran upstairs and locked myself in my closet, where my only company was the crickets chirping away in the attic we never used for storage, thanks to my second bedroom across the hall.

The calls started about forty-five minutes after we got home; my mother screened them in her bedroom, and even though three closed doors separated me from the answering machine I could still hear my father's cursing and yelling. I wandered into her room and found her sitting on the edge of the bed, her head bowed in resignation.

"I just don't know what to do," she said. "He's gone middle-age crazy. Instead of buying a Porsche he bought a bottle of scotch." From that night on I slept in my mother's bed because I didn't want to be alone. Even though he was acting like a madman, my father's absence made me feel incredibly insecure.

My mother spent hours on the phone strategizing with Rita about how to fix her marriage—or not. (Though Arline was closer in age, she and my mother didn't speak anymore, and hadn't in years, though she wouldn't tell me why.) Rita would send my mother bubble envelopes stuffed with Valium, and this relaxed her somewhat. Money was tight, but they hadn't officially declared bankruptcy yet, so we were able to finance our lives with plastic for a while longer. But the clock was ticking—both carpet businesses weren't exactly reaping whirlwind profits now that its CEOs were engaged in a puerile battle royal, one that made me look like an adult in comparison.

One evening in early September my mother got a call from my father. "This is it!" she announced, grabbing her keys and purse and heading for the car.

"What's going on?" I asked.

"It's over," she declared. "Your father has agreed to go to rehab."

"You mean you made up?" I asked excitedly. "He's coming home?"

"Well, we've agreed that he'll go to a treatment facility for a month, and then he can come home. He wants us to come and pack his apartment up with him." She paused by the garage door. "You ready?" she asked, ushering me into the car. We pulled up to my father's apartment and he was waiting outside. He embraced us both.

"I'm so sorry," he said to each of us.

"It's okay, Daddy," I said, relieved to see him back to his old self. He'd been so angry before; if being away from us for another month meant he would return to being Bruce Springboard, it was a sacrifice I was willing to make. We went into his apartment and packed up his clothes and other personal effects. The furniture was all used or borrowed, and we had so much already that there was no need to take it. I spotted the shelf near the sink that held his liquor bottles and made a beeline for them, twisting off the caps and gleefully pouring the contents of each down the sink. Whatever was in those bottles had threatened to break up my parents' marriage, and I couldn't wait to watch it circle the drain. "I never saw someone so happy pouring scotch down the sink," my mother said years later, recalling that night.

My father checked himself in to a detox center for twenty-eight days, and after he returned he seemed heartened; he reached his sixty-day sobriety mark, then ninety. Oddly, in the years that followed he was still able to have a glass of wine with dinner and the occasional scotch, though not right away. But with his mind now clear he faced our financial difficulties head-on and decided we needed to make some changes. Eight months after we'd moved into the darkened domicile on Peacock Street, my father made an announcement at the breakfast table one morning.

"Kids," he said, "we're moving."

CHAPTER 5

Yolanda Street
Aliso Viejo, California
September 1992

. . .

AFTER A SHORT STINT IN A CONDO IN MISSION VIEJO WE FOUND an airy two-story, four-bedroom abode with lots of light on the edge of Laguna Hills. You had to walk through the living room to get to the kitchen and family room, which was an odd setup, and the backyard was big enough for a chair, maybe two. But I had two back-to-back bedrooms that overlooked the street: One was for sleeping and the other was my study, which my parents outfitted with an elegant bleached-wood writing table and white twin Ikea bookcases. My parents' bedroom had a stall shower and a bathtub, plus a walk-in closet, and my father finally had a proper office, where we also kept the computer. The only drawback was that the house looked like every other house on the block. It was so similar, in fact, that one day my father pulled in to the driveway, got the mail, and bounded up the front steps, and only when he tried to put his key in the door did he realize he was at the wrong house.

But soon this perfect little cookie-cutter became host to the wars my mother and I conducted, our screams echoing throughout the house and enraging my father. Once I was grounded for ten days because I'd borrowed my mother's clothes without asking, then had the nerve to act like I didn't give a shit when she demanded to know what I'd done with them.

"I don't know, did you try the hamper?" I asked nonchalantly while barely looking up from my game of Tetris, which was doing a fabulous job of distracting me from writing a term paper.

"What did you say, you little bitch?" she yelled back. My father heard this and intervened.

"Whoa! What the fuck are you yelling from room to room for?" he demanded, emerging from the living room and suddenly agitated. (Yelling from room to room was his biggest pet peeve.) Then he was forced, as always in such scenes, to take the side that would end the fight quickest—usually my mother's.

"Just tell your mother what the fuck you did with her—what was it, El?"

"My DKNY shirt!" she exclaimed.

"Oh! Jenny! Give her shirt back!" he yelled. I said I didn't know where it was, and he commanded me to find it. I rolled my eyes and acted like I didn't care again, and he lunged toward me menacingly, coming upon me so quickly that it seemed like he'd covered twenty feet in a matter of seconds.

Once a scene like this ended with a slap so hard I temporarily lost the hearing in my right ear. My father had cornered me on the upstairs landing and backed me all the way into my study with his yelling; I tripped over my own feet in an effort to avoid him and ended up on the floor, where he nearly climbed on top of me to deliver the blunt smack. It was such a violent scene that my mother, the one who'd instigated the fight, had to physically pull him off me. When he got angry like that, which was happening more and more, it was impossible to calm him down. The look on his face when he hit me haunted me for years after that night, and I recognized it from my childhood: He had lost himself to rage, just drowned in the stuff, and went to a place where even I, his little girl, couldn't reach him.

My mother opted not to send me to a Catholic high school, instead enrolling me in the local public school and shoving me head-first through the honors program, whether I liked it or not. But I didn't know anyone there, and for the first couple of months of my freshman year I wandered around in a solitary haze, eating my lunches alone and burying my head in my books. But I eventually made friends, as kids always do, and my little gang and I would spend afternoons strolling the baking sidewalks that lined the antiseptically pink mini-malls, as none of us was yet old enough to drive. Sometimes we lucked out and one of our moms chauffeured us from place to place. In fact, I'll never forget one particular car ride, when my friend's mother was listening to a call-in radio show that featured a woman justifying her marriage to an ex-convict.

"I love my husband," the caller said. "It doesn't matter what he's done."

"I would *never* marry someone who's been in jail," my friend's mother said disdainfully, shaking her head. Though she didn't look at me, I wondered, did she know? She had met my parents—could she tell just by looking at my father that he had been imprisoned? It was a dim realization, but that day in the car was when it began to grow. For the first time, I understood that this very topic applied to me.

My mother was married to an ex-convict.

But hints of my father's past were suddenly popping up everywhere, and my parents fought less and less to hide them. It was around this time my father got word that one of his New York friends, Vinny Cassese—also known as "Big Vinny" because of his considerable girth—had died of lymphoma. Though I wasn't sure how they'd met, I knew they'd been friends for many years. I never saw him cry over it like my mother had with David, but he did spend an awful lot of time on the phone afterward with Big Vinny's son, Carmine, who was in prison and seeking advice from the next best father figure about whether to testify against the gangsters he used to work for. I'd hear my father on the phone night after night, urging Carmine, "Take the deal. Listen to me, I know what I'm talking about." Over dinner one night he told my mother that the very people Carmine was protecting had been captured on tape ordering his murder. "Can you believe it?" my father asked over his flank steak, so desperate he was even searching my face for wisdom. "They were gonna whack him and he *still* won't cut a deal and testify."

"I thought being a rat was bad, Daddy," I pointed out. I'd learned that much from the Corleone family.

"Yeah, but being stupid is worse," he concluded.

AS HIGH SCHOOL wore on my father would often come home in a good mood, boasting of a job he'd booked that had saved us from financial demise at the last moment. But I sensed the desperation fueling his disposition, and since I had a feeling our situation was tenuous I took a special interest, inquiring from time to time about our finances.

"We're okay," he'd reply, in a rehash of the "How was your day, Daddy?"/"Tiring" routine we'd first honed when I was a child. I thought that if I could see it coming before he did I could head off our financial downfall. But every month before the rent was due he'd come home with relief written all over his face, having swooped in and saved us with a last-minute installation or carpet sale, and a teenager's vigilant inquiries didn't change any of that. Perhaps I was clairvoyant, able to spot the tractor-trailer of disaster heading toward us down the road. Or maybe I just knew my parents too well.

During dinner one summer evening my parents broached the subject of a new car. At first it was all hypothetical fantasizing on my mother's part, but the dishes weren't even cleared when we were out the door and on our way to the Toyota dealership just off the 5 freeway. Our interest in a brand-new maroon Toyota Camry intensified with every hour we stayed on the lot getting sweet-talked by a slick dealer named Dennis. Soon my parents were submitting to credit checks and filling out paperwork against the backdrop of the setting sun.

"Nothing came up under your Social Security number, John," Dennis informed my father. "I guess you cleaned up your shit."

My father nodded and chuckled—Dennis didn't know the half of it. The down payment was $2,500, with lease payments topping $400 a month. Add in the insurance on the Camry, my father's work truck, and the Taurus, which we weren't selling, plus registration on all three—at $450 per car—and my parents found themselves making a hefty financial commitment. It was one they immediately regretted.

"That just ate up our winter savings," my father said bitterly as we drove our new car home. His business routinely slowed in the winter, even though the temperature rarely dipped lower than 50 degrees. "Now we have no cushion."

"But Daddy, look at the CD player!" I said. "The Taurus didn't even have a cassette deck." When we got home we popped a bottle of champagne to celebrate. Later that evening I found my father in the garage, bent over the hood of the Camry and shaking his head.

"I should return it," he said without looking at me.

"No, Daddy, no!" I said, not wanting to part with this shiny new toy, one that I'd probably be taking my driver's test in. My mother came up behind him and patted him on the back. He looked up at her and nodded. I found out later that my mother had been pestering him for several weeks about getting a new car, and she only brought it up in front of me because she knew she'd finally have the majority she needed to win him over.

Almost as soon as I could drive I began ditching school with a vengeance, sometimes joined by my senior friends who only had a few classes a day. We'd hang out in one of their garages and watch movies and eat snacks purchased with my father's gas cards. When I did deign to attend class I put my head down and slept at my desk. I completely missed out on an entire epoch of literature and history this way, and to this day I'm not even sure exactly what I missed because, well, I was asleep. All told, I accrued thirty-nine absences my junior year. No one called my mother to tell her because I forged her name on my all readmit slips—after a legitimate absence I'd traced her signature onto fifty pieces of notebook paper so I could use it whenever I wanted. But it finally caught up with me and I was assigned Saturday school more than once. My father found out, because there was little that went on that he wasn't aware of, but he promised to keep my secret. "Don't worry, I won't tell your mother," he vowed. "Besides, any trouble you could get into is nothing compared to the things I did when I was your age."

Most of my truancies weren't even planned: I'd drag myself out of bed and start out for school, but think better of it and veer south to the beach communities. I spent a great deal of time surveying the hills above Laguna Beach, where the magisterial manses had been charred by fire a few months before. One cul-de-sac after another featured row upon row of brick chimneys, the only physical reminder that the lots had been occupied by houses. It awed me to think that these instruments of fire were all that remained of multimillion-dollar homes. I took most of these trips alone, absorbed in my meandering against the backdrop of early-nineties complaint rock. I don't remember these drives prompting any introspection or catharsis; I was just finding a scenic way to kill time. I packed on the pounds driving and eating my way through my hometown, and even though my mother carefully packed lunches for me every day I threw them out and got fast food instead. Eventually I branched out into cinema, taking in independent films in darkened art house theaters across the county—I must have seen *Muriel's Wedding* six times in a single month. Sometimes I drove to each of the houses we'd lived in and parked on the street, wallowing in the nostalgia of my fading childhood, especially our first bittersweet months in California after being reunited with my father. As it turned out, the timing of my fancy-free sojourns—of which my parents had no clue—was prophetic. It was as if I could already sense our lives in California slipping away amid the sunshine and the eucalyptus.

"JEN? COME 'ERE for a second?"

It was late afternoon in April '94 and my father was calling me into the living room, where he and my mother had been talking. I hadn't been to school that day, so I bowed my head and prepared myself for the guillotine.

"Jen, your mother and I have been talking," he said. "You know the business hasn't been doing well lately, and someone wants to buy it."

My head popped up. "What? What's happening?" I asked.

"Your father's going to sell the business," my mother interjected. Her mouth was pulled into her signature pout.

"El, *please*," my father said, and made a gesture like a chopping motion. "Let me talk!"

"Fine," she said, sitting back on the couch and folding her legs. I hated when he tried to shut her up. I felt so embarrassed for her.

"Jenny, I gave your mother the same choice I'm giving you," he said, sitting forward and talking animatedly with his hands.

"What's that?" I asked with a nervous smile.

"New York or Florida," he said.

"We're moving?" I asked. He nodded.

I looked at my mother. "What did *you* say?"

"What do you think I said?" my mother asked. "I can't stand Florida."

I knew I could count on her. "Dad, I don't want to leave California," I said. "There must be another way."

"Jenny, we've been taking out cash advances to pay the rent," my father admitted. "Every month. And we got more and more behind, and—"

"We busted out the cards again," my mother said, finishing his sentence for him.

What? But they hadn't even given me a chance to buy anything this time. "Jenny, we never should have bought that car," my father said candidly. "The down payment ate up all of our savings—that was our winter money." Why was $2,500 all we had in the world? How had it come to this? "My friend Ron might be coming by today to buy the business," he continued. My father's "business" was a box of extraordinarily detailed index cards with a client history, address, and phone number.

"For much less than it's worth," my mother said bitterly.

"Eleanor, shut up!" my father raged.

"Daddy, please don't tell her to shut up," I implored over the lump in my throat.

"Whaddya want, Johnny?" my mother yelled shrilly. "It's worth much more than ten thousand dollars and you're giving it to that *schmendrick* practically for free. Talk to him, Jenny, because he won't listen to me." At least this explained why she'd started sleeping on the couch.

"Daddy, is it true?" I asked him. But he wouldn't move his sideways glare from my mother's face. I always knew he was angry when he broke out his cold, hard stares. "Daddy!" I said louder. He finally broke his gaze and looked in my direction.

"Jennifer, what your mother doesn't realize is that a lot of my business is tied to real estate, and the real estate situation has been very bad lately," my father said.

"It's true," my mother chimed in. "The market is terrible." A lot of my father's jobs came from real estate agents who had to gussy up a property before renting or selling it, so they hired carpet cleaners and domestics to make it spotless. California was a tenant's market, unlike, say, Manhattan.

"Also," my father said, steering the conversation his way, "my father is getting older, and I'm getting older, and I want to be closer to Florida to see my kids and my grandchildren, and if you and your mother don't want to go to Miami, then New York is close enough."

"I'm not gonna live in Brooklyn," my mother said, anxiously running her hand through her hair.

"El!" my father huffed.

"It's too depressing," she concluded without missing a beat. I felt like telling them they were acting like children again, but I think they already knew that.

"Guys," I said, trying my best to rise above, "I have a year of school left. I cannot move to New York right now. I am not going to New Utrecht High School. No offense, Dad," I said, trying not to slander his alma mater.

"You won't have to go to New Utrecht, Jenny," my mother said, her eyes lingering on my father. I realized they must have discussed this without me, many times.

"Oh, really?" I asked, relieved.

"No," she said. "Because we're not going with him."

"What! You're splitting up again?" I asked, fearful.

"No, Jenny, we're not splitting up," my father said. "Calm down. You and your mother are going to move into a cheaper place around here and I'm going to move to New York this summer, and when you graduate, you two are going to join me. By that time, hopefully, I will have set up the business there."

"We're moving again?" I asked, deflated. I knew the house on Yolanda was too good to be true. I took it all in. This latest plan was impulsive, poorly thought out, and destined to failure. In other words, typical Yonny and Swellenor.

"So you're telling me that this time next year, we'll be living in New York?" I asked.

"Haven't you always said you wanted to move to New York?" my mother asked me, sounding slightly accusatory. If there was anything she hated more than my father's economic instability, it was anyone doubting him.

"When did I say that?" I asked.

"Remember? When you were a kid?" she replied. "You said you wanted to move to New York for college? And I remember you said you wanted me and your father to come with you." She smiled.

"Yeah, I remember that," I said. "Didn't I say that when I was six? When I decided I wanted to go to the Yale School of Drama because Meryl Streep went there? That's New *Haven*, Ma, not New *York*."

"Very funny," she said, lighting a cigarette.

"I also distinctly remember a project in second grade involving red construction paper and a list of my favorite things," I said, "and one of them was red nail polish, but the other was living in Southern California, and I wrote that I never wanted to leave." My mother had kept all of the birthday cards and Christmas cards the three of us ever gave one another, and many of my school projects, something I'd discovered when I'd gone through her night table the week before. I'd cried looking at them, because we'd all seemed so happy before we grew up.

"What are you gonna do, Jenny, huh?" my mother asked, her cigarette hanging out of the corner of her mouth. "Ya gonna go to Saddleback Community College with all your little friends?"

"Hey, that's not fair," I protested. Even though I knew she was trying to break me down, she was right—Saddleback *was* where I was headed, given my recent performance in school. At this point I would have been perfectly happy withdrawing tomorrow and getting my GED. I'd gone from the girl who loved school to the girl who was wasting her life—and her figure—at the Carl's Jr. drive-through.

"Jenny, we're gonna need your help," my father said. He looked at my mother.

"What?" I asked. "Whatever you need." There was no point in fighting this. I was outnumbered.

"Jenny," my mother said, "you might have to get a job."

"Your mother is, too," my father said. "She knows she has to contribute." How many years had he been waiting to say *that*?

I'd never worked before; my one foray into babysitting, at the age of twelve, ended with me starting a small fire by roasting a marshmallow over a pilot light. "I guess it's time I did get a job," I conceded.

"You're going to finish the school year first," my mother emphasized, looking at my father. He nodded. Just then the doorbell rang.

"God, that guy is here now?" I asked. "This is all happening so fast."

And it did—too fast. Ron didn't buy the business that day, but he came back later that week with a wad of bills: $10,000 for fourteen years of sweat and toil. My mother and I were sitting on a bench outside South Coast Plaza—what else is new—when she called home on our new brick-sized cell phone and got the news.

"Did he sell it?" I asked.

She nodded. I started to cry.

"Oh, Jenny, it's gonna be okay, stop *crying*," she said purposely into the phone so he could hear. I was only sixteen and I knew this was a bad decision—why couldn't he see it?

CHAPTER 6

Summerfield Street
Aliso Viejo, California
May 1994
. . .

MY FATHER MOVED US INTO A CONDO IN ALISO VIEJO IN
mid-May and lived there with us until just after Memorial Day, when
he left. My subtle way of protesting the situation was by not lending a
finger to pack up the house, instead hanging out with my friends the
night they loaded the moving van. It was such a disorganized move
that by the end of it my parents were simply dumping the contents of
drawers into boxes. The next morning when I woke in our new place
I stayed home from school and read in bed all day in a near-perfect
imitation of my mother. I was upset that we were breaking our
lease—the Yolanda house had been one of my favorite houses and we
had to move. Again.

If Summerfield was a step down, at least we were slumming in
style—it was a two-story, two-bedroom townhouse with two full
bathrooms, a small dining room and living room, and a decent-sized
kitchen. The development was so new that our "backyard" view consisted of tractor-adorned sand hills awaiting mini-malls and movie
theaters that were at least three years away from being built.

Not all of our furniture would fit into our place on Summerfield,
so we had to sell some of it. This made me more furious than anything. We had to part with the big cushy brown chair I tumbled on as
a kid, the Henredon dining room set with the matching buffet, our
rustic wooden kitchen table—it was all sold off to well-intentioned
couples who perused, smiled, and handed over their cash.

"This sucks!" I announced when the last of our furniture was gone.

"Quiet, you," my mother said sternly. But I felt nothing but bitterness—my parents had failed financially, and it had tanked us as a family. It would take me years to forgive them.

But with my father's departure looming I decided that I couldn't let him leave with animosity between us. Since he had already made up his mind to start over in New York without us—using flawed logic, but whatever—I wanted him to believe we were behind him. Because, let's face it, if he pulled it off he'd be the man of the hour, wouldn't he? *I* needed to believe as well, and why not? The first time he had to leave us, when I was five, didn't he come back? He appeared at Rita's door as if he'd never left, and I had to embrace the possibility that history could repeat itself. After all, this was a man who had taught himself to sew carpets by reading a book. The business had been very good to us, until it wasn't. I was still angry at their inability to plan, but I couldn't be a fair-weather daughter. I would need to stick by him through the bad times, too. My mother had taught me as much. So I drove into the hills above Laguna Beach and parked on a dusty side street and took out a pen and a piece of notebook paper and managed to subsume my anger long enough to compose a letter to my father detailing the sacrifices he'd made for my mother and me, and how brave he was to venture into the unknown to save our family, and how grateful I was. I stuck it inside his slim gray phone book the night before he left.

The next morning he stood at the garage door and said, "Well, kids, this is it." My mother had a present for him: a compass, "so you never lose your way again," she explained, pinning it to the yellow T-shirt on his sobriety teddy bear, the one he'd received after completing his twenty-eight-day detox stint. We hugged him and wished him the best, and he was gone.

He called us every night from the road, Charles Kuralt–like, to report the details of his zany sojourn—like how every Motel 6 from Tulsa to New Orleans was crawling with prostitutes—and each night we begged him to turn around and come home. His absence seemed to bring his miscalculation into stark relief, and perhaps we felt braver pleading our case through a phone line than to his face.

"Can't Daddy just get a job here?" I asked my mother. "Like, with a carpet company? Or maybe doing something else? Why does he have to start his own business?"

"Jenny, your father is losing his teeth," my mother said bluntly. "He doesn't have a college degree—he doesn't even know how to type up a résumé. How can he go around to employers who are so much younger than he is"—he was fifty-seven—"and expect to get a job? This is the only kind of work he can do."

"Why?" I asked, frustrated. "Why must he always stick to this menial blue-collar shit?"

"Jenny!" she snapped, irritated. But she wanted him to come home, too, and one of our wealthy friends even offered to buy him a one-way plane ticket and ship the van back to California. He refused, but he did admit to my mother that when he spotted my letter sticking out of his phone book, just the words "Dear Dad" brought tears to his eyes and very nearly made him turn around.

"Why didn't you, Johnny?" my mother asked when he'd arrived safely in Brooklyn.

"Lemme talk to Dad," I said, and she gave me the phone. "Hey, Daddy. How you doin'?"

"Good," he said. "How yous doin'?" He always used this plural of "you" when he addressed more than one person; it was old-school Brooklyn, my mother said, a variant of colloquial Italian that had been poorly translated in America.

"Fine," I said, my stock response. "Why don't you come home now? We miss you so much. We're no good without you."

"Jennifer," he said sternly, "I am already here, I am not going to leave, I am going to do what I came here to do . . ." I didn't hear the rest because I'd placed the phone on the carpet so he couldn't hear my crying. My mother grabbed the phone.

"Johnny," she said, "don't you see what this is doing to your daughter?"

But he didn't leave New York, and I gave up trying to turn back time. I focused instead on what remained of my youth, holding court at the local coffeehouse and blowing my mother's money on frozen espresso drinks. She resented this, and I'm sure she was lonely—even though I was either too angry or too myopic to empathize at the time—and my going off every night and leaving her in an empty apartment must have depressed her. But I insisted on going—even the night my toilet regurgitated excrement all over my bathroom floor.

"Jenny, ya gotta stay and clean this up," she said as she searched for a plunger.

"Mom, I'm going to be late!" I argued as I settled on an outfit.

"You're leaving me here to clean up your shit?" she yelled, outraged. I paused and watched as she knelt on her hands and knees, sopping up the overflow with paper towels.

"Yes," I said, and headed down the stairs, something I'll never forgive myself for.

That summer I got a job at a local burger joint, and my mother got a job at Budget Carpet, a vast showroom right off the 5 freeway in Laguna Hills. She clashed with her Middle Eastern bosses more than once, not over her religion—we'd never even had a menorah in our house—but over her loopiness. Though she could recite the major factors that contributed to the fall of the Roman Empire, she sometimes suffered from spells of flakiness that robbed her of her ability to add or subtract small amounts on a calculator, or—god forbid—use a computer. She was also getting older—she was now fifty-five—and her social skills seemed to be eroding. She talked a little too loud, for a little too long, and I'm sure this grated on her bosses, who faced an empty showroom most of the time. But at least she was earning $10 an hour, plus my check, which I handed over without complaint each week.

My father wasn't able to restart his carpet business from Brooklyn that summer, and the $10,000 he'd left us from the sale of the business wasn't enough to cover our rent, car insurance, gas, and bills. One day my mother approached me with my red savings account booklet in her hand.

"Jenny . . ." she began.

"It's fine—take it," I said. I'd been expecting as much. The account, my "college fund," contained every birthday check I'd ever received, plus a few $50 bonds Grandpa Frank had purchased for his grandchildren. It had recently topped out at $2,500, but that wouldn't even pay for a semester at a university; it would maybe cover a single semester at a community college, once books were factored in. If I was going to college one day, it certainly wouldn't be financed by that little red booklet.

———

WHEN WE'D LIVED at Summerfield for only five months, my mother invited me to the house of an old Catholic-school friend to talk to her parents. "We're going to Maria's house?" I asked, annoyed. "Why?" I'd seen Maria a few times in the three years since eighth grade because her mother, Marge, occasionally tutored me in geometry, but we said little to each other, as she'd grown a little too arrogant for my taste. But my mother had maintained a friendship with the openhearted Marge, who was very concerned about our situation.

"Jenny, just come," my mother insisted. So one night in October, after we had dinner, we sat in Marge and her husband Akbar's sprawling Laguna Hills living room and they made us an offer: We could live in their downstairs bedroom, for free.

"We have relatives in from Iran all the time," Marge said spiritedly. "It really makes no difference to us."

"Well, why don't I give you my new washer and dryer and refrigerator in exchange," my mother offered. They represented the few purchases my parents had made during their last credit card "bust."

"Wait—Mom, what is going on?" I asked, interrupting the negotiations. Had they all gone mad? Not only had we lost our breadwinner, but now we were going to lose our privacy?

"Marge, clearly we have some discussing to do as a family," my mother explained and bade the couple good night.

"Mother, what the *fuck*?" I asked once we pulled out of the driveway.

"Jenny, we have to be realistic here," she said, lighting a cigarette. "Even though we're both working, we can't afford the apartment anymore. I'm a month behind on the rent."

"What?" I asked, angry. "Daddy's leaving was supposed to help us! And now we're going to be—" I couldn't even say it. This was Orange County. People like us didn't become homeless. We were once the reigning queens of South Coast Plaza! I thought back to this time last year and remembered passing my driver's test, cheering at football games, grilling vegetables on the barbecue in the snug backyard of the Yolanda house, surrounded by palm trees. Now we were fighting to keep a roof over our heads. How had things devolved so quickly?

"Ma! Stop smoking!" I shrieked, braking and shifting the car into park. There was no one behind us, so I knew we wouldn't be rear-ended, but the jerking motion sent my mother into a tizzy.

"Jennifer!" she yelled. I opened her window from the panel by the driver's seat.

"Put. It. Out," I commanded. We had one rule when we got the Camry—which had suddenly become a painful reminder of my father's shortcomings—and that was: no smoking in the car. Certainly not with the windows closed. When everything was falling down around us, I wanted my mother to hold this one thing sacred. Also, I was sick of everyone I knew—including teachers, embarrassingly enough—telling me I smelled like smoke, especially since I'd never put a cigarette to my lips.

She reluctantly put it out, and I took slight comfort in the fact that Marge probably wouldn't let her smoke in the house—I'd be the first to narc on her if she did. After that night I began to notice that streetlights frequently went out as I drove by. I refused to believe it was a coincidence—bad luck was clearly following us.

On the night my mother planned to vacate Summerfield under cover of night, I again refused to help her pack, opting instead to attend the homecoming football game.

"Goddammit, Jenny, I'm not young like you!" she complained as she manically wrapped our precious lamps in brown packing paper. Everything but our clothes, a bookcase, the computer, and a TV would end up in storage. I never realized how much I'd miss eating off my own dishes until they were shut away and all we had were Marge's. Our silverware and appliances were nicer, as my mother had such sophisticated taste. But while Marge may not have lived up to my standards in cutlery, they had a house—many houses, in fact, purchased as investments and scattered throughout the county. Our penchant for finery, it turned out, had gotten us nowhere.

That evening I pulled out of the garage of the Summerfield townhouse; after the game, I pulled in to Marge's driveway in Laguna Hills. We were officially homeless.

CHAPTER 7

Lockwood Avenue
Farmingdale, Long Island, New York
July 1995

. . .

WE LIVED AT MARIA'S HOUSE FOR EIGHT MONTHS, AND I'VE blocked out most of it for the sake of my sanity. When I wasn't sleeping through the remainder of my classes I was raising my low-density lipoprotein by hitting up every In-N-Out Burger between Seal Beach and Oceanside, while my mother got fired from Budget Carpet after three months and spent the rest of our time in California chain-smoking while glued to the O.J. trial. One afternoon a few months before my high school graduation my mother took me into an office located in the mini-mall behind a 7-Eleven in Laguna Hills. It was a welfare office, and she was getting her weekly food stamps.

"I didn't want to tell you," she said.

"Just make it quick," I said, disappointed. I learned that my father had been on food stamps and public assistance for months, and they'd both kept it a secret from me. The shame I felt wasn't just the stigma of welfare—rather, I knew that if we had fallen this far it would take that much longer to pick ourselves back up. Throughout our last depressing months in California I'd beg her to tell me what New York was like: Would I love it? Hate it? Would the indignities we'd just suffered be redeemed by our arrival in the Capital of the World?

"Oh, Jenny, this again?" she'd ask, wary. "You've been there before."

"Yeah, but I don't remember," I said. "It was so long ago."

"You remember the cobblestone streets," she pointed out. "You remember crying because you were afraid the glass on the street would puncture your shoe and cut your feet."

I'd never live that one down. "Yeah, but what's it *like?*" I asked, seeking specifics. "Is it like the way it's depicted in the movies?"

"It's . . ." she started, searching for the words. "It's kind of like Anaheim. Or downtown Santa Ana."

"Yuck!" I said. "Mom, that's terrible!" Both of those places were beset with smog. I don't know why she said it, because I'd eventually find out for myself it wasn't true.

My graduation ceremony was held on a Friday evening, and my father flew in to watch me collect my diploma. But I had little time to celebrate, as he wanted us on the road by Sunday morning. They let me sleep Saturday while they packed, but reality set in when I awoke. I was about to be yanked from my hometown, the one place my mother admitted she never thought we'd leave. My father took us to the storage facility to fetch our things, and I felt a stab of nostalgia when I saw our remaining furniture being moved into the U-Haul; it was like seeing old friends. I missed our life and I wanted it back, and if we had to go to New York for that to happen, so be it.

That night before we left I initiated a discussion about The Future with my mother in the living room. "What are we going to do when we get there?" I asked. "I mean, financially." We were supposed to stay with my parents' friend Cecilia, Big Vinny's widow, with whom we'd briefly stayed while my father was in the facility in 1983, but we didn't know for how long. We'd be "playing it by ear," as my parents were always so fond of saying. Except when they said it, their accents made it sound like they were saying "play it by year"; throughout my childhood I wondered how anyone could play something by year. "I mean," I continued, muting my voice because my father was in Maria's backyard, smoking, "is Daddy even living above the poverty line at this point?" His carpet business hadn't exactly gotten off the ground in Brooklyn because his steam cleaning machine froze in the winter and stayed frozen until April, which is why we were all on welfare.

"I don't know, Jennifer, why don't you ask him yourself?" she replied. A few moments later my father opened the sliding glass door and announced, "Hey, kids, I'm gonna go to bed soon. Oh, and Jennifer, just in case you were still wondering, yes, I live above the poverty line." I was mortified.

Maria was not at all psyched about us leaving; she and my mother had whiled away the days smoking and watching Court TV, and they'd come to rely on each other for emotional support. Even Maria's father was upset; Akbar had come to revere my father for his blue-collar work ethic and often spoke of his attributes in hushed tones. I sensed a slight fear lingering behind the way Akbar regarded my father, though I'm sure Akbar wasn't even aware of it. But my father could evoke a subliminal mixture of fear and respect in people; it was the same quality that lodged a lump in my throat every time he opened his mouth to yell. It defied explanation.

"See you soon! Promise to write!" I yelled out the window of the U-Haul. And with that, we were on the road again.

I was mostly silent during that first day on the highway, comatose from the hypnotic forward motion and the heat, but when we crossed into Blythe, a small town on the California-Arizona border that my mother dubbed "the armpit of the world," I began to cry. This was it, we really weren't going back. I didn't want to freeze my ass off every winter. I wanted to stay in the land of inground pools and fish tacos. How would I survive without the strangely comforting Santa Ana winds, raging through the trees each autumn like static fire? My father stoically tolerated my tears until we got to Illinois.

"I'm going back!" I declared after taking in the baking, desolate landscape for far too many hours in a row. "I have a choice, you know! I don't *have* to go with you guys."

Threatening mutiny put my father over the edge. As it was, stress had turned both of my parents ghostly white. "Then go, Jennifer!" my father erupted. "Go live with Maria's family. Go get a job and buy a car and pay for your own gas and your own bills." Without money I was strapped to them, and I had no choice but to relent.

Somewhere around Ohio I stopped my kvetching and began to embrace an unavoidable fact: I was moving to New York. In a way, it was a great moment: Caught between two lives, we ventured across the country—again—to a future that was wholly uncertain. The next day, as we approached the Goethals Bridge from the New Jersey side, I gazed at New York—well, the backside of Staten Island, really—and remarked to my mother, "I feel like my whole life is leading up to this point."

"That's funny," she said, "I felt the same way when we first came to California." And that's when I understood that my New York would be different from the New York my mother and father had left all those years ago. The majority of their lives was behind them now, while most of mine was still in front of me. Even though we'd taken a few detours, I could finally glimpse the road ahead.

MY FIRST VIEW of "the city" was from the U-Haul place on New Utrecht Avenue in Brooklyn, and I immediately wanted to turn around and go back. It was hot and humid and the streets were dirty—I doubted I could walk barefoot on any of the broken sidewalks I saw before me. We baked in the heat for an hour while we unloaded our furniture into a storage space, and I wondered how long it would be before I saw any of it again.

When I told my friends exactly where I was going to be staying, they seemed confused: "You moved to New York so you could live in *Farmingdale?*" I tried to explain that we moved to New York to be in the city, but when we arrived at Cecilia's we might as well have been right back at Maria's house because we were in the same situation as the one we'd left.

"Johnny! Eleanor!" Celie called from the driveway as we pulled in, holding out her arms. She was petite and blond and resembled a weathered Ellen Barkin. ("A blond-haired, blue-eyed Sicilian," my mother had told me. "Very rare.") Her accent was much thicker than my mother's, a remnant of her Queens childhood. "Is this Jennifah?" she asked, her eyes widening as they settled on my chest. "You're so big! And you've got some breasts there, Jenny!" I nodded and smiled, though I wanted to cry. I'd last seen Celie when I was five. Now I was seventeen and every ounce I gained went straight to my tits. I felt awkward and unsure of myself and I wanted to go hide under the covers after the year I'd just had. But at least my father was with us. As long as the three of us were together, everything would be all right.

Celie lived on the second story of a two-family house in a sleepy town with no Starbucks for miles. The ground floor was occupied by Big Vinny's sister and her husband and son in an arrangement that had evidently survived Big Vinny's death. The biggest attraction in the area was the Amityville horror house, which was apparently the one on which the movie was based. Then there was that strange buzz in the air, a humming, clicking sound that could be heard in every direction.

"What is that?" I asked, but if I'd waited ten seconds I would have gotten my answer. That's when a bug that looked like a flying cock-roach with butterfly wings hit the porch, apparently dead, and a Doberman entered stage left and snapped it up in its mouth.

"That's Ellie," Celie said, gesturing at her dog. "She loves eating the cicadas, don't ask me why."

"What's a chi-cay-da?" I asked, about to vomit.

"They come out in the summer," Celie said. "They're harmless."

"Just wait until you see the Great American Cockroach, Jenny," my mother said, raising her eyebrows. I shivered. We climbed the stairs and came upon a high-ceilinged living room and eat-in kitchen, and three bedrooms arranged back to back down a tight hallway. It was a decent-sized apartment for Celie and her son Anthony—Carmine was still in prison, having ultimately rejected my father's advice four years earlier—but the arrival of a family of three was pushing it. Anthony, who was twenty-four, was sitting at the kitchen table eating lunch with a friend.

"Hey, Johnny!" he said, and gave my father a hug. "How ya been?"

"Good, good," my father said, settling in for some coffee. "Tired." While my mother and I exchanged pleasantries with Celie, my father mentioned to Anthony's friend that he was in desperate search of work.

"Ya ever paint?" Anthony's friend asked. It turned out that Anthony had just returned from a job in Delaware that had him painting the exteriors of Texacos and Taco Bells. Anthony's friend was actually his boss, and he ran a crew.

"Sure, I've painted," my father lied. And with that, he had a job, albeit one that would keep him on the road for weeks at a time. My mother took this as proof that only good things could happen as long as we were together. "Twenty minutes!" she said. "We're here twenty minutes and your father gets a job! See, Johnny? We need to stick together." He nodded. He was to leave the next day, which upset me so much I got diarrhea.

By the time I swallowed some Imodium and took a shower, the sun had set. My parents were having their post-dinner cup of coffee and a cigarette when my father saw the grimace on my face. "You okay, kiddo?" he asked, concerned. "Come sit on my lap."

I obliged, but supported two-thirds of my weight by pressing my legs into the floor. It would be the last time I'd ever sit on my father's lap. "It's just stress, Daddy," I said. I noticed a legal pad sitting nearby and reached for it. I began to make a list.

GOALS

1. Get our own apartment somewhere in the five boroughs
2. Get an apartment in Manhattan
3. Buy our own place, preferably in Manhattan

"Wishful thinking, Jenny," my mother said when she read goal number two. "It got so expensive here. Donald tried to warn me. Jennifer, five years ago no one wanted to live here, the city was crawling with crime, and now you can't get a studio for less than fifteen hundred a month." The Yolanda house had been $1,350, and that was a two-story house with four bedrooms.

"Maybe yous should look at Valley Stream, maybe the Oranges in New Jersey," Celie suggested as she breezed into the kitchen for some coffee. Like my father, she was a fan of "yous."

"Yeah, we'll look into that," my father said, while my mother slowly shook her head so only my father could see. When Celie left, we finished our conversation in hushed tones. "Don't worry, El," he said, making the "quiet down" gesture with his hand. "We're going to live close to the city." My heart soared. "I was thinking maybe Staten Island."

"Because Brooklyn is too depressing," my mother said in agreement, "and Manhattan is out, for obvious reasons. And the Bronx is out, also for obvious reasons. And Queens . . . well, I've never been too crazy about Queens, either."

"Um, guys?" I asked. "What exactly do you mean when you say, 'the city'? I thought the five boroughs were all part of New York City?"

"They are," my father said. "But people who live outside Manhattan call it 'the city.' That's what we do in Brooklyn. Actually, when we were growing up we referred to Manhattan as 'New York.'"

"Yeah, I never understood that," my mother said, and turned to me. "Let's make another list," she said, commandeering my notebook. "Here, I'll start. Paprika, thyme, cumin, rosemary, oregano—we need to replace our spices, you know—extra virgin olive oil, balsamic vinegar, russet potatoes, Dijon mustard, Valencia oranges . . ." It was just like the list we made on the return trip to California in 1983. I smiled at the memory. After an exhausting 2,954-mile journey, there we were, dreaming about ketchup.

"Don't forget U-bet chocolate sauce," I said, remembering how my hand would be covered with chocolate every time I pulled the spoon out of the jar. When List 2.0 was completed I held it up and announced, "The list is life." My mother cracked up at the *Schindler's List* reference.

Just then a lightning bolt cracked the sky open, illuminating the blackness for an instant.

"*Whatthefuckwasthat?*" I asked, jumping off my father's lap and darting to the window just in time to see another tree-branch-shaped strike. "There's another one! What's happening here?"

"It's probably a rainstorm, Jenny," my mother said casually.

"Rain? I'm sorry, did you say *rain*?" I asked, hardly amused.

"Yes, Jenny," she replied. "It rains here in the summer."

"*What?*" My stomach rumbled with this latest predicament. "I didn't sign up for this!"

My father left promptly the next morning, traveling to Georgia or Oklahoma or somewhere to paint. His salary was $100 a day, but the second he signed on he confessed to my mother his plan to overthrow his boss and eventually run the crew. "Your father always gets ahead," she said. It was true, he always found a way to succeed, even if his idea of success was different from most people's. With my father gone I moped around Celie's place watching the *MTV Beach House* and wishing I was in Malibu with Kennedy. My mother was also glued to the TV, often fixing me an iced coffee and pouring a hot one for herself before melting into the couch beside me. Celie found us this way before she went to work one morning and erupted.

"Eleanor, you've got to help Johnny," she pleaded. "You have to get a job, the both of yous. You must help him!" Celie washed hair at a salon in Dix Hills and her day began at 6 A.M.; our laziness must have been an affront to someone who worked so hard. One morning I made the mistake of sitting on the back of one of Celie's couches to watch TV.

"Jenny, goddammit!" she yelled as soon as she walked into the kitchen and spotted me abusing her furniture.

"I'm sorry," I muttered, jumping off the couch like it was on fire.

"Jennifer, what are you doing?" she asked through a nervous half-smile. But what she really seemed to be asking was "What are you doing *with your life?*" I took in her tiny frame, which was lacking any trace of body fat, and felt like I didn't have a reason to exist.

"I don't know," I muttered.

The next morning my mother took me into the city for the first time. Before we hopped the Long Island Rail Road to Penn Station we sat in a diner and munched on bagels and discussed my future. I had to decide where I was going to college, and when. Technically the intention of our Manhattan trip was to look at possibilities, Hunter College on the Upper East Side being my mother's preference.

"But maybe we'd be pushing it if we enrolled you in classes this September," she said, which was slightly more than a month away. I focused on her face: Was she giving me an out? "And we still don't know where we're gonna live," she added.

"And I've always been young for my grade," I chimed in. I was still seventeen, and would be until the end of November.

"Now, this doesn't mean you're not going to college," she warned.

"Of course," I agreed. I wanted to go to college, but I badly needed a break. And that's how I won my gap year. My mother had turned a corner—the woman who had shoved me headfirst into honors classes was giving me room to breathe in a time of tremendous stress.

"Come on," she said with renewed vigor. "Let's go to the city."

After an hour on the train I stepped out of Penn Station into a drizzly July afternoon, and my first impression was that New York was exactly as it appeared in the movies. As I craned my neck to behold the tall buildings and watched all the people scurrying past, I was filled with a familiar feeling, like I'd been here before.

"You have," my mother reminded me.

"But that was a dozen years ago," I reminded her.

She indulged me in the obligatory stroll through Times Square, and when I spotted a newsstand I asked her if we could stop. CROSS-ROADS OF THE WORLD, read the scaffold above the kiosk.

"Can I have the *Los Angeles Times,* please?" I asked the man behind the counter.

"Oh, Jenny, for Christ's sake," my mother said. "You're in New York, we have a much better paper here." I defiantly handed over my money, but when I saw the front page my face fell: It was the national edition.

"No Orange County news," I said sadly.

"Oh, who gives a shit?" my mother replied. "Jenny, *look where you are.*"

My head snapped up: She was right. I was in Manhattan, where all my friends probably wished they could be. After I trashed my newspaper we walked east to the New York Public Library, where my mother showed me the resplendent reading room. "Shh," she whispered. "We have to be very quiet. But isn't it marvelous?" It was. To me it resembled a prestigious law library, with its grand ceilings and smart brass lamps. When we emerged we continued north, gazing at the busy street scene that unfolded before us, and then west, stopping in a café.

"That's Carnegie Hall," she said, pointing out the window at the sturdy brick building on West Fifty-seventh Street.

"Would you like me to wrap the rest of your lunch?" our server asked, pointing to my mother's leftover sandwich.

"No, it's okay," I started, but my mother interjected.

"Yes, we will," she said to our server. Then, to me: "You can take it with you to rehearsal," loud enough for the waitress and the tables around us to hear.

"Mom! What are you doing?" I asked, embarrassed.

"Let them think you're a famous opera singer, on a break from practicing your aria next door." But I wasn't in rehearsals for anything, and I had nothing to look forward to. My life was empty. I wondered if I would ever live up to all that my mother wished for me.

SOON AFTER THAT my father returned in the middle of the night from his two-week painting stint, and I waited up on the couch for him. When I heard him and Anthony being dropped off outside, I bounded down the steps two at a time.

"Daddy!" I said, greeting him with a hug.

"Hey, baby!" he said. His stay would be brief; he was set to hit the road less than a week later. To celebrate his return my parents and I went out to dinner, but before we left I heard my father scolding my mother in the guest room with a suppressed yell that came out as a throaty whisper.

"Eleanor, how could you spend the eight hundred dollars I sent you in two weeks?" he asked, clutching the bundle of cash he was about to hand her, his haul from the last trip. "That was supposed to go toward an apartment. What the fuck were you thinking?"

"I don't know, Johnny," she said, looking bewildered. I watched from the hallway, peering through a crack in the door, and saw her face crumple and give way to tears. She had little recourse; I guess our little jaunts around Long Island and into the city had run us into the red. "I'm so sorry, Johnny," she said. He pulled her into his arms.

"It's all right, El," he said, patting her back gently. "Let's go to dinner."

As we crawled toward autumn we still had no idea where we were going to live. My mother found a real estate agent on Staten Island who showed us a number of apartments, none impressing me as much as the first. It was down the road from the Staten Island Ferry, just off a street called Bay Street. The agent took us up the elevator to the seventh floor, where we were greeted by Flo, a butch, bleach-blond school bus driver in her fifties. The place was gorgeous. Opening up into a kitchen area and a bright living room set against mirrored walls that made it appear twice its size, the apartment featured marble tile in the hallway, which led to a full bathroom opposite a small bedroom, with a master bedroom in the back. The big pink wall in the living room looked like Pepto-Bismol, but the second I stepped onto the balcony I knew we had to live there. There awaited a spectacular view of the sapphire harbor with downtown Manhattan just beyond. The skyline rose majestically over the water, anchored by the World Trade Center, which dominated the view. It was five miles away yet seemed close enough for me to grasp.

"Mommy, this is it," I said, hypnotized by the sight.

"It's a start," my mother conceded, ushering me out. But I knew we would live there, and I was going to make it happen even if I had to beg.

When my father returned from his next trip he informed us it would be a few weeks before he would be on the road again. Even though we had more than enough money for first and last month's rent and a security deposit, we still didn't have enough for the real estate agent's fee, meaning we'd have to wait until he went out on the road again before committing to an apartment. Because both he and Anthony would be out of work for a while, my father went back to Grandpa's place so we could all have a bed to sleep in. It was yet another separation and it upset my mother, so we traveled to Brooklyn every day to see him. One afternoon my father handed me the phone. "Here, talk to your sister, she just had a baby," he said, and I found myself chatting with Angie, still in the hospital after popping out her third child.

"Hey, Jenny," she said lazily.

"Hey, Angie!" I hadn't spoken to my half-sister in years. Could her visit with infant Nicole have been the last time? Did I see her when my father and I took a trip to Florida in '89? For the life of me, I couldn't remember. In fact, I didn't even know she had just been pregnant until my father handed me the phone. I did remember that, like her mother and sister, she was now a nurse.

"How do you like New York?" she asked.

I looked around Grandpa's dingy kitchen, with its coffee-splattered countertops. "It's okay, I guess. You must be so tired. When did you give birth, exactly?" I remembered then that she had another daughter, Krissy, but I couldn't remember when she'd been born. Sometime in the early nineties, maybe?

"Yesterday," she said. "It was a boy. We named him Joey."

"Oh, cool," I said. I handed my mother the phone and watched her face light up as she quizzed her stepdaughter about her delivery. It was strange to think my mother even had a stepdaughter—two, actually, and a stepson—because we'd been so removed from that side of the family.

After the phone call my father escorted us out into the piping hot day. Our first stop was Spumoni Gardens, an old-school pizzeria in Brooklyn with outside tables. "They sell Italian ices here," he said as we waited in line for a slice. I looked around and realized that Brooklyn was also exactly as it appeared in the movies. Other days when we came to Gravesend my father would take me to the neighborhood butcher, where we'd pick up smoked mozzarella and sopressata, a spicy salami my father pronounced "supersod." Then we'd hit the neighborhood pastry shop, where we'd get lemon drop cookies and cannoli, and then the bodega, where we'd get coffee filters and cigarettes. "In Brooklyn you don't need a supermarket," my father proudly declared. "You can go from shop to shop and get everything you need."

One afternoon right before one of our Brooklyn visits I hopped in the shower, and after ten minutes I heard someone stomping on the steps between the two apartments and yelling. A few minutes later the bathroom door flew open and Celie implored, "Jenny, please, you can't take too long in the shower!" I heard a woman's deep voice shouting in the background, and Celie turned away for a moment to address her: "All right, all right, I'll tell her." She turned back to me and said quietly, "Please, Jenny, come out of there now." Apparently Big

Vinny's sister paid the water bill and got out her stopwatch every time someone turned on the faucet. When I emerged from the bathroom with my head hung low Celie was gone, but my mother was irate.

"Did she forget?" she said, aiming her words at the now-empty stairwell. "Huh? Did they forget what your father did for them? Is their memory that short? Huh? Do they have no respect?"

"Mom," I said, my wet hair dripping onto the floor, "what are you talking about?"

"I'm about to get very mad," she said, grabbing her purse. "Let's get the fuck outta here. Come on, get ready, I'll meet you in the car."

The drive to Brooklyn was fraught with my mother's anger: We needed to move, and fast. "We can't stay there anymore," she said frantically. "We need to get the fuck outta there. How can she come up the stairs like that and yell at you? Doesn't she remember what your father is capable of?"

"Which is—? Mom, *what* is Daddy capable of?" I asked, feeling proud that my father would protect my honor but nervous about how far my mother was suggesting he'd go to do it.

"Never mind, I'll just be happy when we see Daddy," she said. When we got to the basement in Gravesend my mother launched into a tirade about the shower incident. As my father listened he didn't seem to get angry, just pensive, like he was storing the information for future use.

"Let's just stay here, with you," she said, climbing onto his lap and mounting him. Thank god they had their clothes on.

"Sorry to rain on your parade, guys, but no," I said. "We can't all stay here." The basement was dank and contained a single bedroom. There was no way I was sleeping there, or on the couch; it smelled like mildew and I didn't even want to consider what lurked under the cushions.

"Jenny, shut up," my mother said, wrapping her arms around my father's neck. "I don't want to go back to Celie's ever again."

"Well, we have to," I said, and addressed my father. "I'm sorry, Dad, but there's no room here." That evening my mother reluctantly drove back to Celie's while I sulked in the car. She was chilly toward me because I was "making" her go back. "Mom, we can't stay at Grandpa's, that place is awful," I argued.

"I just want to be with your father," she said. "And you want to go back. You know, I just don't get you." As we searched for a gas station I decided that I felt bold enough to ask the question I'd held to my chest for years—so many years, in fact, that I had buried my desire for answers, until this afternoon, when my mother had intimated that my father was capable of much more than painting and carpet cleaning.

"Mom, can I ask you something?"

"What, Jenny?" She sounded annoyed, but thawing.

"Why was Daddy arrested that time in Irvine?"

"What?" she said, pretending to scope the horizon for an Exxon.

"You heard me," I said.

"Jenny, we've been over this," she said. "There was another John Mascia, a connected guy in the Bronx."

"Really?" I asked, slightly sarcastic. "You never told me that, that the other John Mascia was a mob guy." It was the first time I'd heard my father's name associated with the Mafia, whether it belonged to him or someone else.

"Yes," she said, at once adopting a reluctantly revelatory tone. She sighed for emphasis. "He was from a family in the Bronx, and your father was mistaken for him."

"Really?" I said, incredulous. "It took five months to figure out that they didn't have the right John Mascia? They couldn't just run his fingerprints and figure it out?" I had her, finally. My intellect had caught up to my memories.

"Well, they did, eventually," she said. "Where is this fucking gas station? Celie said it was—"

"Mom, you know where the gas station is!" I said, suddenly angry. "We go there every day!" She had taken away my summer, stolen me from my home and my friends; the least she could do was stop bull-shitting me.

"Jenny, what do you want?" she asked, matching my irritation.

"I want you to tell me what Daddy did to get arrested!"

"You remember that?" she asked quietly.

"Mom, you know I do!" I said, frustrated. I let a few moments pass before I started again, more gently this time. "I remember when they came to Turtle Rock and Kara took me upstairs and tried to play with me, but I kept running for the door. And she pulled me back, but it didn't matter. I kept running, I wanted to see him, I kept going for that door, over and over again, I just wanted to say goodbye . . ." But the last part of my sentence became entangled in my sobs, which surprised even me. I didn't realize the memory was so raw that it could prompt such spontaneous emotion. But then, I hadn't discussed that night with anyone, ever. The five-year-old in me was finally reacting to having her daddy taken away.

My mother pulled in to the gas station and parked far from the pumps, signaling that she was ready to talk. "I deserve to know what happened," I sobbed, staring at the dashboard. "We live in a place now where everyone knows but me. I want to know, too." Not that I socialized with my father's side of the family enough to risk an accidental revelation about his criminal past, but I did feel left out. I cursed my sudden display of emotion, which made me feel like I was staging a tantrum, like I wasn't entitled to react this way. Too many years of my mother calling bullshit on my tears had taken its toll. But I didn't want her to think I was trying to manipulate the truth out of her with my sobs, because I really wanted to know, apparently much more than I thought I did.

"Your father was in jail before you were born," she began, suddenly calm. "And he was arrested in California when you were young because he had violated his parole. It was a parole violation, for an offense he had already gone to jail for. That was what your father did to get arrested in Irvine."

It didn't sound so terrible; I'd imagined far more sinister stuff. "How long was he in jail before I was born?" I asked.

She stared out the windshield and gave me the slightly comical "I know I'm incriminating myself by saying this but I guess I'm cornered" face scrunch.

"Twelve years," she said.

"Twelve years!" I exclaimed. "Twelve years? Mom! That's such a long time! He missed out on so much! Oh, my god." I couldn't imagine losing twelve years of my life. And he'd lost years in his prime: If I was born when he was forty, that meant he'd been locked up for most of his twenties and thirties. I was forced to immediately reevaluate my father, and realized that he had a piece missing.

"Yes, he was away for that long. 'College,' we used to call it," she said with a smirk. "Your father went away to college." She must have sensed my next question. I couldn't imagine what my father could have done that would have landed him in prison for so long.

"What did he do?" I asked. "It wasn't . . . *rape*, was it?" Whenever I thought back to his arrest and tried to imagine what he'd done, I'd become terrified at the possibility that my father had sexually violated someone. It was the worst crime I could think of.

My mother laughed. "Oh, god, no, Jenny," she said. "What would make you think that?"

I was so relieved that I laughed. "Just something I've always feared, I guess." Her reaction seemed genuine enough that I believed her. And anyway, would my mother really have stayed married to a rapist, even a reformed one?

She read my mind. "I wouldn't have married a rapist!" she said, shooing away the idea with her long nails.

"So what did he do?" I asked as the air conditioner chilled the tears on my face.

She exhaled. "I need a cigarette for this," she said, and rummaged through her relaxed black leather purse for her pack of Benson & Hedges Ultra Light Menthol Deluxe in the box. After years of smoking Carltons she'd gone back to her first love. "Your father was an associate of one of the criminal families in New York," she finally said.

"He was a mobster?" I asked.

"Not exactly," she said. "He was an associate. He wasn't a made guy, but he worked with made guys. Remember in *Goodfellas*, how they weren't 'made' guys?" Being "made" involved an induction ceremony that signified inclusion into a clan. Like Boy Scouts, but with guns.

"Which families?" I asked, wondering if my father was famous.

"I think he was associated with the Gambino family, but before John Gotti controlled it," she said. "Or maybe it was the Profacis, I'm not sure."

"Who?" I asked. I'd heard of the Gambinos but not the Profacis. The name reminded me of my mother's favorite insult, *facia bruta*, meaning "ugly face."

"They worked out of Staten Island, I think," she said. "I don't really know. Actually, one of the families he worked with wanted to make him, but he said no. When I asked him why, he said, 'I didn't want to be running around making money for some fat guy sitting on the corner eating salami all day.'" She grinned.

"Is that why, when you guys would watch those mob documentaries on the History Channel, Daddy would know who all those guys were?" I asked. I'd hear them both commenting from the living room. "Total nutcase," my father said about one.

"Well, one of your father's cousins was also in the business," she said. "So he knew a lot of those guys through him. But your father was in prison with Joey Gallo."

"Who is Joey Gallo?" I asked. I was more intimately acquainted with Vito Corleone than any real-life mobsters.

Young Johnny, about seventeen,
circa 1955.

"Oh, he was a real nutsy fruitcake, Joey Gallo," my mother said. "He murdered Albert Anastasia, the head of Murder Incorporated. You know that Bruce Springsteen song, 'Murder Incorporated'? It was a reference to this famous group of hit men from Brooklyn. Well, Anastasia was the head of Murder Inc., and Joey Gallo killed him."

"Wow," I said, not really knowing what it all meant. A year later, when my grandfather would die of prostate cancer, my father and my uncle Frankie would scour the rows at Green-Wood Cemetery until they found Anastasia's unremarkable gravestone and set down two red roses in memoriam. Though I'd recall this conversation, I wouldn't ask him about it, but I'd remember how they both smirked their way to the tomb and back in recognition of their off-kilter tradition.

"Your father was also in prison with a guy who knew where Jimmy Hoffa's body was buried," she revealed.

"Really?" Now *that* I understood. "Where? Tell me!"

"Oh, I don't think your father ever asked him that," she said, in a tone that communicated that such a query would be uncouth.

"What was it like in prison?" I asked. "I mean, did Dad ever, like, drop the soap, if you know what I mean?" It had to be asked.

"No, nothing like that ever happened," she said. "Most of the guys he was in prison with were Italian, wiseguys from the neighborhood." I pictured Paul Sorvino slicing garlic with a razor blade so it melted into his pasta sauce. "Your father was respected in prison. When he first arrived in Sing Sing, the guys there applauded him. He could have ratted on a lot of people, but he kept his mouth shut. That's why he got twelve years."

"Sing Sing, wow," I said, impressed. She still hadn't clarified what exactly he'd gotten twelve years *for*. "Mom, what did he do? Twelve years is a long time." She stared ahead for a few moments and said nothing. "Mom," I prodded.

"Jenny, he was into a lot of stuff, okay?" she said. "When we met he was selling clothes that came off the back of a truck."

"Like in *Married to the Mob*?" My mother and I always laughed when Michelle Pfeiffer exasperatedly screamed at her gangster husband, "Everything we own fell off a truck!"

"Yes, like *Married to the Mob*," she said. "Your father had a number of odd jobs then, some of them were crooked. He did try construction once, but the first time he was sent up onto a high beam he turned green and said, 'Never again.'" So we shared the same fear of heights. "It's a shame, really, because when he was a kid he wanted to be an electrician, but his teacher told him he needed to be good at math. He wasn't, so the teacher told him he couldn't be an electrician. Can you believe that? Instead of helping him with math, he just told your father, 'You can't do it.' Do you have any idea how much electricians make?"

"How much?"

"A lot," she said, irritated.

"That sucks."

"Did I ever tell you how my uncle Harry got me a job at Zales, in the diamond counting room?"

"No."

"My mother's brother Harry, who had a very successful jewelry business on Forty-seventh Street, made his fortune by sweeping up gold dust from the fillings at dentists' offices," she said. "Those were the days they used real gold to fill teeth." Her tone took on a playful air and she became animated, talking with her hands like a true Italian, not just an Italian-in-law. She got this way whenever she delved into her past and retrieved a particularly amusing memory for my enjoyment. She wanted a companion in remembrance, and I was it. "After my divorce from David," she continued, "Harry got me a job in the diamond counting room at Zales. This is when I was dating your father. And I would, you know, once in a while, sneak out some small stones for your father to fence." She giggled. "I didn't last long there."

"Did you get caught?" I asked, incredulous. I couldn't believe what she was telling me—*my* mother? The do-gooder from Manhattan Beach who chose to teach in the ghetto? Who wouldn't let me go out on school nights—*ever*?

"No," she said. "They had security guards, but I was discreet. I put my hands under the table, pretended like I was scratching my leg or something like that."

"You'd never get away with that with today's technology," I said.

"I was dating your father, but we weren't serious yet," she went on. "And I hadn't heard from him for a while, so I called him up and told him I had something for him." She giggled again. "He started returning my calls after that. Hey, did I ever tell you how your father ran up seventeen flights of stairs with an ice cream cone because the elevator was broken?"

"Only a thousand times," I said.

"You know how he proposed to me?" she asked. "We had just gotten into a huge fight, and I told him to get out, and he said, 'Let's get married.' Just like that: 'Let's get married.' I was fine without getting married, you know, he was staying over more and more, moving his wardrobe over to my place, one pair of socks at a time. Your grandmother Helen was confused because all of his clothes kept disappearing."

"He was living *at home*?" It made sense, I guess, for someone who had just gotten out of jail.

"But he knew I wanted a baby," she went on, ignoring me, "and he said, 'If you want to have a baby, we have to get married.' He was traditional that way. But, oh, I almost killed him once, when he was supposed to take me out and never showed up, and I found your uncle Frankie and asked him where the hell your father was, and he said, 'Don't worry, he'll come around.' And you know why he stood me up?"

"Because he was broke and didn't want to tell you." I knew this story by heart.

"Yes," she said, nodding reverentially. I imagined she must have nodded this way when one of her students finally grasped an elusive concept.

My parents embarking on a new life in California, 1980.

"How did you guys meet, again?" I asked, wondering if her disclosure had altered other parts of our narrative arc.

"Through friends, like I said," she said. "We were very good friends, until this one night when we were over someone's house eating dinner, and we started playing footsie under the table. Well, we went straight home after that and—"

"Mom, ew!" I said, just as I had years ago. Though I always enjoyed trips with my mother down memory lane, this was not the time. "Mommy, what did he *do?*" I asked, frustrated. "It couldn't be *that* bad," I offered, "or he'd still be in jail. I mean, come on. What did he do? Rob the wrong guy? Pull off the Lufthansa heist? What?"

She laughed, and when her laughter stopped her face was still frozen in a forced smile. I knew her expressions all too well: She was deciding what to tell me, or perhaps *how* to tell me. "Like I said, it was mob shit, you know, petty theft, racketeering, that kind of shit," she finally said. "You know, when he was married to Marie, he used to rob houses. When Tina was a baby he got sent away for stealing a car. That's why there's three years between Tina and Angie's births. I bet you didn't know that."

"No, I didn't," I said. "So you mean to tell me that my father has been in and out of prison his whole life?"

"Oh, Jenny, please, ya gotta promise me you won't say anything to him, that I told you all this," she implored, her voice soaked in desperation. "He never, ever wanted you to know," she said, pained. "He liked to think you didn't remember when he got arrested. He used to tell me, 'She doesn't remember, she was too young.'"

"I *do* remember," I said. "I wouldn't say anything to him now— how would I start that kind of conversation, anyway? 'Hey, Dad, why don't you tell me about your time in Attica?'"

"It was actually Sing Sing, Greenhaven, and Fishkill," she corrected. "They tend to transfer prisoners a lot. Your grandmother was always traveling upstate to visit him. Once he got sent to a facility close to the Canadian border. He froze his ass off for years. His brother and his *wonderful* sister"—she was being sarcastic—"must have loved that— that no matter what he did, he was still his parents' favorite."

"Maybe it's because they never saw him," I said.

"You know, your father, when he was younger, he was just like his family, had the same racist views they did," she said.

"No. *Daddy?*"

"Yes, Daddy. Prison changed him. Being in jail opened him up to other walks of life. He was thrown together with blacks and Hispanics, and they learned how to get along. Prison is the great equalizer— it made him a better person, more accepting of different kinds of people." I'd never heard an argument defending imprisonment as a successful tool of social integration. It certainly wasn't depicted that way on TV. "He never wanted you to know," she repeated, sounding forlorn. "You're the only one of his kids who doesn't know any of it." I realized that my sisters knew and I didn't, Rita knew and I didn't, Celie knew and I didn't, my aunts and uncles knew—my father was the black sheep in his family, a criminal, and I was truly the last to know. Perhaps that was because, no matter what he had done to spend fifteen years of his life behind bars, he was still so revered by everyone. Charisma goes a long way.

"Why can't you tell me exactly what he did?" I asked, sensing she was still withholding. "So it was theft, fine. What did he steal?"

"Jenny, he made a mistake," she said, facing me. "He made a lot of mistakes. But don't you see, Jenny? That all ended after we got back from Florida, when you were five. Don't you remember how happy you were to see him that night at Rita's? All of that shit ended that night when he came back to us. He changed his life for us, Jenny. He turned it around—for *us,* because of *us,* because he didn't want to lose his family again."

"Again?" Now I understood why he and his kids were so distant—jail had separated them.

"Yes, again," she said, with a little fight in her, like a defense attorney. "Please, Jenny, no more. Now you know, okay?"

"So it was theft," I said. "He was a thief. Mom, what is so horrible about that?" I said. "Why was that so hard to tell me?

"Well, it was kind of like theft," she said. "It involved racketeering, that's all I'll say."

"Fine," I said. I knew there was more—maybe he'd knocked someone's teeth out as he was stealing their car—but she'd told me all I could handle for one filthy, humid evening. On our way home from the gas station, to cheer me up, my mother began to sing. " 'Even though we ain't got money, I'm so in love with you, honey . . .' "

" 'And everything will bring a chain of lo-o-o-ove,' " I finished for her. She joined me for the rest of the verse: " 'And in the morning when I rise, you bring a tear of joy to my eyes, / And tell me everything is gonna be all right.' "

"It's all gonna be all right, Jenny," she said, and smiled. "Do you trust me?"

"Unfortunately," I said with a smirk.

CHAPTER 8

New Lane
Staten Island, New York
September 1995

. . .

AFTER THE SHOWER INCIDENT OF 1995 MY MOTHER DECIDED
we had to leave Celie's yesterday. Not that staying at Celie's place was
all bad—she made an excellent egg salad that was silky smooth from
whipping the mayo and mustard together—but my mother was desperate to flee after the perceived lack of respect Celie's sister-in-law
seemed to display toward my father and his family, as if some sacred
code had been violated. I took advantage of the situation and rallied
hard for the apartment on the water; my persistence paid off and we
got it around the same time my father returned to work. It was mid-
September and Flo wouldn't be ready to move out until October 1,
but my mother decided we couldn't wait, so while my father was still
on the road we decamped for our real estate agent's place across the
street from the legendary Staten Island garbage dump. Once again we
had no choice but to rely on the generosity of others. Because the
agent was essentially living with her boyfriend in Brooklyn Heights,
she took pity on us—"I get a good feeling about you guys," she said as
she handed us the keys, although she probably felt differently by the
end of the month, when we were only able to give her half of her fee.
Either way, my mother and I were finally, blessedly alone.

In the middle of our fortnight by the dump, my father returned
for two days. He wasn't going to be moving us, though; that we were
going to do on our own. But while he was between jobs he took us
to Flo's to sign the lease, fanning the cash out on her long marble dining room table like we were playing a mid-afternoon hand of poker.

Afterward my father went to run errands and my mother and I went shopping for dinner, and as we pulled in to the parking lot of our temporary apartment building we began to argue about a film we'd rented. The conflict devolved into a frenzy of mutual slapping, ending with my mother threatening, "I'm gonna tell your father when he comes home and he's going to kill you!" Of course, she didn't mean it literally, but I knew I might get hit or spanked. Never mind that I was seventeen, it was old-school—whether I was five or twenty-five, the same punishment applied.

I was tired of my mother's side of the story being the only one my father believed, so I wrote a note that said something like, "Don't bother looking for me, I can't deal with *her* anymore," swiped my mother's latest library book, and hid in the building's parking garage. I figured I'd scare them for a few hours, after which my sudden reappearance would come as such a relief that they'd forgive all of my sins. What I didn't anticipate was that the absence of clocks or sunlight might give a false impression of the passage of time. When I thought a couple of hours might have passed I emerged and called my mother from a pay phone in the mini-mall across the street. She sounded so relieved she was crying a little. "Mom, what's the big deal?" I asked.

"Where are you?" she asked wearily.

"Across the street," I said. "I was reading in the garage. Is dinner almost ready?"

"Dinner? Jennifer, your father has been driving around looking for you for four hours!" she said, distressed. "We even called the police! They kept asking us if you had a boyfriend in the city or something."

Yeah, fat chance. "I'm fine, Ma," I said. "But, wait—did you say four hours?" I'd plopped down in a darkened corner of the garage at around seven.

"Yes! Jenny, you have your father so worried. Do you see his truck around anywhere?"

"No. Ma, what time is it? Ten? Eleven?" I asked, glancing at the invisible watch on my naked wrist.

"Jenny, it's three in the morning!" she boomed. A surge of shame slid down my back like ice. All I'd wanted was to force her to respect me, but instead I'd threatened to tank our fragile new life, which was being held together with fishing line. That much was evident when I entered the apartment to find my mother sitting at the dining room table, looking forlorn.

"Ma," I said. She looked up and shot me an "I'm glad you're all right but I'm going to kill you" look. I took a seat at the table and waited for my father to come home. The phone rang. "Yeah, she's here," my mother murmured into the receiver. I didn't want to cause my father any more heartache; he'd had so much already in the past year. Plus, he was scheduled to drive out early the next morning. Not only had I ruined his last hearty meal, but I'd also robbed him of sleep.

When he trudged in a few minutes later I kept my head hung low, afraid to antagonize him. He barely acknowledged me as he very patiently opened the cupboard, removed a glass, dropped in two ice cubes, and poured three fingers of scotch. He sat down at the head of the table, joining me and my mother in our moment of silence. Finally, he spoke.

"Jenny," he said. His booming bass was deep with exhaustion, and as I raised my head I noticed how bloodshot his eyes were. "I'm going to tell you the same thing I told your mother a few hours ago. It's the same thing I tell everyone. All I have in this life are my girls. You and your mother—that's the only thing I live for, the only thing I work for. If that's taken away, then there's no point to it. Any of it. All I have are my girls." His voice broke at the end of that last sentence, and as if on cue, my mother and I ran over to him and buried our heads in his neck.

"I love you guys so much," I said, weeping openly.

"Oh, Johnny," my mother said, wiping her tears away with her hands. My bad behavior had caused this scene, and even as I stood there holding my parents I knew I'd spend the next day on the toilet, saddled with diarrhea because of what I had done.

But maybe we needed this—it was the emotional catharsis we hadn't made time for. We were mourning our lost year, mourning our lost life, the one we'd so abruptly left behind. I hadn't realized it before, because my parents were in such a rush to leave, but they were probably grieving that loss harder than I was. I was still young enough that I could easily adapt to a new place, but my parents had *chosen* California, pointed to it on a map and said, "There." I had seen them as monsters for making me leave, but they didn't want to leave paradise, either. They felt they had no choice.

After that night I believed that the three of us had been properly reunited and were now working toward a common goal: keeping our family together, in spirit if not in body. My father left the next day as planned, and my mother and I moved onto New Lane. I was in love with our new apartment and all of its expensive touches, like the glass chandelier that I dismantled and soaked in soapy water every six months. I was so proud that we'd found such nice appointments that I'd get down on my hands and knees and Windex the tile floors every month, and when I'd finished the bathrooms and the vacuuming—no more free carpet cleaning, unfortunately—I'd stand on the patio furniture on the balcony and scrub the sliding glass doors, praying I didn't stumble and plummet seven stories. I'd spend hours on the mirrored walls in the living room because it only took two or three weeks for my parents' cigarette smoke to coat them in a hazy yellow sheen. I took pride in keeping our place clean because I understood how quickly we could lose it. Before the inevitable happened I was determined to appreciate what we had, so every morning I would peer out my bedroom window and gaze upon the glorious downtown skyline, and it was the last thing I saw before going to bed. Sometimes I'd stare out at Manhattan to the north and the hills of Staten Island to the south and all the sky in between and wonder what force begat the universe, and what force begat that force, and so on. I spent hours this way, on my knees in bed with my elbows on the windowsill, contemplating the night sky like a stoner without the pot.

Right before our first Christmas in New York I got a job at the Staten Island mall, though I surrendered the bulk of my paychecks to my parents. I actually didn't mind; I liked feeling that I was contributing to our new life. Besides, I didn't need money for anything because I had no life. We were actually treading water financially, until it started snowing. And snowing. And snowing. When it didn't stop, the Weather Channel gave it a name: the Blizzard of '96. It immediately put a halt to my father's work and sank us all into a familiar depression.

"In Brooklyn we call it Mafunzalo disease," my mother cracked one day.

"Oh, my . . . What's that?" I asked, all concerned.

"*My . . . funds . . . are . . . low,*" she said slowly. "Get it?" She cackled.

"Ha *ha*," I said, hardly amused. It really wasn't funny. We were eating meals on my slender writing desk because we hadn't replaced our rustic kitchen table, and we'd traded our sturdy Henredon chairs for folding chairs. All the bills were in my name because my parents' credit had tanked too many times, and watching them go unpaid became so excruciating that I just started mailing checks, even after my parents told me not to.

"I don't want them to cut off the phone," I argued. But there were things I couldn't afford, like a full set of dental implants for my father. I could smell his rotting, infected teeth from the passenger's seat when he drove me to work every day, and even though I begged my mother to force him to see a dentist, she'd always respond, "With what money?" What made it all the more tragic was that a dentist occupied the ground floor of our apartment building, this sleazy guy from New Jersey who whitenened my teeth nearly for free because he wanted to sleep with me. "I love collecting toys," he bragged as he pointed out his Lamborghini in the parking lot, and I couldn't decide whether to puke or pursue dentistry.

Around this time we began getting suspicious phone calls from a woman who said she was from Con Ed asking for Eleanor Mascia. Since the electric bill was in my name, my mother immediately became suspicious. On a whim she called Celie, who revealed she'd also been getting suspicious calls from a woman saying she was from LILCO, the electric company out on Long Island, and asking for my mother. Next my mother called Maria's mother, who said that she'd gotten similar calls from a woman who said she was from San Diego Gas and Electric. There was only one thing in my mother's name: the Camry. My mother was forced to reveal how we'd been affording the monthly payments and insurance.

"We haven't been making the payments," she said quietly.

"Excuse me?" I asked, wondering whose house we were going to live in next. Our next-door neighbor Brian already had a roommate in his second bedroom, so that was out . . .

"We haven't been paying for the car, Jenny," she repeated. In fact, she said they'd left California with no intention of ever making another payment.

"How long did you think you'd get away with this?" I demanded to know. A few weeks later my father gave in and engaged the mysterious Queen of the Utilities, who admitted that she was a private investigator from Toyota Motor Credit and she'd be happy to pick up the car. We left it on a side street during one of the horrific storms that buried us in twenty-six inches of snow. At least my parents had a sense of humor.

My mother had been toying with the idea of substitute teaching at a local high school, but without a car she couldn't get around the Island. And my father had anticipated spending the week after Christmas and before New Year's in Florida, where he was supposed to be painting, and he figured he would use the trip as an excuse to attend his son Tony's wedding on December 31. He'd spent hours with Tony on the phone all fall, asking him about his plans and sounding excited for the big day. We hadn't seen Tony since he came to visit us in the eighties and I wanted to go, too, but I couldn't afford a plane ticket. Now that work wouldn't be taking my father down there, neither could he, and he spent a week in bed, depressed. But instead of calling one of his children and telling them about his money problems, he simply stopped calling. And because he never said he wasn't going, they had no reason to think otherwise.

"Daddy, you've got to tell Tony!" I said, as angry as if Tony was a brother I'd grown up with.

"Stay out of it, Jenny," he said from under the covers.

"Yeah, Johnny, it isn't right," my mother echoed.

"Shut up, Eleanor!" he yelled, which forced him to sit up, which was the most he'd moved in days.

"Don't tell her to shut up, Daddy," I said, fearing that our fragile peace was already eroding. Sometimes when he drove me to work he complained about my mother's laziness, claiming it had bothered him for years. He was partly blaming her for our financial situation, and it wasn't the first time. One evening on the way home he even told me he "didn't know" if they would stay together or split up. I gently argued that she was probably chemically depressed and described all that that entailed, but he didn't seem to understand that such a thing could be biological.

"You can't help the way your mother is, Jenny," he'd told me as we pulled into the mall parking lot one night. "No one can." I became furious, surprising even myself.

"Did I ask you to *apologize* for my mother?" I yelled. "No one has to apologize for my mother! How dare you!" I was crying, but yelling so loud he barely noticed. He looked shocked. "Don't you ever do that again!" I went on. "I don't want to hear about my mother's short-comings from you ever again!" I flushed at the memory.

"Guys," I said, standing at the foot of the bed with my mother at my side, "I know you're depressed because of money. I get it. But it doesn't have to make us all like this," I said, gesturing to my father lying prostrate in the bed.

"Yeah?" my father asked. "Jenny, you can't do anything in this world without money. Nothing."

"But, Daddy," I argued, "not everything in this life demands you spend money. We could go to the city and just walk around . . ."

"Really, Jennifer?" he asked, his nostrils flaring. "And what happens when you get hungry, or your mother gets hungry? We have no money. None." At that moment I remembered how my father always arranged the money in his wallet so it was crisp and straight and facing the same way, and if he ever caught me with a wad crumpled in my pocket he would lecture me: "You should always have respect for money, Jennifer." I wondered what that Daddy would have to say about this.

"But wasn't the whole point just to be together again?" I asked, my voice cracking. "As long as we're together, what does it matter what we do?" I was being naïve, I knew it. I was also crying. I caught sight of myself in the mirrored closet doors: I was still wearing a towel from when I'd stepped out of the shower minutes before, and splotchy red hives covered my chest. My lips were swollen from crying; I looked like a duck. My father said nothing, just sank into the pillows.

"Now, do you think we can stop this stupid fighting about stupid money?" I asked through my sobs. "Because I, for one, am just happy to be out of Maria's house." That night we managed to get my father to agree that he wasn't going to lock himself in the master bedroom and never come out—as a concession, we said we wouldn't complain if he ran out to get a case of beer, which he promptly did—and my mother agreed to get a job. But I got another one first. One day my mother and I drove past a mini-mall on Hylan Boulevard, the Island's main thoroughfare, and noticed a Starbucks being constructed, the first on Staten Island. By the time my father finally got the long-awaited call that he was returning to work in February, I was a barista. Even though I had to wake up at 5:00 A.M. and grab a bus for the morning shift, I was glad to be around people my age again. After I was working there for a few months my mother decided she was going to be a barista, too.

"You?" I asked. "You? Who's manually retarded? Mom, you can't even work the VCR. How is this going to work?"

But she was undeterred. "I'll learn, that's how," she insisted, and called my general manager for recommendations. The store at Seventy-eighth Street and Lexington Avenue in Manhattan was hiring, so every morning she commuted for an hour and a half by bus, ferry, and train to grind coffee for eight dollars an hour. My heart ached for her because she was always tired and this kind of work was demeaning, considering what she was capable of, but she felt she was "contributing" and making my father happy. With three incomes, we pulled ourselves out of the muck.

One night I was making espresso drinks when I heard my co-worker Jenny calling to me, "Hey, do you know anything about . . . who was it again?" she asked the person at the counter, a tall guy with brown hair and penetrating blue eyes.

"Emily Dickinson," he said. "I'm supposed to be writing a paper on her and Walt Whitman but I'm procrastinating real bad." His accent sounded like my parents'.

" 'Because I could not stop for death, he kindly stopped for me,' " I recited. " 'The carriage held but just ourselves and immortality.' " It was the one unit I hadn't slept through in junior year English.

His eyes lit up. "I'm impressed," he said.

"I'm Jennifer," I said, holding out my hand and cursing my green apron for existing.

"Jeff," he said. He worked at Pathmark a couple shopping centers over but admitted he was unhappy in the supermarket industry, despite being named employee of the month several times.

"So apply here," I said, handing him a pad of applications. He filled one out.

"I'd love to work here, are you kidding?" he said. "They give you health insurance, don't they? I actually applied once before but they never called me." I noticed that his handwriting was barely legible.

"I'll make sure they get it this time. Where do you go to school?" I asked.

"Brooklyn College," he said, "but I might go to CSI next year." He was referring to the College of Staten Island, part of the city university system, which I'd also been considering until the car was repossessed.

"My mother went to Brooklyn College," I said. "My parents are from Brooklyn, but I'm from California."

"I'm from Brooklyn, too. Sunset Park," he said. "We moved here five years ago. My mother is from Cuba, though. My Dad's Irish."

"Interesting combination," I remarked. "My Dad's Italian and my mother's Jewish. So I guess that makes me a pizza bagel." One of my regulars had recently called me that, and it took me a second to realize what it meant.

"I'm a McSpic," he joked.

"Funny. Do you speak Spanish?"

"Some," he said. We talked until the store closed, and after he left, my co-worker, Jenny, started jumping up and down.

"He was *so* into you, Jennifer!" she said, her glasses nearly falling off her face. "You should go meet him after work and help him with his paper!"

"Trust me, he was *not* into me," I insisted as I Windexed the pastry case. But I put Jeff's application on the top of the pile. The next time I saw him he was wearing a green apron and receiving a toilet cleaning tutorial.

"Ew, pubes!" he commented from the inside of the bathroom. I was immediately turned off by his immaturity—he was twenty-three and fond of imitating *Beavis and Butt-Head*—and by his conservative views, which were slightly to the right of Rupert Murdoch. I regarded him with overdramatic eye-rolls, until Maria announced that she was coming for a visit and I desperately needed a ride to Newark Airport to pick her up. Jeff told me he might be able to help me out "if you make it worth my while."

"Gross," I said.

Having Maria around for a few weeks lured me out of the dark corner I'd been living in since we left Laguna Hills. Her natural curiosity about my little Italian neighborhood on the water meant I was forced to become acquainted with the church next door, the Garibaldi-Meucci Museum two streets away, and the park under the Verrazano Bridge in order to fulfill my duties as tour guide. And when we wanted to venture into the city, Maria forced me to call Jeff and take him up on his unexpected offer to show us around. I did so only reluctantly, and one night Maria and I donned our short skirts and tight tops and painted our nails and joined Jeff and his friend Carmine as we drove over the Verrazano and through the Brooklyn Battery Tunnel and came out the other side, parking in the Village. There we had dinner and walked all the way down to the ferry, making time for a detour over the Brooklyn Bridge. On our way we proceeded to get blindingly drunk on kamikazes at a bar at the South Street Seaport. I was so tipsy I barely noticed when Jeff handed me a rose he'd bought on the street and kissed me; I leaned in to kiss him back and fell right off the sidewalk. But I loved every minute of it, even the smell of the subway, which didn't smell like urine at all, but had a faint industrial scent. It took Maria's visit for me to finally appreciate the island that beckoned every morning from my bedroom window.

"It's just magical," she said on the final day of her trip as we stood on the balcony watching the sun set. Now that I decided I didn't hate Jeff anymore we hung out regularly after Maria left. Not that our bickering over politics ever ceased, and whenever he came over to pick me up my mother made a point to tear herself away from her *Law & Order* marathon to engage him in a ferocious political debate.

But my father loved Jeff, as he was from Brooklyn and, like my father, he had the accent to prove it ("ask" became "ax," and don't even get me started on how he pronounced "Massachusetts"). Dad liked Jeff so much he even offered him a job painting buildings all summer so he could pay off his considerable credit card bills, but even though it would have grossed him $17,000 he turned it down, as he was on track for management at Starbucks. But my father still trusted Jeff with his daughter, as he was frequently fond of saying, and sometimes took Jeff's side, but my mother never really changed her mind. Whenever Jeff called she would make a point to talk loudly in my free ear, frustrating me to the point of tears. Here I was trying to carve a life out of ice and there she'd be with a blowtorch trying to melt it. I explained that Jeff's slightly militant views were part role-playing and part attention seeking, and his tirades were kind of like epileptic seizures that just had to be waited out. Mostly he was just trying to get a rise out of everyone.

But in fact, he drove me crazy with his use of the *n* word, which he swore everyone from his neck of the woods used. And it was true—his family used it, his friends used it, and no one thought there was anything wrong with it. But there was one person from his neck of the woods who didn't ever use it: my father.

"Yeah, that's because your mother is such a liberal," Jeff pointed out. "I'm sure she beat it out of him." But my mother had confessed the real reason for my father's expanded horizons, something I could never reveal to Jeff.

"You know, if we got married, you'd have to become a Republican," he added.

"Jeff!"

That fall he turned to me and said, "Why don't we just be boyfriend and girlfriend?" It seemed rather perfunctory, but if he wanted me in his life, that was one way to keep me there. But despite my many attempts to forge a more intimate connection, he'd refuse, and we weren't intimate until nearly a year after I met him. When I'd ask him why, he had a number of reasons at the ready, like "I don't want a serious relationship," or "I want to wait until I have my life together, I don't really know what I want to do yet." What Jeff wanted was to be the next Rupert Murdoch, but without doing any of the hard work that that entailed. He was obsessed with people who had attained power, whether it was Hitler or Murdoch—or Madonna. As I soon came to discover, his Madonna obsession dwarfed any other passion in his life. I didn't assign his devotion to the Biggest Icon of Our Time much significance until he took me to see the film version of *Evita,* starring Madge herself. Not just once, but *seven times*.

"Jenny, listen to me," my mother lectured one evening as she diced carrots and celery for her famous chicken soup. "And I know what I'm talking about. Jeff is *gay*." I'd heard it from our co-workers, too, when I caught snatches of conversation that mysteriously evaporated as soon as I approached.

"He's just artistic," I argued.

"Oh, bullshit," she countered. "You're with him because it's safe, and you don't like taking risks." Judging from the ups and downs she'd had with my father, it was clear that she preferred risky.

"He's not David," I said. "He doesn't fit into some category. He's just in a rough place right now, and he doesn't want to commit to me until he has his life together."

"Look, spend time with him," she said, "do what you want, but remember that I warned you: Sex is the glue that holds two people together. If that intimacy isn't there, then you're just friends." And she would know.

But I ignored my mother and continued throwing myself at Jeff, though the rejection started to grate on me. I'd come home crying when one of my advances had been refused, and my parents would comfort me. "Maybe he really isn't ready for a serious relationship, Jenny Penny," my father said, stroking my back as I sobbed into my pillow.

"Jenny, you know you just like the chase," my mother said after he stood me up one night, "and if he ever gave in you'd probably lose interest." She was partly right—sitting on the balcony and anticipating his red Dodge Neon pulling in to the circular driveway below was one of the biggest thrills of my life, mostly because I never knew if we'd still be dating by the end of the night. His unpredictability was stressful but also kind of exciting, and it drew me in, despite the constant rejection.

During our three A.M. breakfasts at Yaffa Café on St. Marks Place, he would regale me with tales of his goth, black-nail-polished East Village days after high school and tell me how my insistence on commuting in to Manhattan each night reminded him of how totally he'd immersed himself in Staten Island life.

"I need to get off the Island," he said one night.

"What, and miss the Can-Can sale at Shop Rite?" I cracked.

When the summer ended I found a way to get off the Island, enrolling at Hunter College at Sixty-eighth and Lex. When it came time to pay the $1,600-per-semester tuition I had to rely on my parents, who had only recently agreed to stop confiscating my paychecks. They enrolled in a payment plan and we had until the end of the term to satisfy it. The week before school started I was enjoying an afternoon nap—one of my guilty pleasures—when the phone rang. It was my father.

"Jenny?" he asked. He was in New Hampshire that week.

"Daddy, how are you?" I asked, waking up.

"Jenny, is your mother home?" I sat up, my heart racing.

"No, she's at work. Daddy, what's wrong?"

"Jenny, eh, I was hoping to talk to your mother first, but . . . I fell off a ladder," he said. "I'm in the hospital."

"How bad is it?" I asked, on the verge of weeping.

"I broke my arm, and it's pretty bad. I have to have surgery," he said.

"Oh, Daddy," I said, crying.

"It's okay, Jenny," he said, crying with me. We wept together for a moment until I finally said, "Okay, I'll have Mommy call you when she gets home." When I heard her keys in the door an hour later I began with, "Don't panic, but . . ." She stayed remarkably calm, immediately calling the hospital and speaking to my father.

"We're going up there," she decided as soon as she hung up.

"How?" I asked. "We don't have a car."

"Your father said we should call Mattie and he'll loan us his Jeep," she said. Mattie was my father's boss, who lived in Flushing and tried his best to appear happily married to his rather rotund wife. But my father had told us the truth: On the road Mattie was a Hoover when it came to cocaine, and a proud patron of prostitutes. My father complained of being forced to act as the crew's boss whenever Mattie was on a bender, waking everyone up in the morning and doling out their daily wages in the evening. One of my father's co-workers picked us up and drove us to Flushing, where Mattie, who hadn't gone on this trip, handed us the keys. "Don't crash it," he joked in his gruff, humorless way. But we didn't get any farther than the on-ramp to the I-95 when the Jeep hydroplaned over some coolant in the street and crashed into the guardrail before sputtering to a halt. The car was totaled. After the tow company hauled it away we walked back into Mattie's house with our heads bowed and handed him the keys.

"Don't worry," my father said on the phone after his surgery. "He was delinquent on the payments and it was about to get repossessed anyway."

When my father returned we looked at his arm and gasped: It was outfitted with a metal contraption that penetrated his skin and held his bones together with screws. The thing jutted out of his arm and turned my legs to Jell-O whenever I looked at it.

"You're the Terminator, Daddy," I remarked. But the Terminator was out of work, and we lived on whatever wages he had saved until they ran out. As soon as the brace came off he went right back to painting, though his doctors advised against it. But this time he hooked up with a crew that paid him on the books, so when they were out of work for weeks or months at a time he could receive unemployment.

One morning, just a few hours after I hung up from one of my middle-of-the-night phone calls with Jeff, my father came into my room and sat on the edge of my bed. His hair was slicked back, like he'd just showered, and he was wearing his black ribbed bathrobe.

"Jenny," he said, "Grandpa died."

"Oh, Daddy," I said, hugging him. "Are you okay?" My father had just placed Grandpa in an assisted living facility because his prostate cancer had returned and metastasized to his bones. In fact, we had planned to visit him that very afternoon.

"Yeah, I'm okay," he said, but he looked tired. At the funeral my mother told me that even though my father appeared calm, he was devastated at losing his last parent. He finally broke down after the final viewing when he leaned in to kiss his father goodbye. I wondered what I would do if I had to kiss one of my parents goodbye, and decided I'd have to be scraped off the floor. As it was, the shock of seeing my grandfather's body instantly reduced me to tears; I'd never seen a dead body before. When it came time to close the coffin my mother ushered me out, leaving Uncle Frankie, my father, and Aunt Rosalie to spend some last moments with their father. "It's always a traumatic moment when the coffin is closed," my mother whispered into my ear. I'd listened through the door and thought I heard wailing, but I wasn't sure whose it was.

My sisters came up from Florida to mourn Grandpa, and because of my father's absence from Tony's wedding I was tense around them at first. I hadn't seen Angie in nine years and I hadn't seen Tina in seven. My sisters and I were pieces of a broken family and I didn't know how to act around them. They didn't stay with us, instead bunking at Uncle Frankie's. Though they made home movies of my mother and father and Frankie showing them around Rockefeller Center and Central Park and their old house in Brooklyn—where they lived as toddlers before moving to Florida—the only time I saw Angie and Tina was at the wake, and then later at the grave site, after I gave Tina my seat in the limousine that would take us there.

"You go with them," I said to her when my parents beckoned me inside. "You're the oldest daughter." And she appeared to be really upset, while I was not—I barely knew Grandpa. "I guess Tina was close to him, huh?" I later asked my mother. I didn't understand why she would be tight with Grandpa but not Dad, but I guessed it had something to do with his being in jail for twelve years.

One night a few months after the funeral I was rummaging through my father's night table searching for a stray Baby Ruth when I found a letter from Angie. It was addressed to my father and it had been opened, so I assumed he'd seen it. He was out of town and my mother was in the living room watching TV, so I read it.

On the first page Angie wrote about how she and her husband, Frankie, and the kids had to move in with Angie's mother, Marie, while their new home in Royal Palm Beach was being constructed. Nicole and Krissy were pulled out of school right before the year ended, which upset them, even though Nicole still earned a 3.9 grade point average for the year. Angie also talked about Krissy, who was six at the time. "She's been obsessed with who her grandfathers are ever since Grandpa died," Angie wrote.

Also, Frankie's father died recently and we never met him, and she's having trouble understanding why she doesn't know who these people are. I always told her about you, she's seen pictures and videos and Nicole remembers you and talks about you to her. I tried to call you so Krissy could talk to you but you were away. So if you could, would you maybe call sometime? I know you're busy, but I feel bad for her and I don't know what to tell her.

I wish we could maybe keep in touch a little bit more than we do, too. I know I'll never have a relationship with you like Jenny, but I feel like we have nothing at all and I don't know why. I really felt awkward seeing you at first at the funeral, but later I became comfortable and thought you did too. But then I leave and I never hear from you and I feel if I don't tell you this now, I may never hear from you again.

I know I'm not great with cards and letters, and I never remember birthdays, but I don't want to never speak again. I can't believe I'm actually telling you all this and if I don't hear from you I'll just forget it, but I have to make an effort. Tony and Tina wonder what's up with you, too. Tony really thought you were going to walk in at his wedding the whole night until it was over and your chair was still empty. I don't know if it's easier for you to forget about us, it may be for you but it only hurts us. We are all grown up now and we're not

looking for a Daddy anymore, but just to know that you still acknowl-
edge our existence and care a little would feel nice. If not for our
sakes, maybe for your grandchildren's sakes.

Well I probably said too much, but I have not said anything for
long enough. Well think about it and I hope to hear from you.

Love, Angela
(561) 753-xxxx

I was in hysterics as soon as I got to the part about how everyone
expected my father at Tony's wedding, holding out hope till the end of
the night, only for him never to materialize. I imagined my brother and
sisters jerking their necks toward the door whenever somebody walked
in and feeling disappointment when they saw it wasn't their father. I
wondered if Angie knew how appalled my mother and I had been at
his withdrawal, but then, how could she? We weren't in touch, either.
But the fact that she left her phone number at the bottom of the letter
just ripped me to bits. It's true that she had just relocated, but I couldn't
imagine my father not having my phone number if I moved. My father
was also her father; how could the same person treat different children
so differently? The tragic part was that after each of his dozen or so
trips to Florida in the eighties he'd come back completely smitten with
his infant granddaughters, talking about nothing but their coos and
quirks. What had happened since then to break the spell?

Letter in hand, I ventured into the living room with tears pouring
down my face. "Mom," I said, holding out the letter, "have you seen
this?" She took it, read a few sentences, and nodded.

"Yes, and your father did, too," she said, handing it back to me.
"What can I tell you?"

"But, Mom," I said, and read aloud the part about the wedding.
"How could he do that? How could my father do something like that?
To me, this is worse than breaking the law."

"I don't know, honey," she said. "I asked him the same thing, but
he didn't want to talk about it."

A thought kept popping into my head. "Would he ever do that to
me?" I asked.

"Don't be silly," she said, "he'd never do that to you."

"Yeah? What makes me so special?" I asked.

"You're his baby," she said. "He'll always be close to you."

I felt guilty that something as random as birth order granted me a relationship with my father. But I realized that while circumstance may have separated them, it hadn't kept them apart. My father did that all by himself.

THAT SPRING JEFF sat me down to dinner and told me that he was finally ready to come out of the closet. He had fallen in love, he said, and couldn't pretend anymore.

"Oh, thank god!" I exclaimed and threw my arms around his neck. We were determined to remain friends, and I was relieved at having discovered the ultimate breakup loophole. When I got home that night I found my parents in the living room watching television. "You guys are not going to believe this," I said, bursting with excitement over having finally defined my stubbornly elusive relationship. "Jeff is gay!"

"I knew it," my mother said.

"No, really, Jenny?" my father asked. "Are you sure? Is he sure?"

My mother and I looked over at my father in disbelief. "Dad, yes," I said, laughing.

"That's too bad," he said. "Tell you the truth, I wanted him as my son-in-law."

"Aw, Daddy," I said sympathetically.

Jeff was relieved he hadn't broken my heart by coming out, and our friendship was sealed. That May he was in the audience alongside my parents as I tore up the stage as the lead in Hunter's spring production. But I could have been dressed as a tree for all the difference it made to my father, who wept silently from start to finish. In fact, he took an interest in all of my collegiate endeavors, reading every story I wrote for the school paper, and when I was accepted into the honors program at Hunter, my father was especially proud, paying for my lifetime membership in the Golden Key Society without my knowledge. One day he came into my room with a small gold membership pin.

"Thank you, Daddy," I said when I opened the little black box, surprised and pleased that he cared so much. However, we were struggling to pay my tuition bill, and when I discovered that I could fill out a FAFSA form to apply for financial aid I brought one home to my parents and laid it out on the living room table.

"Jenny, we can't," my mother said. "They're going to find out we *haven't paid any taxes,*" she added, whispering the second half of the sentence.

"Mom, they're not going to find out," I said, exasperated. "Trust me. This is the only way I can pay for college: with grants and student loans. Please, just fill out the form." When my father ambled in I pleaded my case to him.

"Absolutely not," he said. "Who knows what they'll find on us. No." The only way I could get them to fill out the paperwork was by dragging them both in to my student loan adviser's office so he could convince them that there was no underground IRS Gestapo combing through student loan paperwork desperately searching for tax delinquents. (When it came time for me to file my first 1040 a few months later, I asked my parents what to do. They stared at me blankly before suggesting an accountant who lived in our building.)

But my father did shoulder one cost for me—my credit cards. I'd accrued seven of them, and when the bills overwhelmed me I approached my parents, helpless. I figured they'd been through this so many times they might have some advice for me. But they didn't recommend I "bust out" my cards. Instead, my mother found a consumer credit counseling service that froze the interest and let my father pay them off. Now whenever we fought I couldn't acidly remind my mother that I'd given her my paychecks for two years, because my father's gesture essentially canceled mine out.

With the Jeff situation and the credit situation and my parents' financial situation under control, I ended the school year with one goal in mind: preparing for my upcoming trip to California, my first since we'd moved away. That August I greeted Maria at the airport with "Take me to the ocean," and we watched the waves break at Heisler Park, the whitecaps glowing in the darkness. One night my high school friends took me to Laguna Beach and we dropped in to our old haunts on Forest Avenue. It was then I decided that I could never live in California again. Somewhere between the U-Haul place on New Utrecht Avenue and my perch between the boulders in Central Park where my friends and I sometimes smoked pot between classes, I had fallen in love in spite of myself. It had crept up on me, and without the hum of city streets and the sight of people scurrying up and down sidewalks, I was bored. Who knows what would have become of me if I hadn't moved away? I'd outgrown Orange County, a fact that filled me with pride. I was growing up.

Toward the end of my stay, Maria and I planned a day trip to Mexico in an effort to re-create the senior year trip we took to Tijuana. But instead of sipping margaritas on the water I found myself on a hasty plane that landed in a different New York, one that was filled with sorrow.

"HI, JENNY, IT'S JUST MOMMY. Just making dinner. Call when you get this."

Maria and I had been gone all day and the message was waiting for me when we got back. The time difference meant that she and my father had already consumed her dinner, whatever it had been. I dialed my number. After four rings the answering machine picked up.

"Hey, Mom, it's Jenny, sorry I didn't call you earlier. Gimme call."

I sat in the living room and absentmindedly switched on a summer repeat of *Friends*. I was supposed to meet a couple of Mission Viejo High School alums for a late-night swim but I wanted to touch base with my mother first. It bothered me that she wasn't home. My parents were never not home. I sat and nervously shook my leg as I tried my mother's number once more. (Okay, so she went to the compactor room to take out the garbage.) Twice. (Okay, so my parents are next door at Brian's apartment having coffee and Danish.) Three times. (Could they be . . . having sex? Unlikely.) Four times.

"Jenny, are you coming over?" my friend Natalie asked in a "Where are you?" phone call. I should have been over there by then, but I chose to sit it out in Maria's living room until my mother called back.

But she never did. As the sun disappeared below the horizon and the orange glow of suburban night settled over the Saddleback Valley, I whipped myself into a helpless frenzy. Maria looked on, concerned, as I repeatedly dialed the eleven digits hoping for a different result. At nine o'clock Pacific Daylight Time, somebody answered.

"Hello?" asked my father's weary sandpaper voice.

"Daddy!" I shouted. "Daddy, what is going on? I have been calling for hours! Where is Mommy?"

"Oh, Mommy is fine," he said. "Yeah, Mommy . . . Mommy was stressed. The doctor was worried about her stress level, so they held her overnight."

"She's at the doctor's?" I asked.

"Yeah, honey," he said, his voice level. "He didn't like her stress levels."

"Did she have an appointment today?" I asked, trying to believe. "She called me hours ago, and she didn't mention anything about a doctor's appointment."

Long pause. I heard him exhale. "Jenny," he said, a sob invading his low, guttural tones. "Jenny." My heart was pounding so hard so suddenly I thought I might throw up. "Jenny, it was a heart attack," he finally said. "Mommy had a heart attack."

"What?" I asked, bewildered. "She had a heart attack? When? What happened?" I looked at Maria, who was watching me intently.

"They took her to St. Vincent's, here on the Island," he said.

"Why did no one call me?" I demanded to know.

"Your mother didn't want me to tell you," he said. "She didn't want to ruin your trip."

"Ruin my trip?" I asked incredulously. Did my mother really think I would care more about downing margaritas in Tijuana than this? "Are you kidding me? I'm coming home tomorrow!" I could almost hear him nodding over the phone, picture his relief. Then a thought struck me, threatening to level me: Was my mother still alive?

"Hey, wait, what else aren't you telling me?" I ventured, suddenly suspicious. There was something I didn't know; many things, in fact, and I didn't want my world to collapse without being told first.

"Nothing, Jenny. I'm sitting here in the kitchen, Brian is here with me, and I'm having a scotch, and I just, I was sitting here wondering how I was going to tell you, when I was going to call you . . ." As he spoke I made my way to Maria's backyard, perched high in the hills of Laguna, so her parents wouldn't take me for a madwoman.

"You'd better tell me what the fuck is going on right fucking now!" I boomed into the phone as soon as I stepped outside. My outburst shook tendon and muscle, leaving me wrung out and barely clinging to gravity. I was never permitted to curse at my father; that was his exclusive privilege. The fact that he didn't reprimand my indiscretion

or threaten me with his belt meant that something serious had indeed transpired.

"Jenny," he said, sounding pained. "I am telling you everything." Then he told me the rest. He'd driven up to our apartment building in his big powder-blue Ford van, the one he'd used for carpet cleaning jobs in California but now used for painting gas stations with his crew, and Brian was standing outside waiting for him, along with our landlady, Flo. I could picture my father, healthy and tan, bounding up to the circular drive like a panther and flashing his signature jack-o'-lantern grin when he encountered Brian and Flo looking concerned but trying their best to appear casual.

"Johnny," Brian said. "We have to tell you something."

My father probably paused and looked from one to the other, sizing them up in his laserlike, street-smart manner. It was the same gift that could discern which of my boyfriends were just harmless nincompoops and which were complete and total fuckups.

"What?" he asked them. "What is it?" Realization crept into his voice. I was in California; he knew it must be Eleanor.

"Johnny," Brian had continued, "Eleanor was making dinner and she . . . she had a heart attack, we think. The ambulance came and took her to St. Vincent's. She's there now."

And without a word, he hopped right back into his truck, peeled out, and sped west on Bay Street, probably running lights the whole way.

"Is she going to be okay?" I started to ask, plopping myself down on one of the uneven grassy hills that dotted the backyard, but I found that I couldn't speak because I was crying too hard. I shoved the phone at Maria. She took it, confused but unflappable as always.

"Hello?" she asked. "Mr. Mascia?" I didn't stay sane enough to follow their conversation; I'd begun rolling around on the jagged knolls sobbing and howling.

"Jenny," Maria whispered loudly, her hand over the receiver. "Come on, calm down!" But I couldn't control it. It was pure pain, centered in my chest and erupting from my vocal cords, serenading the houses below like a murder victim moments before extinction. I had never given myself over to grief this way. It wouldn't be the last time.

I'd often wondered which one of my parents would die first, and imagined that perhaps this was the way it was supposed to play out. I was closest to my mother, as girls often are, but I sensed that there were gulfs between me and my father. I mean, the two of us always said we loved each other, and being Italians, we got teary-eyed at the same sentiment, the same nostalgia. But though we never spoke of it, I always got the sense that we both marked time in the same way: by measuring what was lost. Regret colored our emotional life, though I hadn't really earned any regret yet. It must have been something I'd absorbed from him.

Because of our mutual distance, our reluctance to discuss what I sensed he held in the chambers of his heart, I felt my mother might die first, and that it would be appropriate somehow, because without her glue to hold us together, my father and I might finally have to get to know each other. It was perverse—sacrificing one parent for the acquaintance of another—and it was a thought that I didn't even realize I'd fantasized about until now. Was this how it would go down? Me three thousand miles away and rolling around on the grass in agony? Would I at least get to say goodbye?

After a few more minutes of screaming and crying—Maria had taken the phone back into the house and away from my display—I lay on my back and took in the night sky. Just as in New York, suburban sprawl had turned the sky orange and stolen the stars. I panted for a few moments, hearing only my own breath whooshing in and out of my lungs. I felt tiny blades of grass stab my sweaty legs, and it was a jolt—I suddenly realized that all the functions that I relied on to confirm that I was alive, like hunger and fatigue, were on autopilot. I was no longer aware of or connected to my basest bodily reflexes; adrenaline had overwhelmed my receptors. I couldn't tell if my bladder was full, I couldn't imagine ever being hungry again—it was as if someone had removed my stomach. My body had crossed over into some tentative new reality, and as my senses slowly returned, it was as if I was exercising them for the first time. When the dust finally settled, I knew I'd have to take my hunger and my fatigue and my urge to urinate and adapt my senses to this new world, just as I had first adapted, all those years ago, to the old.

Maria was standing over me with her hand extended; the phone was in it. I nodded and climbed to my feet. "Daddy," I said, finally calm. "Are you okay?"

"Well, I have my scotch," he said, with a grunt/laugh.

"I'm coming home," I assured him. "Tomorrow. The next flight I can get." I remembered my parents driving me to the Continental terminal at Newark Airport exactly thirteen days before, walking me all the way up to the gate—you could still do that then—and waving excitedly as I left to return to their Golden Paradise, the one they reluctantly left, the one neither of them would see again. When was the last time I'd spoken to my mother, told her I loved her? Probably that morning. We might have chatted as she chewed her morning toast, and I might have apprised her of my plans for the day, reminding her that I'd be home in two. Now I didn't know whether I'd be greeting her in a hospital or a mortuary.

"Okay. Good," my father said, sounding relieved. What was my mother thinking, trying to keep me out of this loop? Why do that to my lonely father, who had no one else to lend him support? He didn't have friends, he had co-workers; his family was Sicilian and mired in one grudge after another. We three were all we had, and we knew it.

I emerged from the call to a sea of concerned faces: Maria's mother, almost naïvely optimistic and devout; Maria's father, stern yet loving; and Maria, hardheaded yet always sifting and analyzing in her never-ending quest for self-awareness. They were generous and well-meaning people; they'd opened their home to me and my mother when our family unit had collapsed under sudden poverty. It wasn't so long ago that these people were breaking up three A.M. battles between the two of us in this very spot; now I faced them alone, the fragile foundation I'd always taken for granted once again in peril. We'd been so vulnerable before this family, so exposed, and I didn't think we could get any more naked. I was wrong.

Maria and I ambled to the kitchen to talk quietly. "You know," I said, pulling out a chair with unsteady hands, "my dad makes, like, a hundred dollars a day painting gas stations. And last year he broke his arm and was out of work and didn't qualify for worker's comp because he was paid off the books. And my mom is probably going to have to leave her new part-time job at Macy's."

"My parents have health insurance and all that, and if we needed it, god forbid, we could liquidate one of the houses," Maria remarked. She wasn't being snobby; her parents had a safety net and mine didn't. But I felt they deserved one, and I thought about what incredible people they were—so witty, so much fun, so smart, each in their own way, so loving. They didn't deserve to be destitute, not at their age. All they could look forward to was Social Security, and that was still several years off. What would they do until then?

"You don't understand," I told Maria. "If my parents get sick, if one of them dies, they have *nothing*." Panic seared my voice, but I soon realized that all the imploring in the world couldn't make her understand our predicament. Maria's parents were engineers, they owned property. They weren't ostentatious by any means—if anything, they downplayed their wealth—but they had a solid foundation that my parents had somehow forgotten to build for themselves.

Once again I was filled with outrage: Why did everything happen to us? We went broke, went bankrupt, endured multiple separations from my father, and for what? I still didn't really understand. Why couldn't our lives just proceed normally, like the lives of my friends and their parents in California? Why were there always bumps in the road for the Mascia family?

WHEN I LANDED in Newark I spotted my father at the baggage carousel. I was terrified of what he had to tell me, but before I could say anything I saw his face sag with relief. I embraced him, and he collapsed into my arms. I hung on his lean, muscular frame, relieved I had rejected my mother's wishes to stay in California and enjoy the rest of my vacation.

"I'm so glad you're here," he choked, breaking down, his whole body quivering. "I can't do this alone." I had only seen him cry like this once before, a couple of years after his own mother had died. I was ten or eleven, and he was looking through his dresser for the first time since Grandma Helen had succumbed to lung cancer. He pulled a pristine white diaper out of the bottom drawer. "You see, they put her in diapers in the hospital, because she was so sick," he explained, and revealed what was wrapped inside: the rosary that been placed into her hands during her wake, the rosary she worshiped with as a child, and a head scarf she had used to cover the bald patches created by chemotherapy. He held this treasure in his hands, rosary beads spilling from between his fingers, and mid-sentence his words became inaudible, garbled with sobs. My mother had swooped in to rescue the scene, comforting him and explaining to me that my father was very close with his mother, and these things reminded him of a bad time in her life, when she was very sick. Now my mother could be dying, and he cried those same tears of helplessness. This time I understood exactly how he felt.

He grabbed my suitcase and ushered me into a taxi and we braved rush hour traffic to get to St. Vincent's in Manhattan, where she had been transferred overnight. Turns out the "episodes" she'd suffered were actually small heart attacks, and the Staten Island branch of St. Vincent's wasn't equipped to perform angioplasty. The procedure had been completed while I was in the air, and now she was resting comfortably in a hospital bed in the West Village with a stunning view of downtown Manhattan. My father hadn't seen her yet because he'd had to fetch me, but he had been told that her chances for recovery were very good. But we still hadn't heard her voice or laid eyes upon her, and now we were stuck amid a sea of cars in the Lincoln Tunnel. I had never cursed traffic so vehemently in my life.

"Jenny, there's something you need to know," he said as Manhattan emerged on the other side.

"What is it?" I asked, wondering what could be worse than my mother nearly dying.

"Your mother, well, she's older than we thought."

Older than we thought? Than *we* thought?

And then I remembered. About a year earlier, I had been sitting at the kitchen table and my mother was on the couch watching her beloved *Law & Order* when she tested something out on me:

"Jenny, what if I told you I was older than you thought I was?" The scenario seemed ridiculous, as I'd seen her driver's license and birth certificate umpteen times. I wondered how many Xanax she'd taken that day.

"What are you talking about?" I asked. "Is this a joke?"

"No," she said carefully, "but what if I told you that I was older? How would you react?"

"Well, how much older could you be," I asked, playing along, "since I am nineteen and obviously not adopted?"

She thought about it, and dropped the subject with, "Never mind." And now a second source had confirmed that her experiment with the truth wasn't just a benzo-induced yarn.

"The reason I'm telling you," my father explained, "is so you don't see it on her hospital bracelet and get scared."

Scared? "Geez, Dad, how old *is* she?"

My father told me that my mother was born in 1934, not 1939 as she'd always claimed. That made her sixty-four, not fifty-nine. And with that, I was cheated out of five years of her life. Frankly, it pissed me off. I knew she was older than everyone else's parents, but now I had even less time with her than I thought I did. My father looked bewildered; this was new to him, too. I didn't ask why she had changed her age; since she was in fact two years older than my father, I assumed that was the reason. So my mother had given birth to me right after her forty-third birthday, not her thirty-eighth. I suppose this boded well for my own fertility.

When we arrived at St. Vincent's my mother was paralyzed by the sandbags placed over her legs, rooting her to the spot. She looked very tired but managed a weak smile as she saw my father, and then me, an unexpected surprise.

"Hey, how are ya?" I asked like a game-show hostess, all wide eyes and teeth, pretending I wasn't scared to death. And there it was, wrapped around her wrist, the white hospital bracelet that revealed her true age in purple letters and numbers: 10/12/1934. It was a shock, even though I'd been warned, but I decided to roll with it. If I dwelled on this loss, I'd spend five hours crying in my closet because I was scared my parents were going to die.

In a whisper, my mother insisted that my father and I grab a bite to eat, and even though I was certain we could easily go another two days without food I took him to Artepasta on Greenwich Avenue, a frequent haunt of mine and Jeff's.

"Glad I came home?" I asked as I surveyed the humid gray summer day from Greenwich and Bank.

"Oh, Jenny, you kiddin' me?" I knew this rhetorical fragment conveyed miles of gratitude.

"So, Mom's an old lady, huh?" He laughed, as relieved as I was. I examined his smile, and figured that as long as we were on a roll . . .

"It's okay," I said. "She told me your secret, too." He stiffened, almost imperceptibly. But I noticed.

"She did?" He barely glanced at me, keeping his gaze straight ahead. I can still see his distinguished profile, with his almond eyes and naturally bronzed skin that crisis had tinted gray.

"Yes," I said, trying my best to sound like an understanding adult, though at twenty I was still struggling to keep pace with his long-legged stride. "I know all about you."

THE NEXT AFTERNOON my father slowly led my mother into the apartment, and I noticed that she still had the offending hospital bracelet around her wrist revealing her true age. I tried not to look at it as she very slowly craned her neck and smiled at me.

"Hi, Jenny," she said, and I leaned in and gave her a barely-there hug, afraid of hurting her.

"If you wanted me to come home early, Ma, you could have just called," I joked, and she laughed, for exactly one second.

"Ooh, it hurts," she said, grimacing in pain. The three of us led her to bed, where she stayed for the next two weeks. No more smoking, no more fatty foods, and lots of Xanax were the orders from her cardiologist. She recovered very quickly, even if she never returned to work, and when she described her heart attack I realized how much worse it could have been.

"I had just leaned down to take the chicken out of the oven," she said from bed that first afternoon, "and just as I was about to lift up the broiler pan I felt this crushing pain, like an elephant was sitting on my chest. Oh, Jenny, it was awful. But I thought, 'Maybe I'm overreacting,' because I'm thin, you know? I picked the phone up to dial 911 but only pushed 9 before I hung up. Then I started sweating—just pouring out of me, Jenny, like a faucet—and I got so nauseous. That's when I knew, because I read somewhere that people sometimes throw up when they're having a heart attack. So I called 911 and the dispatcher told me to unlock the front door, and I waited."

"Were you scared?" I asked, on the verge of exhaustion but kept awake by the anxiety that coursed through me.

"No, actually, I wasn't scared," she said. "I felt sad. I wasn't ready for my life to be over. It made me sad to think that it would be. There's so much else to do. I haven't seen Paris yet." She was joking; we knew she'd only set foot on a plane when she could be placed in a medically induced coma before boarding. "So now I guess you know the truth," she said. "Your mama's an old lady."

"Very funny," I said, but I couldn't shake the feeling that I'd lost five years of her life, even though I really hadn't. "So you're three years older than Dad?"

"Two and a half," she corrected.

"And I guess you weren't thirty-eight when you had me, but forty-three," I said.

"Forty-two," she corrected.

"Uh, no—I was born in November, and your birthday is October 12, so that would make you forty-three," I said.

"Oh, shut up, you little stinker."

"Did your obstetrician at least know your real age?" I asked.

"You know, I'm not sure," she said pensively. "I don't think he did."

"So who else knew?" I asked.

"Everyone," she said.

"Everyone!"

"Well, except your father," she said.

"I can't believe it," I said. "So Rita isn't seven years younger than you, but . . ."

"Twelve," she said.

"Is Arline still two years younger?" I asked.

"Yes," she said.

"Why did you lie about your age?" I asked, bewildered.

"Well, your father was younger than me, and, I don't know, it was impulsive," she said. "And after we'd been together for so long I couldn't exactly change my age."

"So you're human after all," I said drowsily.

"Looks like it," she said, holding up one of her wrists, which was bandaged where the IV had been inserted. That afternoon I let her sleep, tiptoeing in and out every hour to watch her chest move up and down, proof that she was still alive. I caught my father doing the same thing.

"Hey," he said when we met in the hallway. "Are you—"

"Yeah," I said, leading him to the bedroom. "You?"

"Yeah," he admitted, and I watched as his eyes landed on her chest and stayed fixed there. "I just wanted to check on her, see if she's . . ."

"Breathing?"

He nodded.

"Me, too." Our eyes locked for a moment and I remembered how he'd fallen into my arms at the airport. He could tell me he wanted to leave her every day until the end of his life, but he'd be lost without her. He really truly loved her, in ways I didn't even understand.

THAT DECEMBER, AS PER TRADITION, Brian threw his annual Christmas party next door. My father treated himself to more than a few fingers of scotch and boasted about me to all of Brian's LGBT friends, whom my father had come to embrace. "You see, this is why I love New York, Jenny," he said as we sat on Brian's couch while everyone socialized around us. "There are so many people from different cultures and races who have so many different lifestyles, and they all come together here, you know?"

"Okay, Daddy," I said, close to cutting him off. If his Brooklyn family heard him they'd probably laugh at the liberal he'd become.

"Hey, everyone," he announced. "My daughter is an honors student! She's in the honors program! This one is going to go far in life."

"Daddy, stop," I said, though I couldn't contain my smile. He rarely got tipsy anymore and I wanted him to enjoy it. After a while I got tired and headed back to the apartment to watch TV on the couch with my mother, leaving my father to drink with Brian. He seemed to be in a good mood and only had to commute about ten feet to get home, so I wasn't worried. Until he walked in.

"Hey, girls," he said as he opened the door. He closed it behind him and paused in the front hallway, studying the two of us.

"What is it, Johnny?" my mother asked with a half-smile.

He began to rub his arms, spending extra time on his right shoulder. "I'm always hurting, Eleanor," he said, still drunk and still smiling.

"Really, honey?" she replied, dropping the smile. "Where?"

"Everywhere," he said.

"Everywhere, Daddy?" I repeated, wondering if this was a joke. "Like, pain how? Like, from painting? Maybe you're just sore, Daddy. Maybe when you fell off the ladder you hurt yourself worse than you thought you did." *Or maybe you're drunk and you're about to throw up and in that case, yes, everything would hurt.*

"Johnny," my mother said, rising from the couch, "what's wrong with your shoulder?" He was rubbing it almost exclusively now and grimacing in pain. As she approached he turned and headed toward the bedroom, and I stood outside and eavesdropped as my mother put him to bed. "Johnny, this doesn't look good," she murmured from behind the door. "We have got to get you to a doctor." I knew that would be as difficult as getting him to a dentist.

"Eleanor, no," he said, trying to put up a fight but lacking the energy for much more than a word or two. "It'll be fine. Just need ice."

"For your shoulder?" she asked, speaking so softly I could barely hear.

"Yes," he said. Then: "Ouch! Stop it, Eleanor!"

"Johnny, it's the size of a golf ball," my mother said. I gripped the wall for support. When she emerged from the bedroom her face was white, which was saying a lot—she was so pale that my father had a special nickname for her legs: "milk bottles."

"Mom, what's wrong with him?" I asked, wondering if I should give in to my default state of panic or ignore this scene in the hope that it would just go away.

"I don't know, Jenny," she said, closing the bedroom door. "But it isn't good."

CHAPTER 9

Merle Place
Staten Island, New York
March 1999

. . .

THIS TIME IT WASN'T OUR FAULT WHEN WE HAD TO MOVE. FLO called right after Christmas and told us she had to reoccupy my beloved abode on the water. My parents asked for a little more time on account of my mother's heart condition, and in February we found a three-bedroom just up the road from Flo's apartment in the shadow of the Verrazano Bridge. The apartment was quite large, and cheap—$900, which was $200 less than what we were paying on New Lane—but I hated the green carpeting and the worn linoleum that I just knew I'd never be able to get a hundred percent clean, no matter how hard I scrubbed. And there was this:

"Uncle Frankie might live with us," my mother told me.

"Okay . . ." I said.

"He's splitting from Paulette and needs to live very cheaply in order to demonstrate his eligibility for disability," she explained. "He isn't even telling his kids where he lives because he doesn't want Paulette to know."

"Well, that's not so bad," I reasoned. And the more I thought about it, the more appealing a monthly rent of $450 sounded. I was relieved; my parents could finally relax and stop worrying so much about money. And aside from the few times he emerged from his bedroom in the middle of the night to get ice for his scotch, Frankie mostly kept to himself, fashioning the master bedroom into a mini-apartment where he kept produce, alcohol, and his prized parakeet.

The day of the move I found my father and one of his painting buddies moving us without the benefit of movers, just a rented truck. "Johnny, please hire someone," my mother begged. "You're in such pain." He still hadn't gone to a doctor, and had taken to painting with ice packs on both shoulders.

"Eleanor, please," he said gruffly and continued loading our lives into the U-Haul. When we'd moved to New Lane I had vowed never to move again. *This is the last time I move anywhere with them,* I promised myself as I fell asleep that night, surrounded by boxes. In another not-so-subtle demonstration of my discontent, I refused to unpack for two months.

"Jenny, please clean your fuckin' room," my father commanded over dinner one night.

"Leave me alone," I said.

"What?" he asked, slamming his fork down so hard it nearly broke the plate.

"Easy, Johnny," my mother said as she stood over us, scooping and serving.

"No, she will *not* disrespect me like this!" he boomed, turning to address me next. "Do you have any idea how fucking hard I worked to move us all in here, when the whole time I'm in pain . . ."

"Then go to a fucking doctor!" I screamed. The three of us sat there for a moment and regarded each other: my father, his face molded into anger and disbelief; my mother, watching my father to see how he would respond; and me, aware that there was a foreign presence in our new apartment, and I don't mean Uncle Frankie. After a moment I broke the standoff by retreating to my room without clearing the table. The next week I told my parents I was going to see a therapist.

"Something's just wrong, I don't know what it is," I said from the doorway of the kitchen, where they were rinsing dishes and loading them into the dishwasher.

"Why do you think there's something wrong with you?" my mother asked, barely looking up from her task.

"I don't know, I just feel so empty," I said. Things weren't registering the way I thought they should. I felt numb. For a girl who'd lived her life in a hypersensitive state, this was troubling.

"I don't know why you have to see a therapist," my father snapped. There was an edge to his voice I found strange; he'd been to a therapist before, before rehab, and so had my mother. Why were they suddenly against therapy?

"To complain about her horrible parents," my mother snarled. I was taken aback but undeterred.

"I just feel like I do," I said, sliding down to the kitchen floor like the ten-year-old I once was.

"Then go," my mother remarked, "if it will put a stop to your complaining. But you're going to have to pay for it yourself."

The next week I found a sliding-scale therapist named Susan and began seeing her once a week. Her hair was sandy blond and brittle and she liked to wear big, beefy necklaces. We didn't tackle anything particularly heavy, as I didn't think I had any real problems, just a general feeling of malaise. "I mean, nothing has really happened to me," I began dismissively. "My dad had a problem with alcohol once, but he went to rehab and that was that. My mother has always been a tad controlling, but I do what I want to do, even if she nags me to death."

"Really," Susan said. She didn't write anything down, which led me to wonder if she secretly tape-recorded our sessions. "And your father—what is he like?"

"He's Italian," I began, "and yells a lot. But he can also be mushy and sentimental. He was my favorite for a time when I was a kid. He's so good with children. I should probably tell you that he was arrested in front of me when I was five and taken to jail for five months before he was released. I missed him a lot."

"What was he in jail for?" she asked.

"I don't actually know," I said. "My mother later told me he was an associate of one of the criminal families. He was in jail for twelve years before I was born. He was a thief, but apparently not a very good one."

"Why is that?" she asked.

"Because he got caught. Also, we've been on welfare, so there you go."

THAT WINTER I was so desperate to escape our cramped, brooding existence on Merle Place that I spent most of my time at my new friend

Sarah's sprawling rent-controlled pre-war apartment on the Upper West Side. Sarah and I had just returned from a weekend trip to Boston when I called home to check in, and I was alarmed at how nervous my mother sounded. "What is it, Ma?" I asked, memorizing all the spices in Sarah's glass kitchen cabinets as we talked.

"Your father is in so much pain and I don't know what to do," she said.

"Ma, he needs to go to a doctor." *Paprika, thyme, saffron . . . oh, look, dried apricots!*

"I can't force him, Jenny," she said. "He is so stubborn."

I had pushed our dinnertime outburst out of my mind, as well as his Christmastime complaint, because I figured that if he was really sick he'd be in the hospital. But his pain hadn't evaporated just because I'd forced myself to forget about it. It wasn't going away on its own, I realized: It was getting worse. I stopped studying Sarah's jars of jam and sat up straight. Something was happening and I couldn't ignore it anymore.

"Mom, how can we get him to do this?" I asked. "Now I'm starting to worry. But wait—his lung scan, from when he fell off the ladder, was clean, remember how he told us?"

"Jenny, that was almost two years ago," she said. We didn't even have to say what we thought it was; my mother sometimes tossed around terms like "bursitis" and "arthritis" in a hopeful tone of voice, but we both knew cancer was the only real possibility, given his two-pack-a-day Pall Mall habit. Just then I remembered a quote I'd once heard and remembered because of my father: "Pall Malls are a classy way to commit suicide." Was it Kurt Vonnegut?

"I don't know what to say, Ma," I said. "I love you."

"I love you, too, Jenny," she said. After I hung up I went back to staring at the glass cabinets, but this time my head was swimming with frightening possibilities.

Yet my father refused to see a doctor, which became a source of major hostility between my parents. It came to a head that summer, not long after my mother and I hopped a train to Florida to visit Rita, Kara, and Grandma. Rita and Grandma were now living together in an apartment complex complete with an exercise room and pool, but they couldn't enjoy it because they drove each other crazy. Grandma was ninety-two and her prime objective in life was watching *Bonanza* and screaming "Quiet!" if we dared laugh too loud; this naturally made us laugh harder.

But we didn't enjoy ourselves for long, because my mother and father engaged in a war of words over the phone that began the day we arrived and continued until the night we returned. "I told him that if he doesn't go to a doctor I'm going to leave him," she reported, "and he tells me to shut up. Well, fuck him. I'm gonna leave him, Jenny, I swear." Back on Merle Place, I watched as she slammed her suitcase into her nightstand and swore she wouldn't sleep in the same bed as "that asshole." Strangely enough, remembering the way she looked that night—tan and not looking a day over fifty, her perfectly highlighted bronze waves topped by my straw hat—makes me long to journey back there, even though she was so mad she was spitting bullets. That night we were all still innocent; that night was one of the last before we knew for sure.

HE FINALLY WENT in for a lung scan that week, nine months after he'd confessed to persistent bone pain; it was anyone's guess as to when the pain had actually started. My mother had sent him to her general practitioner, who produced the results in a matter of days. One afternoon I came home from summer school to find the elevator broken, a problem that would plague the building as long as my mother lived there. I lugged myself up four flights of steps, and just as I was approaching my floor I ran into my mother in the stairwell.

"Hey, what's up?" I asked her. "Elevator's broken again. We should call the management company." I seemed to remember that the results were due that day, but for some reason I hadn't been stressing over it. It still wasn't real for me, maybe because my father had denied it for so long.

"Oh, hi, how are you?" she replied cordially. "Yes, someone should." She nodded in farewell and continued down the stairs. She was wearing her sunglasses and holding her keys. To this day I still don't know where she was going, or whether she even knew.

"Um, where are you going?" I asked.

She stopped and looked at me blankly. "Excuse me?" she asked.

"Mom, where are you going? Are you mad at me or something? Hey, weren't Dad's test results supposed to be in today?"

She squinted and took a long, hard look at me. "Jenny? Is that you?" she finally said. "Oh, my god, Jenny, I didn't recognize you."

That's how I knew it was bad.

We walked downstairs and sat on the steps overlooking the street so he'd see us when he walked home from the bus stop. "So I picked up the phone," my mother said, "and you know what Dr. A. tells me? 'Well, Mrs. Mascia, your husband has cancer!' Like he was happy about it or something. 'It's cancer!' What an asshole. He nearly gave me another heart attack."

"Oh, Ma," I said, shaking my head.

"Do you know what this means, Jenny? If they found a tumor in his lung, then the bone pain is caused by *cancer*. Jenny, he's got metastatic lung cancer. We're going to lose him again," she said, sobbing into my shoulder.

"We've got to call his kids," I managed before dissolving into sobs myself. "Do you want to tell him, or should I?"

"Oh, you tell him, Jenny," she decided. "You have theater training." And that's how my father found us, leaning on each other for support on a bright summer afternoon. He was muscular and tan and wearing a white T-shirt with paint-splattered jeans, and just before he spotted us I'd spied him bounding up the leaf-strewn sidewalk like the picture of health. It seemed such a shame to shatter his innocence the way mine had just been. I nudged my mother and stood up.

"What's going on?" he asked, still smiling.

"Daddy, I have somethingtotellyou," I spat out before exploding into hysterical sobs. So much for the Meisner technique.

"Johnny, the results came back," my mother said, rising.

"Yeah? And?"

She nodded. "It's what we thought," she said. "You need a biopsy to make sure, though."

"Okay," my father said, nodding as if he was bracing for a heavier blow but was instead told that we'd have to move again. "Okay," he said again, and grabbed his Pall Malls. The second the red wrapper became visible my mother knocked it out of his hand. Hard. In the process she hit his arm, which had cancer growing inside it. He flinched.

"Ouch, El," he said, irritated, but stopped just short of angry. He didn't instinctively lunge for her, though, just nodded again, perhaps absorbing her violence as a necessary punishment for fifty years of smoking.

The following week was filled with tests and X-rays, all conducted at St. Vincent's on Staten Island, where he'd have to stay for a full week to qualify for Medicaid. Once he was covered he'd never have to worry about another medical bill as long as he lived. I visited every day after my summer school class ended, and on the final day a doctor pulled me and my mother into the hall. "It's very bad," he said. "It's stage IV. The primary tumor is in his lung, with metastases to his bones and adrenal gland. The gland doesn't seem to be a threat, and it doesn't seem to be spreading to his liver or brain yet, but the bones are worrisome. There is a rather large lump on his shoulder that can be radiated to relieve the pain, but I must tell you, any treatment he stands to receive will be palliative."

Palliative. Pain relief.

"How long do you think he has?" my mother asked as I absentmindedly focused on the charts stacked up on the counter at the nurses' station.

"I'd say three to six months," he said, and immediately I felt a falling sensation, except I wasn't falling. My center of gravity had shifted, moving from my head down through my stomach and resting somewhere at my feet. This lopsided feeling was pulling me down to the floor and I had to grip the counter in order not to end up there. I now knew what it meant to be "floored" by something. This was the worst news I'd ever received.

"Ma, this can't be happening," I said, straining to focus on her face. "What are we going to tell him?"

"The truth," she said, moving wordlessly into his room, where he was putting on his pants, then his socks. "Let's go home," she said, hugging him.

"Just a sec, gotta go pee, meet you out front," I spat, and moved as quickly as I could out of the hallway where I'd received my family's death sentence. Because like it or not, our lives as we knew them were over. My family was finished. After my father died it would be like the spring of 1983 all over again, except this time he wouldn't come sashaying through Rita's front door. This time he was going to die.

I walked quickly toward the front of the hospital with my tears still in check. I spotted the gift shop and went in, choosing a pack of gum with little awareness of what I was doing. Now I knew why my mother hadn't recognized me in the stairwell. In this state of pitched panic I might not have even recognized my own face in the mirror.

"Thank you," I said, paying for the gum. The lady behind the counter looked older than my father. He had just turned sixty-two; it seemed like such a young age to die. I realized that he'd never reach the age belonging to the lady behind the counter. It didn't seem fair that he should die so young when there were so many old people in the world. I started crying; I couldn't hold it in anymore.

"Oh, honey," the lady said, handing me a pack of tissues. "What's wrong?"

I blew my nose. "My father's going to die," I said, and cried harder.

"There, there, now," she said, "it's going to be okay, because whatever happens, it's the Lord's will. You do believe in God, don't you?"

"Um . . ." I started.

"Only God can get you through something like this," she said. "You should go to the chapel here if you need to." I nodded, too upset to argue. My father, I realized, would never see me become self-sufficient, an adult. I would lose him, and a memory would be all that remained. I didn't want him to just be a memory, I decided as I exited the hospital on shaky legs, and I repeated it over and over in my mind until the thought threatened to strike me down right there in the street:

I don't want him to just be a memory. I don't want him to just be a memory. I don't want him to just be a memory.

MY MOTHER KNEW exactly where to go for a second opinion: Memorial Sloan-Kettering Cancer Center at Sixty-eighth and York, where my father's uncle Joey had been successfully treated for lung cancer two years before, undergoing an operation that put him into remission against steep odds. A few weeks after receiving my father's first death sentence we braced for another, driving into the city in the beat-up white Subaru station wagon for which my father had traded his powder-blue Econoline van. It had 130,000 miles on it, so we were screwed if it broke down, but he could hardly drag himself onto a subway train, ferry, and bus after daily chemotherapy sessions.

We were sent to the Rockefeller Pavilion at Fifty-third and Third, a luxuriously appointed branch of the hospital that had just opened a month earlier. It didn't look like a cancer hospital; it looked more like a hotel, with concierges dressed in black manning a reception area on the first floor, directly across from a soothing waterfall. The door to each treatment room was emblazoned with a plaque that read CHEMOTHERAPY SUITE, and receptionists read patient records on flat-screen computer monitors. The floor we were headed to, the thoracic unit, opened up into a waiting area with flat-screen TVs and a mini-fridge stocked with ginger ale and orange juice. It was all so state-of-the-art. "This is a hospital?" I asked in disbelief as we were ushered into an examination room by two doctors. They'd been forwarded the slides and the biopsy results and they had the same opinion as the doctors at St. Vincent's, except for one thing.

"Some people want to know how long they have," one of the doctors said as he addressed the three of us. "Is that something you'd also like to know?"

My father nodded. The doctor paused for so long I didn't think he was going to answer. "A little more than a year," he finally said.

"Excuse me," I said, and slipped into the bathroom. I couldn't help breaking down—I'd stopped wearing eyeliner for precisely this reason. When I came out, the doctors were still speaking to my parents.

". . . standard chemotherapy, with radiation to the bone metastases, beginning as soon as possible so as to shrink the rather large tumor at the upper end of the humerus," one of the doctors was saying. "In addition to the shoulder, there are metastases in both the right and left femur, which is a weight-bearing bone, and without immediate radiation it may break."

"Uh-huh," my mother said, looking like she was trying to memorize everything that came out of their mouths. "And what about surgery? My husband's uncle was successfully operated on here and his lung cancer was put into remission."

"Yes, well, Mrs. Mascia," the other doctor said, massacring our name so it sounded like mass-KEY-a, "we need to first see if chemo and radiation can shrink the primary tumor, but I think I speak for both of us when I say that we never normally operate on cancer this advanced. Your husband will be receiving palliative care."

"They say 'palliative care,'" she whispered when my father went to get the car, "but don't listen to them. Your father is so strong, there's no telling what he can do. He could beat this, Jenny. He's got to." That night we had a somber meal at a diner on Staten Island, but no one ate; my father nursed a scotch as we sat in silence. As soon as we got home my mother sat down at my desk and stared into the bulky monitor of my brand-new student-loan-financed PC and said, "Show me how this thing works." By the end of the week, the same woman who still typed a hard return at the end of each line whenever she wrote an email had located every major clinical trial for lung cancer on the East Coast of the United States, becoming fluent in the language of cancer: Taxol, carboplatin, cisplatin, Herceptin, Gemzar, endostatin, Tarceva, Iressa. Plus, she'd stumbled onto an online support group for lung cancer patients and their primary caregivers, which my mother now was.

"My husband was diagnosed with a tumor (large cell carcinoma) in the left lung (3 centimeters) and adrenal glands and bones," she wrote. "We've been granted an appointment at #1 this Monday. I have several questions in case someone would be kind enough to answer them. We want him to live, we love him, and even knowing that life is not fair, I'll still say it. It's just not fair." In industry parlance, #1 meant Sloan-Kettering, which should have given us comfort but didn't. Having my mother on the case did, though. If anyone could solve this problem, it was her.

"If they can get rid of the secondary cancer, there is a chance they can operate on the primary tumor," she explained during one of her all-night research benders. "England has an interesting clinical trial right now. I just want to extend his life for as long as possible."

My father continued to work with ice packs on his shoulders, despite my mother's tearful pleading. "But you could break a bone, Johnny," she argued, but to no avail. One night over dinner my father seemed strangely upbeat. "I'm not afraid to die," he announced as he passed the broccoli rabe.

"No?" I asked.

"No," he said. "I just want to see my parents again." His place at the table faced the terrace, and I'll always remember how the sun cast its warm glow on his features as he sat ramrod-straight, triumphant even, not the least bit afraid of death. "Of course, I don't want to leave yous," he added. "I worry about you and your mother, you know."

"So don't leave us," I suggested.

"I've been trying," he said. "Doing a lot of visualizing. Little soldiers marching back and forth through my bloodstream, stomping on the cancer cells."

"Wow, Daddy," I said. He made me believe; he could make anyone believe.

By the next morning, though, he didn't seem so at peace with his diagnosis. "I had a dream that I was dying," he said over breakfast, looking jarred, "but when I woke up I realized that it was only a dream. I'm not dead yet. I just kept telling myself when I woke up, 'I'm not dead yet.'"

The next time I started up my computer and searched through the My Documents folder I found this:

July 7, 1999

These are our last wishes as to the disposal of our mortal remains.

1. There is to be no funeral in any traditional sense.

2. There is to be no casket, no makeup, no viewing, no dressing, etc.

3. There is to be no religious service or service of any kind except that which any person or persons wishes to conduct privately after the death of either one of us.

4. Immediately following death, and as soon as arrangements can be made, the body of John Mascia or Eleanor Mascia shall be cremated. The remains, in an urn, or box, or whatever shall be given to the living spouse, or if both are deceased, to their daughter, Jennifer Mascia. The person who receives the remains knows our wishes as to their ultimate disposal.

The above are the last wishes of John and Eleanor Mascia.
There is to be no interference, and since we are both of sound
mind and do execute this document in sound mind, there is no
cause for interference.

Signed this ____ day of _____, 1999

They never signed it, and as far as I know they never really
needed it. But they'd written it, which meant they were thinking
about the end. Since this nightmare began I'd been worried how my
mother's heart was going to survive this—her literal heart. She took
Xanax for stress, but at five pills a day she was still a basket case. It was
quite possible that my father's illness could trigger another heart
attack.

It was then that my vampire existence began. I'd stay in bed all day,
dodging phone calls instead of answering them on the first ring as
usual. By the time darkness fell I was too wired to fall asleep so I'd stay
up watching *World News Now* and keep the television on all night
because if I didn't I'd be left with the silence, which was louder than
the television could ever be, because the silence left me room to think.
I began to wonder what the purpose of life was if all we do is love one
another and watch our loved ones die. The three of us were a unit and
it seemed incredibly unfair that we were going to be broken up.

My work performance began to suffer, but I was determined not
to tell anyone about my father. I didn't want to ride a wave of sympathy; I wanted to pretend my life was normal. So fearful of pity was
I that I didn't bother telling my manager at my cocktail-waitressing
job that my life had been irreparably altered; instead I sulked and
moped until he sat me down at the bar after a dreadfully slow lunch
shift and told me that the owners wanted me gone because I "don't
really smile anymore," and "we can't have you working here with a
bad attitude."

"Um, there's a lot going on in my life," I said, my heart pounding
because I hated getting fired. "I don't know if anyone mentioned it to
you, but my father is dying of cancer." I didn't particularly want to stay
there but I did feel compelled to explain myself to these schmucks who

thought they were special because mortgage traders and Yankee players were regulars at their bar.

"Oh, really?" he asked, looking surprised. "Hey, I'm really sorry about that. Maybe this break will be good for you, then. Why don't you order something before you leave," he offered, and walked back into the kitchen. I found myself face-to-face with the afternoon bartender, a natural comedian named Mike who was fond of doling out sloppy kisses when he was drunk.

"I'm really sorry," he said as he polished glasses.

"Thanks," I mumbled, rising to leave.

"My father died of liver cancer," he said.

I paused. "I'm so sorry," I said.

"You know, even if he dies, he'll always be with you," he said. "You're a part of him. You came from him. You can never be separated."

"Thank you," I said, and ran out before the tears spilled from my eyes.

Even though I was out of work there was something I wanted to do for my mother while I still had some money. She had hocked all of her jewelry during one of our rough patches on New Lane, and while my father was still alive I wanted to rescue his mother's diamond cocktail ring, my mother's wedding ring, and my father's chunky gold insignia ring from Tiffany. My father sometimes wore the latter as a wedding ring, and it had a crest pressed onto the front that my mother jokingly dubbed "the Mascia family crest." I rummaged through his nightstand for the receipt to the consignment place on Fifth Avenue in Brooklyn and called to say I was coming in to pick up my jewelry. After a bus ride across the Verrazano and a swift $300 transaction I placed the box on the dining room table while my parents were out. When my mother opened the front door I hid in my bedroom and listened as her footsteps echoed throughout the entryway. They abruptly halted and I heard no sound for a full minute, so I walked out. "Mom?" I called, and found her bent over the table, weeping silently. She turned to me.

"Oh, Jenny, thank you," she said, reaching for me. "Thank you so much."

If only it had stayed that way between us.

———

I OFFERED TO TAKE the next semester off from school, and possibly the entire year. I'd offered before, when my father was initially given three to six months, but she refused to allow it. She hadn't changed her mind.

"Stay in school," she said. "Daddy wouldn't want you to leave school on account of him." I was leery at first, because my biggest fear was that I'd be in class or, even worse, waiting on a table when I got the call that my father had died. I wanted to be there at the very end. But not knowing when the end would be was excruciating; in a way I wanted it to happen now, because the uncertainty threatened to crush me.

Money was another constant source of worry for me; my parents had no savings, and my mother had just started receiving Social Security, but it was just enough to cover the rent and nothing else. I grew angry that my parents had gone through so much money over the course of our lives, and when we needed it most we had nothing. In California, moving to a cheaper place was always a solution when we were broke; moving to New York was sold to me as some kind of financial miracle, but it hadn't panned out that way. One day when I was feeling brave I sat down with my mother at the dining room table and expressed just how worried I was about them financially.

"Mom, usually people have some kind of savings," I began. That's when she told me that she and my father were selling all the Percocet and OxyContin that his doctors threw at him. Apparently getting stage IV cancer is like hitting the Big Pharma jackpot, because suddenly my father was knee-deep in powerful drugs he didn't even need yet. "These fucking pills make me so groggy," he complained, so my parents FedExed them to Rita, who sold each prescription for $1,500.

I was relieved, but frightened all over again: What if they blew through this money like it was 1987 all over again? "I just wish that you and Daddy had invested in something in California," I continued. "Remember when we had the contract at Chapman, all that money we went through? Why didn't we save anything?"

"Oh, and *you're* qualified to give me financial advice?" she asked rhetorically.

"Well, I'm just say—" But I never finished because she slapped me across the face. Maybe she was irritable because my father had forced her to quit smoking. She'd quit after her heart attack but she'd recently started again, insisting that she wasn't inhaling. Which created another source of friction, as I let her know she wasn't fooling anyone with the "didn't inhale" crap.

"Hey!" I yelped, but she was on fire.

"You have no job," she yelled, "and you go out and spend money with your friends, and you're lecturing *me* about finances?"

"I'll be fine as soon as I move out," I muttered under my breath.

"Oh, not this again," she snapped.

"Mom, it's bound to happen sooner or later, I'm kind of at the age where I'm ready to move out," I said.

"Oh yeah? Just watch—you'll have to drop out of school and work full time to pay for rent."

"No, I won't!"

"And what exactly do you think is going to happen when your wonderful uncle Frankie decides *he* wants to move out?" she asked. "We're going to be responsible for the full rent, and there's no way we can afford that. And you're going to escape just when we need you most so you can re-create your fun years—"

"My *fun years*?" I asked. "You think I want to move out so I can party whenever I want? Is that what you think of me?" I certainly hadn't demonstrated an aptitude for partying now that I was legally eligible to do so.

"Well, aren't you trying to recapture some lost youth? Apparently we robbed you of your childhood by not saving enough money or investing—"

"What I meant was that I would have been happier not knowing every time we were about to go bankrupt or bust out the credit cards," I argued. "Whenever you had a problem with money I had to hear about it, whether I was six or twelve or seventeen, and I'm sick of it! I am sick of having to live with *your* failures!" The blood had rushed into my face and I felt like my eyes were going to pop out.

"Oh, I'm sorry, did you miss your childhood because you were taking care of your poverty-stricken parents, like some street urchin in a Dickens novel?" she asked, dripping with sarcasm. "Who put this moving-out idea in your head, anyway?"

"No one!" I insisted. "I want to be independent, I want to stand on my own. I feel like I have no control over my own life!" Sobs rose in my throat.

"Oh, Jenny, that's bullshit," she said with disgust in her voice.

"How dare you! These are my real feelings here!" I screamed, my throat straining.

"Okay, fine," she said, reaching for her cigarettes. "So you're going to spend money on an apartment when your father's dying and we might need it to live?"

"I'm going to tell Daddy you're smoking!" I snapped. She froze. I rushed to fill the silence before she could. "Look, I am going to survive on my own, I will be fine," I said. "Sarah thinks so, Jeff thinks so—even Tina thinks it might be a good idea to give you guys some space." Tina and I had been emailing lately, as I needed advice from someone who knew my parents. My mother had been emailing her, too, asking her professional opinion about certain clinical trials. "I don't know what she's talking about half the time," Tina had confessed. "She knows much more about cancer than I do."

"Oh, *Tina* said it would be a good idea?" my mother raged, and I knew I'd given her the ammunition she could kill me with. "Tina has no idea what's going on in this house. She's always been jealous of you, *and,* she's always smoked pot and used coke, I'll bet you didn't know that—"

"So *what?*" I asked, realizing how ruthless my mother could be, attacking her own stepdaughter this way. I shuddered to imagine how she might have pitted her biological children against one another if she'd had more. "Why are you trying to discredit my sister? Moving out is *my* idea, and let me tell you, it's sounding better every moment we stand here and scream. Why can't you just say what you're really feeling? Instead of trying to undermine my confidence, tell me, 'Jenny, I'm going to miss you.'" I had been merely threatening it before, but now I was convinced I should move out, as soon as I could.

"Jenny, need I remind you, *you* are the one who begged me to take care of myself because you didn't want to be an orphan—"

"What does this have to do with anything—"

"Let me finish! And when I told you I wanted you to have your own life, what did you tell me? Huh?" I shrugged. "You said you didn't want to leave me. But now all of a sudden when your father is being treated for cancer, a cancer he will probably never recover from, when just physically taking care of him is going to be almost impossible for me alone, now you don't want to miss out on finding yourself and all that shit. What's the matter? Can't you wait a few months? I need someone to help and support me, not someone who is still living in the past, someone who's acting like a seventeen-year-old, who is afraid she might have to help with a few bucks, who has the nerve to scold me about how we didn't *handle our finances properly* to make things right for you. I made things as right as I could, and I'll never let you put me in the position of feeling guilty again. You *did* help when we were in California for a while by ourselves, and I was very grateful. We were in real trouble, but I did the best I could and you never forgave either of us, or, obviously, forgot."

"Mom, we're not having *that* argument again—"

"Your aunt Rita certainly thinks your leaving would be incredibly insensitive," she quickly countered.

"Rita? You mean, the person you're selling drugs to?"

"Don't you dare talk about my sister that way! She's done nothing but good for us, tried to help us whenever we've needed it—"

"Mom, why don't you just let me leave! It's obvious we're not getting along here—"

"Because you're a selfish bitch and your timing is so shitty it's unbelievable," she spat. "I've been trying to tell you that *your father is dying* and you're in denial—"

"*Au contraire*, mother, it's *you* who are in denial," I countered, "always asking the doctors, 'Are you sure you can't operate? Are you sure it's bone cancer?'"

"I'll tell you something, kids," my father said as he walked out of his bedroom, his hair slicked back from a recent shower. "I'd rather die in peace than live with this shit."

We both froze and turned to face my father. "See?" my mother said, breaking the silence. "This is your fault."

"This is not my fucking fault!" I screamed.

"What did you say to your mother?" my father asked, approaching me menacingly.

"I was just saying that if I think about moving out it's not because I don't love you guys or because I'm unhappy," I stammered, clearly not prepared to argue this in front of my father. "And she told me my feelings were bullshit. I am so sick of being invalidated by that woman!" I turned and addressed her next. "You have no right to tell me my feelings are bullshit! I am so tired of this!"

"Hey, don't curse at your mother," my father warned.

"Her?" I asked, nearly laughing. "Don't curse at *her*? *Fuck* her." I'd meant to say "Forget her," but my true feelings emerged. My father ran up to me and kicked me in both shins. He had terminal cancer and kicked me in the shins.

"Look what you made your father do," my mother hissed as she slipped out of the room. My father flipped off the lights and followed after her. I stood there, shocked. I was twenty-one years old; I wondered, should I still be getting hit?

Later that night I found my father sitting in the darkened living room, stirring his scotch with one of his meaty fingers. "Your mother's getting worse as she gets older," he said, shaking his head slightly and staring off into space.

THAT FALL, BECAUSE WE all thought my father was mere months away from dying, our apartment became a revolving door of visitors. My father's cousin Camille came, and cried the second she saw my father, even though he wasn't even thin yet. "God damn her, he doesn't need that right now!" my mother privately hissed. Tina flew in a few days before my twenty-second birthday, which she, Jeff, and my parents celebrated at Trattoria Romana, our favorite Italian restaurant on the Island. Even though Tina had to leave the house once or twice to let me and my mother scream at each other in peace, all was forgotten by the time we sat down to dinner, when my parents gifted me and Jeff with a verbal promise for an all-expenses-paid trip to London. We never ended up going, but the gesture was nice. It turns out we were the benefactors of the sale of my grandfather's house, which left my parents with $25,000 in cash. In typical fashion, they stored it in a suitcase under the bed. Coupled with their grassroots pharmaceutical operation, they now had enough money that I didn't need to worry about them. It was a relief.

"Dad," I began one weekend when the three of us sat down to a lunch of cold cuts. "I was reading in *New York magazine* how Long Island City is the next neighborhood to gentrify, and I was thinking if we bought some property there, something small, it would appreciate over the next few years."

"Jenny, we need that money," my father said. "We can't spend it on a house."

"Yeah, besides," my mother chimed in, "twenty-five thousand dollars isn't nearly enough to get anything, even around there. Haven't they been saying that about Long Island City for years now, anyway?"

"Guys, you can't just keep that money under the bed," I argued. "Why not invest it in something so we don't go through it so fast, like we always do? I mean, it's not like you guys don't have *other money* coming in."

"Jenny, can you keep your mouth shut?" my father huffed. "This is our money, not yours, and we will do with it what we see fit. Okay? Thank you." I nodded and concentrated on my salami. Later when my father was out of earshot my mother explained why they wouldn't be Donald Trumping their loot.

"I may have to live on that money," she whispered. "*After*. That will be all I have." I never brought it up again.

Our final visitor was Rita, who called and told my mother that she hadn't been really selling all that OxyContin and Percocet, she'd been taking them herself and paying for them with money she'd stolen from her daughter, Kara. Also, she was addicted to cocaine, and could she come to New York to "dry out" with the help of my mother's stern discipline and famous chicken soup? It would be her first visit since we'd moved to New York five years before—in fact, it was her first visit to the Mascia family in seven years. My mother was bewildered. "My sister is a drug addict," she said sadly. It was unbelievably shitty timing, and it meant that she would be caring for two sick people at once, but she relented.

My mother had specifically asked Rita not to cry when she saw my father, who was hardly the stick figure most cancer patients are reduced to; mostly he looked troubled by something in the middle distance that neither my mother nor I could discern. But despite my mother's orders, Rita cracked as soon as she crossed the threshold. My mother and I ushered her into the bedroom before she could wail in front of him and begged her to keep her composure, which she did, but just barely. I spent the next five days massaging her cramped legs and tight temples and feeding her Jell-O, which she spilled on my mother's sheets, leaving a permanent stain that was somehow blamed on me. All the while Rita whimpered, "I don't want to be addicted to cocaine anymore. It's terrible, Jenny." I'd never heard her utter the word aloud; it seemed beneath her. She was my idol growing up, but all along she'd been an addict. I felt bad for her, but not as bad as I felt for my father. I couldn't understand how Rita received the princess treatment while my father had poison flowing through his veins. Neither could my mother, who finally came to her senses a week later when Rita missed her flight back to Miami; the next one wasn't for another three hours. She turned to my parents, helpless, and asked them if they could take her in to Manhattan with them, where my dad was scheduled for chemo, and then drive her back to Newark for the next plane. My parents refused, and in lieu of a goodbye they gave her a handful of OxyContin just to shut her up. A few days after she left I sat with my parents in the living room and shook my head at what she had devolved into. "She's nothing but a selfish drug addict," I spat. Without warning, my father flipped his rage switch and went from zero to incensed.

"Don't you *ever* say anything like that about your aunt!" he shouted. "You have *no idea* what she has done for this family!"

"Uh, okay," I said, backing away. I looked at my mother, who sat silently. Had I missed something?

THE UPCOMING NEW YEAR'S EVE was a special one, and not just because it was the turn of the millennium. New Year's meant that my father had surpassed at least one doctor's expectations: He had lived longer than three to six months. That night we went to Uncle Joey's daughter Linda's house on the Island, but the celebration was bittersweet. Joey had just been told that his cancer had returned, meaning he and my father would be carpooling to chemotherapy. Joey's wife, Emma—my father referred to her as "my favorite aunt"—acted cheerful as always, though we knew her heart was breaking. We had that in common. We weren't sure if this would be the last New Year's for either of them.

At least my father had finally quit working, which thrilled my mother, as she no longer had to worry about his bones breaking. "Do you miss it, Daddy?" I asked, mistaking his diligent hard work for actual love of carpet cleaning and painting.

"You kiddin'?" he asked, shaking his head and smiling. "No way."

"Do you miss smoking?" I asked.

"You kiddin'?" he replied. "Every day." I certainly didn't miss his smoking, and I didn't miss his working, either—he no longer had to drag himself out of bed at seven, and for the first time in memory his hands were soft, not rough like the sandpaper he'd worked with. His face was relaxed and his gut persisted, which my mother and I took as hopeful signs. But he looked older than he had six months ago; worry lines now threatened to drown his eyes. I, on the other hand, look at photos of myself from that night and cringe: My waist was expanding by the month, and even though I cried about it to my therapist I felt powerless over what was happening to me. My mother had also gained weight, and she insisted on wearing her sunglasses indoors, which baffled me, as I thought they looked ridiculous, but she took great pains to hide the bags under her eyes and no one could convince her to stop.

When the clock struck midnight, the revelers arrayed around Linda's spacious, smartly appointed house and toasted while my parents and I gathered into a tight circle and hugged each other, weeping in disbelief that we had made it this far. My father nodded repeatedly, which he always did when he cried, as if each nod would dry up his tears. "We made it," my mother said, her eyes watering. What I didn't know then was that the three of us would see one more New Year's before cancer came to claim my father, and that the coming year would be one of the worst of my life.

IF MY FATHER'S illness taught me anything about myself, it was that (a) I was more than capable of finding comfort in food, and (b) all I needed when the shit hit the fan was a romance in which to drown myself. Kareem was a fellow student who'd appeared with me in a play that fall, and though I knew he liked me I didn't feel the same way. But by winter I'd begun to warm to him slightly: He was energetic and witty, with a flair for writing and excellent comic timing. I recruited him to review films for the school paper, and he in turn recruited me as an on-air personality for the radio station. One day a mutual friend of ours whispered in my ear, "You know, I bet you and Kareem would be a good match," and that was all it took. I was in love—it happened that fast. Before long he was my sun, my earth, and my stars. I discovered that love could be a decision I made, and once I opened my mind to it, my body followed. So deep was my need to escape that logic was bypassed completely. By February we were officially a couple, in the throes of full-blown emanating-from-our-pores lust; two months later we were talking about moving in together. This perplexed my mother, who knew I wasn't initially attracted to him. There was also a cultural divide: His parents were Egyptian Muslims, who'd immigrated a short time before Kareem was born. His mother wore the hijab, as did his younger sister, who tattled on her brother and his "slutty" American girlfriend at every turn.

When Jeff and I went to San Francisco that spring to visit my high school chum Natalie, the two of them wanted to kill me because every time they turned around I was on the phone with Kareem. The eight hours we spent driving up the coast was the longest I spent without talking to him and I cursed myself for not having a cell-phone. In his absence I opened up to Jeff and Natalie about the situation with my parents, even recounting the heated argument that ended with my shins getting kicked.

"Whoa, Jen, what are you saying?" Natalie asked. "Your father *kicked* you?"

"Yeah," I said sheepishly. "What, your parents don't hit you any-more?"

"*No,*" Jeff and Natalie said in unison.

"Not since I was a kid," Jeff said. "Jen, you didn't tell me this was going on."

"Wait—you're telling me your parents don't hit you anymore?" I asked. I was driving and it was getting dark and I struggled to keep my eyes on the road.

"Uh, no," Jeff said. Natalie shook her head in the passenger's seat.

"Jen, I think it's time to move out," she said.

"Yeah, Jen, you need to move out as soon as you can," Jeff echoed.

"I didn't realize that your parents didn't hit you anymore," I mumbled, wondering if I could possibly afford an apartment by the summer. I returned from California to find that Uncle Frankie had moved out. With my parents in the master bedroom I now had two rooms to myself. My mother bought me a new computer desk from Ikea in a last-ditch attempt to keep me on Merle Place, but it remained in a corner, unassembled. I hadn't wavered in my goal to branch out on my own, and it was all I thought about—until an afternoon in June, when I picked up the *New York Post* and turned to page 24.

> With a few keystrokes, worried victims and survivors can get information on 500,000 past and present inmates of New York's 70 state prisons—through the state Department of Correctional Services web site. Just visit www.docs.state.ny.us and click on "inmate lookup."

My eyes were glued to the page. I reread the sentence over and over until it stopped making sense. On the train, on the express bus, in the privacy of my bedroom, my eyes kept wandering back to the article, which explained how to find criminal records online. It was what I'd been waiting for. I sensed it would only be a matter of time before my father's information would be accessible to me somehow, and now I could finally confirm whether my mother had, in fact, told me the whole truth five years earlier.

It was late afternoon when my mouse hovered over "Inmate Lookup," and the shades filtered the sun so my bedroom was bathed in amber. Despite the fact that I was closer than I'd ever been to an answer that had eluded me for seventeen years, I didn't realize that this could be one of the defining moments of my life; I don't remember my heart pounding or my breath quickening or any of that. I just typed his last name—my last name—and waited.

He was the only *Mascia, John* listed—if there was in fact another John Mascia in the Bronx with whom my father had been confused, he never did time—and I clicked on his department identification number. Date of Birth: 04/10/1937; check. Race/Ethnicity: White; check. Date received: 01/16/1964. Latest Release Date: 10/16/1975. Almost twelve years, like my mother had said. The table below was labeled "Crimes of Conviction," and there was only one entry.

Murder.

It couldn't be. My father had killed someone. No wonder my mother had lied to me. As I sat there staring at the screen I heard my parents preparing dinner in the kitchen—innocuous, everyday sounds—and all I could think was, "Gotcha." I was now in the loop.

No longer did I feel shame for wondering—this was real. I hadn't just been overdramatizing, as my mother suggested scornfully whenever I broached this topic. My father—my funny, selfless, streetwise father—had killed someone. He had shot them or strangled them or stabbed them until the life drained from their body. And soon he would lose his life. Some might say that he deserved his fate.

His crime opened up a new line of thought: Why? How did he do it, how could she have married him, how could I have lived with someone who had taken life and not known it? I had been prepared to find a slew of charges for thievery that added up to a twelve-year sentence. But this, the only item on his rap sheet—at least, the only item that had survived the transformation from paper to digital—caught me off guard. Next to "Murder" it said in parentheses, "Deg'less prior 9-1-74." What did that mean? Twelve years meant he'd missed out on raising his children; twelve years meant he'd missed the sixties and all that entailed; he'd been in jail for the Kennedy assassination, women's lib, free love, both *Godfather* films. Thank god he'd been released when he was, or I never would have been born.

So now what? Should I waltz into the living room and ask my father about this? I had a feeling, bolstered by my mother's past sentiments, that he would wither under my questioning—me, his only child unburdened by the truth. In my eyes he wasn't a murderer. How could I take that away from him?

I called Kareem and told him everything; I had to tell someone. I knew I was going to confront my mother, but I didn't know when. She might very well react in anger—I could almost hear her yelling, "How could you do this when your father is so sick!"—but she had been using his imminent death to keep me in line for the past year. When he died she'd find another way to discourage my curiosity, then another. I had to cut through all that while he was still alive. Even if I never spoke with him about it, at least the option would be there.

I waited a few more days before telling my mother, and I didn't choose the moment; it just spilled out the morning my mother drove into the city to meet my father at Sloan-Kettering, where he had been admitted. The clinical trials he'd been participating in had minimized the amount of cancer in his bones, which nobody expected, but he'd been in and out of the hospital with minor chemo fevers. He was only going to get sicker; I had to act now.

"Mom?" I asked as we pulled up to Thomas Hunter Hall on Lexington Avenue and Sixty-eighth Street. After she dropped me off she would veer east and park the dusty old Subaru in the hospital's underground garage.

"Yes?" she said. I felt like I was dangling off a precipice. I was going against her now, and I felt it.

"I have to tell you something," I started. I took a breath and tried to find some comfort in her eyes. They looked tired. "I read an article the other day in the *Post* that said you could look up criminal records online. And I looked up Daddy's." I waited for her reaction. She stared straight ahead. "Do you know what I'm going to say?" I asked, giving her the option of moving first.

She made a "tsk" sound with her tongue and said, "Jenny, why did you do that?"

"Because I wanted to know," I said. "You know that. I have always wanted to know." It hadn't exactly eaten me alive every day for the last six thousand days, but it had always been there, running under our lives like a river, undetected. My desire to know may have been moved to the back burner—by boyfriends, by feeble explanations that satisfied me for a time—but it was always there.

"And what did it say?" she asked, even though she knew the answer. Her tone was slightly angry and gaining steam.

"It said murder, Mom. *Murder*. Now tell me what happened," I insisted. "This time you can't hold out on me. I know the truth."

"Goddammit, Jenny, he never wanted you to know," she said. "And you found this where? On the *Internet*?" Now her tone was angry and mocking.

"Yes, on the New York State Department of Corrections website," I said, calmly. "His record is there. It said he went in January of 'sixty-four and was paroled in October of 'seventy-five. So I guess he didn't get twelve years for racketeering?" It was a little snotty, but I felt I had the right. She'd lied to me, long after I was old enough to understand.

"So anyone with an Internet can see this record?" Her computer savvy, I noticed, had not extended to a general awareness of modems and connections.

"Yes, anyone with *access to the Internet* can see his record," I clarified.

"Your father would be very upset to know that," she said. "I think it's a violation of privacy that anyone can go on there and see that."

She was sulking and staring out the window at the traffic slowly chugging its way down Lex in fits and starts.

"Mom," I argued, "I'm sorry, but if you kill someone? I think that kind of nullifies your right to privacy, no?"

"No!" she said, staring me down. "No, I do not, especially when the person in question has changed his life for his family and all that is in the past." She turned toward the traffic again in protest, but she didn't demand I leave the car.

"Tell me what happened, because I don't want to go and ask him. In fact," I said, sweetening the pot, "if you tell me everything, I *won't* go to him. How about that?" Then I'd have a built-in excuse not to broach the subject with my father: I had cut a deal with my mother. Maybe I was a coward, but I decided then and there that confronting a (probably) dying man with his past at a time when he was most certainly preoccupied with what would become of him after death was not something I was willing to do. I would not be responsible for his leaving this earth scared. As it was, he must have been terrified, and I worried about what must be going through his head whenever I laid eyes on him.

"Oh, Jenny," she said. And she told me.

MY MOTHER WAS on the verge of breaking up with David for the last time when she met a man named Paul. He was a black ex-convict, and they began an affair that lasted two years. He was also married with children, but that didn't stop them. "All the guys in the joint claim to be innocent," she said of Paul, "but he really was." Framed, she claimed. Because of Paul my mother had become involved in the prison reform movement, and to that end she joined a Quaker group that ministered to prisoners. Paul told her that if she really wanted to know about prison reform she needed to go speak with a real mover and shaker behind bars up at Fishkill Correctional, a man named John Mascia.

"And that's how I met your father," she said, a guilty smile forming on her lips.

"*What?*" I asked, astonished. "You said you met 'through friends'!" As I said it I heard how vague it sounded, and realized I'd been duped.

"Yeah, that's what we told you," she said, "but everyone else knew the truth."

"Everyone knows?" I asked. "Rita?" She nodded. "Arline?" Another nod. *"Angie?"* Nod. "His other kids know?"

"Yeah," she said. "But *I* had to tell them." When my parents first moved down to Florida, my mother explained, Angie was fifteen and working at a fried chicken joint. Her life was drudgery; she hated coming home smelling like chicken every night, and she didn't have a lot of clothes, so my mother took her shopping. "We bonded, Angie and I." She smiled. "She must have felt close to me because she eventually asked me, 'Eleanor, why did my father go to jail?'"

"She didn't know?" I asked. She had been curious like me, but at least she hadn't been alone in the dark.

"I guess Marie never told them," she said. "So I went to your father and said, 'Johnny, your daughter is asking questions about you. She wants to know why you were in jail.' He said, 'You tell her,' and left the room. So I told her."

So my instincts had been right, that I shouldn't go to him with what I'd found. "So what did you tell her?" I asked.

"I told her the truth," she said.

My father grew up in Bay Ridge at a time when young kids could be lured by "the element," and some got absorbed into the orbit of the city's criminal families. My father belonged to a crew of scrappy Italian kids called the Eighth Avenue Boys—he had told me as much when I was younger, but had never revealed their criminal aims—and they brushed up against wiseguys. But he wasn't a mobster, mostly he robbed houses and sometimes dealt drugs. Like she'd said five years earlier, he resisted being "made."

When my father was married to his first wife he had a partner named Bobby Wyler. "A Jew, which was rare in those days," my mother pointed out. Bobby was in prison around the time my father moved his young family down to Florida in 1963. He was going down there, she said, to escape "the life," and got a job at a restaurant. "But it was owned by a relative of Al Capone, or someone like that, so your father really wasn't escaping the life." In any case, the life found him when Bobby needed a favor.

"There was this guy, a drug addict, who was informing on them to the cops," she said. "Bobby was in jail, so he asked your father to drive up to New York and take care of it. And he did."

"He killed a guy, for *that*?" I asked. "How did he do it?" I pictured a saw and a wood chipper.

"Shot him," she said flatly. "Took him to some park out in Brooklyn and shot him. But Jenny, you have to understand, this isn't something he did lightly. He had to work himself up to do it. He had to psych himself into thinking he was a monster who could do something like this. He had nightmares about it, you know."

"I didn't know," I said. He'd rescued me from so many of my nightmares, but I hadn't been wise to any of his.

"He was very upset by what he had to do," she said. "And after he did it he went back to Florida, but he knew the cops were after him—someone had dropped a dime on him. So he checked himself in to a hotel and waited there, so his family couldn't see him get arrested."

"Like I saw him get arrested," I said quietly.

"Your father always liked to think you didn't remember that," she said. "He'd say to me, 'She was so young, there's no way she remembers.'"

"But I do," I insisted, flinching at the memory.

"I know," she said. "You remember everything."

In order to avoid the electric chair, he pleaded guilty. "He was very scared of getting the chair. And your grandmother was very afraid, too. In those days there were no degrees for murder—like murder one, murder two—there was just life in prison or death. One of the results of the prison reform movement was that degrees were instituted, and sentences were reviewed and some prisoners were retroactively sentenced."

"Is that why, on his record, it says 'Degreeless prior to 1974'?"

"It says that?" she asked. "Then I guess that's what it means."

"So his sentence was shortened?"

"He was paroled," she said. "In jail he had been involved in the reform movement and advocated on behalf of prisoners—wrote legal briefs for them, edited the in-house newsletter, even became the warden's pet."

"Like *Shawshank Redemption*?" I asked. It was a movie he loved.

"Sort of," she said. "But they also staged actions against what they viewed as harsh treatment, and it got your father thrown in solitary a few times. He'd go days without food, and had to live among the rats and the roaches and—*oy*. You have to remember, Jenny, this was around the time of the uprising at Attica. Even though he was never in Attica, the movement swept all the prisons."

"No wonder he didn't go to college," I said. I'd always wondered about that.

"Well, we used to say he was 'in college,'" she said.

"Yeah, I remember, you told me," I said.

"He did get his high school equivalency there," she said. "Though they didn't call it a GED then."

"I thought he quit New Utrecht High School but went back later?" I asked, realizing that this truth, too, had been upended.

"He did go back later," she said. "In prison." She smiled.

I sighed. "So, he was paroled . . ."

"So. When he got out, he was actually seeing another woman in the Quaker group I was with. Her name was Nancy something, I forget her last name, she was married to a television executive, and she was having an affair with your father. At this time, your father and I were just friends."

"But you liked him," I said.

"*We-e*-e-ell," she said, in her twisty-turny way, "we were friends first, just friends. But I remember the first time I saw him, when he walked up to the glass and sat down, and I thought, 'He is so graceful, he walks like a panther.' He moves so gracefully and so silently that he could come up behind you and you wouldn't even know it."

"That must have come in handy for certain pursuits," I said wryly.

"When your father got his parole," she continued, "I was the one who picked him up, and I drove him to my apartment, but we were still just friends. I drove him to my apartment so he could be with Nancy, because she was still married. And I was still with Paul."

"You drove your future husband to your apartment so he and his girlfriend could have sex? On *your* bed?" It was mind-boggling.

"Well, he was technically my boyfriend's friend. Paul was the reason I lied about my age," she admitted.

"What? You told me it was because of Dad," I said.

"Well, I was dating Paul before your father, and Paul was also younger. They were friends, so when I started dating your father I couldn't exactly tell him I'd lied about my age for Paul."

"Why not?" I asked.

"It didn't seem right," she said. "He knew me one way, and then to tell him I was older, it would have been a huge *kasha varnishkes*," she said. "I mean, my driver's license said I was born in 1939, my birth certificate had been changed, everything."

"How were you able to forge all that stuff on official documents?" I asked.

"With a pencil," she said. "There were no computers then. It was easy."

"Hm. So, you and Daddy got together . . ."

"So we got together, and I wanted to have a baby, and we did," she said. "I was already forty, so I was worried I wouldn't conceive. But I did, and we had you. But then he started up again with his shit."

"What shit?"

"Oh, dealing," she said, feigning nonchalance.

"Which drugs?" I asked.

"Pot, mostly," she said. "He would tell me stories about pulling in bales of marijuana floating in the Intracoastal, just waiting to be picked up. No one had really cracked down yet, not like they did later. And he was staying out later and later, and you were born, and even then he was out somewhere. After I had you I spent three days in the hospital mostly by myself. Rita was there, but he was out doing his thing. And finally I threatened to leave him."

"Why didn't you?"

"Well, a few months after you were born, he got arrested," she said. "He was driving in a car with someone, and there was coke in the car. We think he was set up, that the guy with him was an informant who planted it under the seat, because your father was mostly done with that shit by then. But he got arrested. We knew it was a parole violation, and for a murder charge—they could have locked him up for a long time. So I went down to the jail with you in the stroller to try to garner some sympathy—that was Celie's idea—and begged them to release my husband. And they did. But they made a mistake—he was a parole violator. They shouldn't have released him, and today they wouldn't have, because they'd just pull up his record on a computer. But they didn't do that then, and they let me bail him out. And when we got home he said, 'I'm going to end up in jail or dead. I have to get out of here. You can either stay here with the baby, or you and the baby can come with me.'"

"And what did you say?"

"I said, 'What, are you nuts? Of course I'm coming with you.' And we went to Houston."

"Wait—*that's* why we went to Houston?" What was she telling me, exactly?

"That's why we went to Houston," she said. "But before we left, your father had about sixty thousand dollars' worth of pot he was supposed to sell, and a cut was supposed to go to these Mafia associates he'd been dealing with. But they never got it, because he sold it all, and that's how we financed the move. And just like that, he quit everything, he went legit. In Houston he ran a little mailbox franchise, like a Mail Boxes Etc. type of thing. And when I couldn't take Houston anymore we went to California, which turned out to be perfect timing, because later we found out that the FBI was right on our tail. And a few years later, when you were five and we were living in Turtle Rock, I got a ticket, and that's how they found us, because— stupid us!—we never sold our old car and they traced the VIN number. And that's when they came to take Daddy away."

"Mom, are you saying we went on the lam?" I asked, stunned.

"Jenny, don't you remember how you were Jennifer Cassese?" she asked. "We used Celie and Vinny's last name. Daddy took his father's name, Frank, and was known as Frank Cassese. Before that, in Houston, he used Nicholas." As she said it I realized that I'd never questioned why we'd gone by Cassese, even when we lived with Celie that summer and my mother told me my father had been in jail before I was born. As a child I'd simply accepted it, and I guess that part of me had remained a child while the rest of me grew up.

"You know, I thought for years that 'Frank' and 'John' were derivatives of the same name," I said, putting it together. "I thought Frank was another name for John, like Bill and William, or Richard and Dick."

"Well, it isn't," she said. "I was Eleanor Cassese, and we couldn't call anyone, have anyone visit—the FBI went to my mother's house and questioned her, and they questioned David because, before I went to Houston, I came to New York to sell some jewelry, and we stayed at a very nice hotel, the Pierre or the Plaza, I can't remember, and they found out. He told them to fuck off," she said, chuckling at the memory.

"But Rita came to visit," I pointed out, "and Grandma and Grandpa."

"They came after we'd been out there a couple of years," she said. "I was always worried about them opening their mouths, though. Always. And I felt so bad about getting the ticket, like it was my fault we got caught. We should have ditched the car," she lamented. At least now I knew why they had been using fake Social Security numbers when they went bankrupt.

"Why, so we could be like *Running on Empty* for the rest of our lives?" I said. "No, thank you. I'd rather this happened, don't you?" If he'd been arrested when I was older, when I could remember every detail, god only knows how much worse it would have been for me.

"Yes, I suppose," she said. "And when they came for him the second time, he went willingly. The agents came over and I fed them coffee and pie—"

"I'm sorry, did you say the second time?" I asked.

"Yes," she said. "They came for him the first time when you were home with him, just the two of you."

"What! They did?"

"Yes. The FBI called me at work, and my boss Jesse drove me home," she said, "because they couldn't leave you home alone. And I came in and found them cuffing your father, and do you remember what you said to me then?"

"No," I said, cringing. I felt like an amnesiac being told about a life I could no longer remember.

"You said, 'Are they arresting my daddy?' And do you remember what Jesse said?"

"No," I said, honestly not remembering.

"Jesse said, 'No, honey, it's not real. They're making a movie.'" Jesse's words struck a vague chord of recognition, shrouded in so much fog it seemed like they were spoken in a past life. "My heart broke for you, Jenny, it really did," she said. "He was released just in time for Christmas, remember? But they told us they were going to come back for him. And, *in mitten drinnen,* your aunt Rita decides it's the perfect time to send Kara there to separate her from Miguel."

"Now *that* I remember," I said, faintly recalling how Kara allowed me to overdose on grape jelly sandwiches.

"And when they did come back for him, I told Kara to keep you in your room because I didn't want you to see him get arrested again."

"Bad move," I said. "I remember lunging for that door for what seemed like hours, just trying to get to him."

"I know," she said, "but what else could I do? I didn't want you to see him taken away. They took him to the jail in Santa Ana, and they arranged for his extradition. I didn't have money for lawyers, so Rita paid for everything."

"She did?" Now I knew why my father had gotten so angry when I'd criticized her.

"Jenny, she was so very good to us," she said. "Then a friend of mine from New York found us a lawyer, a good one, to fight his extradition, and because your father had led a crime-free life for the five years he was on the run, a special deal was going to be worked out where he could fight the parole violation from California. But Governor Deukmejian had just taken office, and he wanted to appear tough on crime, so his office called off the deal. So we had two options: go on trial for the parole violation charges in New York, or go to Florida to deal with the five-year-old cocaine charges."

"That's why we went to New York?" I asked, remembering my week aboard Amtrak.

"Yes," she said. "I pushed your father's lawyers to try their luck in New York, knowing that if he was cleared of the parole violation then maybe Florida would dismiss the charges. So that's what we did. They took him to New York by bus, and oh, Jenny, it was awful. They'd take him to Burger King for breakfast, lunch, and dinner, and the ride took days and days, and I had no contact with him until he got to New York. And when it became obvious that all this would take longer than we thought, I sent you down to Florida to stay with Rita, and I stayed with David at his place in the Village."

"I hated that you left me down there," I said. "Remember how I cried as the train pulled away?"

"Yeah, and I also remember how Rita said the words 'ice cream' and you stopped crying almost immediately," she said, shooting me a sly smile.

"Yeah, yeah," I said. I also remembered trying to conjure my father from thin air, and Rita's Turkish cigarettes. "Oh, and thanks, by the way, for leaving me with a druggie and her druggie friends," I said, finally able to discern the situation.

"Jenny, I didn't know that," she said. "If I'd known she was a drug addict I never would have let you stay there."

"Mom! You did know!" I said. "She told me they were Turkish cigarettes, and you totally backed her up."

She shrugged. "Well, nothing happened to you, did it?" she asked.

"Well, no," I admitted, "but it could have! Jesus—coke dealers, pot smokers, members of the Medellín cartel. Not good. What if someone had come looking for drug money and killed us all?"

"But they didn't, did they?" she asked, eyebrows cocked.

"No," I said, defeated.

"No," she said, vindicated.

"So when did he get out?" I asked. "How long was he in for?"

"He had his hearing in the summer, and a lot of people flew in from California to testify on his behalf. Gay, Maureen," she said, ticking off clients of his, "his partner Phil . . ."

"Really?" I asked, surprised. "They knew about him, too?"

"Yes, and it helped," she said. "Even the FBI agent who arrested your father, I'll never forget him, his name was John O'Neill, and after he testified he stepped down and, in full view of the judge, shook your father's hand and wished him luck. It was wonderful, I'll never forget it." If anyone could be a murderer *and* a charmer, it was my father. "But Florida still wanted him," she went on, "so he got sent down to Florida. But right when he got there they dismissed the charges, and he was released. Just like that. On my birthday. It was the best birthday present I ever got."

"And that's when he showed up at Rita's front door?" I asked. "I still remember the sweater he was wearing."

"Yep, that's when he came home," she said, and slowly shook her head. "Shit, Jenny, we never should have left California."

"He'd still be sick," I reminded her. "Location wouldn't change that."

"I know," she said. "But we had a good life there."

"Tell me about it. So he went back to carpet cleaning, and that was that?" I asked, wondering if murderers can be "cured."

"Yes," she said. "Just like that. Jenny, he changed his life for us. For *you*. He turned his whole life around so he could have a family. He didn't want what happened with his other children to happen with you. You know, Marie was pregnant with Tony right before your father went away, and he didn't meet him until he was a teenager. He never wanted Tina or Angie visiting him in jail, seeing him that way. And he didn't want you to, either, but I said, 'Absolutely not. Your daughter wants to see you and I'm bringing her.' And I did, remember?"

"Yes, of course," I said. "I remember the facility where I could sit on his lap, and the one where I had to talk through the phone, through the glass." I hadn't thought about this stuff in years. I couldn't believe it was still there.

"I don't regret it, and I don't care if your father was mad at me for it," she said. "He got over it. But we knew he'd be released eventually. The first time he went away, he thought that was it. He sent Marie a letter asking her to divorce him, to live her life. Doing time is very, very difficult, and he said he had to bury his feelings very deep in order to survive. It's a certain mindset you have to adopt, and he did: You have to go deep down inside yourself and cut yourself off from the outside world, otherwise it's too painful. He never thought he was going to be released, and he certainly never thought he'd have another family again. But he did. We had you."

"Yeah, and you met because he was in jail for murder," I pointed out. "If he hadn't killed somebody, I wouldn't even be here." The possibilities made me shudder.

"Jesus, Jenny, why do you have to see it that way?" she said, annoyed.

"Mom, I'm just trying to understand," I said, and I was. I now understood the grisly legacy I'd inherited before I'd even been born. I was the product of a murder, in a way. It was horrifying.

"He felt he could never escape what he was," she said, "and he doesn't deserve to have you treat him like everyone else."

"I'm not, remember?" I said. "I'm not going to talk to him about this, I agreed."

"Because when we lived in Lake Forest," she continued, "there was a guy who saw your father working on his carpet cleaning machine in the front yard, and he noticed your father's tattoos, and he said, 'So, how much time did you do?' because the tattoos were a giveaway that he'd been in prison. Maybe the guy had also been in prison, I don't know. But your father came home that night so demoralized. He said to me, 'I'll never escape it, people will always know.'"

"No one knew—did Maria's parents know? No one from California knows, just people here."

"Please don't tell your friends, or, god forbid, your *boyfriend*," she pleaded, saying "boyfriend" like the word was gagging her.

"I won't," I lied. "I promise. So where is Bobby Wyler now? I mean, did he know what Daddy did for him? Whatever became of him?"

"Dead, I think," she said. "Lung cancer, maybe? I'm not sure. But your father almost killed him once, and I bet he never knew."

"What?" I asked. "I thought you said he changed his life for us."

"He did, he did," she said. "But when he got out he found out that Bobby, who was supposed to help Marie and the kids with money when he got out of jail, didn't—he hadn't done a thing for them. And your father got very angry, because it's kind of understood that your partner, especially someone you've helped out like your father had, is supposed to take care of your family. But he didn't. So he drove to Bobby's place with a gun, and he had worked himself up into thinking he was gonna kill him. And I tried to talk him down in the car—"

"You were *there*?" I tried to imagine my mother desperately trying to talk her new boyfriend out of killing someone as he zigzagged his way through the streets of Brooklyn, his jaw clenched with quiet rage. I remember how quickly my father could conjure fury; it came on without warning, like an earthquake. I now saw how that tornado of rage was honed and perfected, and to what sordid purposes it had been applied.

"Yes, and I managed to talk him down," she said. "When he got there, he saw that Bobby Wyler wasn't alone, and he calmed down, because he said, 'I can't kill them all.' Don't you see, Jenny? He changed his life for us."

Avoiding a bloodbath because of a logistical headache involving body disposal meant he had changed his life for us? I let it slide. I'd raked her over the coals enough for one afternoon. I still had classes after this, though I'd already decided to ditch them.

"I bet you never knew this," she said, smiling at the memory, "but when we used to toast at dinner, before you were old enough to understand what we were saying, we used to toast 'To prison reform!'

If it hadn't been for the prison reform movement, he never would have been released, and we wouldn't have been a family. It was so important that he had this chance, Jenny. He wanted another chance so badly. And he was a good father to you."

"He was," I agreed. "He *is*." He wasn't dead yet, and I had no intention of burying him with my past tense verbs.

I sighed and cracked my knuckles, a nervous habit since childhood. So my father was a murderer. "Let me ask you something," I said. "What would you think if I came home with a guy who had done time for murder? You wouldn't be so happy, would you."

"No," she said. "Your father and I would think you were making a big mistake."

"So why was this so different?" I asked.

At this she smiled again. "Because it's your father we're talking about. Your father was different."

"Well, what did your family say when they found out—Rita? Your mother? David? Your father?"

"Everyone loved Johnny," she said.

"Even though they knew what he did?"

"Yes," she said. "He was so magnetic, Jenny, he could make you forget all that. My mother loved Johnny; my father, as far as I know, for the little time he knew him, he liked him, too. And Rita—well, you know how well Johnny and Rita get along."

"Yes, I remember," I said.

"You know, Paul used to tell me when we were dating, 'Johnny will never love anyone as much as he loved Marie. Marie was the love of his life.' And I thought, 'Oh, yeah? We'll see.' He never told Marie as much as he told me. We were close in a way he never was with anyone else."

I believed it. The two of them—the three of us, actually—were fused in ways I'd never understood, until now. We'd been fugitives together. *Fugitives*. Any anger I felt toward my mother for lying to me all these years was superseded by the wonderment I found myself feeling at all that we'd gone through.

"You know, you told me years ago that the reason Dad went to jail in Irvine was because there was another John Mascia and it was a case of mistaken identity," I reminded her.

"Well, there *was* a John Mascia in the Bronx," she said.

"Yeah, you tried for years to pass him off as the reason Dad got pinched."

"Did I?" she asked, feigning innocence. I couldn't help but laugh.

"Oh, my god, Mom!" I said with a start. "When you had your heart attack and Daddy told me about your real age, do you know what I said to him?"

"What?" she asked.

"I told him, 'It's okay, Dad, because I know your secret, too.' But Ma, I didn't know about this. He thought I was talking about *this*."

"Well, you don't have to tell him differently now. Jenny, he's paid the price," she said. "He's had a shitty relationship with his kids—"

"Yeah, but why, do you think?" I asked. "I really want to know. Was it guilt? Like, he let the estrangement get so deep that even trying to mend it only reminded him of what he had done?"

"I don't know, Jenny," she said, "but he's going to die of cancer."

"Ma! Enough with that, I know!" I looked out the window at the crowd of students on the steps. I had a feeling their Monday was a lot different from mine. "Mom, this guy was the only person Daddy killed, right?"

"Of course, Jenny," she said.

"I just need to make sure," I said. "Please understand." A sob caught in my throat; I swallowed it and kissed my mother goodbye.

"He's the love of my life, Jenbo," she said as I slammed the car door.

HIS NAME WAS Joseph Vitale. I discovered the identity of my father's victim later that week, when I was combing through my mother's nightstand and found a clipping from the *Daily News* dated January 9, 1964. It had been there all along, I just hadn't known what to look for. The headline read MASCIA GIVEN 20-TO-LIFE IN DOPE MURDER, and the story went on to describe him as a big-time narcotics pusher from Miami Beach. Assigning him that provenance was awfully funny, since he'd lived there only a short time when he was arrested for murder. I showed it to my mother, now that I was no longer timid when it came to these matters.

"Your grandparents saved it when he was sentenced," she said. "And now you know everything, so you can stop looking."

———

AS SOON AS the semester ended I got a job at Houston's, a fine-dining restaurant on Park Avenue South that eschewed advertising, instead relying on word of mouth to jam the dining room. And that it did— there was no reservation system, so the waits could be monstrous. It took me the entire summer to make $3,500, which would cover first and last months' rent, a security deposit, and the real estate agent's fee. When I was halfway there I knocked on my parents' bedroom door and sat down on their bed and finally told them what they probably already knew.

"Guys," I started, but broke down. "Sorry, hang on, I want to do this right." Memories of running into this very bed during a lightning storm or after a nightmare came flooding back. It would be hard to close this door, but it had to happen.

"Okay, now, what I wanted to say," I said, blowing my nose, "is that I'm moving out." I looked at them for a reaction. They listened, patiently. "We just can't live together anymore. Mom, we're screaming at each other all the time. It's not fair to Daddy." Which was definitely a factor, but not the real reason. The real reason was that I knew I needed to move out before my father got really sick, because I certainly wouldn't have the courage to leave my mother after he died. I might have ended up living with her into my late twenties, and then we would have killed each other. I didn't want to always be at odds with my mother. I was doing this to save our relationship, even though I knew it would hurt my father.

"It's not like I won't be back all the time," I assured them. "I have no intention of abandoning my family. But it's time. I love you guys so much," I said, breaking down again.

"Jenny, it'll be fine," my father said. "You do what you have to do."

"Let's see if she can save the money and move without dropping out of school," my mother murmured to my father.

"I won't be dropping out of school," I snapped, "because I'm not moving out alone."

"I knew it," my mother said. "You're moving out with Kareem, right?" I nodded. "Well, at least you'll be splitting the rent. *If* he gets his act together."

"A lot of things are still up in the air," I said, wanting to take it all back. "But I just wanted to let you know." I was still crying; I didn't seem to know how to turn it off.

"Okay," my mother said.

"Okay," my father said.

"Okay," I said, and left the room. It was official: I was going to cohabit with my boyfriend.

"I really want to live on my own," I told my therapist, "but I don't think I can afford it by myself."

"Are you sure?" she asked. "You've worked out the math?"

"The problem is that most of these apartments require that you earn forty to fifty times the monthly rent, and even though I certainly make enough to cover a thousand-a-month rent, I don't make forty to fifty times that," I explained. "So I guess Mo and I will move in together. I know, we've only been together a few months."

"Nothing is irreversible," she said. "Even if you move in together and it doesn't work out, you can always find another place."

"I guess," I said.

"Do you think he's ready?" She had a point; he didn't even have a job, and didn't seem eager to bust his ass like I was.

Kareem remained unemployed throughout the summer, finally landing a gig as telemarketer for a theater company in September. Unfortunately, it paid $9 an hour. I accused him of not taking our life together seriously, and in addition to one-bedrooms, I also started circling studio apartments in the classifieds, ready for the possibility of each.

The first place we looked at was a two-bedroom on East 110th Street in East Harlem. "Such a bargain, thirteen hundred," the real estate agent informed us at the precise moment that two giant rats scurried past.

"No," I said, and we returned to school to plot our next move. On the train we continued an argument we'd been having about god knows what, and when we emerged he insisted on continuing the fight, even chasing me down Sixty-eighth Street and over to Third Avenue despite my pleas to leave me alone. It was a side of him I'd never seen before, and it was frightening.

"Is this how it's going to be when we move in together?" I asked him. "Is this how your parents are with you? Chasing you down until you submit? Haven't you ever heard of *space*?"

After he reluctantly returned to campus I was about to throw away the *Voice* when I glanced at the back page. "1 bdrm, 1 bath, 103rd Street and 2nd Ave, $925." *Could this be real?* I wondered as I dialed the agent's number. She agreed to meet us there in thirty minutes.

For years East Ninety-sixth Street was considered to be Manhattan's version of the San Diego–Tijuana border, the line in the sand where all Upper East Side development stopped, and few ventured north of that east-west corridor, which ran from First Avenue to Central Park. Crossing it meant entering a world of housing projects and drug dealers, but once you did, you found yourself in a gray zone: East Harlem was not quite Spanish Harlem, but it was definitely not Yorkville. But where others saw decay I saw an opportunity to live cheaply in Manhattan, which had, after all, been number two on the list of goals I'd drawn up at Celie's house.

The apartment was above JFK Fried Chicken, which is a low-budget version of Kennedy Fried Chicken, which is itself an homage to KFC—a knockoff of a knockoff. While we waited for the real estate agent, two unmarked SUVs pulled up and a gaggle of officers jumped out and slapped handcuffs on a man standing right in front of the building in what appeared to be an undercover drug bust. I turned to Kareem.

"Well, maybe it's a good sign," I reasoned. "Could mean the neighborhood's getting better." Once inside, I knew I wanted it before I'd even reached the avenue-facing bedroom. It had a decent-sized kitchen and hardwood floors, which, as the child of a carpet cleaner, I'd always coveted. It was a walk-up, but the apartment was on the second floor, and there was lots of light.

"I'll take it," I said. We had less than twenty-four hours to gather the requisite bank statements, money orders, and letters of recommendation from our employers. Kareem had only been at the telemarketing gig for a week, so I took the company letterhead from his introduction package and forged a proof-of-employment letter. He snagged one of his father's bank statements and I scanned it and created a new paragraph stating that he had many more thousands in the bank than he actually did. I was a little criminal, just like my parents. The real estate agent altered my credit history, which was blighted with my credit blunders from college. "The whole packet is going to be faxed," she explained, "so it's okay if we cut and paste." The next morning, Kareem and my parents crowded into the agent's tiny one-room apartment in Kips Bay and watched as I handed her $3,700 in cash. Kareem had contributed none of it; my parents even had to lend him $75 for his credit check because I had nothing left. We agreed to split the rent, but that didn't do anything to change my parents' opinion of the person I'd chosen to make my life with.

"You worked all summer to pay for this and he didn't do shit," my mother complained.

"I know," I said. What could I say? They were right.

"Your father is very disappointed in Kareem, but he would never tell you that," she added.

"He won't let me down," I told her. "Trust me." Four days later I got the call: The apartment was ours. I jumped up and down, unable to believe my luck: I was going to live in Manhattan. My dream, realized. Even my mother shared my enthusiasm.

"Manhattan, Jenny, that's wonderful," she gushed. When I took my parents to see the place a few weeks before we moved in, they were impressed.

"For a first apartment, this is great," my father said, scoping out the kitchen. "Really, Jenny, this is terrific." Just then a small cockroach made its ascent up the wall next to where my father was standing; his thick hand came down on it without missing a beat. "Yeah, this place is real great, Jenny," he said, smiling like nothing had happened. "Real great."

Later that month my parents took me to Pier One to pick out new furniture. At the register I held out the sum in cash, but my mother shook her head.

"No," she said. "Your father and I will take care of it."

"No, Mom, you can't!" I protested, but they had their way. Officially it was a gift in celebration of their daughter's milestone; my mother soon revealed the unofficial reason.

"Because when you break up," she said, "your father doesn't want there to be a war over the furniture." I didn't get angry at her comment. I knew she was right.

CHAPTER 10

East 103rd Street
Manhattan, New York
November 2000

. . .

RUE TO MY PROCRASTINATING NATURE, I WAITED UNTIL FIVE
in the morning on the day of the move to start packing, and I hadn't
finished by the time one of our friends went to get the U-Haul. In the
end I was dumping drawers into boxes, just like my parents used to.
Naturally, the elevator got stuck so we had to run the thing manually.
My father couldn't help, and I could tell it bothered him, so he hung
back, drinking his Looza pear nectar and his Ensure, which my
mother offered at every opportunity. "Gotta keep your strength up,"
she'd say. He'd gotten thinner in recent months, and his eyes, once
squeezed by his retirement girth, were now sunken and hollow. His
morale had taken a serious hit when a chemotherapy needle leaked
the deadly potion into his hand, the work of a careless doctor. The
resulting wound looked like a volcano on the brink of eruption rising
from the back of his hand. "Number one my ass," my mother vented.
"I should sue this motherfucking hospital, I swear to god."

As we loaded the truck I tried my best to avoid my parents, which
wasn't easy. I knew what would happen when the time came to say
goodbye, and I agonized over it. After several hours I'd finally packed
all I wanted to take—one of my rooms, however, was an absolute disaster that I vowed to return and clean—and I found myself alone;
everyone was waiting downstairs. I took a deep breath and walked
slowly into the living room. My father was sitting on the couch. I
froze. I couldn't avoid this, I had to face him. I ambled over to the sofa
and plopped down next to him. We took one look at each other and

burst into tears, so loud it sounded like howling. We knew that this goodbye meant more than just "see you in a few days." This could very well be his last lucid goodbye, a surrogate for a time when he wouldn't be able to say anything at all. After a few moments of this we looked up at each other and started crying all over again. Neither of us seemed able to stand up. My mother walked in, took in this scene, and shook her head.

"Two sentimental Italians," she said. "Unbelievable." My mother would be following the truck to the apartment, but my father didn't feel strong enough to go. I'll never know if that was the truth, or whether he was too sad to prolong our farewell. We sat there for a minute more until my mother said, "Come on, Jen. Let's go." She managed to resist being taken in by our display, and I realized that her maternal instinct must have kicked in—she was being strong for the both of us because we had fallen apart.

"Goodbye, Daddy," I said. I reached out for him and he returned my embrace. I smiled. "See you soon."

Kareem told his parents we'd gotten married so they couldn't protest our living arrangements, and it took a month for them to discover our lie. Soon his father was demanding to see our marriage certificate. Within a week Kareem's brother was leaving death threats on our answering machine, accusing us of destroying the family honor, and his father followed suit with tirades designed to make Kareem feel guilty for breaking his mother's heart. "That's it, I'm done," I said, and called the precinct down the street. The next morning two officers paid us a visit and listened to the messages, and later that week Kareem's father was slapped with a restraining order and his brother was arrested for aggravated harassment, spending the night in jail. Perhaps he finally realized the consequences of doing his parents' dirty work, because after his jail stint the calls stopped and we were finally free to live together in peace.

But we never did. Kareem had lost his home, and he sought to replicate it on 103rd Street. We engaged in maddening, logic-bending arguments during which Kareem blocked my exit from the apartment with his hulking physique. One night he pounded on my locked bedroom door for three hours, inflicting gashes where he attempted to rip it off its hinges. All the while I sat at my computer desk trying not to breathe. The next morning I silently crept out of the apartment, but he heard me open the front door and chased me out onto the street and into a cab. I jumped out and hailed another, but he pushed his way into that one, too. Four cabs later I was able to shove him out for good and speed away. The driver must have thought we were nuts.

"My father is dying and you choose to act this way?" I said over the phone a few hours later. "What is wrong with you?"

"I told you, I'm going to be there for you," he said.

"*This* is being there for me?" I asked, incredulous. "You're torturing me!"

Our fighting took us so far from the baseline that we entered a kind of hyper-reality where logic didn't penetrate; it was eerily reminiscent of my mother's irrational explosions. But his rage always subsided, and afterward he'd admit that he'd been out of line. I was reeled in by his sudden clarity—he wanted to change! "I can't believe what I've done, Jennifer, I'm so sorry. It's not me. They fucked with my head," he confessed through body-wracking sobs. He claimed only one thing could save him: therapy. He was committed to getting better, he said, for *us*. He began talking to someone, and I was thrilled. I had the old Kareem back, and these explosions had just been a blip.

But by February I had bigger problems. "Daddy," I said when I called home one evening, "I just got fired. Please don't tell Mommy."

He laughed; it was just like when he spotted me at Saturday school and vowed to keep it from my mother. "I won't, don't worry. Whatever you need, we're here."

"I love you, Daddy," I said. But his relaxed manner belied something more profound.

"Jenny, he's not doing well," my mother confessed in a late-night phone call. "I'm taking him to the hospital tomorrow, okay? Meet us there?" We'd just celebrated our last New Year's—apart, because I'd been stuck at work, cursing myself because I knew he wouldn't be alive this time next year.

"Of course I'll be there," I said. When I walked in the next morning his legs were swollen from the sudden infusion of liquid, meaning he'd been severely dehydrated. But even worse, his scrotum was grotesquely enlarged, looking like a water balloon ready to pop, causing him terrible pain. As the nurses inserted his IV and catheter my mother kept trying to cover his nether regions with his hospital gown. I was horrified at my father's state; when had this happened?

When I was fighting around with Kareem, that's when, and I felt terrible. My mother was right: My priorities were fucked. And they remained that way, as I ran out into the hallway every few hours to alternately argue and make up with Kareem. "Jenny, please," my mother implored. "Your father's sick. Will you give it a rest?"

"It's okay, let her talk if she wants," my father said, his voice cutting out every few words like a shaky cellphone connection. When he was wheeled away for tests later that day I asked my mother, "How sick is he? I mean, is this it?"

"I don't know, honey," she said. "We've got to keep him hydrated, and when he's stronger he'll start another clinical trial." I knew it was a pipe dream, but I wasn't sure if she did.

Since the bulk of his fellow patients were terminal, visiting hours didn't exist, and as days turned to weeks my mother essentially relocated to Sloan, sleeping every night in the unoccupied bed across the room. If someone was assigned to it she'd sleep with him in his bed, careful not to disturb his IVs. One night when she was asleep he went to the bathroom unaided and tripped and hit his head; the subsequent X-ray revealed that the cancer had spread to his brain.

"We did a PET scan and there's also some activity on the spine and one of the ribs," one of the doctors confirmed.

"Can the brain be radiated?" my mother asked, not pausing for a moment to absorb this setback.

"Only if he builds his strength up," the doctor said. My father half paid attention. With minor exceptions he had ceased connecting with most people, and his face wore the grimace of someone retreating from this world and entering the universe of pain. He never left.

"Then that's what we gotta do," my mother said. She fed him more Ensure and tried to get him to eat the hospital's offerings but he refused, and his weight peeled away in layers until his skin shrank so much that his tattoos appeared darker. Because Sloan was four blocks from Hunter I made it my second home, eventually mastering the underground passageways that led to the elevator that took me to my father's room, where I'd plop myself down on a chair and curl up with a book. When the fighting between me and Kareem became unbearable I would sleep there, too. (A few times he tried to follow me but I outran him.) My mother invariably asked me to bring ice cream, which she hoped would entice my father to eat, but he was often asleep by the time I got there. Because my mother got the bed, I got the chair, but I didn't mind, comforted by the sight of my sleeping parents and the sound of their light snoring. It was just the three of us again.

WHAT ULTIMATELY SANK my relationship with Kareem was the night he physically prevented me from leaving school. I was about to head to Sloan when he placed his bulky mass between me and the door, and when I'd attempt to escape he'd mirror my every move. Thankfully there were people milling about the halls, and I shouted for someone, anyone, to call security. As soon as I started screaming, Kareem panicked and ran downstairs. I followed and caught up with him just in time to see him restrained by eight security guards who seemed to appear out of nowhere. I watched from just inside Thomas Hunter Hall as they spent half an hour calming him down, and I felt responsible somehow, like I had caused his breakdown because I'd asked him to change his life. But I also felt betrayed, because he had become unbalanced, and I hadn't committed to this Kareem. I had committed to the Kareem I'd first met, the Kareem who was harmless as a puppy. How could I have connected so strongly with someone so unstable? Was it in my DNA to forge connections with troubled people, people with unbalanced personalities, people with dubious sexuality? A crowd formed around me and I tried to act like a bystander, but my cover was blown when one of the guards popped his head in and said, "He says he just wants to talk to you."

"What, are you kidding?" I asked, astounded they were entertaining his whims. The guard even asked me a few more times—"No, no, no!" I yelled. "How many times do I have to say it—*he refused to let me leave!*"—until Kareem tried to slip from their grip, charging a few feet down Lexington Avenue before the guards pounced again. A few minutes later a different guard popped his head in and asked me if I wanted to press charges, telling me that because we lived together I had a textbook domestic violence case on my hands. "We just did this with his brother," I muttered, kicking myself for not foreseeing this turn of events—the apple and the tree and all that. "I can't," I said to the guard. "Just please accompany me to Sixty-eighth and First? I have to visit my father in the hospital." I was supposed to pick my mother up hours before and drive her to Staten Island to get a fresh change of clothes. When she saw me she began whisper-screaming, *"Where the fuck have you been!"* but I shook my head and beckoned her into the hall and finally confessed the hell I had been living with Kareem.

"It's over, Ma," I said.

"Thank God," she said, and held me.

"It's over, Daddy," I said, returning to the room.

"Good," he whispered, barely audible. "Because I want to kill him."

ONE AFTERNOON I came to Sloan to find my half-brother, Tony, sitting at my father's bedside; he'd brought his wife, Carrie, and she sat quietly in a chair next to him.

"Hi," I said to my brother, who I hadn't seen in thirteen years. He was prematurely gray, just like our father, and shared his round, welcoming eyes. His features were a little broader, though, and his accent was Florida all the way.

"Hey, Jenny," he said, leaning in for a hug. "How ya been?"

Terrific. Thrilled. Titillated. "I'm okay," I responded. "How are you?"

"Oh, good, you know, same old," he said. I didn't even know what the "same old" was.

"How are your . . . kids?" I didn't know even know if they had any. Where had I been?

"Good, good," he said, addressing my father. "Toni is almost three now, and little Timmy is going to be one in December. Can't believe it." He spoke with an openmouthed smile and a hint of wonder, just like Grandpa used to. It was childlike without being juvenile. It was charming.

"Hey, Johnny," my mother said, kneeling down to meet his face. "Would you eat some pizza if I got some? Just a slice?"

"I might," he said. Dried spittle caked the sides of his mouth; when he drank from the plastic hospital cups he'd leave some behind on the rim.

"Come on, Jen, Tony, Carrie—let's get pizza," my mother suggested. We grabbed a pie from around the corner and made small talk; my mother did the heavy lifting because it was awkward. I wanted to pull Tony and Carrie aside and tell them how sorry I was that my father had missed their wedding, and how we'd pleaded with him to go, but I didn't. I could barely handle what was in front of me.

When we got back my father took a few bites of pizza and promptly set it down. My mother didn't force him, just whispered "pistachio ice cream" in my ear when I left that day. When I returned the next afternoon, Tony and Carrie were still there, their eyes focused on the television, along with my father's. He reminded me of a child then, absorbing the images with a blank expression, as though they were beyond his comprehension. I wondered how much of my father's brain the cancer had infiltrated, then wondered if he was playing dumb to avoid a confrontation with the son he'd publicly stood up. Either way, father and son said very little to each other, and when Tony finally hugged his father for the last time there was no scene, no tears. My moving out had been more emotional than their final goodbye. My heart would have been breaking for Tony if it hadn't already been cannibalized by loss.

A few days after they left, Sloan-Kettering informed us that my father wasn't rehabilitating as fast as they liked, and since he wasn't ready for hospice they recommended a rehab facility in Staten Island, after which he was welcome to return for brain radiation. Two months after he was brought to Sloan for what was supposed to be an overnight stay, I watched from Sixty-seventh Street as he was loaded into an ambulance and taken to a rehabilitation center not far from my parents' apartment. I monitored his progress by phone, planning to visit him over the weekend, but at 11:30 on Friday night, my mother called.

"Jenny, when I went in to see him today, he was, like, in a trance," she said.

"Was he dehydrated?" I asked, by now somewhat versed in end-stage cancer.

"I don't know," she said. "How can you tell?"

"How can you tell?" I asked her rhetorically. "Mom, you know this. I know you know this."

"I don't," she said, her voice threatening to break.

"What color was the urine in his output bag?"

"Um . . ."

"Was it orange, Ma?" I asked, worried I was losing her, too.

"It was very dark. It was very, very dark, like you said, almost orange," she said, coming back.

"I'm getting in a cab and coming over," I said, not caring that it would cost fifty bucks. We managed a few hours of sleep before rising at dawn.

"Let's go," I said as soon as I opened my eyes, and my mother hopped into the car without even a cup of coffee—a first for her.

"I'm sorry, it's not visiting hours," a nurse called after us as we barged through the door.

"Fuck visiting hours," I mumbled.

"Jenny!" my mom scolded, but followed me down the hall toward his room. I glanced at the patients in the hallway and noticed that each one ranged from partial awareness to catatonia; for a moment I thought I'd stepped onto the set of *Awakenings*. We came to my father's room; he was despondent and his lips were drier than bone. I checked his urine bag and extended it toward my mother: orange juice. His eyelids hovered somewhere between Tommy Chong and Kurt Cobain. I knelt down next to him.

"Daddy, are you ready to get out of here?" I asked.

"Yes," he said in a squeaky whisper, and began to cry. "I been meaning to tell yous all week, but I hate it here."

INSTEAD OF BULKING him up, his stay at the rehab center had set my father back to the point where brain radiation wasn't possible. No one had to tell us this, nor did they try to sell us on hospice; he still wasn't sick enough for that. But my mother had an idea: She was going to get home care. "I can't take care of him myself," she said, and enlisted the Visiting Nurse Service. She told them she needed a hospital bed and 24-hour aides to care for my father, "until he's strong enough for another clinical trial," even though we knew he'd never get there.

"Mrs. Mascia," one of the nurses at Sloan said, "Medicaid doesn't cover round-the-clock care. Maybe eight hours a day, but no more than that."

"Wanna bet?" she asked, and a few phone calls later we were assigned two nurses to oversee my father's care in twelve-hour shifts. "You're coming home, Johnny," she whispered in his ear; he smiled.

I wasn't there when his hospital bed was installed in the living room at Merle Place, and when I finally laid eyes upon it a week later, the horror of the scene was eclipsed by another tragedy.

"Jenny," my mother whispered over the phone one night.

"What is it, Ma? Is Daddy okay?"

"Uncle Joey died," she said, and out of her mouth came a sound I'd never heard—whispered, suppressed tears, punctuated with tiny coughs. It sounded like someone being strangled in a library.

"*What*? Oh, Ma, what happened?" My parents and Joey had driven to chemo together for the better part of 2000, indulging in a little gallows humor along the way. They'd shared the same disease, and now they would share the same death.

"Emma found him in the hallway, collapsed and writhing," she said quietly. "She called 911 but it was too late. She thinks it was a heart attack. A massive, massive heart attack. It was just so unexpected," she said, weeping softly.

"Oh, Mommy," I said. "How did Daddy take it?"

"I didn't tell Daddy," she said.

"Well, you are, aren't you?"

"Jenny, how can I?" she asked. "To do this too him now—you've seen him, he's out of it. Emma said not to tell him. In his state he might not even understand." My father had crossed a line and I hadn't even caught it. I wanted to reach back and find the exact moment when my father had stopped being my father and instead become his shadow.

"I guess you're right," I said. Now I knew why she was whispering.

"Please come to the funeral with me, Jenny," she said. "I don't want to go alone. It's Saturday morning. Please."

"Of course."

"Because I know his family will be there and I—"

"I'll go, I promise."

"Jenny, don't let me down. Please."

"Mom, listen—could this happen to Daddy?" I asked. "Because if it was so sudden, I mean—I want to be there, I don't want to miss . . . *it*." I tried to say it as gently as possible, but a painless death was now our best-case scenario.

"Don't know," she said numbly. "What was really awful was when the paramedics came and they restarted his heart and put him on a tube, and Emma tried to stop them, screaming, 'He has a DNR! Don't you dare stick that tube down his throat!' But they did anyway, and it was only after he got to the hospital and they called to check with Sloan that they removed it."

"Oh, god," I said. A DNR, or Do Not Resuscitate order is a medical directive that prohibits taking extreme measures to prolong life. My father had signed one, too.

"Joey didn't want to be kept alive by a machine," she said. "Emma was adamant that his wishes were carried out. Oh, I feel so bad for them, Jenny."

"So do I," I said. "I feel bad for all of us."

I took the express bus to Merle Place on Saturday morning to find my father lying in a hospital bed in the middle of the living room and a young black man sitting on the couch next to him. A commode and a wheelchair were parked nearby, as was a walker, in case my father felt inspired to take a few steps. The setup made me hate the apartment even more than I already did.

"You must be Jennifer," the young man said, rising and offering me his hand. "I'm Yaw." He pronounced it "Yow."

"Hi," I said. "You're taking care of my father?"

"Yes," he said. "Such a good man. So funny."

I nodded. "So funny." Even when I was a teenager and his jokes stopped being funny, he was still funny. My mother emerged from her bedroom wearing black. I considered my own black shirt and walked over to my father's bed. "Well, Mommy and I are going to, uh, have breakfast now," I said. My mother hooked her arm in mine.

"Yeah, we're going to eat a little something," she said. I was worried he'd catch on because I rarely rose before noon. But in a way I wanted him to know. I wanted him to keep him in this world, keep him with us. But his body had other ideas.

"Have fun, girls," he said. When the church service was over my mother took my hand and led me into the sunshine, where I cried tears of futility; I knew my father was next.

Despite Emma's considerable pain, she brought her daughter Linda over to the apartment on April 10, my father's sixty-fourth birthday. "Hiya, Johnny," Emma said, smiling bravely. My mother had helped him onto the couch for the occasion and dressed him in a gray short-sleeved button-down. He wore a warm smile when he wasn't staring off into space, and I couldn't tell whether his disorientation was caused by the fentanyl patch stuck to his back, the liquid morphine my mother dropped into his mouth every hour, or the brain cancer.

"Hey, Emma!" he said, his eyes slowly finding her face. My mother told me that Emma and Linda had changed their black clothes in the stairwell so as not to arouse my father's suspicion. But as they were leaving they very nearly broke down at my father's final words.

"Say hi to Joey," he said, waving. Emma froze her smile in place and nodded ever so slightly.

"I will, I will," she said. "Goodbye, Johnny."

After they left, Yaw helped my father navigate the living room with the help of the walker. Inch by delicate inch he staked his claim on the green carpet, chugging into his bedroom and back. "Look at you, Daddy!" I said, hopeful. He was dressed and upright; it was almost like having my old father back. He nodded and paused, drawing a deep breath so he could speak.

"I just want to get well," he said.

He would never walk again.

WE DIDN'T REALLY become close with Steven, the overnight nurse, because we spent most of our time sleeping when he was on call—as did he—but my mother and I quickly warmed to Yaw, who spent most of his time writing letters to his girlfriend in Ghana. He was a Christian, he said, and believed that the spirit lived on after death.

"Really?" I asked, wanting so much to believe that my father wouldn't be gone forever.

"Of course," he said. "He believes it, too." He tilted his head toward my sleeping father.

One afternoon my mother moved my father to the couch and gave him a haircut. Chemo had been kind to his follicles, leaving him just enough hair to comb over into his signature gray shell. When she was done snipping she held up her mirrored vanity tray so he could check her work. He stared at it for a while before looking at my mother and shrugging.

"Go ahead, Johnny," she said, nodding and smiling. "Look." Once again he looked at the mirror, but not into it. I shot my mother a look, and she took the mirror and put it back in her bedroom. I followed.

"Mom, why—"

"I don't think he can see," she said flatly.

"No," I said, disbelieving.

"Yes," she said. "Jenny, I don't know if I can take much more." Even though we had nurses, it was my mother who wiped his backside after he sat on the commode; she was the one chugging the choo-choo train of applesauce into his mouth and holding the straw up to his lips so he could sip some water. The one time I tried to administer his morphine drops he refused. "Ask your mother first," he wheezed, even though it was her orders I was following. Around me, my father acted much less aware than when my mother would walk into the room; her presence made him focus. He was tied to her now, and because of this she had her hands full.

"Mommy, please, we can't put him into a home," I begged. The thought of him being dumped in someone else's lap, like we didn't care about him—it haunted me. "He needs to be with us, Mommy, please. I'm here, I'll help."

"But you saw him, he only takes orders from me. It's my heart I'm worried about, Jenny," she said. "The physical and emotional strain may be too much. If we knew how much longer he had I'd take him up to Calvary in the Bronx. It's an incredible hospice—that's where Vinny went."

"You heard what the nurses at Sloan said," I reminded her. "You need to be three to six weeks away from dying to be admitted to hospice. Who knows where he's at?" Since we didn't know, my mother brought in someone who could tell us. Her wealthy aunt Adele, who lived on Fifth Avenue and had come to see my father once at Sloan, sat on the board of Mount Sinai and called in a favor. That favor was Diane Meier.

Judging from her slim, spritelike physique and casual attire of sweatshirt and jeans, you'd never be able to tell that Diane, a geriatrician, was one of the leading palliative care experts in the field, frequently quoted in *The New York Times*. Eight years later, she would go on to win a MacArthur genius grant for her pioneering work in the field of palliative medicine, but on this night, she was just an overworked physician who had driven all the way to Staten Island from East Harlem after a long day at the hospital to examine my father and determine how far he was from the end. "Hi, there," she said to him quietly, stooping slightly to meet his eyes as he lay in bed. After my mother and I stood behind them for a few minutes, waiting, she looked up and said, "Is there somewhere we can talk?" We led her to the back bedroom—the one I'd actually cleaned when I moved out—and the three of us sat Indian-style on the carpet.

"I'd say he's about three to four weeks away," she said. My eyes darted to my mother, and I expected her to cry, but she didn't break, just nodded grimly. "Would you like to know exactly what will happen?" Dr. Meier asked us, and I nodded.

"Please," I said. She explained how my father's sleep would get deeper and deeper, and last longer than we were used to. "Until one day he'll just keep sleeping," she said. "He'll enter a coma, and soon the death rattle will begin."

"That sounds awful," my mother said.

"It does, literally, sound awful," she said, explaining how we use a number of muscles to swallow all the saliva and mucus that accumulates in our mouths, and when we're weakened by cancer we can't control those muscles anymore but the mucus still accumulates, and when breath travels over it, it becomes audible. "It can go on for weeks sometimes," she said. "When you hear that, you will know he is close." My mother and I held each other's eyes for a moment; we still had this to look forward to? "And then he'll take long, deep breaths," Dr. Meier continued, "and the spaces between each breath will get longer, too—so long, in fact, that you might think he has passed, but then, just like that, he'll breathe again. And this may carry on for a few hours, until he'll breathe and not breathe out."

We sat there quietly as the late spring wind rustled the Venetian blinds.

"Dr. Meier, do you believe that there's life after this?" I asked.

"Oh, I do," she said. "In fact, I believe that everyone has a spirit that leaves the body during death."

I smiled. "Good. If you believe it, I feel better," I said, though it didn't make swallowing this information any easier.

"Dr. Meier," my mother said, "I'll tell you the truth, with all of this, I'm concerned about my heart. I'm not sure if my aunt Adele told you, but I had a heart attack three years ago and I'm a little worried that the stress of all this will aggravate my heart condition."

"Are you on nitroglycerin?" Dr. Meier asked.

"No, but I've heard of it."

"Ask your cardiologist to call in a prescription for nitro. It strengthens the heart muscle, and when you feel any tightness in your chest just place one under your tongue and let it dissolve."

"Thank you so much, Dr. Meier," my mother said. "For everything. I can't believe you came all this way."

Dr. Meier considered me and my mother for a moment. "John is a very lucky man," she said. "There is a lot of love in this house. The three of you are very connected, and it's apparent to anyone who walks in. Eleanor, you're doing a brave thing by not taking him to hospice, and it's a decision you made out of love. But if this becomes too much for you, it does not mean you have failed him. This is incredibly difficult, even for medical professionals. If you change your mind, *do not hesitate* to call me, and we will have a bed set up for him at Sinai."

My mother nodded, tears flooding her eyes. "Thank you, Dr. Meier."

"Now, I would recommend you do something, and it is going to be very difficult, but it's necessary, and many people never get the chance. You should tell him how you feel about him very soon. If you don't, you might regret it."

"Oh, my god," I said. "How am I going to do that?" I looked down at the carpet. Eulogize him to his face?

"Yes," Dr. Meier said, addressing me. "You must tell him how you feel about him." My mother nodded.

"She's right, Jenny," she said. "Thank you again, Dr. Meier. Really, I can't think of another doctor who would do something like this."

"Oh, it's nothing, and let me give you my number," she said, scribbling on a piece of paper. On her way out she stopped at my father's bed and leaned in and grabbed his hand. "You have a wife and daughter who love you very much, Mr. Mascia," she said. "I wish you good luck."

"Thank you," my father politely whispered, but as soon as she left he added, "I don't like her, El." He spoke almost exclusively to my mother now.

"Why not, Daddy?" I asked, but my mother shushed me. She led me into her bedroom and shut the door. "What?" I asked her.

"He doesn't like her because he knows what she's doing here," my mother explained. "Your father is very smart. Even now. Well, you heard her, Jenny. We've got to do this."

My face began to crumple but my mother took my chin in her hands. "Hey," she said. "We can do this." We stepped out into the living room and my mother asked Yaw to move my father to the couch so we could sit next to him. I sat on his left side and my mother on his right. I didn't want him to know that I was spilling my guts because he was dying, because then he'd have no choice but to face his imminent passing. I didn't want to make it worse for him.

"Um, Daddy," I said, whimpering slightly. "Well, I love you guys," I began. "Dad, you're, like, my hero," I said, thinking about how he changed his life for us, how he gave up the thrills and the riches of the criminal sphere to paint buildings and clean carpets. "I wish—if I could— I wish I could take your place," I stammered. "If it was possible, I would take your place." I meant it. He lifted one of his bony arms and wrapped it around my shoulders without shifting his gaze from the floor.

"No, baby, no," he said. "You have your whole life to live."

"She loves you so much, Johnny," my mother said, nuzzling up to his other side. "I love you so much, Johnny."

"I love yous too," he said. "My girls."

I WAS STILL TIED to the city by my final term papers, so after scenes like that one I had to drag myself onto the subway and blend in with a sea of faces registering their quotidian concerns while death hovered nearby, waiting.

"I don't understand why this is hap-p-p-pening to h-h-him," I'd call my mother and cry when I found myself unable to conform to the rigors of academia.

"I don't know, either, Jenny Penny," she'd say, her voice low so my father couldn't hear.

"It's just so unfair," I said. "I can't believe that after all of our separations, now it's for real. This is it. He's going to die." The fact that he had taken life didn't factor into my grief; my mother and I discussed his past in these conversations, even the unflattering bits, but we didn't feel it made him less worthy of our love, and we didn't feel he deserved to die because of it. The fact that he had killed didn't diminish our pain one iota.

"I know, Jenny, stop crying, it's gonna be all right," she'd coo into the phone. She never cried when I cried, as if we were rationing tears.

"Mommy, you'll be there when this is over, right?"

"Of course I will, baby. Now make your daddy proud and finish your paper. Steven is leaving now and I have to see if Daddy needs anything before Yaw comes, okay?"

"I love you so much, Mommy," I sobbed.

"I love you, and Daddy loves you, too."

I set to work on my paper, a piece for my honors class, which was due in a matter of hours. My father had been so proud of my honors status, and his pride inspired me as I finessed my final act of procrastination, capping a career of leaving things to the last minute. I wanted to see how long I could put a paper off and still turn it in on time; the answer was three in the morning. I laughed despite a throat full of sobs—my academic career was finally over.

The sun was high in the sky as I printed out my paper, and I parted the shades in my living room—which was now completely mine, how I'd really wanted it all along—and basked in the warmth of the sun. It seemed especially cruel that a brilliant New York spring waited right outside my window but I couldn't enjoy it. Worse—neither could my father. As I sailed down the FDR that afternoon on the express bus and beheld the sparkling river and the fluttering leaves on the trees that lined the East River Walk, I understood that this spring wasn't for me. I'd catch the next one, though, and the one after that. And just like that, I realized that the black cloud above me would, in fact, lift. This crushing pain in my chest would not last forever. My father—my beloved Bruce Springboard—might be leaving this earth, but I was not. It was simply not my turn. This gave me a kind of perverse comfort, because I knew one day it *would* be me sucking on a morphine dropper in a hospital bed in the living room. On that day I wouldn't be getting a pass, but this time I was. It was incredibly unfair for him, but death was not yet coming for me. I was still alive.

"JENNY, COME HERE," my mother said one night about two weeks before my father died. She brought me into her bedroom and closed the door. She'd placed one of our dining room chairs in front of the closet.

"Ma, what—"

"Hush," she said, climbing onto the chair and reaching to the back of the closet, past my father's sewing kit—how funny that he'd been the mender in the family, while my mother couldn't even thread a needle. She pulled out what looked like a photo album, but it didn't have a cover, just weathered black pages covered with snapshots. It was wrapped in a plastic linen bag.

"Is that construction paper?" I asked, unzipping the bag. I flipped through pages adorned with photographs of Angie and Tina when they were young—class pictures, pictures of the girls with Grandpa Frank and Grandma Helen.

"What's that?" I asked. She had something in her other hand, what looked like another homemade photo album, the cover of which spelled "My Family" in red embroidery. I opened that one and gasped: It was my teenaged father and his first wife, Marie, beaming in black-and-white. "Ma, she looks just like Angie!" I said. The resemblance was uncanny. "And Tina looks like Daddy!" Tina began as an adorably petulant duckling and blossomed into a voluptuous yet self-effacing teen; Angie wore her gregarious personality on her sleeve but matured into a steely cool surfer chick with a chipped front tooth. There were pages and pages of Marie and my father holding my sisters when they were babies, their faces angelic and eager. It was hard to believe that a few years after these photos were taken my father would shoot a man to death. I pointed to long-forgotten relatives posing with the young family. "Who are these people?" I asked.

"I haven't a clue, my dear," my mother replied. I turned my attention back to the other album, thumbing through the soft black pages.

"Who are these kids?" I asked, pointing to a photo of Angie, Tony, and Tina with two younger children.

"Those are Marie's other kids, Cindy and Marty, the ones she had with her second husband," she said. I turned one of the photographs over and noticed a stamp on the back.

"Correspondence Department, SSP?" I asked.

"Sing Sing Prison," she said. "He never wanted you to find this. It was the photo album he kept in prison. Most of these pictures were sent to him by his parents, who stayed close with your brother and sisters when your father was in jail. They were close to Cindy and Marty, too, when they were young." I flipped to a page covered with Polaroids; they were of my father with a very young Frankie, Paulette, and their kids, and others I didn't recognize. In each they stood before a pale blue background. "Taken in prison," my mother said. "See? The background is the same." In every photo he had a cigarette dangling from his fingers, just as he did in many of the photos taken during my childhood. Damn Pall Malls.

"Wow," I said. "This was here the whole time and I never knew?" To think that my curious little fingers had been inches away from discovery all those times I'd gone rummaging through their closet. A piece of paper fell out of the big album; it was a program from a piano recital at Robert Whitford Music School. I opened it and skimmed the performers for a familiar name. Lo and behold, an eleven-year-old named Angie Mascia had played Tchaikovsky on May 12, 1972, at 7:00 P.M.

"Mommy, he saved this?" I asked, holding it out for her to see. Just like he'd saved my report cards and articles from the school paper and even the scripts from shows I'd starred in.

"I guess he did," she said, taking the delicate paper.

"He really did care about them," I said. "What happened?"

She shook her head. "Don't know," she said, clipped, as if too much thought on the topic might cause her to get angry at him, a feeling she was not about to indulge now. I flipped through white-bordered photos of Uncle Frankie in his Navy uniform, posing with an infant Tony; Angie and Tina captured in each of their young life stages, complete with frizzy hair, braces, and bikinis; and Grandma and Grandpa posing in the driveway of their old house in Brooklyn and poolside with their grandkids in Miami. I retrieved a photo from the back of the album and held it up for my mother to see: It was my father, looking to be in his early twenties—with teeth! A full set of white teeth!—standing with his arm around a brunette with heavily drawn eyebrows.

"Who's this with Daddy?" I asked.

"Ah, that was the mistress," she said, studying the photo. "A friend of Marie's, I think."

So he really had cheated on Marie with all of her friends. "He had pictures of the two of them just lying around?" I asked, spotting her in another picture; in it she was wearing a sequined dress and had a fur stole draped around her shoulders.

"I guess," she said, "and Marie found them and left him because of it."

"Really? He was that stupid?" When I was younger he'd warned me that "all men are snakes. Well, except me." Looks like he was right about the first part and wrong about the second.

"Yeah, and I don't know why, she hardly seemed worth it," my mother said, holding up a picture of my father and Marie, whose round eyes and angelic face were beyond compare. "A real *facia bruta*, the other one was," she said.

"Yeah, my god, Marie is so much prettier," I said. "I don't understand."

My mother shrugged. "That was the life," she said. "It was accepted behavior in that line of work."

"But he didn't do that with you," I said, reaching for a manila folder filled with black-and-white eight-by-ten photos.

"Oh, no," my mother said, following my eyes. "He was way past that shit when he met me." As she spoke I pulled out one glossy photo after another, some of my father with two dozen other men, lined up in three rows, all wearing cardigans or sweatshirts. A sign in the front row read SPARTANS FOOTBALL, 1965 CHAMPS.

"Ma?" I asked, and she chuckled.

"Prison," she said, anticipating my question. "It looks like an Ivy League sports team, doesn't it?" I nodded. All of his teammates were white; times certainly had changed. There were other photos, some with fewer players, some with signs that trumpeted their baseball successes as well. In another picture my father looks like he's in an auditorium and he's cradling a frame in his hand—perhaps it's a diploma?—and he's shaking someone's hand; there's a band playing behind him and a banquet table with food off to his right. Another photo depicts what looks like a talent show—there are two men wearing suits who look like they're performing a skit while someone plays a piano behind them; yet another photo features my grandparents and some other people seated around a table, and I deduced that this one was taken on visiting day. My father is also at the table, sporting seventies-era sideburns and laughing over his plate of food.

"That's her, that's Nancy," my mother said, pointing to a compact blonde with a faraway look on her face and a head full of curls. "The one your father was seeing."

"That's her?" I asked. She looked like a young Bette Midler.

"And that," she said, pointing to another photo, "is Paul." I could see why she'd been so stuck on him—a six-inch-tall Afro framed genial eyes, a neat black mustache, and a dazzling smile. He was lean, like my father, and sitting with a white woman—could that have been his wife, the one who confronted my mother, or another mistress?

"Cute," I said, handing her the picture. "But then, you've always had impeccable taste." She smiled.

As the hourglass ran out I kept in constant contact with Angie and Tina, calling them so often that my mother began to resent the time I spent away from her. Because my mother was busy with my father I supplanted her as the Florida liaison, and I grew closer to my sisters because of it. Since they were nurses they knew what questions to ask, and when I told them about the liquid morphine and the fentanyl they knew it wouldn't be long. They weren't flying up, though. They really didn't need to, I explained, as he was barely lucid and they had both seen him in December.

"I wish you would come down this summer, Jenny," Angie said. "You have a family here, too, you know."

"I know," I said. "Well, now I know."

"We've always been here," she said. "We'll always be here."

I took to sleeping in the living room on an inflatable mattress, and Steven would watch TV while I watched my father's chest rise and fall dramatically. It looked like his heart was trying to escape, because his stick-figure physique made his rib cage more prominent. In the morning I would wake to the sounds of my mother trying in vain to feed him applesauce. I glanced at the seat he'd occupied at the dining room table and remembered him sitting there just two years before, assuring us that he wasn't scared to die. I couldn't believe the man in the bed was the same person.

"Good morning, Daddy," I said, rubbing my eyes. "Hey, did I tell you I'm going to visit my family this summer?" My mother shot me a look when I said "my family."

"Really?" he asked, far away.

"Yeah, my sisters and brother and nieces and nephews—they're all waiting for me, Dad." The family he'd jettisoned, for whatever reason, was now mine. As an inheritance, it was priceless. My mother came around to the foot of the bed and fixed my father in her sights. I read it clearly: These might be his final lucid moments.

"We love you so much, Johnny," she said. "Jenny loves you so, so much, Johnny, and she knows what you did, and she loves you anyway."

"Ma!" I said, but pushed it down. "Yes, Daddy, I love you so much, it doesn't matter what you did," I said, but it had a bitter tinge. I grabbed her arm and took her into the bedroom.

"Why did you tell him that?" I asked, furious. "He's barely lucid. He can't even ask me anything or answer me back. He's trapped in his head and you're telling him his youngest daughter knows he killed someone."

"Jenny, I'm sorry, I just wanted him to know."

"This isn't knowing, Ma," I said. "He doesn't talk anymore, and I bet he only sometimes understands what we're saying." I closed my eyes. "You know how much I love you, Mom. I'm sorry, I just wish you hadn't done that." She nodded and left the room.

THE DEATH RATTLE began the morning of May 5, a Saturday, and it sounded just like coffee percolating. Thankfully, it didn't last for weeks. When my father hadn't woken by noon, my mother hovered over him and made a pronouncement: "I think he's in a coma." His breathing was exactly like Dr. Meier described—deep breaths followed by long pauses.

"Ooh, Jenny, look at his mouth," she said, pointing a long nail at his lips.

"No, Ma, just tell me," I said, keeping my distance at the foot of the bed.

"It's swollen, with what looks like cold sores," she said, and stood up. "Like he gets when he's stressed. Oh, Jenny, he's stressed. His whole mouth is broken out in those things."

"His body is fighting death," I mused. I slept on and off all day and sulked through dinner, which we'd ordered from the Italian place down the street.

"Why did you have to get so much food?" my mother asked when she saw my pasta, bruschetta, and Caesar salad, which I couldn't shovel into my mouth fast enough, prompting endless sniping between my mother and me for the remainder of the evening. My size 14 jeans were tight on me by this point, but I didn't give a shit, eating her portion, too. Just to prove how little I cared about my body, I made rigatoni with garlic, oil, and parmesan for breakfast the next morning. I brought it into my old bedroom and ate a few pieces while my mother sat down next to me.

"Jen, we need to get along right now," she said. "Your father is dying out there. We cannot fight in front of him anymore. Please." I hemmed and hawed and sulked for a good ten minutes before I gave in and handed her the pasta dish, realizing I didn't even want it. I reluctantly hauled my girth into the living room, where my mother and I watched TV—and my father's rising and falling chest—for the next seven hours. Around eight o'clock his breath caught for a moment, and we thought that was it. Yaw stood up from the couch and soundlessly went out onto the terrace, his head bowed respectfully. My mother leapt off the couch and ran toward her bedroom, bypassing the hospital bed altogether. She hovered in the doorway, watching. I sat in the chair next to the bed and was too frightened to move; I started shaking all over. We both peered at his body and waited. And waited.

"Jenny!" my mother shouted from the doorway. "What's happening? Is it happening?!"

I met her eyes for a moment, then returned my gaze to my father. And just like Dr. Meier predicted, he exhaled a ragged breath.

"Sometimes the spirit wants to leave the body," Yaw said, emerging from the terrace, "and it can't, because it will cause pain to those it will leave behind."

"Are you saying we should leave?" I asked, popping two of my mother's Xanax with lightning-fast fingers.

"Maybe, yes," Yaw said. "Maybe he wants to go, but he can't because you and your mother are so distressed." It was all he had to say; I grabbed my mother's purse and in ten minutes flat we were sitting at Royal Crown Bakery over a plate of tuna and onion sandwiches on ciabatta.

"I got so scared when I thought that was it, Mommy," I said, too wired to cry, despite the Xanax. I was still shaking.

"Me, too, Jenny," she said. "All I wanted to do was crawl in the bed with him, but I got so scared. Oh, I got so scared."

"It's okay, Mom. It's okay to be scared." I picked at the sandwich, my favorite, but I couldn't summon an appetite. "What do you think we'll find when we get back? Do you think he'll be gone?"

"I don't know," my mother said sorrowfully. If we'd been in our right minds we never would have left his bedside to go for a sandwich, so that should tell you how panic-stricken we were. When we got back Yaw was standing over him, and he shook his head; my father was still alive. I guess he did want his girls with him at the end. I took the phone and lay on my mother's bed and called Angie, then Tina, and told them our father was close to death. My mother sat on the couch and waited.

"Jenny!" she yelled in the middle of a particularly deep conversation I was having with Tina.

"Wait, Tina, hang on," I said, and took the phone into the living room. "Ma, what's up?"

"Jenny, I think he just . . . Yaw said he, he went to the bathroom." My father was wearing diapers, so there was no mess, but Tina overheard and said, "Jenny? Jenny?"

"Yeah, Tina, Mom said—"

"Jenny, this is what happens," she said. "The muscles relax and the bowel empties. You should go." I threw down the phone and resumed my place on the chair by his bed. My mother stood behind me, close enough to her bedroom that she could dash back inside if it became too overwhelming. Together we watched his breath go in and out, deeper and longer, until it caught. It released, then caught again. It released, then nothing.

"Oh, Jenny," my mother said, and darted into her bedroom. I expected the fear to overtake me again, and I was surprised when it didn't. Instead I was filled with a surge of calm; it's as if my fight-or-flight response had flipped in the two hours since it was first tested, and all I felt was peace. I had a choice: I could stay with my father's body as his spirit departed, or I could look after my mother, who needed me.

I shot up and ran to my mother. I grabbed her shoulders, looked her straight in the eyes, and said, "It's okay, Ma, I am not scared anymore. Do you hear me? *I am not scared anymore.*"

Tears soaked her cheeks and snot dripped from her nose; she nodded, looking lost. I held her close and walked her back into the living room, where my father's body lay. She took one look at him and buried her head in my shoulder. "Oh, Johnny," she cried, and reached out toward him. She kissed his cheek. "I'm so sorry, Johnny," she said, and turned to me. "I should have gotten into bed with him, I should have—"

"Mommy, it's okay," I said. "We were with him."

"No, I fucked it up," she said, kneading her forehead.

"Ma, he knows we were here. He waited for us. We did not let him down." I glanced at the clock; it was 10:40. I noted the time and, struck by a thought, calmly walked into the kitchen and fetched a pair of scissors. I went back into the living room and, with only slightly trembling hands, snipped a lock of his hair. I looked around and grabbed one of his pill bottles, emptied it, and inserted the gray snippet.

"I have to call the mortuary," my mother said, but climbed into bed with him and held him for a moment. When she finally rose I noticed that Yaw was gathering his things. His shift had ended two hours before.

"Yaw, thank you so much," I said. "For everything."

"God bless you, Jennifer," he said, and left.

My mother decided she'd wait downstairs for the mortician, and I figured it was because she didn't want to stay with my father's body anymore. When she left I sat back down in the chair and studied his still chest. I was struck by how white his lips were; I didn't know that could happen, but when I thought about it, it made sense. His mouth was partly open and I could see all his broken teeth and the spaces between. I considered climbing into bed with him but I didn't want to disturb his body, so I sat at the foot of the bed and hugged his bony legs. The tears came fast, and with each heave I clutched the sheets, until my cries turned to screaming.

"I love you so fucking much!" I screamed. "I love you SO. FUCKING. MUCH." I sobbed over my father's dead body until I heard the door open, and I quickly rose and threw on my poker face. There were two morticians, a man and a woman, and they lifted my father, sheets and all, and placed him in a long red bag that looked more like a duffel than a body bag. He seemed like a rag doll, his limp limbs jutting out at odd angles. When they zipped the bag over his head my mother gasped.

"You're sure he's dead?" she asked the morticians, who paused and nodded, businesslike.

"Mom," I said gently, "we know he's dead." The man and woman left, and for the first time in months, the apartment was quiet. We looked at each other and pressed our foreheads together. He was gone.

"Ma?" I asked. "Where is he, do you think?"

"I don't know, honey," she said, "but wherever he is, he has all the answers now."

CHAPTER 11

May 2001

. . .

T HE NEXT DAY WAS A BLUR, SPENT EITHER IN FRONT OF THE TV or running errands, but I can't remember a minute of it. I do remember Tuesday, when my mother and I drove to Brooklyn to pick up my father's death certificate, and then to a funeral home in Staten Island to receive his ashes. After that we headed into the city to pick up Arline, who'd hopped a train to Grand Central.

"Oh, Eleanor," she said, hugging my mother under the painted constellation in the Main Concourse. Then she reached out to me and brought me in for an embrace; it was the first time we'd met. She was short and squat, with a curly light-brown bob. "Oh, Jenny," she said. "Look at you. You look just like your mother." Her words were carried on a deep, husky whine, just like Rita's when she was upset. "I brought babka?" she said, elevating the word into a question, and my mother and I laughed for the first time in two days.

On our drive back to the Island my mother said, "Hey, Jenbo, you want to see where Arline and I grew up?"

"Sure," I said, eager to see a piece of my mother's past I'd only heard about. I checked my watch; I should have been in my honors Roman architecture colloquium—not that I cared. I was restless and raw, keenly aware that I'd crossed the line from B.C. to A.D.

"That's Abraham Lincoln, where I went to high school," my mother said as we passed an official-looking building visible from the expressway. "And we used to play hooky at the sweet shop across the street, but that's closed now."

A few minutes later we were coasting down a wide, tree-lined boulevard called Oriental, and from there we made a right on Hastings.

"Yep, that's it," Arline said, pointing to the house on the corner. "375" was emblazoned on the front.

"It looks like it's been redone," my mother said, surveying the façade.

"Don't you want to go in?" I asked, thinking that I'd want to if I had lived there.

"Nah," my mother said. "Arl, how much do you think it's worth now? Half a million? Three-quarters?"

"Oh, Eleanor, millions," she said. "I still can't believe he made her sell it. What an asshole."

"Wow, I can't imagine calling my father an asshole," I said, popping my head into the front seat.

"That's because your father wasn't," Arline said.

"Did you ever meet Daddy?" I asked her.

"Once, before you were born," she said. "At my father's funeral, actually."

"What did you think of him?" I asked Arline.

"Handsome," she said quickly. "So handsome, and so nice, and *funny*. He was so funny." She turned to my mother. "You were so lucky, Eleanor."

My mother shook her head. "I didn't do what I was supposed to do."

"Ma, enough with that! Just because you didn't climb into bed with him when he wasn't even lucid—"

"Eleanor," Arline interjected, "the way you took care of him—you kept him *alive*. They gave him six months and you got on the computer and extended that by two years. It was you, finding clinical trials and doctors and second and third opinions—"

"Lotta good it did," my mother mumbled.

"He would have been dead a long time ago if it wasn't for you," Arline said. "You gotta stop blaming yourself."

"All right, enough," she said with a wave of her hand, but I could tell it wasn't an angry gesture. She just wasn't ready to hear it.

The next afternoon I started going through my father's drawers. My mother wasn't ready to clean out his closet—"I just can't part with his clothes, not yet," she said—but his nightstand seemed harmless enough. I opened the familiar black-lacquered drawers and found pens, pencils, a few Stephen Kings, and the white cardboard bookmark I'd made him in sixth grade with "This Bookmark Belongs to Daddy and No One Else" written in puffy paint at the top. He'd saved it all these years, and still used it, apparently, because it was holding his place in *The Dark Half.* I thumbed through his wallet and found two driver's licenses, one current and one expired. I couldn't help but notice the expiration date on the current one: 04-10-2003. He expired two years before his license did. Because I knew my mother would want to keep the current one, I stuck the expired one in my wallet. I also found his slim gray telephone book, the one he'd carried for years, and when I set it aside I spotted a roll of undeveloped film. I jumped up and grabbed my mother's keys.

"Be right back," I said, and sped to the CVS on Bay Street, which had a one-hour photo. As soon as I opened the photo envelope the girl at the counter offered me a roll of paper towels. "Thanks," I said through heaving sobs. Judging by the contents the roll was from 1996—there were a few shots of his broken arm, replete with the metal contraption; a few exteriors of Burger Kings and Taco Bells; a photo of him, and a few of me, taken on a day long forgotten. It was the day my parents took me into the city, the first time we all went together, when my mother lamented the Village's transformation into "one big mall." There were a few photos of me smiling and posing in the parking lot of New Lane, my long brown hair blown pin-straight and flecked with red highlights from the sun. In my father's headshot he's facing the camera and smiling with a slight shrug, except he wasn't really shrugging; the camera caught him just as he was raising a cigarette to his mouth. It's classic John Mascia, a photo depicting him at his zenith. Two years later his bones would start aching, and we all knew how that story ended.

As I cried at the CVS counter—harder than I ever remembered crying—I decided that I would focus on the way he looked in the picture, as opposed to the way he looked when he was sick, which was the only way I could remember him now. I peeled myself off of the counter and threw myself behind the wheel of the Subaru and scream-cried the whole way home. As I looked for parking on Merle Place I also decided this would be the last time I cried with abandon over my father, because if I gave myself over to the horror of what I had just experienced I wouldn't be able to function.

As per my parents' computerized "Last Wishes," my father didn't want a showing or burial, but I insisted on a memorial service. My mother oscillated between embracing the idea and decrying it as an unnecessary hassle, but I couldn't live with the fact that my father would die without at least a few people sitting in a room and acknowledging it. So after Arline left we began scouting locations. My mother mentioned that David's memorial service had been at the Ethical Culture Society on the Upper West Side, and she wanted to have my father's there, too, but we couldn't afford the fee. "You should try our Brooklyn location," they suggested when we called. So my mother and I drove to Brooklyn and located the Gothic mansion across the street from Prospect Park. We decided on the ground-floor space that led to a lovely garden out back. We scheduled the service for June 6, exactly a month after he died, and, true to form, every time my mother and I argued she threatened to cancel it. "Yeah, Mom, because this is a party I just have my *heart set on attending*," I zinged. She gave it a rest after that.

The one-week anniversary of my father's death fell on, of all things, Mother's Day. It was oppressively hot that weekend and my mother came up to my apartment. "Well, happy Mother's Day, I guess," I said as she made coffee. My mother snorted and waited for the water to boil. "Look at it this way," I added, "at least today's not your anniversary. Especially this year." He'd died six months shy of their twenty-fifth.

"Yeah, well, whaddya gonna do," she said.

"I'm so sorry, Ma," I said. "But at least you had a good marriage." I was romanticizing a little, but they really did love each other. I'd seen how close they were at the end, how she'd conquered the enigmatic world of computers to try to find him a cure, how he wouldn't take medicine from anyone else. I'd be lucky to find a love like theirs.

"He cheated on me," she said.

"*What?*"

She nodded. "With this white-trash waitress he met when he was painting on the road," she revealed. "We almost broke up over it, but I forgave him because, well, he was your father. And really, he wasn't about to start over with someone else, not at his age." Her jaw was tense and her lips pursed, just like when she'd been forced to admit his crimes to me.

"You said he never cheated on you!" I said, rising from the couch.

"Well, he did."

"Mom, hang on," I said. "You mean, when I was living in the same apartment with you guys, you were, like, embroiled in a love triangle and I had no idea?"

"It was hardly a love triangle," she said. "You didn't see that skank dropping morphine into his mouth."

"Well, what—how . . . what happened?" I stammered.

"She followed him up here after he broke his arm," she said. "Daddy told me everything—he had to, because she was going to tell me." A mischievous grin appeared on her face; I tried to imagine my mother kicking Britney Spears's ass.

"This sucks," I said, collapsing into my futon. "I feel like he cheated on me, too."

"Oh, don't be silly," she said. "*I* was married to him, not you."

"True," I conceded. "But he spent all that time away, and he was with some chick probably not that much older than me," I pointed out. "He was *enjoying* his time away from us. That, to me, is cheating."

"It's over now," she said, pouring half & half into her coffee and slurping away.

Graduation wasn't for another couple of weeks so I returned to Merle Place with my mother. We had to prepare for the memorial service and decide what to do with my father's things, an obligation that called attention to itself every time we opened the refrigerator.

"*Jenn*-n-n-y," my mother whined when she found herself face-to-face with a dozen bottles of applesauce. We took pleasure in trashing them—"I never want to look at applesauce again as long as I live," she muttered—but we decided we couldn't throw away my father's eye-drops, which he'd been taking to control an eye infection for the last eighteen years. He'd transferred herpes simplex to his eye when he was in prison in 1983, and he almost lost his cornea, so he had to take drops for the rest of his life. I remembered how he used to come home from work and lean his head back and blink rapidly as they hit their target. "Not yet," my mother said. In fact, she was never able to throw them away; I was the one who ultimately had to part with them when she died four years later.

Then there was the matter of his wardrobe, which he'd been wearing with few variations since the late seventies. My mother began removing his good suits and laying them on the bed, but she stopped. "Jenny, I can't do this," she said, her face crumpling.

"We don't have to do it now," I said. "We can wait."

"But I want you here to do it with me," she said. "I can't do this alone."

"And you won't be," I said. "I'll be here."

"You promise?" my mother asked me, hanging up his suits. On a whim she reached into the pocket of one of them and produced a small glass vial. It was empty. "What is this?" she said, examining it.

"Hell if I know," I said. "I've never seen anything like that before." She reached deeper into the pocket and pulled out another one.

"Jenny, it looks like a crack vial," she said, holding it up. While I was well versed in marijuana, I'd seen cocaine exactly once.

"Mom, it could be anything," I said.

She closely inspected the suit. "This is the suit he wore to Grandpa's funeral," she said. "And there's no way anyone was doing coke at Grandpa's funeral. Jenny, I bet these belong to Rita," she said, holding up the vials. "Remember? When she came here to 'dry out'?"

"You think she did drugs here?" I asked. "But how would she get drugs on the plane?"

"I don't know," she said, and cased the bedroom. I could almost see the wheels in her head turning. "If she was standing here, maybe," she said, pointing to the space where the bedroom door hit the closet, a design flaw, "and she heard someone coming, she could have stuffed these in his pocket. Yeah, that's what must have happened."

"Really?" I asked. "You think?"

"Well, how else would you explain why there's a crack vial in the suit your father wore to his father's funeral? Nothing else makes sense."

"I can't believe Rita, man," I said. I felt like she'd sullied my father's reputation by infecting his clothing with her drug paraphernalia. My mother didn't tackle my father's suits for a year after that, and when she did I wasn't there. I broke my promise to her, probably because I wasn't ready to revisit his death yet. And as punishment I had to hear about how she lugged the garbage bags to the Salvation Army by herself, and how I didn't really love her. "Right, Ma, I'm just here for the fresh-squeezed orange juice," I joked.

But there was something else I helped her with whenever I came over, a chore that seemed to rise above all else. The scene played out the same way every time: I'd unlock her door and she'd grab my arm, frantic, and lead me into her bedroom. She'd get on her knees and reach under the bed and pull out the suitcase of money left over from the sale of my grandfather's house.

"Count it," she'd command, dumping the bundles of cash on the bed. I'd give her the same wary look each time.

"Really?" I'd ask.

"Really," she'd answer. "I have to know how much I have, if I'm running out." And I'd count it, bill by bill, until I reached a number. "Thirty thousand," I'd announce; later, "twenty-five thousand," then "fifteen thousand." She lived on that money for two years after my father died, just as she predicted she would.

The memorial service drew twenty-five people, mostly my college friends. Aunt Emma and her daughter Linda came, along with a few of my father's cousins I didn't know. A couple of my father's painting buddies showed up, but neither his sister nor his brother was invited. My mother had asked my father as he lay dying if he'd like to see them, but he said no, probably because they hadn't called him in years. Frankie's disappearance was the most baffling, as they hadn't had a falling-out; Frankie just seemed to disappear when my father got sick. Tony, Angela, and Tina didn't fly up, instead sending a bouquet that we set in the center of the table in front, along with his ashes, which had been placed in a dark wooden box from Bombay Company. My mother bought a wrap dress for the occasion, black and sleek, and it marked the beginning of her "mourning in style" phase. Instead of donning a baggy black schmatte like a Sicilian widow, over the course of the next few years she fashioned herself after Juliette Binoche in *Trois Couleurs: Bleu,* the 1993 film in which Binoche loses her daughter and husband in a car crash. Throughout the film Juliette is a picture of neat, low-key casual, and my mother's emulation prompted her to buy a tan leather messenger bag, cut her hair into a short brown bob, and wear smart little blazers over her jeans. I must say, she looked great.

"You like?" she asked, modeling the wrap dress in the dressing room in Macy's.

"Looks great," I said. I, on the other hand, had outgrown all my clothes, so I picked out some sleek black pants in multiple sizes. "These fit," I said as I slid into one pair. I looked at the tag: size 16.

"Jenny—" my mother started.

"Don't say it," I said. I was disgusted at the way I'd neglected myself, but it would be a few months before I cared again. For the entire week before the service I focused on my eulogy and the printed program, which we passed out in lieu of a mass card. My mother and I took some ideas to my college newspaper office and one of the designers created a double-sided white card, the front of which was decorated with a portrait of my father from his prison days, though the location isn't evident. He looks Roman and distinguished, and he's gazing at a point just beyond the camera lens. Next to that my mother placed a stanza from the Song of Solomon—"Set me as a seal on your heart, as a seal on your arm, for love is strong as death, jealousy as cruel as the grave." The back of the card featured the photo of my father that I'd found on that undeveloped roll—with the cigarette cropped out, of course—arranged next to the death notice I'd called in to *The New York Times* the day after his death:

Beloved husband of Eleanor and father of Jennifer, Angela, Tina and Tony. A man who lived his life with vitality and grace, with intelligence, wit and an incredible sense of humor. He had the nobility and strength to turn his life around for his family and create a loving home. A hard worker who gave everything he had to his wife and youngest daughter, he was a cut above, a class act. He will be mourned by his daughter Jennifer for the rest of her days.

I'd originally called in a brief four-line death notice, but I wanted something more personal on the record about my father. At the service, my mother read the W. H. Auden poem popularized by *Four Weddings and a Funeral:* "Stop all the clocks, cut off the telephone, / Prevent the dog from barking with a juicy bone. . . ." My eulogy was next. I took a breath and ignored the constant opening and closing of the massive front door and soldiered on through my strained crying. I told the group how my father had made mistakes, lots of them, but also how he had moved past them, with wisdom and strength of character, "with a grace and elegance unmatched in the most moral of citizens." I recounted how badly he'd wanted to be respectable, and how highly he was regarded by everyone he encountered, from the nuns at my Catholic school to the guys on his painting crew. I told them how in love he was with my mother, and how he'd climbed seventeen stories to give her an ice cream cone when the elevator in her apartment building was busted. I told them how he treated me like a little princess, fixing shoes I didn't even know needed fixing and patiently hanging around the video store for hours, waiting for someone to return *Dirty Dancing* so I could watch it again and again.

"We don't get to choose our own parents," I said in closing. "But if I had been given the choice to pick my father, I would have chosen him without question. And even if I wasn't his daughter, I would still think it a tragedy that John Mascia has died."

I stepped down and reached for a cassette player. "I'm going to play a song for you now," I said to the group, "that my father would play in bars all over the country when he'd go for a drink after a long day of painting buildings. He said it reminded him of the good times he had with his crew. It's called 'Friends in Low Places.'" As Garth Brooks's voice filled the cavernous space I felt bad that there weren't more people there to mourn him. He'd lived to sixty-four—where were his friends? The answer, of course, is that he didn't really have any. It was then I realized the extent to which my father had kept himself in reserve. No wonder his children weren't there—he didn't give, so he didn't get.

My mother had specific plans for the disposal of my father's ashes: She wanted to sprinkle two-thirds at his parents' grave site at Green-Wood Cemetery in Brooklyn, and she planned to keep the other third. But I remembered that he once said he wanted some of his ashes to be placed in the Pacific, so my mother reluctantly set aside a third for that purpose. The portion she planned to keep was poured into a blue and white Crabtree & Evelyn jar and placed in her linen closet, nestled among the blankets and the towels. Whenever I took a shower I made sure to say hi.

Graduation a few days later was a long, sticky affair in Central Park, and in the photos all four of my chins are on display. Afterward Aunt Adele and her daughter and granddaughter took me and my mother to Orsay to make up for my father not being there. "I'm so proud of you for graduating," my mother told me over crème brûlée, "after everything you went through this year."

Though I'd wanted to be an actress for as long as I could remember, I didn't go on one audition. Instead, the day after graduation I donned all black, printed out a résumé, and hit up a dozen restaurants for a server position. I was hired at the first place I interviewed, a seafood restaurant called Lundy's at Fiftieth Street and Broadway. It was the Times Square offshoot of the venerated Sheepshead Bay seafood house where my mother and her family had eaten every Sunday back in the day. But the week I started they were hit with a blistering review from the *Post,* and when I'd been on the job three months the entire restaurant industry took an economic hit, thanks to September 11. That day and its aftermath reopened a barely healed wound for me and my mother. Fortunately, we didn't know anyone who died, but to walk outside and see grief etched on everyone's face was devastating. It meant there was nowhere for us to hide from ours.

It was right after the attacks that I started running. The impulse actually began with a dream I'd had when I was still with Kareem, in which I effortlessly sprinted through the city streets, darting from sunlight to shadow. My dream felt like freedom, which is what I'd desired in my waking life. I found a park on the Upper East Side riverfront called Carl Schurz Park, which featured a pier-shaped deck jutting out over the water, and it stuck in my memory because I thought it peculiar, even Californiaesque. That summer I began walking there in the middle of the night when I was grieving and restless. Once in a while I'd project arias out over the black water, and when my throat was ragged, I'd plant myself on the towering steps nearby and watch the sunrise, which was something to behold: The eastern sky moved through sapphire and turquoise and lime and the rest of the spectrum until each color was represented by a stripe in the sky. Soon I began walking there in sweatpants, then with a Walkman in my ears, and within a month I'd begun alternating walking blocks with jogging blocks. Before I knew it I was running three miles, then four miles, then four and a half miles, then five miles, from my apartment to the Fifty-ninth Street Bridge and back, every night after I got home from work. I blazed a path through the Upper East Side, trailing fat cells in my wake, and I kept it up through shin splints, sprained ankles, blisters, and a strange popping sensation in my right hip.

"Are you sure it's safe to go running after midnight?" my mother asked me. "Yes," I'd assure her, "it's perfectly safe, I'm usually the only person in the park." Of course, I didn't mention that that was because

I was the only person in New York crazy enough to go running as late as 2 A.M. I'd tried running during the day but I felt freer when cloaked by darkness; under the sun I felt the eyes of the world upon me and I couldn't handle the scrutiny. But by running so late it was almost as if I was issuing a challenge: *Go ahead, I dare you to fuck with me. I can outrun you.* I finally took back some control—over my body, my mind, my broken heart. All I had tethering me to the earth was the sound of my breath in the dark, and a ritual: Whenever I reached a certain part of the park I'd whisper, "Love you, Dad." I hadn't been to church in years, but that became my church.

Within six months I had melted down to a size eight, and my progress impressed me even more than it impressed my mother. I didn't tell her I'd started running until the weight began dropping because I knew she'd appoint herself my personal exercise coach and essentially take over my project with her suggestions, and with blistering criticism if my stamina ever failed me. I'd gone from a bit of a lump to running thirty miles a week, but in my vulnerable moments I began to question whether I had, in fact, done it alone. I began to fantasize that maybe I'd somehow inherited my father's considerable physical strength when his spirit departed, and this process had transpired on some cosmic physiological level that living humans can't see or understand. How else could I have acquired this remarkable strength? *Maybe there is something out there,* I thought. *Maybe he can see me.*

Or maybe some things in this life aren't supposed to mean anything at all.

THAT WINTER MY MOTHER and I took a trip to Florida to see Rita and Grandma Vivian. Arline joined us and refereed when my mother and Rita got into a huge fight over her drug use. Rita had a habit of leaving the house every few hours and my mother suspected she was smoking crack, and when she confronted her about it, Rita acted like a typical drug addict in denial.

Meanwhile, Grandma Vivian was still addicted to *Bonanza,* and I noticed she hadn't lost her signature spunk. When I sparked a conversation with her about my mother's teaching career, which ended at age forty-two when she married my father, Grandma griped, "She could have made more of her life. She could have been a principal."

"*Oy*, Ma," my mother snapped, and it was refreshing to see that my mother had issues with her mother, too. Grandma would die that October, on the day before my mother's sixty-eighth birthday. She took it pretty well, but admitted, "Sometimes I still wish my mom was around to kiss my boo-boos, so to speak. I guess you never grow out of that." I shuddered and hoped that wouldn't be me.

The last two days of the trip I spent with Angie, just like I'd promised my father on his deathbed. I still hadn't met two of her three children, and my failure to keep in touch made me feel awkward and slightly ashamed. A year before my father died my mother gave me Krissy's and Joey's wallet-sized school pictures with an admonishment: "You really should get to know your nieces and nephews, Jenny. You know how nice it is to have a good aunt." She was talking about Rita, who had gifted me with diamond earrings and gold hoops and frequent visits. But it was hard to start a correspondence with my nieces and nephews when my father wasn't communicating with their mother. After he died I finally had my entrée.

My mother drove me to Angie's house in Royal Palm Beach, and we were late because we nearly got lost in the Everglades. When we finally turned onto her dusty road it was pitch-black outside, but Angie and Frank waited for us to start dinner. And there we sat around the dinner table, two sides of a shattered family: Nicole was sixteen and tall, somehow blessed with ample breasts but slender hips; Krissy was eleven, hyperactive and prone to fits of giggles, just as I'd been a decade earlier; and Joey was six, rambunctious and a human garbage disposal when it came to sour candy, just like me. "I'm not satisfied till my tongue is burning," I told him.

"Me, too!" he chirped before turning his attention to his toy helicopter. As Angie and the kids cleared the table, tears sprang to my eyes; I couldn't hold them back. "I can't believe he missed all this," I whispered in my mother's ear.

"She okay?" Angie asked her. I could feel my mother nodding as she held me. Angie gently rubbed my back.

"Hey, it's okay," she said. "You're here now." My mother didn't stay that night but I did, enjoying a midnight game of Monopoly with Krissy and her cousin David, who was Cindy's son. Oddly enough, the entire Florida branch of the Mascia family was littered with first and second marriages that produced half-siblings, just like the one that had produced me. I felt like my situation wasn't so odd, then, and this feeling was bolstered by Angie's immediate acceptance of me, her long-lost little sister. Her kids seemed thrilled to have another aunt and welcomed me like they'd last seen me the day before yesterday.

My mother came to get me the next afternoon, and she walked headlong into a quasi–family reunion, complete with Tina and Cindy's families, though I'd come to learn that these gatherings were commonplace. Even Marie, my father's first wife, was there, and I finally got to see the inspiration for my father's tattoos up close: She was tan as a deer, with shoulder-length white hair and a welcoming smile—the same one my father had, actually. In fact, her laid-back manner reminded me of a side of my father's personality, the one that was affable and soft-spoken and a product of the old neighborhood. She was a semiretired nurse who'd taken up painting in recent years, and her creations, which adorned the walls of Angie's one-story house, were quite good. "Just like Daddy," I whispered to my mother, struck by the coincidence.

Though my mother and I said our goodbyes that night, I'd return a dozen times over the next several years, joining the gang on camping trips and eighteenth-birthday celebrations, and laser hair removal appointments with my sister Tina and her strong-willed daughter Veronica, now fifteen. A recovering tomboy with an almond tan and naturally white-blond hair, Veronica was happiest spending her days on fishing boats and chasing after golden retrievers, and I envied her fully formed sense of self, something I desperately could have used at fifteen.

After a camping trip late that summer I spent a few days at Tina's house in Fort Pierce, which featured less activity than Angie's but proved more conducive to probing conversation. The first thing I noticed when I walked in was the card my mother and I had created for the memorial service taped up on one of Tina's kitchen cupboards. "Wow," I said, pointing to it.

"Yeah, it reminds me of him. This way I see his face every day," she said with tears in her eyes. Tina had appointed herself the family historian, and as such she had amassed photo albums and letters sent between family members over the years, some not even addressed to her. I opened one of her albums filled with photos, many of them Polaroids, taken right before I was born.

"A lot of people are doing things they're not supposed to be doing in these pictures," she said with a smirk, and I spotted a birthday cake adorned with a gigantic marijuana leaf. It was rumored that Tina enjoyed the occasional joint, and even though we had that in common I didn't dare mention it. I flipped through the years and there were my parents, looking young and happy, and *stoned*.

"Tina, did my mom smoke pot?" I asked, making a mental note to rake my mother over the coals for her hypocrisy.

"Miss Ellie did enjoy the occasional joint," she said, "but it was probably because she was always around it, because Dad smoked so much."

"My dad—I mean, Dad smoked a lot?" I felt embarrassed for my slip; I had to remember that he was Tina's father long before he was mine.

"Oh, yeah," she said. "Everyone did then." The photos of my parents were few and far between, which was an accurate representation of their appearance in Tina, Angie, and Tony's lives.

"Tina, when are these from?" I asked when I reached a set of photos depicting my father in what looked like the early 1980s hurling snowballs at his brother, sister, and cousins.

"Oh, that was Grandma's funeral," she said, and on the next page was a photo of Tina with Grandma Helen right before she died; Tina's eyes are red and full of tears. I looked at the pictures of my father from that day and recognized the black mustache, later shaved off; the mole on his cheek that he later removed because it turned out to be cancerous; his salt-and-pepper hair before the white had taken over; and his smile, which was all teeth and took over his face without betraying the deep crow's feet he'd go on to develop. It was too much—I ran into the bathroom and locked the door so I could weep in peace. At Tina's house I would come to feel my father's presence more acutely than anywhere else—other than on Merle Place—and whenever I returned I went back to those photo albums so I could see another side of my father, the side his older children had glimpsed. And then there were the letters.

"He wrote these to Tony when he was away," she said, and the first letter she handed me brought back a flood of memories: drawings of Snoopy and Linus, just like the cards he'd sent me from behind bars when I was five.

"Hi Tony," the first typewritten card read, "I send you pictures of a . . ." and on the inside were precise renderings of a squirrel, a dog, a billy goat, and finally, a "Dad," and here he'd inserted a photo of himself from the early seventies, a profile shot most likely taken in prison. I turned to her with tears spilling down my cheeks.

"I had no idea they were ever close," I sobbed.

"Oh, they weren't really," she said. "Dad tried for a while, but it didn't really work out. At first my stepfather resented Dad so much that he destroyed every picture we had of him. When he left, Dad reached out to Tony, who was about ten. My mother was always worried that Dad would disappoint Tony, so she was apprehensive about letting him write, and later, letting him visit."

"Disappoint?" I asked, already skimming the second letter in the pile.

"He'd come around and then fall out of touch," she explained, "and he had a habit of doing that with everyone and Mom didn't want Tony to get hurt. In the end, of course, he did."

"Oh, Tina," I sighed, and read the second letter, also typewritten: " 'I received your letter and I was very happy to hear from you. I have heard a lot about you from your Nanny, and I think she is so impressed with you because of all your little friends.' Little friends?" I asked.

"Oh, Tony was really into snakes and bugs and things," she said.

"Oh," I said, and read on.

Your poor Nanny comes close to having a heart attack every time you show her a bug or a snake, but the truth is, she tells me you're a fine boy. She thinks you look a lot like me when I was your age, and judging from your pictures, I do see a little of me in you. This isn't the worst thing that could happen, as I don't think I am that ugly. Well, maybe a little ugly. Anyway protect your nose with your life. As you can see from my picture, if I followed my nose I would walk in circles.

He'd broken it three times—probably, I now realized, in prison.

Speaking of your "Little Friends," I spent a half hour in the library trying to see what the snakes you caught look like. I saw

the picture of the Banded water snake, but I could not find pictures of
the Glass snake. I looked at so many snakes that I will probably have
nightmares tonight.

I had to put the letter down because I was crying so hard. "Aw, what
is it, Jenny?" Tina asked with a look that told me she already knew.

"Just imagining him in some prison library," I wept, "looking up
snakes so he could impress his son, who he's never even seen—my
god, it's so painful to read this. His heart must have been breaking,
Tina." I felt a searing pain in my chest, right above my heart, and I
read a little more about turtles and fishing—how he'd gone with Tina
when she was five or six, which was a year before the murder—until I
got to the last paragraph, which sent me running into the bathroom
again to sob in peace:

> *Dad would like to touch you and show his love for you, but under*
> *these circumstances this is not possible. But, I would like to be your*
> *father in more than name only, so though I can't take you by the hand*
> *and take you to stores to buy things, I ask you to do your own shop-*
> *ping until your Dad can make the scene with you.*
>
> *Your Nanny is coming to Florida in June, so be sure to give her a nice*
> *big hug as a present, and tell her I told you to give it to her. She will just*
> *love this. I am going to tell her to take a lot of pictures of all of you, so*
> *make sure you get in front of the camera whenever Nanny tells you to*
> *take a picture. This is the only way I can see how big my boy is getting.*
>
> *Well Son, I guess that's it for now. Take care of yourself, and be a*
> *good boy. I will write again soon.*
>
> *Love you,*
> *Dad*

P.S. *You have no idea how much I enjoyed using the word "Son."*

> *Love again*
> *John Mascia #10332*

When I emerged from the bathroom I sat back down on a bar
stool in her kitchen and shook my head. "What happened?" I asked.

"Was it because we went on the lam? That just ended any opportunity for a relationship? I mean, Tony came to California a few times, and I remember they bonded over their shared love of guns." As soon as I said it I realized how perverse it sounded, that a killer should have a fascination with guns, but I suppose it made sense.

"We were all really surprised when you guys skipped town," she said. "One day you were here, and then one day Angie called me and asked me what I knew about Dad's arrest, and I was like, 'What arrest?' And I went to your house in Plantation but no one answered the door. I peeked in the window and everything was gone. My mom suggested I check the newspaper, so I drove to the *Sun-Sentinel* and went through some of their back copies, and there it was."

"And that was it?" I asked, blowing my nose and reaching for a Diet Coke. "You didn't hear from us until 'eighty-three?"

"Actually, he called me from the road," she said, "and he seemed to know so much about my life. It was really strange—he'd ask me questions about things he couldn't possibly have known about."

"Yeah?" I asked, touched that at least he hadn't let one of his children drift away.

"Yeah, it was uncanny. I always thought he had people looking after me," she said. "You know, wiseguys." Later, when I told my mother that, she was shocked. "Really? He really did that? I had no idea. Well, she was his oldest daughter," she reasoned, but the tone of her voice said, *"What an idiot. He could have jeopardized everything."*

"Do you remember when he was arrested for the murder, in 1963?" I asked Tina.

"No," she said, "because he wasn't arrested at the house. I kept getting letters from him, though, saying how he couldn't get home because there was a hurricane coming, or his car broke down, or this or that. I wish I'd kept those. And I remember my mother taking me out to the causeway on Seventy-ninth Street, and I asked my mom, 'Is my dad dead or in jail?' And she had to tell me. Then she took me to Burger King for a chocolate milkshake, and I even told the cashier lady, 'My daddy's in jail,' and I started crying. I remember sending him little presents, like stationery—I mean, what else do you give a guy in jail?" I laughed. "Then there was the *PT-109* coconut."

"What's the *PT-109* coconut?" I asked.

"*PT-109* was a movie about how John Kennedy's boat got shot up during World War II," Tina explained. "He ended up on an island, and all his men were starving and sick, and he comes across these natives and writes a message on a coconut so they can get the word out that they need rescuing. Since my stepfather frowned upon any mention of Johnny, I carved 'I miss you and I love you Daddy' on a coconut, and Nanny and Grandpa Frank brought it up to the jail."

"He actually received this coconut?" I asked, wishing I could have seen his reaction, though I'm not sure he would have understood the gesture's reference—the movie was released a few weeks after he murdered Joseph Vitale.

"Yep, I'm pretty sure he did. And whenever I see that movie now, it reminds me of my childhood. But after that I didn't really ask my mom about Dad because I was so afraid it would upset her. Like, she was handling so much at once that I didn't want to remind her of her husband, the murderer."

"God, Tina," I said, my tears drying but capable of being restarted at a moment's notice. "You were, what, six?"

"Yep," she said. "Almost seven."

"I was six, too," I said. "Well, almost six." It had been May, in 1983, when he was taken from my mother and me and shipped to New York, and it was also in May, exactly twenty years before that, when he'd been taken from Tina and shipped to New York. I was lucky— I got him back in five months. Tina never really got him back— a child's nightmare come true.

"Did he ever tell you to keep your boogers in a box?" Tina asked me out of the blue.

I snorted. "No, but he did tell me that the oceans were formed from dinosaur pee," I said. I picked up a different album, and the first set of pictures showed the extended family arranged on the beach, with everyone save the newborns holding up a sign with a different letter or number that spelled out "Summer Vacation 1990." My father isn't holding up a letter; he wasn't there. All told, he appears in no more than a half a dozen pictures, a guest star in the family he started. Marie got all the vacations with their spanking-new grandchildren, and he got nothing. Rather, he chose nothing.

On one of my later trips I handed Tina the album with "My Family" embroidered on the front. "It really belongs to you," I admitted. "In a way, it's like your baby book. It doesn't feel right keeping it."

"Are you sure, Jenny?" she asked me.

"Yes, please take it," I replied. I'd swiped it without telling my mother, but I decided then and there that perhaps some decisions regarding my father's memory were up to me, and me alone.

CHAPTER 12

July 2004

. . .

I SPENT THE NEXT FOUR YEARS MIRED IN A QUARTER-LIFE CRISIS seemingly without end. I waited tables and lamented my lack of direction—acting was a child's dream, and I was no longer a child. But I had found nothing to replace it, so I coasted, traveling a bit and making repeat visits to Florida to see my family. In 2004 I joined the whole gang on a Caribbean cruise: Angie, Frank, Nicole, Krissy, and Joey; Tina, Bill, and Veronica; and Marie. I was nervous around Marie, unsure of what she really thought of my father, and of my mother for being married to him. He had deep-sixed his relationship with their kids, and while I still loved him I didn't want to be associated with such neglect, and I didn't want my sisters to think I excused him for it. But Marie, with her easygoing sandpapery voice and reflexive smile, was never anything but nice to me. I couldn't shake the way she reminded me of my father whenever her face was in repose. My mother would never forgive me for thinking it, but I wondered whether he and Marie were more suited to each other than he and my mother were. Marie and my father were cut from the same Bay Ridge cloth, easygoing and uncomplicated in manner, while my mother was layered, sophisticated, complex, dramatic. I wondered whether my father's divorce from Marie went down the way my mother described it, and whether her second husband really did leave because my father wrote from prison that he'd kill him if he continued to terrorize his kids. I wondered many things I didn't have the nerve to ask about.

But I finally did gather the nerve to ask about one thing. Just before I was scheduled to fly home after the cruise, I accompanied Angie as she drove Krissy to her high school, where she was getting bused off to cheerleading camp. As Krissy hauled her bag and pillow over her shoulder and sleepily boarded her bus, Angie's eyes welled with tears. She caught herself and turned to me and laughed, her doe eyes shining.

"Those were the days," I said, remembering my own time at cheerleading camp, which I'd also attended with a mouthful of metal.

"Yeah, god, she's growin' up so fast," Angie said, pulling out of the parking lot and heading toward the house. I wanted to tell Angie how much I admired her life, and the way she had raised her children, given the shit she had to go through as a teenager. But I didn't. Instead we found ourselves talking about Dad. It was funny—all the brothers and sisters I had begged my mother for when I was growing up were alive, just living in another state. My wish had been fulfilled after all.

"I know," I said, "I remember when Nicole was a baby, and you guys brought her out to California. Now look at her—she's old enough to vote! Dad really missed out."

"Yeah, but I don't let it bother me anymore," she said. "It used to really bother me, that he didn't come around more, but I got over it, ya know?"

I didn't know what to say. It wasn't fair that I'd gotten to be an entrenched part of his life and they hadn't, and I wanted to reassure her that it wasn't personal. If I was Marie's daughter I would have experienced the same neglect, I was sure of it.

"He was never going to be what I wanted him to be," she continued. "I knew we were never going to have the relationship he had with you, so I stopped looking for a father." She shrugged and looked at me, more tears in her eyes.

"He fucked up," I said, at a loss. There was something I'd always wanted to discuss with her, and I figured we had reached a candid, all-bets-are-off kind of moment. "I found your letter," I said. "The one you wrote to Dad after he didn't show up at Tony's wedding. I cried my eyes out when I read the part about his chair being empty all night, and how you expected him to walk in. It just broke my heart. My mother and I were very angry at him for that, I wanted you to know."

She nodded. "Yeah, Tony was upset at that, but Carrie was *really* angry. Actually, when they came to see Dad in the hospital, Carrie had it in her head that she was going to tell Dad off, but then she saw how weak and sick he was and they decided not to say anything." Wow, I wondered what my mother was going to say when I told her that. Angie must have read my mind: "Don't tell your mom," she added.

"I don't blame Carrie for being mad," I said. "*I* was mad. I just don't get why he dropped the ball so badly. He could have remained close with you guys after he got paroled, after we'd been on the lam." It was the first time I'd acknowledged our secret history in front of Angie, which had only been a secret as far as I was concerned. I felt like I'd finally been brought up to speed, albeit a decade or two late.

"It's funny, cuz we'd be kinda close, then I wouldn't hear from him for years," she said. "He was just like that—he'd fade away."

I wondered what it was like to have grown up without a father's love. As dysfunctional as my parents were, as much as we yelled at each other, I couldn't imagine not having him in my life. If he had lived until I'd reached Angie's age, would he have drifted from me, too?

"I remember once, he came home after a trip to Florida," I recalled. "I was ten or eleven, and he kept playing this song over and over again because it reminded him of Nicole and Veronica. It was 'Two Hearts' by Phil Collins. I guess he'd been playing around with them and dancing to this song. I was almost jealous," I admitted. "He seemed to really dote on them."

"Yeah, but then where did he go?" she said. "When Krissy started asking questions about her other grandfather, I didn't know what to tell her—like, who is he? Why isn't he around? I asked him to please write, call, anything, get to know her."

Her words made me angry. Here I was, upset that he'd never know the grandchildren I would someday provide, and he hadn't even paid attention to the ones he already had. None of his six grandchildren had been born after his death. He had no excuse not to get to know them. When Angie had packed her family into their camper and driven up to New York only to stay with Uncle Frankie and Paulette instead of us, it was glaringly obvious just how far their relationship had veered off track. His estrangement had a ripple effect on those only remotely involved, like me. I had nieces and nephews I had never met, until he died and *I* sought a relationship with them. Didn't he think of me, of my desire for family? I was an only child, and because of him I nearly stayed that way.

"I don't know what happened, I wish I could tell you," I said mournfully. "Maybe he felt guilty because he killed someone and felt he wasn't worthy of you guys, or maybe he felt bad that your step-father was such a monster. Maybe once you began to grow distant he figured the relationship was too far gone to resurrect. Maybe it was just easier for him to do nothing. I don't know."

"Yeah, well, it's over now," she said. "I feel bad for you, though, because you had him and then lost him. I feel bad for your mom, too. She fought for him, hard."

"It's okay," I said, my automatic response. "I'm fine." We'd pulled into her driveway a few moments before and sat there, idling under the light over the garage door. After a few moments I decided to go for broke. "Angie?" I asked.

"Yeah?"

"Did you ever get the feeling that something happened between Dad and Rita? Because ever since I was a kid, I kinda had this feeling that something did."

As soon as it came out of my mouth I realized I'd never said it aloud. I hadn't even let it evolve into a fully formed thought until that moment; it had lived for years as a feeling, unarticulated. Angie looked down at the steering wheel and said nothing for a long moment, but I could tell what the verdict would be by studying her face.

"Ugh," she finally said. "I don't want to hurt your mom."

It was confirmation. I started crying.

"Jenny," she said, and started crying, too. "It's just something we all kind of suspected, you know, because he came here so much, and they were . . . in business together. Oh, Jenny, don't cry."

"How could they do that to her?" I asked, snot threatening to drip into my mouth. "I knew it! I knew it! I always knew it. For some rea-son, it's like I always knew, I don't know how. Wait—what do you mean, they were *in business* together?"

"Oh, boy," Angie said, rubbing her nose. She breathed in and out a couple of times and stared out the window. "I don't want your mom to think I'm filling your head with this stuff, I love your mom so much—"

"No, Angie, really, it's okay," I said, sitting up straight and damming my tears through sheer force of will. "You can tell me. I'm fine. Tell me what happened. You mean like the OxyContin they sold together when Dad was sick?"

"Well, yeah, like that," she said. "I didn't know if your mom knew about it, which is why I don't want to say anything that she wouldn't want you to know."

"Oh, Angie, I know everything," I said. "She has such a big mouth. I know he killed someone, I know he was in rehab, I know he cheated on my mom with that waitress. I know he dealt drugs in Miami before we went on the lam." I felt the need to demonstrate that my mother's mouth was so big that this information might come flying out of it next week even without Angie tipping me off.

"He and Rita were dealing cocaine," she revealed. "He'd come

My favorite aunt and my father, Christmas 1987.

here and they'd package it up and sell it." This didn't surprise me. "This one time, though, he disappeared with Rita for a couple days, and he took my car. While he was gone I was in his room cleaning and I found all this stuff under the bed, brown wrapping paper and packing stuff, like for shipping. My husband came in and saw it and had a fit, like, 'That's it, he's leaving!' And I begged him, 'Please, don't kick Johnny out,' because he visited so rarely and I finally had a chance to spend time with him."

My heart heaved in sympathy. Angie wanted a father so badly she was willing to accept the absentee, drug-dealing version. I started crying again, I couldn't help it. How could they do this to my mother? She had done so much to keep him alive! To keep him out of jail! And how could Rita have carried on a normal relationship with my mother after screwing her husband?

"Oh, Jenny," Angie said, shaking her head and staring out the window.

"No," I said, nodding, "I'm fine. I just can't believe they would do this to her! I loved Rita, I looked up to her, I wanted to *be* her, and probably so did my mother. And now she can't even confront him and yell at him because he's *dead*."

"Jenny, please don't tell her," she begged. "Besides, we don't know for sure, we only suspected." I brightened a bit.

"What else made you suspect?" I asked, ready to weigh the evidence myself.

"Well, they came to Tina's house once, just the two of them, and they were laughing, and the way they were looking at each other, they were just really playful with each other, and Tina and I looked at each other, like, 'I wonder what's going on *there*?'"

"You never asked him?" How was I not going to tell my mother this? But how *could* I? To whom, besides Rita, could she direct her anger? Would she regret the last twenty-five years of her life if I opened my mouth? With one sentence, I had the power to destroy her.

"No, we just always had a feeling," she said. "Like you did."

Rita had visited at least a dozen times when I was growing up. How could they have kept it a secret? How could my mother not suspect? It seemed preposterous that his daughters could pick up on his sexual tension with Rita but my mother couldn't. I wanted to go back to believing it hadn't really happened, and without a smoking gun, it almost felt like I could.

When I got back to New York I spent a few days at my mother's apartment in Staten Island and successfully pushed my conversation with Angie out of my mind. I plugged my new camera into the computer—an Olympus digital my mother had bought me for Christmas—and showed her my photos from the trip, jabbering on about how the water in Grand Cayman was as blue as 2000 Flushes, the pointlessness of cruises in general, and the staggering amount of room charges I'd been saddled with—$600, on her credit card, incidentally, which she'd given me to use on an emergency basis.

"Goddammit, Jenny!" she cursed. "I just got credit again and now it's gonna be shot to shit."

"Ma, don't worry," I said. "I'll pay you back, you know I will."

"Yeah?" she shot back. "With what job?" She had me there. I'd been fired from my last waitressing job that winter and my unemployment benefits were about to dry up, signaling an end to my leisurely holiday from toil.

"I'll get a job," I said. "I'm going to look next week." And I did, when we met after her therapy session on Fifty-seventh Street, right next door to Carnegie Hall. As we crossed the avenue I noticed a spacious restaurant with floor-to-ceiling windows on the corner. I walked in, and while my mother waited, I interviewed with the general manager and was hired on the spot. My experience had spoken volumes, which made me profoundly sad—I did not want to be a professional waiter. Plus, I was dismayed when I saw what I would be wearing, as servers passed by in tuxedo pants, bow ties, and vests with enormous airplanes ironed on the back. I swore to myself that this would be my last waitressing gig, even if I had no idea what could possibly take its place.

My colleagues at the Redeye Grill were your typical actor/student/career waiter mix. Whenever any of them asked me what my aspirations were I muttered "actress" and slunk away, ashamed that I had done nothing to further the only goal I'd ever really had. Meanwhile, my passion for current events was coming to a boil, thanks to my disenchantment with the Bush administration, and I felt increasingly restless spending eight hours a day among people who didn't place much value on the news. So I'd fold napkins while quietly reading my copy of the *Times* and remind myself that there was a world outside this one, and that one day I would join it.

"That Kristof is a genius, isn't he?" said a voice from behind me as I sat at the back of the dining room between shifts, poking at my pasta. He was dark and lanky, with thin, perfectly groomed black hair, searching brown eyes, and a peanut-shaped face.

"Who?" I asked.

"Nicholas Kristof. Don't tell me you don't read him?" His accent was Bengali with a distinctive British tinge. He was wearing a red vest, which meant he was a food runner. I'd seen him around the restaurant, effortlessly lifting hulking trays of food with just the tips of his long, slim fingers.

"No," I was sorry to report, "I read Maureen Dowd and Thomas Friedman, mostly." He gently shook his head back and forth, clicking his tongue and feigning disappointment.

"You're really missing out," he said, pulling out the chair next to me and taking a seat at the table. "This man is amazing. I've been following his career since before he became a columnist. He and his wife won a Pulitzer for their reporting from Tiananmen Square. Did you know that last year he bought two Cambodian prostitutes their freedom and gave them money to start a new life? He's going to win a Pulitzer this year, mark my words."

"What's your name?" I asked. "Sorry, I've had to remember so many this week."

He held out his hand. "Tutul," he said. *Too-tool.*

"Jennifer," I said, and shook it. "So you read the *Times*?"

"Every day," he said. "Do you read Somini Sengupta? She writes from India and Pakistan, and she's brilliant. She will be a columnist one day, you just watch. I predicted Kristof would be a columnist one day, too. I'm usually right about these things." Thus commenced an intellectual alliance bursting with discourse and debate about world affairs that was sweeping in its scope and would go on to change the course of my life. Whenever we worked together we would parse the issues of the day from hot spots around the world while the restaurant whirred around us. The Orange Revolution: covered. The Oil for Food scandal? Check. FARC, Chechnya, Musharraf and Arafat: analyzed, dissected, and digested. Co-workers began to notice our mutual admiration society, as I was the only waitress who hung around the kitchen killing time with the food runners. The kitchen boasted a decent-sized television, oddly enough—the line cooks depended on the bleached blondes of Telemundo to get them through each steamy, exhausting shift—and the two of us spent most of the fall glued to the presidential debates. It seemed like we were the only people in the place who cared.

"What do you want to do with all this?" I asked him during a slow dinner shift, referring to his vast stores of knowledge. Surely he didn't want to be a food runner much longer; he was already thirty-four.

"I am going to be a professor," he declared. "I'm going to sharpen and challenge young minds." To that end, he was taking graduate courses at City College. "And what about you?" he asked.

I hesitated; what *did* I want to do? Wait tables and talk politics all day long? That sounded nice, but I needed to be going somewhere. I certainly wasn't going to turn thirty with a check presenter in my pocket and an apron tied around my waist. He recognized my ambivalence.

"I think you should go to Columbia School of Journalism," he said.

"Eh, I always thought I was done with school," I said.

"Oh, no," he said. "You really should consider it."

"Well," I said, my mind slowly embracing the concept, "I used to edit the arts section of my college paper. But I never thought I'd make a career out of writing. How do you know I'd be a good reporter? You've never seen my stuff."

"I can tell just by reading your emails," he said. "You've got what it takes. Consider it."

More school? More loans? I hadn't even paid off my loans from Hunter, and I only owed ten grand. But perhaps grad school would save me, put me on a track that led to something. And unlike law or med school, journalism school didn't sound like it involved memorizing hundreds of pages from dusty tomes. By the time I'd cashed out that evening I was certain Tutul was right. I'd already subconsciously absorbed the writing styles of the journalists I admired, so why not apply that rudimentary education toward an actual career? I was tired of breathing the rancid air in my claustrophobic little world populated with lobster forks and Bordeaux glasses. I longed to care about someone else for a change. There were people suffering in silence, screwed by poverty and their governments, and I could write about them. I could use my talent for good, instead of auditioning until I was forty and praying for a husband to rescue me from terminal uncertainty. My future had chosen me, and Tutul had given it a voice.

"Mom," I said when I called my mother during my walk home that evening, "Guess what I decided? I'm going to go to Columbia School of Journalism and become a reporter."

"Really?" she said. "But Jenny, are you sure you want to give up acting? You used to make your father cry whenever you were onstage."

"Ma!" I protested. "That's not real! This is!"

The application was due in eleven days; I emailed it in ten. Now all I had to do was wait.

"HEY, MA?" I SQUEAKED. It was chilly, so we were sitting in her car where we waited for the express bus that would take me to work. She had finally ditched the beat-up Subaru and charged a 1998 Honda Accord on her Discover card; the afternoon she came back from the used car dealership she proudly showed off the detachable radio she didn't even know how to detach.

"Ye-*es*?" she replied in her loopy singsong. I'd wanted to broach the topic many times, but we'd been discussing Rita and now I couldn't chase it out of my mind. My mother had just vowed never to speak to her youngest sister again—"I get on the phone and all she wants to talk about is Brad Pitt and Angelina Jolie! Who cares why he left Jennifer Aniston? Someone should tell her that there's other news in this world"—and if that was truly the case, then there was something I needed to know.

"Ever since I was a kid," I began, "I've always thought—and I don't know why or how or when this started—but I've always kind of suspected that, maybe, um, did you ever get the feeling that . . . somethinghappenedbetweenDaddyandRita?"

She stared straight ahead, seemingly stuck in a never-ending pause. She turned to me, her eyes flat. "Why would you say that?" she asked slowly, carefully.

I shrugged. "Just something I've always felt," I said. "And, well, I brought it up with Angie, you know, to see if she also felt that."

"And what did your sister have to say?" she asked in measured tones. *Your sister.*

"Well, she said that she and Tina always kind of suspected, because he took so many trips down there, and they were so close when they were together, you know, they acted very familiar with each other." I felt like I was ganging up on her. I didn't want her to feel cornered, but how else was this information supposed to make her feel? I was selfish to bring it up, I knew it, but I had to know. Perhaps she already knew and had forgiven Rita, though that seemed unlikely. If I truly knew my mother, there was only so much she was willing to forgive.

"Did they?" she said. "Is that what she said?"

"Mom, I basically forced it out of her," I explained. "She didn't want to tell me. She loves you so much. She has no proof. It's just that I was so certain, dating from childhood, that I was right."

She inhaled resolutely, her jaw clenched. "The only thing your father and Rita ever did was sell drugs together," she said. "They were in business together. I knew all about it, so your sisters don't really know the whole story."

So there was more she hadn't told me about my father. "Angie mentioned that, about the drugs," I said. "She said that Daddy would come down to Florida and prepare packages with Rita and ship them off, or whatever."

"That's all that was happening," she said, her lips pursing. She seemed lobotomized, and as she spoke her eyes robotically moved from me, to the windshield, and back.

"So, wait, Daddy sold cocaine?" I asked. My mother sighed; this was clearly another subject she had never wanted broached.

"When we were struggling in California—do you remember all those times we went bankrupt?" she started.

"Yes, busting out the credit cards. *That* was fun," I said sarcastically.

"Yes, busting out the credit cards. Well, we'd just lost the contract at Chapman, and your father was panicking. You were in private school, and that was expensive, not to mention the dance lessons and the cheerleading and the clothes and—"

"I get it," I snapped.

"We were living way above our means," she said. "I was guilty of it, too. Your father once pulled me aside and told me he was going to divorce me unless I got a job and contributed, because he was breaking his back cleaning carpets."

I'd known he and my mother split when he was drinking, but I didn't know about this. "When was this?" I asked. "Before he went to rehab?"

"Yeah, maybe, 'eighty-six or 'eighty-seven," she replied. "Right after we lost Chapman. And he called Rita and she helped us. She helped us by giving him drugs to sell. We made quite a lot of money that way and we lived on it for a long time. And the reason he went to rehab was because he started taking more than he was selling."

"What do you mean?" I said, shocked. "I remember emptying the liquor bottles into Daddy's sink."

"Yes, well, he had a drinking problem, too," she said. "But he did coke because it enabled him to drink more."

How was that possible? The one time I'd chased coke with rum I'd nearly vomited an internal organ. "So that was the real reason he went to rehab?" I asked. No wonder he was able to drink after he got out. "And Rita became addicted as well." I began putting it together. Couldn't my mother see the images in my mind, of Rita and my father doing coke and fucking like rabbits?

"Yes, Jenny, don't you remember breaking up that fight between us?" she asked. "Remember? He took the box of bills and threw it up at the ceiling? And you came downstairs and told us to shut up? I'll never forget that. Oh, we were so embarrassed. He was acting that way with his big fucking mouth because of the coke."

I remembered that night. He kept telling her to "Shut up!" and I couldn't stand it. I knew my mother was more than capable of standing up to him with her own sizable mouth, and she never cowered before him, but still.

"What eventually sent him running to rehab was this one night when he ran out of coke and could only get his hands on crystal meth," she continued. "He snorted it and went on to hallucinate for something like eight hours. He scared the absolute shit out of himself."

"Christ," I said.

"Angie had a problem with coke at one point, too," my mother revealed. "When she was young. And your father did nothing to help the situation—and I was very mad at this—because he did it right along with her. With Tina, too."

"He did drugs with his kids?" I asked, feeling icky.

"Yes, and it got so bad that at one point Angie brought him to her therapist, and the therapist told him, 'You cannot do drugs with your children.'"

"Um, I would assume that's Parenting 101," I said, still reeling.

"Well, your father didn't raise them, Jenny," she said in his defense. "They didn't have that bond. He would never have done that with you—he *didn't* do that with you. But I never understood how he could have done that with them. There are some lines you just do not cross. That's one of them."

"When was this, when he got out of jail? Before we went on . . . *the lam*?" I couldn't get over that one.

"Yeah, around then," she said. "It was what a lot of people did then, and in Miami, especially."

"Did you?" I asked. My mother had a glass of wine maybe once every six months.

"No," she said unequivocally. "Maybe a little hit of a joint every once in a while, but no."

"Well, thank god he went to rehab," I said.

"Yes," she said, staring off into space.

"So Rita and Daddy were just in business together, nothing more?" I asked. "You're sure?"

"There is no way he would do that to me, Jenny, and my sister wouldn't, either. She's helped us so much, whenever we needed it. I may get angry with her, but she's my *schvesta*. Whatever Tina and Angie told you, they misinterpreted what was going on between Rita and Daddy. It was just business, and I knew all about it."

"And you're sure that guy in the sixties was the only guy he ever killed?" I asked. I threw that in once every couple of years, just to keep her on her toes.

"I'm sure," she said.

"You promise?"

"I promise."

And that was that.

CHAPTER 13

December 2004

. . .

"JENNY, SHUT UP. THEY FOUND SOMETHING."

I was seated on the couch in my living room, glued to coverage of the recent tsunami in an effort to deflect the argument she was having with me, an argument that came to a full stop with these six words. She'd just had a small carcinoma removed from her nose and her pre-op lung X-ray picked up something that shouldn't have been there.

I don't know why I was surprised. My mother and father smoked for fifty years, and for half of that they treated each other to secondhand doses of each other's smoke on top of their own. It seemed silly to assume my mother was exempt from developing lung cancer—maybe I figured her ordeal with my father somehow made her immune? Perhaps I subconsciously credited my father's demise with faulty genetics: His parents had both died of cancer, and in the decade after his death, lung cancer would go on to claim his brother and his sister. I believed my mother would be around for as long as her mother had been, dying of that old saw "natural causes" at the age of ninety-five.

But that wasn't to be. "They" had found "something," and she didn't have to elaborate—I knew exactly what she meant. Two years of Oncology Studies at Memorial Sloan-Kettering University had taught us that "something" meant "cancer" and that "they" meant the white coats. At first I thought she was being overly dramatic, because if anything was seriously wrong, wouldn't she have told me about it the moment she got off the phone with her doctor, voice trembling and hands shaking?

"So I got a referral for a doctor at Mount Sinai," she told me, "and I need you to go with me. I'm getting more X-rays so they can figure out what this is." She sounded levelheaded. Sane. A much different reaction from the one that followed Dr. A.'s oddly cheerful "Your husband has cancer!" phone call from five years earlier.

"It'll be fine, I'm sure," I managed.

Later that week we entered the East Ninety-eighth Street office of Dr. T., internal medicine and pulmonary disease specialist. Dr. T. was in his late seventies, with a craggy, wizened face and raspy voice. The preliminaries were mundane—consultation ("I stopped smoking after my first heart attack eight years ago," "My husband died of stage IV non-small-cell adenocarcinoma in 2001"), checkup ("Okay, Eleanor, breathe in, hold it, okay, now breathe out"), X-rays, and the verdict.

"Jennifer, may I speak with you for a moment, please?" Dr. T. asked from the open door of his exam room.

"Me?" I asked. I followed him into another exam room bathed in fluorescent light. He waited until I was inside before shutting the door behind us. He turned toward me. His face was solemn.

"This is very bad, I'm afraid," he said. "I just wanted someone in her family to know."

It was the same feeling I'd had when the doctors at St. Vincent's estimated that my father had three to six months to live: My center of gravity sank like a stone, past my stomach, and headed straight for the floor.

"What are you saying?" I asked, but I couldn't hear myself speak. This instant reversal of fortune had sent the blood flooding into my ears, blocking out anything but the thumping of my heart. He pointed to the X-ray hanging on the wall behind him and flipped on the backlight so I could see the spots. There were small masses on one of her lungs and some more splattered throughout her thoracic cavity. "At this point, I would characterize the progression as stage IIB-IIIA," he gravely informed me. "I need a biopsy to be sure that it's cancer, but even without one, I'm pretty certain. I mean, I don't really need a biopsy to see what this is."

I knew enough about cancer staging to understand that my mother's condition straddled the border between treatable and terminal cancer. "Um, her heart . . . she has a heart condition. How—I mean, can she survive chemotherapy?" I stammered. "My uncle Joey, he had lung cancer, and all the chemo and radiation, it—heart attack, he died, very suddenly—" I leaned back against the counter that held oversized glass jars of swabs and tongue depressors and slowly slid to the floor.

"You don't understand," I said, trying to reason with this man who really had very little power over how sick my mother suddenly was. "I only have one parent left. This can't happen to me again. She's all I have! You must understand. *This can't be happening to me again.*"

He obviously hadn't expected this kind of reaction. His face changed, became softer. "Um, listen, I report to a cardiothoracic board with oncologists and surgeons, and I'm sure I could recommend her case for treatment, perhaps even surgery . . ." It was no use. He looked at me, bewildered: My legs had given out from under me and my heart hammered a lethal drumbeat on the left side of my chest. My face was drenched with tears, and the sudden migration of eyeliner and mascara down my cheeks was not something I could easily explain to my mother.

"Listen," he said, "I have to go into the office now and talk to her. It's just outside the exam room. Take a few minutes to compose yourself." He walked out and closed the door behind him.

I shuffled into the bathroom and washed my face. I caught my reflection in the mirror, and as much as I tried to avoid looking into my own eyes, I couldn't help it. *Jennifer,* I silently implored, *whatever will become of you?*

I cried harder. My mother might never see me get my master's degree, should I be accepted to Columbia. She would never see my kids. She wouldn't even see me turn thirty. Neither of them would. This time I would be really, truly alone. And worse, she'd be dying the same death that had thrown its long, suffocating shadow over us as it came to claim my father. We'd escaped it that day in May, but it was back, this time for her. And one day it would come for me.

I was still crying when I heard rapping on the bathroom door. It was Dr. T. "Gimme a minute!" I said, flushing the toilet a couple of times. When I finally dragged myself into his office I encountered my mother, seated, but no sign of Dr. T. He must have given up waiting for me. "There you are," she said to me. Seeing her face, nervous but still relatively innocent, calmed me. If she still didn't know, it was almost like it hadn't happened yet.

Dr. T. arrived shortly thereafter. He had the X-rays illuminated on another white board behind him and pointed out a few spots to my mother. *Here it comes . . .*

"We won't know anything without a biopsy," he said, "and to get that we'll need to do a bronchoscopy. It's unpleasant, but you'll be heavily sedated."

"I know," my mother said with a groan. "My husband had one. Not pleasant."

Wait—what was happening? Where was his "pretty certain" diagnosis of stage III lung cancer? My head whipped from his placid mug to my mother's ignorance and back again. When was he going to tell her?

"Okay, so we'll set up an appointment for your bronchoscopy," Dr. T. said in closing. "Any questions?"

We left Dr. T.'s office and ambled across the street to One Fish Two Fish and ordered an early bird special. I grabbed my phone and quickly excused myself to go to the bathroom. I hit speed dial #4 and prayed I didn't get voice mail.

"Sarah!" I said when she answered. I was crying again.

"Jenny, my god, what is it?" Only in times of stress did she call me Jenny; usually she called me Fuh, her original nickname for me. As in Jenni-*fuh*. Ha, ha.

"Sarah, what do I do?" I explained what Dr. T. had done to me— turned me into the bearer of unbearable news—"and I can't face her and not tell her," I sobbed. "How do I tell her? But how can I look into her eyes and *not* tell her?"

"What kind of doctor goes over a patient's head to tell her family but doesn't even tell her?" Sarah fumed.

"Well," I said, slowly returning to life, "I'd say he got his medical degree at Target, but I don't think that place was around in the 1910s."

"Jenny," she said, her steady composure rising to the occasion, "you have to tell her. You just do."

"I do?" I asked, but I knew I did. Sarah was right—how could this doctor have handed me this burden? Wasn't this stuff covered during his residency?

"Yes. Go."

I left the bathroom on wobbly knees and sat across from my mother. It was just the two of us now, and this role, by default, fell to me. Maybe my father was watching me, rooting for me, from wherever he was. I silently begged for any strength he could lend me, and realized that despite all he'd been through, he'd never had to do something like this.

"I have to tell you something," I began as we waited for our salads.

My mother addressed me with a bemused expression, one she might use when entertaining the ramblings of a child. "Yes?"

"Mommy." I breathed in and out a couple of times. "Mommy. You have cancer. He told me, when he pulled me aside. I don't know why he didn't tell you. It's in your lymph nodes. He said he could see it on the X-ray. It's stage IIB—still treatable," I noted, omitting the IIIA part of the equation. "He said that the doctors could give you chemo and it wouldn't necessarily hurt your heart. There are therapies now that aren't that hard on your heart. It's *treatable*, Mom. It's not like Dad. And he even mentioned operating. See? They never said that to Dad."

I let the news sink in. I think it may have been because I was there watching her, but she didn't fall apart. She leaned back in her chair and kept her stare fixed on an imaginary point in space slightly off to the right and nodded, slowly. I thought I caught a tear in her eye, but it quickly evaporated. Her maternal instinct must have kicked in, preventing her from exploding with grief until she was alone. Now that my duty had been performed, my head slumped between my shoulders and nearly hit the table. I stifled another sob and looked up at her as she sat, expressionless.

"Mommy, I am so sorry," I mumbled. "Mommy, you have to fight. For me. *Please.*"

She nodded, appearing to calculate something in her head. "I will, baby," she said. "I want to see you graduate. I want to see you have a baby. I'll stay around, for you. I *have* to." I mindlessly picked at my salmon as she implored me to eat. I seemed to be taking this harder than she was. I remembered her reaction on September 11, as we watched the towers fall in the city in which she grew up: She was placid, soothing, never betraying her emotions as long as I couldn't handle mine. And a few months before that, when I forced myself to kick Kareem out of my apartment, she was there to catch me when I fell apart. I'd never really appreciated it before, but it was this steady, solid quality that made her a mother—a strong mother, a very *good* mother. She met my eyes then, and I wondered how we got to this point. What she had been for my father, I now was for her, and it had happened in less than an hour. I had become a primary caregiver.

Afterward we strolled up Madison Avenue to Starbucks like it was any other night. But it wasn't, and I could feel it in my adrenalized, worn-out muscles. There would be calls to make, battle plans to be drawn up, setbacks against which to steel ourselves. We returned to my apartment and settled in for the sleep of our lives—for my mother, a sobering countdown had begun; for me, an inexorable slide into certain grief, protracted and life-altering. Grief, I realized, would be a state that would infuse the rest of my life; it would be the lens through which everything else would be seen, felt, and heard. To say that I wouldn't be the same would be inadequate; I didn't know who I would become, that person now just a dot in the distance.

"JENNY . . . CALL ME *baaaaack!* You're going to be *very interested* in what I have to *saaaay!*"

I retrieved the message in the bathroom stall at work on a lazy April afternoon. I'd been expecting an envelope from Columbia, and I knew the mailman delivered his bundles at 1:30 P.M., but my mother swore she didn't know that when, at 1:31, she impulsively descended the stairs and unlocked my mailbox and ripped open my acceptance letter. My future was set, and not a moment too soon. At that point my mother had been receiving chemo and radiation for three months, and just as we'd essentially moved to Sloan-Kettering when my father became ill, my mother and I spent enough time in Mount Sinai's sunlit atrium and above-average cafeteria to call it home. Since it was just four avenue blocks from my apartment she lived with me during the week, an arrangement that drove us both a little nuts. But she was overjoyed that at least one piece of my life had finally clicked into place—perhaps I'd finally get the master's degree from Columbia that had ultimately eluded her. She took to calling me "Brenda Starr, Girl Reporter" after the comic strip character, and even though I didn't get the reference I'd giggle at how tickled she seemed by my newly chosen profession.

But our celebration was tempered by a return, the following morning, to the grind: radiation five times a week and chemotherapy on Tuesdays. Radiation was the lesser of the two evils, as the only side effect was a slight sunburn, and she loved Dr. C., her easygoing radiation oncologist. Of all her new doctors at Sinai—cardiologist, pulmonologist, pulmonary oncologist, cardiothoracic surgeon—she liked Dr. C. the best. When she asked him why the sunny disposition, he explained that radiation oncologists never really see anyone at their sickest, they generally don't see anyone die, and patients are in and out in fifteen minutes. We also loved Dr. S., her cardiothoracic surgeon, but he wasn't really *her* surgeon; he'd been "retained" in the hope that her cancer could be excised. But since the primary tumor was wrapped around her pulmonary artery, and taking the lung wasn't an option because five decades of cigarette smoking had diminished the breathing capacity in her other lung by 40 percent, we didn't see him very often.

While I had physically been there for my mother during the first half of her yearlong cancer ordeal, in the shadows of my mind I felt that I wasn't really there for her at all. True, I woke up every morning for the first couple of months and went with her to radiation, sat with her in Dr. C.'s office and ate the graham crackers and drank the orange juice they provided, and every Tuesday I accompanied her down the hall to chemo. "I'm a human pincushion!" she'd habitually remark as the nurses struggled to find a plump vein among the multitude that were collapsing in her arms. Chemotherapy was actually semi-entertaining for both of us; as her Benadryl took hold she became woozier and woozier until she spoke so nonsensically she sounded thoroughly sloshed. I then took her back to my apartment, where she slept off the chemo like a drunk, and since they loaded her up with gallons of Compazine, she mercifully never threw up. She also didn't fully lose her hair, though at the end it did get thin and patchy in spots and she got creative with an assortment of colorful scarves.

But around month three I started to get lazy, and she noticed. Since radiation only took fifteen minutes and Sinai was so close to my apartment, I let her go without me once, then twice, then a few times a week. I'd sleep in and arrive for chemo when it was already in progress. I was still working at the restaurant twenty hours a week and attending my first reporting class at Columbia, but class time and outside reporting only absorbed fifteen hours of my week. So why did I feel so exhausted all the time? I couldn't, for the life of me, wake myself up, and sometimes even when I came late to chemo I slept in the bed next to her if it was empty. This annoyed her, as she wanted a person there to give her moral support and allay her fears, not fall asleep. I was useless to her. I had read a few years before that Céline Dion attended every single one of her husband's radiation appointments when he had throat cancer. She was a superstar, busy with recording and touring, not

to mention angling to freeze her husband's sperm for future pollina-
tion. If a woman with these demands could do it, why couldn't I? I wish
I could have been there for her the way she wanted me to, instead of
running to a friend's apartment every night to smoke a joint, despite
the protests my mother hurled at my back as I ran out the door: "Jenny!
You shouldn't be taking *anything* into your lungs, not with your genetics!" But what she really meant was, *Don't leave me and tune out. Stay
with me.*

Which is what she must have been trying to express the morning
she crawled into bed with me as I slept past noon. In my twilight
sleep I felt her reach tentatively for my back; I'd fallen asleep facing
the wall. We shared a bed in these days, reminding me uncomfortably
of our forced cohabitation during that last year in California, and I
assumed she was waking up and wanted me to wake up, too. She
hated making coffee and eating breakfast alone, and here she was,
saddled with a late sleeper. But I felt her nails on my shoulders as she
brushed away my hair, followed by sobbing. It sounded at first like
she was laughing, then choking. I stirred, then froze. Soon I felt
sweaty hair and hot, wet cheeks on my back. I heard her suck in her
snot and imagined it dripping from her nose. My heart went out to
her, but I decided to feign sleep until I figured out what to do.

"Jenny, I am so fuckin' scared," she said, her voice dipping into an
octave I only heard her use when she cried over my father. I remained
in my semicomatose state, waiting for a sign. "Jenny," she said, rocking me slightly. "I need you." I murmured something incomprehensi-
ble. She rocked me again. "Jenny." She wasn't yelling at me, like she
did during one of our regular battles of will. She was *needing* me; it
was infused in each of her half-swallowed sentences and the little
gasps for breath she emitted after each sob. "Jenny, I am so fucking
scared," she wept. "I don't want to die."

She was killing me. But I didn't stir. What was I supposed to say?
That I, too, had severe bouts of death anxiety, the kind that everybody
has but no one except Woody Allen likes to talk about? That I'd begun
having them again, that they'd wrenched my insides, beginning the
day she called me and informed me that yes, the results had defini-
tively come back positive for cancer, and I hung up and collapsed hysterically on West Fifty-seventh Street because that was the moment I
knew for certain I was going to lose her? That the clock had started

that night, ticking away the seconds until the demise of what was left of my family? That I'd wandered Columbus Circle in a haze, weighed down by the devastating heaviness of it all until Sarah picked up her phone and took me in for the night, and even then I couldn't shake the crushing doom that awaited us both? Should I have used the opportunity on the morning she cried to my back to compound her fears by telling her the truth—that yes, she was going to die, and yes, I knew it? Should I have mourned her death with her right there and then? Tried to articulate that my fear of living without her had been buried so deep for so long that it was in a place I was only vaguely aware of and couldn't even begin to access? Should I have brought her on that journey with me, even though I feared it would have been selfish to do so?

While I sensed all this that morning and accepted it as fact for the duration of her illness, I felt that speaking these things aloud deposited me in the land of cliché, and anyway, it was tiny compared to what she was going through. Really, who wanted to hear what I thought? This was her death, not mine. But here she was, reaching out to me in desperation, laying herself bare in a way I bet she'd never done with anyone. When she'd cried hardest over my father, the day she said she realized she was going to lose him after all those years of fighting for him, she grieved alone, sobbing into his bedsheets at Sloan-Kettering after they wheeled him off to get a scan. So when she needed me—or anyone—with an unprecedented ache, why didn't I open myself up in kind? Why couldn't I just turn around and comfort her? Really, what would it have cost me? Maybe I decided, in a place somewhere deep down where these decisions are made, that I would instead act brave and say little, that it was better for both of us—that if we started mourning our impending separation now we'd get lost in a big dark hole that had two full bottles of Xanax at the bottom. I am satisfied that my mother knew how I felt about her; I am not so sure she knew how I felt about *losing* her. Not that morning, anyway.

My aunt Arline later told me that my mother expressed many times that year how scared she was for me in the event of her death—that I'd be lost without her, that I wouldn't finish school, that I wouldn't have anyone. She hid from me most of her fears regarding the effect her death might have on me. And for that, I'm glad. She spared us both a lot of agony.

CHAPTER 14

December 2005

· · ·

M Y MOTHER LIKED TO QUOTE THAT LINE FROM THE MOVIE *Seabiscuit,* which we saw a couple of years before she got sick, when the famed horse's trainer says to its owner, "You don't throw away a whole life just 'cause he's banged up a little." I knew why she connected with it: She'd always felt discarded by her father, and his cold, dismissive treatment unleashed feelings of worthlessness she'd have to battle over the course of her entire life. But this quote seemed especially apt as she stared down her final months. And as her banged-up body got weaker from the chemo and the hulking oxygen machine made its first appearance in her apartment, it could have applied literally as well. Though she claimed she only needed the oxygen once in a while "to catch my breath," she was drowning in fluid: It was in her lungs and around her heart, cutting off her breathing if she fell asleep in any other position but sitting up. Of course she didn't tell me that; instead she'd call in the middle of the night, breathlessly requesting my companionship under the guise of benign chitchat. She either knew what was wrong and pretended not to, or convinced herself that her breathlessness would subside. But by the time Christmas Eve rolled around, we came to understand how severely we'd both underestimated her condition.

I'd taken an afternoon express bus straight from a dismal $25 lunch shift and arrived at my mother's apartment around three. Instead of cooking we settled at the last minute on takeout from our old Italian haunt, Trattoria Romana. We returned to the apartment with calamari and zuppa di mussels, and I set the table with napkins, knives, and forks, put ice cubes in our wineglasses, laid out dinner and

salad plates, and began to apportion the food. My mother sat down
and began picking at a handful of calamari. After squeezing lemon
over a piece or two and popping them into her mouth, she said, "Oh,
Jenny, my head hurts so much right now."

"Do you want me to get you something?" I asked.

"No, *oy*, Jenny, I just need some air," she said and rose suddenly,
bolting for the terrace. She opened the door and faced the breeze,
rocking gently back and forth, which seemed to calm her. I remained
in my seat and squeezed lemon over the calamari, eager for this
episode to end so I could stop worrying. But it didn't end—as she
straddled the doorway, one foot in the cold and one in the warmth,
her features knotted themselves into a fist and she squinted in agony.
She slowly turned around and said, "Jenny? For some reason I can't
picture what the inside of your apartment looks like."

"Wh-what?" I asked, the first half of the word carried on a laugh
that sank like a stone as I absorbed her words. I'd had that apartment
for five years, it was the only place I'd ever lived outside of my parents' house—and it was where she had just spent the better part of
the year recuperating from cancer treatment.

"Jenny, I can't picture what the inside of your apartment looks like,"
she repeated. She put her hand to her head and massaged her temple. I
followed her eyes as they beheld the dinner table, crowded with our
feast. "Where did all this food come from?" she asked, mystified.

And that's when something sprang up in me like a hot coil my
body couldn't contain; it was as if everything that made me Jennifer,
Eleanor's daughter, stood at attention and threatened to escape
through the top of my head. It was panic, surging and rigid, informing me that it would be in charge for the rest of the evening.

"What do you mean, where did this food come from?" I demanded,
sounding almost angry. "Mom, don't you remember? We drove to
Trattoria Romana to get it."

"No . . . we *did*?"

"Yes! Mom, this is our Christmas dinner," I insisted, coming closer
to her. She was squinting with pain, and I knew it was a stroke. I half
expected her to collapse right there. I had to act fast—I wasn't going
to wait for an ambulance to arrive so she could be taken to a subpar
hospital on Staten Island that wasn't versed in her medical history. I
was going to drive her to Sinai. Me, whose license had expired in

2000. Why hadn't I taken that stupid driver's ed course she'd been nagging me about for the last five years?

I ran into her bedroom and swept all twenty of her pill bottles into a bag lying nearby. I emerged having no idea how I was going to persuade her to abandon an untouched dinner and accompany me to Manhattan, but I was determined to make it happen. "Mom," I said urgently, "we have to go!" As soon as I said it I quickly darted back into the bedroom, grabbing her wallet and keys.

She flinched. "Why? What is it? Did you see something?"

Vermin! That's how I could get her to leave! Nothing scared her more than vermin, roaches, or, even worse, flying roaches. "I saw a rat," I improvised, "and we have to leave this house *right now.*"

"Wha—" she said, her eyes following me as, bag slung over my shoulder, I shoved the dishes into the sink, food and all, and opened the door. I held it open and stood in the doorway, waiting for her to follow.

"Jenny," she said, "we can't just leave! There's food . . ."

"Forget the food!" I said, adrenaline pumping through my body and threatening to paralyze my limbs unless I moved fast enough to burn it off. "Mom, do you trust me?"

"Jenny, where are we going?" I weighed my options: I could try to explain what was happening to her, or I could continue to alarm her enough so that she would follow me into the car. How could I tell her she was having a stroke? I had no idea what it would ultimately do to her—notifying her of her condition was, to me, the same as leveling with her about her mortality. I couldn't do it in the summer and I sure as hell couldn't do it now.

"Mom!" I yelled, hoping to stun her with volume.

"What?" she asked, finally paying attention.

"Do. You. Trust. Me."

"Should I?"

"MOM!" I shouted, almost wanting to laugh. I think it was her attempt at humor, but under the circumstances I couldn't be sure.

"Yes?"

"We have to go."

"We do?" Her blithely questioning tone lacked the urgency that could have propelled me to Manhattan on foot, if need be. This disparity was beginning to annoy me.

"Mom," I said, "you can stay in here with a *rat,* but I am taking your car and going to Manhattan. So you can either come with me or be left here without a car. Your choice."

She considered this. "Do you have my wallet and my keys?" she asked.

"Yes."

"Well, if you insist." I peeled out like a stock car driver and somehow averted a dozen fender benders as I raced over the bridge and up the FDR. Around Fourteenth Street, much to my surprise, she seemed to return to me.

"Jenny, what are we doing?" she asked, joining our regularly scheduled programming, which was already in progress.

"Mom?" I asked.

"Yeah, what happened to dinner?" she asked.

I laughed. Had I overreacted? "Oh, Mom," I said, "You're back! Oh, I'm so relieved. Do you know how I had to get you out of the house? *Oy,* I didn't think I was going to be able to convince you—"

"Convince me? Jenny, how did we get into this car?"

My insides turned to stone. "What? You mean you don't remember . . . forgetting? Mom, you looked at the dinner table and didn't know how the food had gotten there!"

"Forgetting? What do you mean? We were just sitting at the table, and now we're here," she said. "Jenny, what is going on?" I gripped the steering wheel and felt utterly alone. She was gone again.

Over the course of the drive I kept quizzing her, peppering her with questions I can no longer remember, having lost them years ago in a blur of horror. Her memory seemed to come and go every three or four minutes, moving from fuzzy to self-aware with the onset of each new headache. As I pulled off the FDR and neared Ninety-sixth Street, I realized I'd have to think of a cover story in case she wanted to know why we weren't going to my apartment as promised.

"Mom, we need half and half for your coffee, so I'm just going to stop off here, okay?" I said as we raced up Madison. I pulled in to the emergency entrance on 101st Street and instructed her to wait there. I dashed out, hoping she didn't notice that there weren't any delis nearby, and rushed headlong into a group of ambulance drivers.

"Stroke! My mother is having a stroke!" I shouted, and they ushered me inside. A couple of doctors and nurses followed me to the car and opened the passenger side door. I watched as my mother swiveled her head from side to side, probably wondering where she was and how she got there. As they eased her out of the car and onto a waiting gurney I felt relief: She was in their hands now. For a moment I was worried she'd yell at me and demand to know what she was doing there, but she didn't. Somewhere, perhaps, she understood.

"Mom, I'm here," I said as I followed her gurney into the emergency room.

"What's going on? Where are we?" she asked, but didn't seem confused or angry, only curious.

"Mom, we're at Sinai," I said, marveling that I'd gotten us here without getting pulled over or killed. "It'll be okay now." They took her to a bed in a corner of the emergency room, and as we waited to be seen she looked at me with clear eyes, and I knew she was right again.

"Mom? Geez, you scared me," I said, stroking her pale, leathery hand, free of liver spots thanks to the laser treatments she'd treated herself to before her cancer diagnosis.

"I did?" she asked. "What happened?" I went through it all: the dinner, the headache, the rat—"Jenny, you're brilliant! You know how scared I am of vermin"—and I pulled up a chair, relaxing into it. We sat in silence for a time, bracing ourselves for the interminable wait. Twenty minutes into it my mother muttered, "Ooh, Jenny, my head," and I saw what the dim lighting in her apartment had obscured: skin that turned deathly white before my eyes. Her head lolled a little to the left and she appeared to be fainting.

"It's happening again!" I screamed, which summoned a young intern. He took one look at her and said, "Her BP is dropping." And then to another doctor nearby: "We need to move her into the code room, her stats are dropping." And to me: "You'll have to wait in the hall."

"Oh, do I have to?" I asked. During chemo I'd been able to stay with her at all times, just as we'd been able to stay with my father at Sloan.

"Yes, I'm afraid so," he said, and wheeled her into the code room.

On my way out I heard, "Eleanor? Eleanor, can you hear me?" I lingered for a few moments more, hoping to bear witness to her revival.

"You have to leave now, I'm sorry," a nurse said, and closed the double doors in my face.

The hallway was empty but for me. After a few stunned moments I shuffled to the nearest bench, where I sat and folded my hands and felt captured in this moment like it was amber. There was no five minutes ago, no five minutes from now—everything hung on this brief pause between concern and catastrophe. I slouched forward and frankly addressed myself: *Jennifer, this could be it. She could die right now. You must be prepared.* But worse than her suddenly dying was my not being there when she did. I'd vowed to be there when my father died and I'd extended that promise to her, though I'd never voiced this.

"Ma'am?" a nurse said about ten minutes later. "You can go back in now." My mother was still in the code room, but stable. Her skin was so translucent I could see blue veins peeking through. They moved us back to ER holding and an ambitious, fresh-faced resident swung by her bed and studied her scans. Since my mother last coded, her memory had stayed intact, probably a result of the drugs they were giving her.

"I think your mother had what is called a transient ischemic attack," Fresh-faced Resident said. "It's commonly referred to as a mini-stroke. That's when the blood flow to the brain is temporarily interrupted but restored in time to prevent any lasting damage, unlike a real stroke."

"So it wasn't an actual stroke?" I asked.

"No, and in all probability it didn't do any serious damage, like, for instance, brain tissue death," he said. "People often have many of these leading up to an actual stroke, but they can have them for quite some time and not sustain any permanent memory loss."

"So she *could* have a real stroke?"

"She might, but not immediately. In the meantime, I suggest making an appointment with her cardiologist as soon as possible," he said, and left.

For the life of me I wish I could remember how we started talking about my father. Maybe I pointed out that if my father had been there when I was panicking about how to treat my mother's mini-stroke, he would have turned green. I remembered how helpless he'd seemed during her first heart attack, and maybe I told her that right then, to let her know how she'd been fretted over and loved. But my memory of those few moments in ER holding was erased by what my mother said next as she sat slumped in her dingy hospital bed, a tale delivered in an unnaturally even voice that seemed to come to me across oceans of time and space.

"Jenny," she said, "I have to tell you something about Daddy."

I looked up from my book. Another affair? I braced myself for the sordid. "What's up?"

"You know how I told you he did . . . what he did?" she asked.

How could I forget? Every time I brought it up she shamed me into silence, so fearful that this one act would define him. I didn't repeat it for nearby patients to hear, instead nodding.

"Well," she continued, "what if I told you it wasn't the only time? That he did it other times?"

"What?" I asked, shocked, but on second thought, not entirely surprised. Her pattern of conveying partial truths had immunized me against expecting any less. "Well, how many other times?" I asked, trying to sound nonchalant. *You're a reporter,* I told myself. *This is just another interview.*

She shrugged slightly, perhaps trying to seem nonchalant as well. "Four, maybe five," she said hesitantly.

"When was this?" I asked, skating quickly over my agony.

"After he left prison, right after you were born," she said, her whole face seeming to shrug. She sounded so matter-of-fact, her voice so free of affect, it was almost as if she was afraid to place any judgment upon her sentences because after years of defending and advocating for my father, she'd forgotten how.

"Why? How did it happen?"

She sighed. Maybe she was already sorry she told me. "You remember how I told you that when I gave birth to you, your father was gone a lot, running around, getting back into The Life? How he was out doing *business?*"

I understood *business* to mean dealing marijuana or cocaine. "Yes," I said.

"Well . . ." she trailed off, expecting me to guess the rest.

"He was out killing people?" I asked, dropping my restrained tone.

This was the reformer I'd been taught to revere, who'd *changed his life for us?* "Mom! Who were these people?"

"Drug dealers, mostly," she said. "People who owed him money, people who double-crossed him. They were bad guys, Jenny."

"Mom, how can you say that? I don't believe in that." Then a thought even more unbearable reached up and grabbed me around the throat. Perhaps there was a darker reason she'd always tried to discourage my curiosity when it came to his crimes. "Mom, did you know this was going on when it was happening?"

"No, no, he told me afterward," she said.

"Like, the day afterward? The week afterward? What?" I demanded.

"Like, in the eighties." It was so vague I almost laughed.

"In the eighties? Like, when? Before he got arrested again? When he went to rehab? When?"

"When he went to rehab," she said, and I cursed myself for giving her an assortment from which to choose. Of course she'd choose the latest possible date. She should have just told me he confessed before he died.

"And you *stayed with him?*" I yelled, suddenly not caring about being overheard. What, were they going to charge her as an accessory after the fact? She was already facing a death sentence.

"Jenny, keep your voice down!" she snapped, for the first time sounding irritated that she'd aroused my anger. And my tears: I was crying now, my composure slipping from my grasp like butter.

"No! How could you stay with a man you knew was killing people?" I asked, hysterical and dismayed. No wonder she hated me bringing it up—she had known this for the better part of their marriage and done nothing. She'd let a monster raise her child.

But he wasn't a monster. Sure, I'd seen his rage race from zero to sixty in .02 seconds, but aside from a few temper tantrums he hadn't been a monster. I certainly wouldn't have guessed that he was a multiple murderer. Did that make him a serial killer? No, that was different. That was bloodlust. This was . . . what, exactly?

"It was a part of that *life,* Jenny," she said, trying to calm me down. "He was doing a job, and one of the by-products of that job was to do what he did."

Was it possible that my mother was defending murder? I sobbed, erupting in torrents. This was too much. We went back and forth in clipped tones for a few more moments before I fled to the hallway. She yelled after me, asking why I was so mad. I didn't ever want to return, though I knew I'd have to. How would I explain my defection to her sisters, to her friends? I paced the hallway and stared at my cellphone, but who on earth could I call? Who could withstand a confession like this, and who did I want to know about it? No wonder the three of us had been so close, yet so insulated, moving through life as a unit, ignoring anyone who told us what to do or how to live and instead doing what we felt was right for us. This ugly secret must have bound my parents together, and though I didn't know it growing up, it bound them to me. I considered with a start whether anyone else knew what he had done. Maybe his other kids, maybe Rita? They'd all been living near us in Miami before we went on the lam. How many people shared this dirty secret?

"I can't believe this shit," I muttered to myself in the very hallway I'd paced in despair just an hour before. How could this be? But then, hadn't I always sensed that this truth was out there, waiting for me to find it? Why had I asked my mother so many times whether he'd fired his gun into anyone else's head if I didn't suspect there was more she was hiding? I'd come to the hospital fearful for my mother's life only to wind up despising her. How could she defend him? She acted like erasing drug dealers was a necessary duty, like my restaurant sidework. Is systematic elimination—a quick antiseptic hit—any less brutal than the grisly hobbies of Jeffrey Dahmer or John Wayne Gacy? Was there a hierarchy when it came to murder, and was my mother really expecting me to classify my father's brand of killing? And to think I'd stood before my closest friends and family and eulogized him, calling him a hero who had learned from his mistakes and turned his life around, while my mother listened and nodded approvingly, never suggesting I change a single word. But my eulogy was a lie. He hadn't changed anything for us. The threat of jail was probably what reversed his killing streak, not a crisis of conscience.

One thought halted my racing mind: My mother must have assumed she was going to die, otherwise why would she have relinquished this secret? She'd kept it buried deep despite his dying, despite my insatiable curiosity. I shivered when I considered how close I'd come to never finding out. If I wanted to know the whole story, I realized, I'd have to shut up and stop judging her. Because I was. Because no matter how wonderful a father John had been to me, if I had been his wife I would have left him after such a confession. I marveled at my mother's choice, to stay with a person who had admitted to murders that were never solved. I felt betrayed for trusting the two of them like I had. Underneath every dinner we shared together, every weekend trip to San Diego, every morning car ride to school, this secret was hiding. I wondered what else there was to discover that could upend my life.

When I returned to the emergency room my mother was angry with me for being angry, but she didn't have time to scold me because the attending physician was at her bedside.

"I think we can release you, you seem to have stabilized," she was saying. "Your scans don't show an occlusion."

"So what happened to her?" I asked "The resident said it was a mini-stroke?"

"Yes, well, I don't really think she had a TIA," the attending said. "This was more of a global event, while a mini-stroke tends to affect one side of the body. That was not the case here."

"Well, um, *something* happened to her, she was crashing," I pointed out. "She suffered memory loss. You're sure it wasn't a stroke?"

"It doesn't appear to be, from her scans," she said, and reached for my mother's chart. "Your mother was treated here in September for vasovagal syncope?"

"Yes, she fainted, essentially, but—"

"Perhaps this is another reaction to the chemotherapy? Perhaps she needs to build up her nutrients again," she suggested.

"But she hasn't had chemo for months," I objected. But the attending was convinced, and there was nothing I could do. I sighed and complied with the checkout procedures. It was 3:00 A.M., and after the scene at her apartment six hours before I couldn't believe she was going home.

We went back to my place and settled into sleep, neither of us interested in sifting through the past. Or at least that's what I think we did. I really don't remember.

AFTER MY MOTHER'S release from the hospital I persuaded her to stay at my apartment so I could watch her—despite her insistence that she needed to return to Merle Place to clean up all the dirty plates of cala-mari I'd dumped in her kitchen sink—and every hour I'd ask her ques-tions to make sure she was sentient. She feigned annoyance but patiently complied, leading me to believe she was just as worried about her mental state as I was. As for her dramatic post-stroke confession, concern over my mother's health had moved it to the back burner, and I didn't share what I knew with any of my friends. I was alone with the truth, just as she had been, and I buried it, just as she had.

I came home the next night bearing gifts—fresh mozzarella, toma-toes, basil, baguette, and chicken noodle soup for good measure, none of which she ate. Her throbbing head stole her appetite but proved a powerful sleep aid. After rejecting my mini-feast she poured a glass of water from the Brita filter and took her cocktail of pills—Xanax, Lopressor, Zocor, Zantac, and indomethacin for the fluid around her heart—and sat down at my drop-leaf living room table. She was wearing one of my old T-shirts that was two sizes too big and a pair of fuzzy white socks. Two minutes later she reached for her pills again.

"Ma, what are you doing?" I asked. "You need another Xanax already?"

"No, I'm just taking my pills," she said, and opened her bottle of indomethacin.

"Ma, you just took those."

"No, I didn't," she said matter-of-factly.

"Ma! Yes you did! I saw you! Don't you remember? You got up to get water and took them and drank it." I rose from the futon and walked over to her to prevent her from swallowing another.

"Oh, Jenny, you're lying," she said, sounding quite convinced.

"Mom!"

"Jenny, I did not just take my pills," she insisted. But she said it without emotion, deadpan, like her heart really wasn't in this fight. Again I felt helpless and alone; I was the only person in the room who knew the truth and it was like shouting into a wind tunnel.

"Mother, I just watched you take them! Why would I lie to you?" And again I went for the heartstrings: "Don't you trust me?"

"Oh-kaaaay," she said, overarticulating to let me know she was humoring me. She poured the contents of the bottle on the table and began counting. I paced the living room and wandered into the kitchen while I waited. This was uncharted territory, and it terrified me in ways I wouldn't allow myself to deeply consider.

"Forty-six, forty-seven, forty-eight." She paused, staring at the pile of pills. "Forty-eight," she repeated. She looked up at me.

"I told you that you took them," I muttered, hardly triumphant over my victory. She leaned back in her chair, then leaned forward slightly, weighing her options. I walked into the living room and sat back down on the futon. "Do you think this is happening when I'm not here?"

"I don't know," she said, wringing her hands slightly. "Maybe." She met my eyes, leveling with me. Silence. And then, in a voice that once again seemed to float into my ears from someplace else:

"Jenny, I have lived for seventy-one years."

It was a declaration, like seventy-one had been long enough. Well, it wasn't long enough for me. "Mom, no," I said. "I can't lose you, too." I was sitting up, pleading with her. I didn't want her to give up. "I already lost Daddy. *Please.*"

"Jenny," she said, "your father and I will always be with you."

It was a rare moment; her concern for me seemed to overrule her fear of dying. I don't know if I would have been capable of such grace in the face of my own demise. It was a generous gesture, and I often wonder now whether it was a promise, and whether she has fulfilled it. Was she explaining why, when I come home from work sometimes and flip on the TV in my living room, my cable box is tuned to her favorite channel—QVC—even though I never watch it? Did she know I'd search for them in the shadows whenever I turned off the lights, or in the gaping blue sky during a particularly clear day, or out over the river from my perch in Carl Schurz Park? Could she see me, in my future incarnation, trying to imagine the two of them sitting across from me on the N train? Was she able to transcend her fear on that late December night and achieve a state of grace? If so, then she was right. After seventy-one years, maybe she was ready to die.

I MADE STATEN ISLAND my base for the next week, shuttling to and from work on the X1 express bus. I vowed to call her every hour, but as each stroke-free day passed, I relaxed a little, even avoiding her mid-shift calls like I used to. So she rang and rang, wheezing and gasping, frantic for someone to assuage her fears. Or perhaps she called me nearly every hour because she didn't remember calling me in the first place.

We had the whole place to ourselves for a change; my mother had taken on a boarder to fill one of the spare bedrooms the year before, but she'd moved out after Thanksgiving. This development deprived me of my favorite of my mother's quirks: Whenever she came to stay at my place, she brought with her a candy-apple-red gym bag filled with every piece of jewelry she owned.

"Mom, who is going to steal that from you?" I'd ask. This was especially baffling since she always locked her bedroom door.

"Jenny, your grandmother Helen's ring is in here"—a diamond cocktail ring that looked like a starburst—"and I just bought some rings from QVC, including an imperial topaz for you." She'd become obsessed with jewels, particularly imperial topaz from Brazil. "I also bought that platinum ring with the three rows of diamonds, and you can keep that and sell it one day." I only half-listened to my mother tell me how she was basically stockpiling my inheritance. She was charging everything, bills she'd never pay, and she didn't seem to care. She continued to bring the gym bag over to my house even after the boarder moved out. I guess some habits never die.

I will always regret that in the week between Christmas and New Year's I didn't insist that she stay close to her doctors at Sinai. But in truth, she never felt completely at home in my apartment. Her apartment felt more like home, and it's where my father died. Maybe that's why she always gravitated back there, where he reliably returned her gaze from the silver picture frame, unaware that he was dead. But I felt his emptiness there, always. I remembered the difference between May 6, when he lay comatose on a hospital bed in the living room, and May 7, when the coffee table took his place. I always crossed the threshold of that apartment and envisioned the life that should have been unfolding there, the laughing, the fighting, the cooking. Merle Place felt a little bit like home to me only because she lived there, and because it's where I spent holidays, and it had carpeting, which reminded me of my childhood. But my father's absence was palpable, and I felt terrible that my mother lived with it. But maybe she liked living with ghosts, just as I am now.

I DIDN'T CONFRONT my mother about her confession until after New Year's. Normally I would have prodded her into telling me everything until she relented, but the way she had scolded my emotional blubbering that night had had a chilling effect. She must have realized I would bring it up again, though, and when I did she was ready for me. I think we were driving when it started. We were always in the car when these things began: the "Your father was in prison before you were born" conversation, the "We used to be fugitives" conversation, the "Mommy, did Daddy have an affair with Rita?" conversation—talk about doorknob therapy. It could have been a nod to our tradition of packing a thousand years of history into a single car ride, or perhaps it unfolded this way so we didn't have to walk into the living room afterward and hear the echoes of our painful secrets.

I asked my mother for the final time if those "four, maybe five" people my father had killed were his only victims. She said they were.

"Who were they?"

"Like I said, they were drug dealers, people who had done business with your father and crossed him. One guy was black, I remember. And he had a family," she said.

And he had a family. She knew that, I suppose, because she asked my father and he told her. *"Johnny, how could you do that! Did he have a family?"* I'm sure at one time this must have bothered her; the fact that it didn't now was simply proof that years of dubious morality had desensitized her. When he told her about this man with his family, and the "four or five" others like him, did she take solace in the fact that his victims had been the scum of the earth?

"This was when he was in Florida? Before we left?" I asked. So, 1978.

"Yes," she said. "He was starting up with his shit again, and it was a part of his business." Again I decided to suppress my judgment. I wanted information, not an argument.

"And then there was Tommy Palermo," she said. Tommy Palermo, she explained, was a guy my father occasionally worked with, but who was more closely associated at that time with my father's dear friend Vinny Cassese, whose last name we had taken on the lam.

"Wait, Vinny was involved in this stuff, too?" I asked. I never thought to ask where my father had met Vinny, though I'd heard about him my whole life and knew his son was half a wiseguy. They'd called him "Big Vinny" because he was overweight, though I remember my father sadly informing us that cancer had stolen his girth. Vinny shared such a close bond with my father because, as it turned out, they'd met in prison.

"What?" I asked. "So *that's* how Daddy and Vinny met?"

She nodded. "They were in Sing Sing together," she admitted. "So Tommy had ripped off a bunch of people, and one of the guys he stole from was a made guy." This wiseguy naturally wanted to kill Tommy for his foolhardy deed, my mother said, and since Vinny was Tommy's partner, Vinny was marked for death as well. "We had already moved down to Florida," she went on. "And your father caught wind of this and went back up to New York to try to reason with this wiseguy who'd been ripped off. He and some members of his crew granted your father an audience because they respected him, because he'd done time, but also because he was known as a shooter." *Great.* "They told Daddy they were going to kill Vinny because Vinny was Tommy's partner, and even though Vinny probably had nothing to do this mess, they couldn't know that for sure. What's funny is, Vinny had even been ripped off by Tommy—they all knew he was no good. Johnny had even warned Vinny not to do business with Tommy anymore, but he did. And this is what happened.

"I didn't want him to go," she continued. "I was scared for your father, that this thing might backfire. But he knew these guys. They told Daddy, 'If you want to save your friend's life, you can do away with Tommy yourself.' And he did."

"Was he scared?" I asked, enthralled.

"No, I don't think so. Your father wasn't scareda nobody," she said with her best *Goodfellas* affect. "But I was."

I could just imagine two beefy Italians in dark suits and solid shirts with matching ties and slicked-back black hair sitting across a table from my father in a dimly lit room, offering this compromise in hushed tones. Espresso may have been involved, but I can't be sure. My father, alone on his side of the table, leans back in his chair, a bit nervous but never betraying his fear, thinks for a second, then leans forward again, looks Wiseguy #1 in the eye, and nods wordlessly. It was the same nod he employed to assure my mother and me that even though the world might be falling down around our ears, "Everything's gonna be all right." No wonder I never trusted that nod. In my experience, the security it offered was fleeting, something I realized as my father disappointed us, and himself, over and over again. That nod had made my mother an accomplice, which, technically, was what she was. And she knew it.

"Vinny never knew what your father did for him," she said. "But his son Carmine did. He never forgot." Carmine had followed in his father's footsteps by spending much of his life in jail. He'd been incarcerated when we moved to New York and he might still be, I wasn't sure. I couldn't believe Vinny had never known what my father did for him. It seemed like such a waste, in a way.

Whenever my mother spoke of the life she lived with my father and Rita and her husband in south Florida in the late 1970s, before she was pregnant with me, I always wished I could have known them then, gone on their adventures, too, been a part of their gang. How interesting, then, that I should yearn for what was actually the darkest time in their lives. Or at least in my mother's life, as she discovered that my father was not who he had purported to be. I recognized that bitter snap of disappointment, when a lover has sold you a shoddy bill of goods dressed up as the perfect man. I'd felt it all my romantic life.

And that was all I gleaned from my mother, the final mystery. I don't know what else she hid from the world, because that was our last conversation about it.

CHAPTER 15

Friday, January 6, 2006, 10:30 A.M.

"Jenny, I (*gasp*) think I'm having a (*gasp*) heart attack," my mother said over the phone as I walked in to work.

"Mom, are you serious?" I asked. "Are you *sure* you're having a heart attack?"

"Jenny," she said, her voice gravelly, "I'm pretty sure. Yep."

"You *must* call the hospital, then." I instructed. "Did you?"

"No, I'm going to do it now. Let me hang up."

I had to walk to the back of the emergency room of Staten Island University Hospital to find her, and when I did I encountered a ghost. She looked irritated and miserable, writhing around in search of the most comfortable position, the one from which she could breathe easiest. But she was alive.

"Hi," I said, and hugged her awkwardly. She was so frail I could probably have lifted her off the bed with one hand.

"Hi," she said, a bit dazed. She leaned forward and stayed there, inhaling as deeply as she could. She'd stay hunched over like this for days.

"So what did they say?" I asked, pulling up a chair.

She shrugged. "They said the EKG didn't seem to show anything. But Jenny, my stomach hurts. I feel so nauseous."

"They said it was nothing?" I asked. Nausea indicated a heart attack. "Okay, then, you just need a stent to open your artery, and you'll be fine," I decided. I took in her ghostly pallor: Would she be able to handle another angioplasty in her condition? Like my father,

her attention now seemed to be fixed someplace in the middle distance, her ears trained on a tune none of the rest of us could hear.

"Go get me Xanax," she said, nudging my arm. I marched up to the nurses' station and requested Xanax; I ended up chasing nurses down for Xanax half a dozen times that day. Around midday I ran into the bathroom with my cellphone—a no-no in any hospital—and called Arline.

"Oh, Jenny, not again!" she said, pained.

"She's going to be fine, Arline," I said. "They're not fussing over her, so I take that as a sign that she's stable."

"Okay, Jenny, but call me as soon as anything changes," she pleaded.

"Sure thing." We languished in the ER for the next several hours. My mother spent the entire time struggling to find a position from which she could breathe, while I rested my head at the foot of her bed without catching a wink of sleep. I was wide awake when a technician came to give her a bedside EKG around 11:30.

"I'm getting a positive reading for cardiac enzymes," a nurse said after a few minutes. He looked up at my mother. "You're having a heart attack right now," he said. "We need to move you back to the ER."

IT WAS JUST before dawn and the world hadn't woken yet. I'd spent the entire night trying to get my mother to keep her oxygen mask on after her levels dipped precipitously, and she was finally dozing. It had been an epic struggle; without the mask they would have put her on a breathing tube. I heard murmurs just outside the curtain around our bed. Through the thin sheet I could hear that an old woman was being brought in. "The home has been called—her family should be here soon," one of the nurses said in a thick Noo Yawk accent. I heard a bed being moved into the space next to us. It came to a stop. I heard the nurses' footsteps padding down the hall. I waited a moment, listening for movement, but there was none. Slowly, quietly, I peeled the curtain back.

Her hair was long and white and she stared at the ceiling with wide-open eyes, eyes that had absorbed at least a century of living. I knew she was dead because she wasn't breathing, but she looked as if she had expired mid-breath, right as she inhaled for the final time—

her neck muscles were strained, skin stretched taut over collarbones. I tried not to breathe; it seemed unfair somehow, since she'd been chasing breath till it outran her. I released the curtain and stood, stunned, scared that this woman was a bad omen.

When midday rolled around, Sarah arrived with H&H bagels and, in typical fashion, began bossing the hospital staff around until a few nurses finally conceded that my mother would get a room around six. I'd been up for thirty hours straight and coffee seemed appropriate, so I showed Sarah the Hylan Boulevard Starbucks where Jeff and I had met a decade earlier. I ordered a gingerbread latte and sat on one of the comfortable couchlike chairs. Sarah sat across from me.

"I have something to tell you," I said, and launched into the gory details of my mother's near-deathbed confession from two weeks before. It wasn't the first time I'd unloaded a morsel of our unsavory past onto Sarah, and even though she was one of my best friends, I felt shame every time, as if I was betraying my parents. But it was becoming more and more apparent that they were my past, and if I wanted to connect to my future I'd have to learn to trust outsiders.

"Well?" I asked. "What do you think?"

"Well, she does have a flair for the dramatic," Sarah said. "And I'm not surprised."

"Me neither," I conceded. If he'd killed once, why would it be hard for anyone to believe he'd done it several times? The sun hit my face through the window, reminding me how exhausted I was, and also how close to hallucinating. I sipped my brown-sugar-covered whipped cream and said, "You'd better drive."

Sarah vowed to stay until we got a room, and at 8:30 we finally did. I was pleasantly surprised by our accommodations and understood why it had taken so long to secure them: Each room was private and clean, with glass enclosures and state-of-the-art monitors. I gave my mother's history to Philomena, the nurse on duty, who asked me what I'd brought her in the way of clothes "for when she checks out." I felt a surge of joy: Philomena seemed to think that my mother was going to get out of this mess alive.

I kissed my mother goodbye and returned to her apartment. I was drifting off when I got the call.

"Ms. Mascia?"

"Yes, hello?"

"This is Dr. S., the attending at the Heart Institute. You'd better come down here. It looks like it won't be very long now, I can tell by the way your mother is breathing."

I shot up. "Excuse me? What do you mean, it won't be long now?" I paced my way into the living room and fought the urge to fall to the floor the way I had in Dr. T.'s office.

"Well, she's laboring now," he said. "You really should come down."

It was 2:00 A.M. I frantically dialed Arline's number. "Ar-liiiiine?" I said, fighting tears.

"What? What is it?" She'd answered on the first ring, proving she was just as on edge as I was.

"Arline, they just called me to go down there," I said. "They said they think she might die soon!" *Did I really just say that word?* "You need to come here, I need you. I can't do this alone."

"I'll come down first thing in the morning, okay?" she said, and I wondered if she already had a bag packed. "Gosh, Jenny, I didn't think it was that bad!"

"Yeah, me neither," I said sadly.

"Oh, Jenny, I feel so bad for you," she said. "Are you okay?" It was a question I'd have to deal with for the rest of my life.

"Yeah, I'm fine." My stock answer, signifying nothing. I raced to the hospital. When I arrived she was sleeping, but her breathing was heavy and labored and her chest rose up and down so violently it once again looked like she was already on a breathing tube. I stood in the hallway and stared at her distressed form through the glass doors of her room and emphasized again to the doctor on duty that she'd come in for a heart attack, one that should not be killing her, and all she needed was a stent. Dr. S., clearly the second string, told me she was too unstable for an angioplasty.

"Yeah, she is *now*," I said, "after being neglected for thirty-six hours."

"There is nothing we can do, Ms. Mascia, because she has signed a Do Not Intubate form."

"Let me see it," I demanded, holding out my hand. He showed me the form, and I gasped when I saw the signature: It was feeble and meandering and falling off the dotted line. I had no choice but to drive home and return during normal visiting hours when I could sort out the medical-directive mess.

Monday, January 9, 10 A.M.

As I crossed the hospital parking lot I spied two turkeys out of the corner of my eye, just wandering around the asphalt. I figured sleep deprivation and emotional exhaustion had finally caught up with me, until I remembered reading that parts of Staten Island were inundated with wild turkeys. "I hate this fucking place," I muttered as I headed upstairs. When I arrived I had my first encounter with Dr. M., who would be coordinating my mother's care for the duration. Which was fortunate, because the man was full of hope.

"I'm sorry, Ms. Mascia, but she's signed a DNI. There's nothing that can be done," he told me in an accent that I pegged for Greek.

"Look, my mother was obviously not lucid when she signed the DNI," I explained. "She did not understand what she was signing."

"She requested the DNI," he pointed out.

"After the nurses threatened her with intubation," I countered, realizing that she'd probably wanted to avoid the same fate as my father's uncle Joey, who was tubed despite being brain-dead. "Tell me, doctor, did my mother also fill out a DNR?"

"Did she?" he asked, reaching for her chart.

"No, she didn't," I answered before he could find it. "Don't you find that a little odd? Aren't those two forms usually filled out in tandem?"

He considered this. "Yes," he said, "I will concede that is a little unusual. Look," he said, sighing, "I take it you are her primary caregiver?"

"Yes," I said, as if that wasn't already apparent.

"I will have our legal team go over this situation, okay?" he said. I started to smile. "But I can't promise anything."

"Okay," I said. "By the way, her doctor at Mount Sinai wants her transferred."

He gave a wry chuckle. "Do you think, if she is not stable enough for angioplasty, that she is stable enough to get transferred?"

I decided against kicking him in the teeth. For now. "Could you please call her doctor?" I asked, in the most conciliatory tone I could muster. "He is very nice and wants to discuss her care with you."

"Tell him to call me," he replied.

With all this behind-the-scenes maneuvering I nearly forgot about the patient beyond the glass doors. My mother was still asleep, still rhythmically slumping with each breath. I suddenly didn't want to be near her. Illness was transforming her into something else, something not quite my mother, and I didn't want to meet this new Eleanor. I just wanted the old one back.

Arline arrived just as I drew up the courage to enter my mother's room, and I was relieved to spot her rotund form wobbling through the halls. I greeted her with a hug and gently shook my mother awake. Her left eye opened and took in the sight of her sister.

"Hi," my mother said softly. She smiled. I wondered if she realized how serious the situation was, that her easily exhaustible sister had trudged down from Connecticut in what must have seemed like a flash.

"Hey, honey," Arline said. "How ya doin'?"

My mother shrugged slightly. "Back hurts," she managed through the oxygen mask, apparently reduced to sentence fragments now. Unable to handle the scene for more than a few minutes, I ducked into the hall and called my mother's doctor, who regretted that she couldn't be transferred.

"You know, I think it would be a tragedy if Eleanor came in for a heart attack, of all things, and didn't make it out," he said.

"Yes," I agreed. "Especially since it was caught so early."

By mid-afternoon the DNI had been successfully rescinded. The medical team would intubate my mother to raise her oxygen back to normal functioning levels so she could be eventually transferred to Mount Sinai. Arline and I tentatively approached my mother's bed with Dr. M. and a respiratory nurse in tow. This was it—the hardest thing I would ever have to do.

"Mom," I said, bending over the left side of her bed and speaking gently to soften the blow, "they want to tube you, but it won't be forever. They want to improve your oxygen so you won't have to keep taking that mask off."

She shook her head. "No," she said.

"It's. Going. To. Be. Just. Fine, Eleanor," Arline said, taking the slow-and-loud approach, "Everything. Is going. To be. Okay." I silently prayed that my mother didn't say anything that would cause her DNI to be reinstated. She didn't realize that this was her only chance, that even with the oxygen mask her numbers were—85? When did her oxygen drop to 85? The mask was securely fastened, but it didn't seem to make a difference. How could I articulate how dire the situation was? As each hour separated her from her heart attack, the more lethargic she became and the less she seemed to understand. I'd have to try my best. Dr. M. stood behind me, allowing me to finesse the consent.

"Mama, do you remember how Aunt Emma had to be on a breathing tube after her open-heart surgery?" I asked. "They took her off it after a day, and she didn't feel anything, she was asleep the whole time. It would be like that—it would only be temporary." I was speaking in kindergarten tones to a woman who'd read Dostoyevsky for fun at the age of twelve. It was surreal.

Dr. M., standing on the other side of her bed, chimed in. "We just want to get you over this hump," he said. I looked up, struck by his sudden enthusiasm for invasive treatment. He seemed to be relying on me for cues. "It will only be temporary," he echoed.

"Is this okay, Mom?" I asked her one final time. At this, she said nothing, didn't nod or shake her head, perhaps sensing that intubation was what I wanted and she didn't want to contradict me in front of the doctors. She stayed silent at the exact moment that a "no" would have spelled the end of her life. "Ma, if we don't do this," I added, "something bad will happen. Are you ready for that?" She shook her head vehemently.

I reached for her hand. "Do you love me?" I asked. She nodded.

"Do you trust me?"

She shook her head slowly, melodramatically, and attempted a faint smile. Arline and I laughed. Always cracking a joke at my expense, my mother was.

That was the last exchange we ever had.

Arline and I were ushered into the hallway and the staff hastily closed the curtains to obscure the view through the glass doors. As soon as the tube was inserted, doctors began shoving consent forms in my face: for a cardiac catheterization, for a urinary catheter, for a femoral line because chemo had collapsed all the veins in her arms. My hand was barely off the page when a cardiologist wheeled in a giant X-ray machine and an EKG and finally performed a cardiac catheterization. He determined the location of the blockage to be the left anterior descending artery.

A single artery. I was relieved for a moment: That could be easily fixed! Then I became infuriated: One lousy artery had caused all this? That was a problem that surely could have been solved three days before with an angioplasty. In the space of thirty minutes, my mother had been hooked up to tubes and machines in at least five places, à la *The Matrix*. What had I done?

"She can't stay this way," I said to no one in particular. I wondered what thoughts were running through her coma-ridden brain. Was she dreaming? Did she know what had happened to her? Was she angry with me for tubing her?

"She's not mad at you, Jenny," Arline said. I must have vocalized that last part.

"How can you be sure?" My mother's eyes were half-open, like the Sphinx in *The Neverending Story*. I feared she could see me.

"Jenny, she would have wanted you to do everything you could," Arline said. "This had to happen. She needs this breathing tube."

"I know. I didn't give up on her," I said, remembering that quote from *Seabiscuit*. "I don't want her to think I gave up on her." It was suddenly very important to me that she knew what I was trying to do to keep her alive. I didn't want her to think I passively sat around while a bunch of doctors called the shots. We headed out of the building and toward the parking lot to get something to eat. We had nothing else to do until the next visiting period. *Visiting period*. I chuckled bitterly at the thought. She was down for the count; we'd only be visiting her doctors now.

"Ooh!" Arline exclaimed, pointing at something moving toward us in the distance. "Jenny, oh my god, what is that?"

"A turkey," I said bitterly as I crossed the lot ahead of her to fetch the car. I drove without any clear direction, just accelerated up Hylan Boulevard. I stopped when I saw an automotive shop. I pulled in. "Where are we going?" Arline asked.

"We're going to replace her tires," I said. During one of our last conversations, she had complained that two of her four tires were bald.

"Actually, they're all bald," the mechanic informed me. I laid $260 on the counter. "Replace them," I said. I wanted her car to be ready for her when she came home. I wanted her to see that I had taken care of everything.

Next we stopped at the Victory Diner on Richmond Road, a boxcar-shaped relic. From our crusty window booth I called each of my mother's doctors and a few of her friends, all of whom were horrified at this latest predicament. I couldn't believe I was discussing my mother like she wasn't here. I half expected to turn around and see her sitting next to me. How could she not be carrying me through this, just as she had carried me through my father's death? Her absence was becoming a permanent fact now; I could feel it begin to take shape in the shadows around me, where it still resides, and always will.

"Jenny," Arline said when we returned to my mother's apartment that night, "can you believe this is happening? I can't believe she was so sick."

I smiled evenly. "I guess she was."

"I just don't believe it," she said. She glanced at a framed photo on my mother's baker's rack, a Polaroid of the two of us in the hospital after she gave birth to me. I'd blown it up and put it in a frame for Mother's Day. She's got me in her arms and she's looking proudly into the camera. I'm clutching the neck of her hospital gown for dear life and trying to bury my head in her chest.

"She was so beautiful, Jenny. So beautiful. It's so unfair." Arline's voice sounded weepy but I knew she wasn't breaking down because of me.

I nodded. "Yep."

I climbed into bed and closed my eyes, and there they were:

My parents and I are in the kitchen of a house we've never lived in. My father sits at the table with his hands folded while my mother faces the sink, her back to me. "Mom," I say, "you have to come with me. You simply can't miss this." Although I don't say what "this" is, I am dressed for a cocktail party. "I'll help you get dressed," I volunteer, "and help you put on some makeup. Come on."

She turns and looks at me helplessly, shaking her head. She is wearing a long white tunic and sports dark, slicked-back hair. "Mom, please!" I say, growing desperate. "Please come with me!" She isn't fighting me on this, as she would have in real life; she simply shrugs calmly, expending as little emotional energy as possible. While she seems concerned that I am so frustrated, her serene demeanor conveys the impression that her inability to attend is something that cannot be changed. She can't go, and there's nothing anyone can do about it.

"Mom, we must hurry if we're going to go," I warn. Her eyes widen and she finally speaks, at last appearing animated.

"I can't," she says, shaking her head from side to side, trying to make me understand. "Jenny, I just can't." I look to my father for an answer but he doesn't say a word, merely stares straight ahead. She doesn't engage him, either, only me, as if I am the only one who doesn't understand, as if I am the only one who needs an explanation.

"I can't go with you," she says one final time.

Tuesday, January 10, 10:00 A.M.

Arline and I approached my mother's room just as the alarm on the adjacent wall was blinking red; she was crashing. I peeked through a gap in the curtain and saw a team of doctors on top of her, working on her, frantically trying to bring her vitals back up. I watched as her bed was adjusted up and then down to get the best access, and she seemed like a rag doll, bending to the whims of others with no fight of her own. Arline and I sat down in the chairs by the nurses' station and shot each other worried glances. At any moment our lives could change direction depending on what happened in that room, and once again I felt the jittery sensation of being suspended uncomfortably in the present.

A few minutes later she was stabilized. Dr. M. emerged and informed us that her blood pressure was jumping all over the place and things didn't look good.

"I would say her prognosis is very poor," he said. The words hit my spine like electric spikes. "We think she might have pneumonia."

"Pneumonia?" Arline said. Pneumonia was never good.

"Well, I'm not entirely sure it's pneumonia, actually," Dr. M. clarified. "Something is causing her white blood cell count to spike, I'm just not sure what it is. It's an infection of some kind, maybe sepsis." I called Dr. G., my mother's cardiologist, who relayed that Dr. M. had called earlier and told him that my mother hadn't released urine in twenty-four hours, an indication that her kidneys were shutting down.

"I love how *you're* the one to tell me this," I said, "and not her actual doctor."

"The only thing that will help her produce urine is dialysis," Dr. G. explained, "which would serve as a stop-gap that will hopefully jump-start her kidneys into action. Once she's able to produce urine again we can resume treatment for the heart attack. We just want to get her stable again so we can transfer her here."

"You know what I want more than anything?" I said in a rare moment of whimsy. "I want to be able to tell her everything we went through this week and I want her to laugh and say, 'Aw, honey, it's all right now, I'm fine.' Maybe not perfect, because she's still going to have cancer, but alive. That is what I want."

"I would like that very much," he said. "I would love to meet your mom and talk about all this with her, and tell her what a wonderful and caring daughter she has. That's our goal, and we need to keep sight of that goal. Okay?"

"Yes," I said. "But I need you to level with me. How bad is this, really? Because I keep hearing 'poor prognosis.' You're not here, but you do have some perspective. And even though five doctors seem to have sprouted up around my mother's bed overnight, you're the only one who is really on the case. I need to know what *you* think."

He sighed. "Honestly? We need to get her kidneys working again. This is a turning point. If her kidneys shut down completely, all of her organs will eventually follow suit. If we can get them restarted, I think she has a good chance."

So this was it. I really *was* suspended in the present, prey to a wind that could knock me to the ground if it chose. I left the hospital soon after to collect my sister Tina from JFK airport. I can't remember when I'd called her; it must have been sometime the day before. Or maybe it was Saturday?

"Tina," I'd started.

"Well, hello, Miss Jennifer," she said in her Florida twang. "What's goin' on?"

"Oh, not much," I said. "Tina, my mom had another heart attack."

"Oh, *no*," she said in hushed tones. I remembered giving her and Angie a play-by-play of the last hours of my father's life via telephone, an arrangement that seemed to be repeating itself now. But this time Tina said she was flying up. A couple of phone calls later she reported that Angie would be a few flights ahead of her.

"Really?" I asked. "You're coming up here?"

"Of course, Jenny," she said. I was pleasantly surprised that my half-sisters, who hadn't flown up to watch my father die, would travel here with very little notice to be with their stepmother as she fought for her life. Maybe they were closer to Eleanor than I thought. Maybe her nagging phone calls about her ungrateful daughter and my father's awful family and insensitive oncologists had ingratiated her in ways I didn't appreciate.

It didn't hit me until later, as I roamed the JetBlue baggage carousel that afternoon, scoffing at the dingy floor and the paint peeling off the walls: They were coming for *me*. They were coming up because, after my parents, they were the closest family I had. I looked around. This was it for me—they were all I had left.

"Tina," I said, collapsing into her arms as soon as I saw her. She looked so much like my father it startled me, especially since she was allowing her prematurely gray hair to overtake the auburn. I wondered if he'd be happy knowing his girls would all be together, then realized I already knew the answer.

Wednesday, January 11, 11:30 A.M.

When I signed off on my mother's dialysis I didn't really know what it would entail. I knew end-stage diabetics require the procedure several times a week and it's a major hindrance, but I visualized an IV that takes blood out and another that puts it back in, with some kind of a filter in between. So nothing prepared me for the horror I found when I opened the sliding glass door that morning.

My eye was immediately drawn to the tubes, dozens of them now, flowing from bags and machines into every possible orifice save her ears. But the dialyzer was appalling: It looked like a giant stand-alone reel-to-reel tape player. I watched aghast as her blood was pumped through a plastic tube into the reel-to-reel, looped around, separated from the urine, and sent back into her body through another plastic tube. All this while the ventilator made a soft whooshing sound to remind me that it was breathing for her, just in case I'd forgotten. For such a busy room with so many vital processes occurring at once, it was relatively quiet, which made the atmosphere rather eerie. I moved a few inches toward her and noticed that her face had grown puffy from the accumulation of fluids, but her eyes, thankfully, were tightly closed. Though the monitors' discordant minor notes dutifully registered her heartbeats, I knew that she was gone.

"It's not her," I said to Arline and Tina. "She's not here anymore."

"No," Arline immediately agreed with me. "She's not." She moved to my mother's side, took her hand, and began weeping gently. Tina flipped through my mother's chart and shook her head. "Jenny, her lab values are really poor," she said. "Her levels are not good at all." She drew aside the blanket warming my mother's feet and said, "Oh, no, Jenny, *look*." I walked over and she pointed out the red dots that had broken out all over her hands, arms, and legs. "Her capillaries are breaking down," she said. "They're no longer carrying oxygen to her skin." She ran her finger along my mother's right leg. "Her extremities are cold." Tears sprang to her eyes. "Oh, Miss Eleanor," she said, her nose flushing red.

I sat in a chair across the room. I wanted to be as far from my mother as possible without ending up in the hall. I didn't want to appear cold, but I was anxious and numb and devoid of hope. I knew the rest of her hospital stay would consist of nothing more than waiting for her to die, and I couldn't handle the agony of not knowing when. If I was going to have to spend the rest of my life without her, I wanted the rest of my life to begin as soon as possible.

From my seat in the back of the room I overheard Dr. M. discuss dilating the breathing tube with his staff. Within minutes he walked in and asked for my consent to open the tube to the maximum capacity. As I signed the form, I remembered less than twenty-four hours before when we all thought the breathing tube would be temporary. Now it couldn't even get her enough air.

"I want a DNR," I said to Dr. M.

"You want the DNR?" he asked, probably leery of entrusting me with anything I might later fight to overturn.

"Yes," I replied. "Now." I wasn't going to spend the next six months studying fluttering eyelids for signs of life, a perpetual captive to false hope. He produced the form and I signed it. Later that day Dr. M. told me that he thought her liver might be shutting down, and I knew it was over. My only decision now was how long I wanted this grisly scene to play out.

AS UNNECESSARY AS I considered it to be at that point, we needed to eat. I took Tina and Arline to a gaudy diner where all the Italians convened for two A.M. Sambuca.

"Rita's coming tomorrow," I informed Tina. Rita and my mother hadn't gotten along for the past couple of years because of Rita's drug problems, and I specifically remember my mother telling me after her cancer diagnosis that if anything happened to her there would be no need to call her youngest sister. But that was how they all spoke about each other, depending on the day. My mother had ranted about me so much over the years that I'm sure both of my aunts thought I was the Bad Seed. But Rita wanted to be there. She was, after all, my godmother, and isn't this the very reason why she'd stood over me in 1978 as the priest poured water on my forehead? Christ, if my mother thought for a second that Rita would be assuming parental responsibilities—even though at twenty-eight I was too old to need parenting—she'd yank out the breathing tube herself and walk home from the hospital.

"And how is Rita?" Tina asked. Arline and I looked at each other.

"Good," Arline said.

"She's fine, I guess," I said. The truth was that Rita's drug of choice—currently Percocet—left her rambling only slightly coherently about subjects that ran the gamut from Rita to Rita. Occasionally she'd gripe about her daughter and marvel at celebrity breakups. Addicts are notoriously self-absorbed and feel the need to discuss themselves with anyone who will listen. It's exhausting, and after a while my mother's patience had simply run out.

"Tina, I should tell you something," I said. "It's about Dad." I hadn't expected to do this—if my mother hadn't been dying I don't know when I would have—but since Tina was sitting in front of me I decided this was the time. "Mom told me something after she had that mini-stroke a few weeks ago. She told me more about Dad." I dipped a fry in Russian dressing and stuck it in my mouth, but only because I was nervous. "She said that after he came out of jail in 1975 he didn't really stop being a criminal."

"Oh, I know," Tina said. "I remember when he came down to Florida with your mom, he had wiseguys over all the time. Bill and I would listen to their stories and we were, like, mesmerized."

I nodded, knowing full well that the bomb I was about to drop would dispel the gossipy atmosphere for good. I drew a breath and blurted:

"Mom told me he killed four or five people during that time and never got caught." I let it hang there for a moment.

"Are you serious?" Tina asked, incredulous.

"Your mother said *what*?" Arline said.

I turned to Arline in shock. "You didn't know?" I asked her. *"You?"*

"She never told me," Arline said. I hadn't expected this. I thought for sure my mother had told her sisters. She'd talked to Arline five times a day in recent years. Maybe she told Rita, to whom she was closer at the time. I'd have to ask her. Jesus, what if I was the only person my mother told? No wonder she felt so compelled to unload as the end of her life was looming.

"Wow," Tina said. I thought I could see tears in her eyes.

"Yeah," I said. "She said they were all drug dealers, though, people who stole money from him, shit like that, and from what I gathered it stopped the second we left Florida. But one of the people he killed was sacrificed for Big Vinny." That didn't sound right. "You remember Big Vinny, don't you, Tina?" I relayed the tale of Vincenzo "Big Vinny" Cassese and his dead partner, courtesy of our father. "Can you believe it?" I asked no one in particular. "He was a killer. And I lived with him and I didn't know it."

"So did we," Tina said. "So did my mom."

"But *my* mom *stayed* with him," I pointed out. "Your mom got out and got herself a career. She didn't stay married to a murderer." She nodded. Two months later I'd visit Tina, and over seared tuna Caesar salads in Fort Pierce she'd ask me to tell her this story again, the story of Dad's killing streak. She'd sit across from me and patiently listen, and when I finished she'd remark, "He must have been so scared," and her brow would crumple and her eyes would turn pink and a tear would roll down her cheek. And it would take me a few minutes to figure out what she meant: that as our father faced the end of his life, he feared he'd end up in hell for what he had done.

THOUGH RITA WANTED me to wait until she got there to take my mother off life support, no one expected me to acquiesce. My mind was made up the second I saw her blood going through the dialyzer, and nothing would give me more satisfaction than screaming, "Get every fucking tube out of my mother's body!" right in Dr. M.'s face. I was also afraid that she'd die without me there—I feared that even more than I feared her death. The decision was mine, and

Arline's, and we both agreed: She wouldn't want to hang around in this state. We'd look at each other every so often and say, "She's not there anymore. It's not her." Whatever had been done or not done during the course of her treatment was a matter for lawyers, if we so chose. Regret and bitterness could keep me visiting her dying, mechanized body in this goddamn hospital for months on end. I knew what she wanted, and as soon as I decided to carry it out I marched through the dimming parking lot, past the turkeys, up the elevator, and into the waiting room of the cardiac intensive care unit. I had with me Arline, Tina, and a college friend, Ji Young—who arrived as soon as her classes were dismissed; she ran an after-school program in East New York—and my father's favorite aunt, Emma, who'd taken a car service from Brooklyn.

"I remember how ya motha and fatha drove Uncle Joey back and forth to chemo," Emma said in the waiting room, her face pinched with her signature brand of bittersweet grief, "and how ya motha called me all the time after my heart surgery to see how I was doin'. I'll never forget whatcha motha did."

My friend Sarah arrived soon after with her father, Jack. They'd left her grandfather's posthumous birthday dinner, the first milestone since he'd died in October. She said that as soon as she got the call, she and her father hopped in his car and sped to Staten Island.

"Jennifer," Jack called to me. "Come over here for a second." I followed him to a corner of the waiting room. "I just went through this, you know, with my own father. He was much older, and I'm older than you are, but if you ever need to talk, you can always call me."

"Thanks, Jack," I said, knowing I would never call him—or anyone—about this, but supremely grateful that he'd left his own father's birthday party to bring Sarah to me.

"You know," he continued, "when I went through this, I realized that there are two kinds of people in life: practice players and game players." He paused a moment for emphasis. "Some people in your life will show up to every practice but skip the game; others will show up to the game even though they've been skipping practice, and those are the people you least expect. People are funny like that."

"Thanks, Jack," I said. "I'll remember that." I'd learned this lesson when my father died. Some of the people closest to me couldn't handle it and faded into the background, and their absence came as a shock, while others—always the ones I never expected—entered my life out of the blue to help shoulder the burden. I didn't have time to wonder who would fall into which category, but I was sure I'd find out soon enough.

I turned to my group. "Well, this is it," I said. It was 8:00 P.M. I wondered what my mother's time of death would be. Her gravestone, if she hadn't requested to be cremated, would have read 10/12/1934–1/11/2006. A life lived, with all the important stuff obscured by a dash. I marched through the double doors and into the nurses' station. Dr. S. was there, as was a slightly nervous young resident named Dr. O. "My mother is Eleanor Mascia," I declared, "and I want to withdraw care." They both looked at me like I was an oncoming truck.

"Um," Dr. O. said, looking around for backup, "we need to consult with each department first. Can you wait in the waiting room, please?" She looked about my age. Her hair was long and wavy, like mine, and she wore it loose. In every restaurant I worked I'd had to tie it back, but here she was dealing with life and death, and hers was permitted to hang free.

"Okay, I'll be in the waiting room," I said. I spun around and marched back out, despite the fact that the nurses' station faced my mother's room. Perhaps another daughter would have gone in there and spent every last second she could with her mother, but I couldn't stand to see her that way. I felt deeply ashamed about it, too, because I knew that if the tables were turned, if I had been mangled in a car accident and rendered brain-dead, for instance, she would have been right there, wiping the blood off my broken flesh with a washcloth, ignoring the fact that I couldn't hear the lullabies she'd be singing into my ear. My mother would be strong enough to confront the death of her one and only reason for living, so why couldn't I even summon the courage to approach her room when she was at her most vulnerable?

There was something else: I felt I had betrayed her. Not for taking her off life support, but for putting her on it in the first place. "What were you supposed to do?" Arline asked me a dozen times that week. "You did what you had to do at the time, with that particular set of circumstances. What, were you going to just let her die without giving her a chance? You gave her a *chance*, Jenny." Every friend to whom I'd expressed my doubts on that day and every day afterward said the same thing. "But she doesn't know that," I'd say to them. "She was promised a breathing tube so she could have an angioplasty. I tricked her. I told her it was temporary. She didn't know she was going to die."

But maybe it was better this way. Maybe it was better she died without realizing it. Not from a long, protracted battle with cancer that robbed her of her hair and every ounce of her body fat, but in a twilight sleep that slowly dimmed until it was extinguished. There would be no goodbye for my mother and me, except perhaps in my dreams. But I preferred it to the alternative: an excruciating scene with the two of us sobbing, struggling with the cruelty of our separation. No, we never would have been able to say goodbye to each other. It just wasn't possible. It took me until now to realize that "goodbye" was not something I could have ever said to the two people who had been closest to me. "Goodbye" was inadequate, "goodbye" was unimaginable; "goodbye" was simply not intended for the three of us.

When I emerged from the ICU, half a dozen curious faces searched mine for information. "We have to wait while they get their shit together," I said, and plopped down in a chair in front of the TV. The news was on but nothing penetrated. We weren't alone in the waiting room, and around ten o'clock a family poured out of the ICU, collapsing into chairs. From their sobs I gathered that the matriarch of the family was the one who had crashed; a man and his adult daughter and son leaned into each other and cried hysterically over their concern for "her."

"I feel so bad for them," I said to Ji Young on my right and Sarah on my left. "To lose their mother like that." They must have thought I was nuts, since I was about to lose my mother like that. But my heart really went out to them because they wouldn't be there when it happened. I glanced up at the clock. "I think I should go in there again," I said, and returned the ICU, where I was told not to come back unless someone came for me. "Pulling someone's plug is awfully hard," I remarked quietly to the group when I emerged once again. The wait dragged on and Jack had to leave. As midnight rolled around, Emma decided she'd go, too.

"I'm gonna go back there and say g'bye ta her," she said, and returned ten minutes later with wet cheeks. "I made my peace," she said. "I don't need ta see her die." I kissed Emma and walked her to the elevator.

"Thank you, Aunt Em," I said to my father's favorite aunt. "She would have loved that you came."

"Oh, Jenny," she said, "ya motha loved you so much. You do know that, don'tcha?"

I did. "Yes," I said, "and she knew how much I loved her." And I know she did.

AT 1:00 A.M. THE double doors opened and a woman on a limited-mobility scooter buzzed into the nearly empty waiting room. She was flanked by two security guards. "I need to speak to the daughter," she announced.

"Yes," I said, and rose to meet her. "We've been waiting since eight o'clock. What is the delay?"

"I'm sorry, but we can't do this tonight," she said.

"Excuse me?" I said, flabbergasted. "Why?"

"Because of certain *legalities*, every specialist who signed off on all of the equipment that is keeping your mother alive must also sign off on its removal," she explained, as if she were reciting from a hospital policy handbook. "A representative from respiratory, nephrology, pulmonology, cardiology, and also your mother's general practioner all need to sign off on the order, and they're not here."

"Are you joking?" I asked her, getting angry. "Is there a reason you couldn't have told us this *five hours ago*?"

"I'm really very sorry, ma'am, but you're going to have to leave and come back tomorrow morning, okay?" As if on cue, the two burly security guards stepped forward.

"The elevators are right around to your right," one of them said.

"Yeah, I know where the elevators are," I mumbled. I was about to pitch a fit but realized that I had a goal, and if I caused a scene they'd bar me from the place and never let me back in. "I didn't realize this was a nightclub," I managed as the five of us piled into the elevator.

That night Ji Young, Sarah, and I shared my mother's bed and Arline slept on the couch. But after I lay restlessly on top of the covers for an hour I took my phone into my mother's bathroom. I kept the light off and called one of my mother's friends in California to tell her the news; she instantly pledged money to subsidize some of my tuition. My mother would have been relieved knowing that her death wasn't going to bankrupt me. I returned some calls from my restaurant friends and confirmed that, yes, this was for real, my mother was going to die. I also learned that my colleagues were starting a collection for me at work.

"I don't think I'm going to be a waitress anymore," I announced to one of them, a charismatic actor-writer named Turhan. He'd called me earlier with news that his grandfather had died.

"Jen?" he asked me during a candid moment. "What's it like?" He wanted to know how it felt to lose my last parent. He was thirty-one and hadn't yet lost his first. I considered my answer while staring at the strip of light under the door.

"What's it like?" I repeated, fingering my mother's wedding ring, which now hung from one of her beefy gold chains around my neck. I recalled how I'd lived the past year—hell, my entire life—in fear of losing my mother. I'd spent hours crying at the prospect of losing her—of losing both of them—and yet here I was, experiencing the Big One. Sitting there in the dark with Turhan's question hanging in the air, I realized I'd never have to lose her again. For this, I was thankful.

"The fear is worse than the reality," I told him.

And it's true.

Thursday, January 12, 11:30 A.M.

Arline decided that she didn't want to see my mother die, especially after preparing herself for the event only to be sent home. I totally understood and bade her goodbye on the way back to the hospital with a promise that Rita and I would drive up to see her in Connecticut later that week. It had dawned on me during all those drives back and forth to and from the hospital that I would inherit a car, one I'd be driving without a license for the foreseeable future. "Get your ass to the DMV and take that damn test!" my mother had commanded me for the last five years. Maybe this was the reason.

I was nervous as I drove Ji Young, Sarah, and Tina to the ICU. I felt like I was on the spot, maybe because I knew I would only have this one chance to be there for her as she breathed her last. It sounds awfully strange to me now, but I wanted to get it right. I know—what does "right" even mean? To me it meant hitting all the right notes, but even from my perch in the present I can't tell you exactly what that entailed, only that it went the way I wanted and I have no regrets. Especially this part:

"I want you to get every tube out of her," I told Dr. M.

"Yes, I know," he said. "You were here last night? I could have told you—"

"Last night was last night," I said. "I want to get on with this. The breathing tube, the dialyzer, the femoral line, the IV, the catheter—everything, gone." We were allowed to sit with my mother as he gathered the necessary signatures, and Ji Young, Sarah, and Tina had a moment with my mother. Ji Young, who lived upstairs and saw my mother throughout her yearlong ordeal at Sinai, was particularly struck by seeing her like that. Before her father suddenly died of a cerebral hemorrhage a few years before, he'd lived a couple of days on a breathing tube, brain-dead, so doctors could harvest his organs. I only realized months later how traumatic it must have been for her to see my mother with the same tubes down her throat. And for Sarah, who had just seen her grandfather as he lay dying, and for Tina, who knew my mother the longest, even longer than I did, and who had just lost her mother-in-law, with whom she had been very close. Tina was a nurse, so I knew she could handle it, but I realized just how few people in the world can say that they've seen someone die. Nurses, doctors, cops, conflict reporters, killers. It's an exclusive group.

Dr. M. asked for my signature last. I stared at the paper and found the empty line. My pen hovered over the form as I read. If my mother saw my signature there, would she feel I'd sold her out? I was signing off on her death. I was the one sending her to the grave.

Then I remembered the alternative: a lifetime of breathing tubes and dialyzers. I wasn't killing her, I was releasing her. I signed my full name on the line, big and clear like John Hancock: Jennifer Nicole Mascia.

"What will happen once we withdraw care?" I asked.

"Well," he said, "she's in cardiogenic shock, she has severe arrhythmia—"

"No," I said. "I'm not asking about her chances of survival. I mean, what will happen exactly? How long will it take?" I wanted to know what to expect, step by step, just as Dr. Meier had done as my father lay dying in the living room. Dr. M. said she could expire anywhere from twenty minutes to an hour after they removed the breathing tube.

I went back into my mother's room and waited. Around 11:30 A.M. a group of doctors came in to remove the tube. We waited outside for about ten minutes. Tina and Sarah broke the silence by reinforcing my belief that she wasn't there anymore and that her spirit had been gone for days.

"You do know that, don't you, Jenny?" Tina said.

"Your mom isn't there anymore, it's just her body," Sarah echoed. I was later told I said nothing in reply, just stared back at them blankly. Even though I'd expressed this earlier, I guess they just wanted to make sure I really believed it.

"She wants to be with your dad," Ji Young said, petting my hair. "She can be with him now." She was right. My mother had spent four and a half years missing him, and for her his death would always feel like it happened yesterday. Perhaps that's why she resented my ability to move past it. Maybe her place was with him now, if such a thing is possible. Maybe her aching for him ultimately outweighed my need for her.

The curtain parted and the doctors filed out. We came in to find the IVs gone and the breathing tube replaced by an oxygen mask. We closed the sliding glass door and there we were, the four of us. Not a combination I would have imagined, but every single one of them deserved to be there.

I approached her from the left and half-crawled into bed with her. It was my mother's one regret with my father's death, that she was so consumed by fear that she'd run out of the room instead of crawling into bed with him, so I imagined myself fulfilling her wish. But she was firmly situated in the middle of the bed and swollen, and I didn't want to disturb her, so I wiggled my torso onto the bed and kept my bottom in the chair. I gently stroked her hair, which had grown in gray before she had a chance to dye it brown.

"I'm so sorry this happened to you," I said. I didn't cry. My stoicism surprised me. I was hovering above my emotions, separated from them by a jet stream of cold air. Tina, Ji Young, and Sarah stood closer to the foot of the bed. Tina started crying; Ji Young followed suit. Every ten seconds or so the heart monitor emitted its dissonant bleeps. I'd had enough.

"Can we shut this thing off?" I asked no one. Tina found the right button and turned it off. "And she hated that oxygen mask, she couldn't wait to rip it off," I said, on a roll now. "Why did they put it on her?"

"I know," Tina said, "it's like they just don't get it." She removed the oxygen mask. My mother's mouth looked black from my vantage point, and I wondered when she had last brushed her teeth, drunk a cup of coffee, eaten a meal. Had she known it would be her last time? Her breath was still ragged, and her cheeks puffed in and out with each new exhalation, completely devoid of control, and her lips got sucked into her mouth each time she inhaled. Her body was merely functioning now, nothing more.

We sat with her for five minutes, ten minutes. Once in a while someone would say something to her, stroke her hand, or cry, and I continued playing with her hair, just as she loved me and my father to do. "I'm like a kitten," she'd say. Softly, I sang a single verse of what I considered to be "our song," the song she rasped on car rides, and aboard Amtrak, and all the times we weren't sure where we were going or where we had been:

And even though we ain't got money,
I'm so in love with ya honey,
And everything will bring a chain of love.
And in the morning when I rise,
You bring a tear of joy to my eyes,
And tell me everything is gonna be all right.

I couldn't stand the waiting. I didn't want her to exist in this ephemeral state between living and dying for another minute. She was half a person this way, and anyone who knew her could attest that she had been so much more. Maybe she was waiting for me to say something? Could Yaw have been right—was she waiting for me to leave so she could depart the earth in peace? Or maybe, even without brain activity, she couldn't rest until she heard her only child speak to her one last time. I watched her body inhale and exhale a few times. As she took in another breath I said the first thing that came to my mind:

"Don't worry about me, Mom. I'm going to be the first woman executive editor of *The New York Times*."

Her chest froze mid-breath. She never exhaled.

My head snapped up and I looked from Tina to Ji Young to Sarah, stunned. We waited a moment, then all at once the four of us burst out laughing.

"She heard you!" Ji Young said. "Jen, I know your mom, she heard you!"

"Oh, Jenny," Tina said through her tears, "you just made her so happy."

"Well, I guess that's the last thing a Jewish mother needs to hear before she can rest in peace," I said, still laughing. "No pressure or anything." I walked over to the counter, picked up a pair of scissors, cut off a lock of her hair, just as I'd done with my father, and put it in a pill bottle I'd emptied for the occasion. I was about to walk away when a thought occurred to me.

"Sarah, can you do me a favor?" I asked. Four years ealier, when my grandmother Vivian died, my mother had asked Sarah to look up the Jewish mourner's prayer, the Kaddish, in Hebrew, so she could say it for her mother. With this request in mind I calmly turned to Sarah and said, "Could you say Kaddish for my mother, Sarah?"

The significance of my request flickered across her face; she remembered. She closed her eyes and began, squinting to remember the Hebrew perfectly:

Yitgadal v'yitkadash sh'mei raba b'alma di-v'ra
chirutei, v'yamlich malchutei b'chayeichon
uvyomeichon uvchayei d'chol beit yisrael, ba'agala
uvizman kariv, v'im'ru: amen.

A few lines in, her face turned beet-red and her hand instinctively went up to her eyes to conceal her weeping. She continued to recite the prayer through sobs that threatened to cut off her voice, a rare loss of control for a girl who always seemed to have it.

"Thank you," I said to Sarah when she was done. I gathered the clothes I'd brought for my mother—the clothes she was supposed to wear when she checked out of the hospital—and I left, closing the sliding glass door behind me.

HAVING HAD MY FILL of cardiac intensive care, I ducked into the bathroom just outside the unit. I closed the door and flipped on the light, and when I caught myself in the mirror I stopped: I was totally alone for the first time since she'd died. I studied my reflection: I looked pretty much the same as I had before Friday, save for the gray circles under my eyes. I caught sight of my mother's wedding ring, which I'd placed on a chain around my neck, destined never again to grace her finger. She'd worn my father's ring around her neck for four years, and now I was wearing hers; the circle was complete. I studied my face again. No one would be able to tell my mother had died by just looking at me. How was I breathing? How was I standing upright? I wasn't even crying. There was no sound in the bathroom, only quiet. She was gone. It was palpable.

And that's when I felt it. Not a crack, it wasn't that dramatic, but a slow tearing of the fiber that had connected the three of us. I stood there in the unforgiving fluorescent glow, and for the first time I saw that I was standing alone. They weren't waiting outside for me; they weren't waiting at home for me. They wouldn't be calling me. They were gone; they belonged to my memory now. My father's death had muted a part of my life; my mother's death silenced it completely. The space she had occupied was empty, like a street cut off from traffic. I was the only one left. Would I be enough?

When I emerged, Tina, Ji Young, and Sarah were all in agreement: They were going to take me out of Staten Island for a few hours. We piled into Ji Young's green Volvo and hit the expressway. I called Arline and told her that her sister had breathed her last at 12:14 Eastern Standard Time; I called work and relayed the news and said I didn't know when I'd be back. I also called one of my professors, because I felt that someone at school should know what happened. I had at least a dozen voice mails, and as I listened to them I made a mental note of calls I needed to return. And then, after my sixth new voice message:

"You have one message whose retention time is about to expire. First voice message."

"Hi gaw-geous. I tried to call you before but you must have been in the tunnel or the subway, probably the subway because it's nine-thirty. So I just want to wish you to have a happy day. And . . . uh, that's all. I love you! And . . . thanks for everything. It means a lot to me. And . . . it really does. Okay? 'Cause it's, it's like, it's like emotional support, and . . . I'm gonna start crying, so . . . I really love you, okay? And I appreciate everything that you do, and I don't want you to sacrifice any part of your life. It's enough! I love you. Byebye."

She'd left the message just after she was diagnosed with cancer, and I'd saved it all this time. I must have been on my way back to Manhattan after staying at her apartment when she told me not to sacrifice any part of my life for her care and treatment. I think she meant that she didn't want me to put off going to journalism school on account of her cancer. I can't remember what kind of emotional support I lent her that day—perhaps that was the day I pledged to accompany her to every treatment, à la Céline. Maybe I pointed out the difference between my father's terminal diagnosis and her treatable and not-yet-advanced cancer. Her doctors also had to remind her that her cancer was more treatable than my father's, because she could not shake the vision of his once-strapping physique reduced to shriveled skin that hung off a crippled skeleton. My mother did not want to go out like that, and maybe that was the day I assured her she wouldn't.

I didn't want anyone to see me crying, so I focused my tears on the brilliant blue behind the Manhattan skyline, which was just coming into view as we sailed along the BQE. "Thanks for everything," she'd said in a deeper, more serious tone than the "I love you!" just before it. It was an emotional octave below her normal pitch, her way of leveling with me. She'd left the message eleven months ago but I pretended for a moment that it was from today, and that the "thanks for everything" was her voice from beyond the grave telling me that she knew how I'd tried to keep her alive, and how I'd agonized over how best to do it, and even though she couldn't stay, *thank you for trying*. All I wanted was to tell her that I hadn't given up on her, especially in the face of doctors who seemingly had, and maybe—somewhere, somehow—she'd actually heard me.

We sat for lunch at Pampano, a Mexican restaurant on East Forty-ninth Street where my mother and I had celebrated Father's Day a couple of years after his death. I stared at the smoked swordfish dip and ignored everyone's pleas to eat. My stomach had shut down; the prospect of eating made me feel guilty for some reason. I also didn't want a drop of alcohol, as I was afraid altering my state would somehow compound my grief. Monika, a friend of mine from the Redeye Grill, joined us mid-meal; Rita and Angie were scheduled to fly in that evening. Everyone at the table eyed me warily, and I realized that, unlike when my father died, I was mourning alone. I selfishly wished

Arline had stayed. But more than that, I wished my mother was sitting in the empty seat at the head of the table—she'd tell everyone to leave me alone and let me sulk. No one knew what I needed like she did.

Afterward we drove to my apartment so I could get some clothes, and as I peered out the window the familiar streets of my city suddenly seemed foreign to me. The sensation, exacerbated by the cruelly vivid sunlight, was akin to an acid trip: I was seeing everything as if for the first time, through eyes that had never before been used. As Ji Young looked for parking I hopped out and went upstairs by myself. The apartment was just as I had left it on Friday as I'd rushed off to work, but it seemed much quieter than I remembered. The air had been sucked from the room. She was gone—from here, too. Her energy had been zapped right out of my life. I felt her absence from my kitchen, my living room, my bathroom, and my bedroom. I'd never be able to escape the void her death had created. I rested my elbows on the kitchen counter and put my head in my hands and wept.

I wept all the way to my bedroom, where I began packing fresh underwear and socks. As I folded a few shirts on my bed I remembered some of Eleanor's quirks, which made me laugh through my sobs. Like her habit of bringing her gym bag full of jewelry to my apartment. I suddenly remembered her telling me sometime before Christmas that she'd hidden her jewelry somewhere. Up until last Friday, in fact, she'd reminded me at least half a dozen times that she had stored everything in my closet. Which I'd found strange, because why would she do this even after her roommate moved out? In a flash everything she nagged me about that I'd shrugged off came to the fore: "Jenny," she'd been saying for the last month, "don't forget—my jewelry is in your closet. *Don't forget.*"

"Okay, okay, I got it," I'd said dismissively, clueless as to why she was so adamant about it.

Like lightning I ripped open my closet doors and tossed shoeboxes aside until I spotted the red gym bag. The last time she'd come to my apartment was the night of the mini-stroke—an unexpected trip, which meant she must have put it in my closet long before that. I hurled it onto my bed and unzipped it, and it was all there waiting for me in little black boxes: the imperial topaz, the platinum and diamonds, my grandmother's cocktail ring. I cried harder as I opened each box, embracing the meaningless stones as if they were pieces of her, until I got to the last one, a nondescript white box. I snapped it open and gasped: There, on her long gold chain, was my father's ring—the ring she never took off, the ring she kept around her neck as a symbol of her boundless grief. When had she stopped wearing it? She didn't tell me she had, which was strange. It seems like a decision she would have made, to take off my father's ring, and one she definitely would have shared with me. That ring was a piece of my father that she proudly showed the world—she wanted people to know her husband had existed, and that she still loved him even though he was gone, just as I now wore a piece of her around my neck because I wanted her to be more than just a memory. For me, there was only one answer.

"She knew," I repeated to myself, over and over, through my tears. "She knew. She knew. She knew."

WE MADE OUR WAY back to Staten Island plus one: Monika had decided to follow our little grieving party across the Verrazano. I wasn't sure what to do once we got there except mope and wait for Rita and Angie to join us. But as the night wore on I noticed Sarah pulling Tina and Ji Young aside and murmuring things I couldn't hear. Ji Young later told me that Sarah was coordinating the cremation, the sale of some of my mother's furniture, and the transport to my apartment of the things of my mother's that I wanted to keep. Sarah had a mission: to pack me up as soon as possible and get me the hell out of Staten Island. It was a good plan—my mother didn't own the apartment, so I didn't need to sell it—and if left to my own devices I might have wound up sprawled among the detritus, examining every slip of paper until four months had passed and the city marshal was banging down the door. I would have to go through dishes, papers, dirty laundry that my mother had let pile up, pots, pans, patio furniture, a closet full of clothes that still included a few items of my father's, and my old bedroom, the same room my mother had begged me for five years to empty so she could rent it out. She'd laugh if she knew it took something as monumental as her dying to finally get my ass in gear.

My mother couldn't bear to part with my father's clothing for a year after he died, but under Sarah's direction I zipped through my mother's closet in an hour, placing items to be donated in big black trash bags that I'd drive to the Goodwill the following week. I kept a lot less than I thought I would, coming away with one suitcase full of clothes that I saved mostly for sentimental value, as my mother's waist had been the size of my thigh. Shedding her 1980s finery—the fruit of all those shopping sprees—wasn't as hard as I thought it would be. Monika went through my mother's drawers and held up socks, panties, old makeup: "Keep or toss?" she'd ask, her strong, capable hands emptying and sorting and stacking so fast my head was spinning. Sarah placed ads in the *Staten Island Advance* for an open house to take place that weekend, at which we'd sell the treadmill my mother had bought and never used, various kitchenware, the patio furniture, even my childhood board games. I was adamant about keeping the baker's rack, as acquiring one had been a dream of hers, and the mahogany dining room table, which could fit in my living room with a little tinkering. Tina shoved a box of my father's video-cassettes under my nose and made me choose. There were hundreds of them, all movies taped off the television in the 1980s.

"Jenny, do you really need a fifteen-year-old copy of *The China Syndrome?*" she asked.

"Yes," I replied.

"*Jen*-ny," she said, rolling her eyes and sounding very much like my mother, "do you *really* need *Flashdance? Foul Play?*"

"*Yes!*"

"Ooh, look at this," Tina said, unscathed. "'Eleanor's Childhood Movies.' You want this, right?" I'd seen those movies only once before, when Arline had them transferred to VHS a few years ago: a collection of images of my mother's family from the thirties and forties, recorded on her father's movie camera. Since the medium was fairly new, the tape consisted mainly of random clusters of aunts and uncles huddled together and waving, a family portrait come to life. I'd forgotten it existed. The sketchy bits I remembered featured my mother, aged four or five, sitting on the grass at summer camp with her nose shoved in a book, oblivious, while rambunctious children gallivanted around her. I grabbed the tape from Tina. God only knew when I'd gather up the courage to watch it.

Angie, who arrived on Friday morning, helped me go through the laundry basket full of papers and bills that had accumulated, because my mother's idea of dealing with financial obligation meant randomly tossing bills onto her bedroom floor until the collection agencies started calling. Rita, who pulled up in a Town Car on Thursday night, stayed in her nightgown for the entire weekend and only left my mother's bedroom to pay for the cremation and eat pretzels.

"Rita, put some clothes on!" Monika barked in her rigid Polish accent. "Your ass is hanging out!"

Rita, massaged into submission by her daily cocktail of Xanax and Percocet, obeyed and sheepishly headed back to the bedroom. Which was a relief—before Rita arrived I'd hidden my mother's Percocet, Xanax, Ambien, and whatever else was small, round, and white in the trunk of my mother's car, paranoid that Rita would have a narcotic field day on my mother's tab. I knew exactly how my mother would want me to deal with Rita and acted accordingly, as if she was issuing instructions from the hereafter. After Sunday, the day we made the big move, Rita would lounge on my futon—hemmed in by boxes and hastily assembled furniture and wearing the same nightgown and eating the same pretzels—for a week.

"Rita," I'd ask her one day while we watched my mother's TV, newly installed in my living room, "did anything ever happen between you and my father?" It was random and impulsive and it left my mouth before I could think twice about it, just as it had when I'd asked my mother the same thing.

"No," she'd say, shaking her head, adding: "I wish."

I was taken aback by the way she volunteered that last part—admitting to a lesser degree of guilt is the hallmark of the guilty—and figured she had something to hide, but perhaps that "something" was all the cocaine she and my father sold, which she probably figured I didn't know about. I filed the conversation away, my mind too muddled to pursue any line of questioning to its terminus.

Going from an empty apartment to an apartment suddenly filled with worker ants boxing up a precious part of my life was a shock, but if someone hadn't directed me toward a firm goal, grief and pity would have gotten the better of me. I was determined to return to school in ten days—my mother didn't want me to sacrifice any part of my life, that's what she had said—and ripping off the past like a Band-Aid was probably the best approach. Though they could never substitute for my mother's company, having this motley bunch around me was therapeutic, and before I knew it the mop-up operation had morphed into something else entirely: We were sitting shiva, albeit in our own nonreligious way. I wished she could have seen just how alone I wasn't—in addition to our core group of mourners, Jeff, who had popped in and out of my life since my father's illness, stopped by on Saturday to sample the seemingly endless supply of Italian pastries.

But my shiva couldn't last forever, and Sarah, Ji Young, Monika, Tina, Angie, and Jeff couldn't hold my hand through everything. Like during the last week of January, when I had to cross the Verrazano alone to clean out the scattered bits we hadn't had time to pack into the U-Haul. I took everything that wasn't broken or worn out, incorporating even my mother's everyday items into my life: towels, shower caddy and shampoos, bottles of Windex and Tide. My gang couldn't be there when I cleaned under the bed one last time and found a folder containing the small calendars my father had kept on the road when he was painting. I gasped when I saw that each day in calendar years 1996, 1997, and 1998 was marked with either "Work" or "Rain," including my birthday. I'd forgotten how meticulously he'd recorded everything having to do with his business, and I suddenly missed that quality of his very much. I was alone when I located my father's gun, an unlicensed .22 he kept for "protection," which I promptly unloaded and hid in my closet as soon as I got home. And no one was with me when I finally cleaned out my old bedroom, distilling my entire childhood into two or three boxes.

I remember that it was a Saturday and I'd grown tired and sad from packing in utter silence and I went into my mother's bedroom and lay down on her mattress, which had been stripped bare. The canary sun began to set, and as the rays hit my face through the bare window they forced my eyes closed. I rested my chin on the mattress, and it was quiet. Too quiet. And that is when I felt the void most acutely: a dull pain, located in my chest, just behind my heart. It was such an empty ache, an utter abyss, like someone or something had gouged out my soul. I remembered how my father had moved us onto Merle Place six years earlier and wondered if he'd be surprised to see how I'd finally vacated it. Would he feel sorry for me? A thought raced through my mind and repeated over and over again:

I am the only one left. I am the only one left. I am the only one left.

For a long while after that I felt I was still in that room, on that bare mattress, where my parents had slept and made love and suffered chemo fevers. And that afternoon, as my twilight sleep gave way to dreams under the setting sun, I thought that maybe a part of me would always be in that room, no matter how old I got, because that was the room in which I'd finally lost them for good.

But I wasn't alone, thankfully, for the moment that transcended all the packing and the moving and the hospital directives and the take-out Chinese food—the moment when I found my mother's will. There were two of them, actually, and I discovered them as I was erasing the hard drive on her computer before I sold it. They weren't notarized, and I printed them out and resumed my place on the floor, where I'd been sorting all the files my mother kept under the bed—birth certificates, death certificates, marriage licenses, all of my report cards from every grade, teaching credentials, old checkbooks, both my parents' lung X-rays, programs from all my plays, and the letter dated 1988 informing my father that he'd been released from his parole. My parents' rich past, reduced to a stack of papers.

The first will was dated June 10, 2003, and it was brief: a few paragraphs leaving everything to me, including any potential future earnings, because even though "I have no property and/or money nor insurance, one never knows what this life could bring." She hoped, if this mystery wealth ever materialized, that "my daughter will put her business affairs in good hands, wise hands, as I wish with all my heart I could have made her financially secure." She left directions for the dissemination of her ashes: a third to go to Laguna Beach, where I'd scattered some of my father's ashes in 2004; a third to be sprinkled on the Mascia family plot at Green-Wood Cemetery, where she'd scattered a third of my father's ashes in 2002; and the other third "commingled with my husband's and scattered in any part of Central Park my daughter deems fit." That explained why she'd kept a third of my father's ashes in a blue and white ceramic jar in the linen closet. The way she ended it thickened my throat into a lump:

> I do not want a memorial service. I just want to go and I hope there is a place where we three can sometime meet again, although I know in my heart it is not to be.
>
> I love my daughter with all my heart. She is my heart. She is the best.

But it was nothing compared to the second will, also not notarized, and twice as long. It was dated the day before she'd had the mole on her nose removed, right before her cancer diagnosis. Reading it aloud to Sarah and Angie and Tina on the living room floor, I know I didn't cry—at first I chuckled at my mother's obsession with credit cards and jewelry hocking, not knowing what awaited me at the end, and maybe even then I simply whimpered, too numb to do much else. But later, when the numbness wore off, the pull of these words, her final act of grace, did their work, and I was forever changed.

"Hey, guys," I said. "Check this out." I began to read:

I, Eleanor Mascia, being of sound mind, hereby declare this to be my last will and my wishes for the disposal of my body and belongings.

I will type this in the form of a letter to my daughter.

Dear Jen,

Have me cremated. Call Social Security and ask how much they will contribute toward a funeral. I think it's $250 dollars. Use a credit card of mine for the rest or hock some of my jewelry.

I don't want to wait three or more years to be with Daddy. My last wish is to be with him, floating around the Pacific Rim or wherever, and I want you to scatter my ashes on the beach where you scattered Daddy's. Use the debit card to get any money out of my bank account. Take out everything. Wait until the third of the month and take out my Social Security check. Don't worry—they won't find out, and if they do, screw them.

At this we all laughed.

Try to hold onto the apartment and sublet it for $1200 a month. Add $60 or more for the parking spot. Take anything you want from the apartment—sell it or keep it. If you want to move to the apartment, tell them I am living here and that you stay with me when I don't feel well.

"Like *Weekend at Bernie's*," I remarked. "So morbid!" I continued reading:

I have some new Cuisinart pots I haven't used—take them. Take the dining room set, TVs, treadmill—all the dishes in the buffet. Put into storage whatever you don't want.

I looked over at Sarah—everything my mother had instructed was already in motion or completed. I felt a deep sense of pride that I'd been one step ahead of her all week without even knowing it.

Take all the credit cards and max them out. Try to have Ji Young do it, if she will, because they will think the cards are stolen. Buy her a couple of things in return, or talk to Arline. She has a larcenous streak, like me, I think.

"I can't wait to read this to Ji Young," I said, laughing. "My mother sold her down the river for a fifty-five-hundred-dollar line of credit." I read on:

Buy stuff you can sell for the most part—jewelry, etc. If you want cash advances I think you need a pin number. If I'm okay after this surgery I will get them. The Fleet, Bank One and Discover Card have quite a bit of money left on them. Call customer service, they have automated balances: S.S.# 130-26-XXXX, mother's maiden name is Funt.

"She wanted me to clean her out!" I said, shaking my head. I had already emptied her checking account, but I didn't have it in me to perpetrate fraud. I silently read ahead to the final paragraph and my breath caught in my throat. "Oh, my god," I said, and my hand started shaking. Sarah came up behind me and followed over my shoulder as I read the last part aloud:

I have some last wishes. Please try to keep Daddy's ring—the one around my neck. Please offer Arline anything she wants—jewelry and/or furniture, etc., and if you are ever in a position to help her with anything please do. I'm sure there is lots more I wish I could do for you or others.
I loved you very much. I loved you very much. I was astonished that at my age I could have had such a lovely, funny, beautiful child. Your father and I both loved you so much. I hope you really know this,

that in spite of the times we were separated, or fought with you and each other, we showed you that love again and again, in spite of imagined or real hurts. I hope you remember that we three were a family, a real one that sat down to eat dinner together, that explored and traveled together, even if we didn't go to the Grand Canyon, and showed each other the real love we felt.

Wherever I am, even though I am not a believer, I know that part of me will belong to this earth somewhere, and thus part of the earth will always remember and love you.

CHAPTER 16

February 2006

. . .

I AWOKE WITH A GASP. IT WAS NEARLY THREE IN THE AFTERNOON and I'd let myself sleep the day away. I stumbled into the living room and tried to avoid the detritus in my path but bashed into everything anyway. Boxes of books stacked atop boxes of pans, my mother's beloved baker's rack—which had cracked in the U-Haul—her dining room table, and dishes upon glasses upon silverware now crowded my tiny flat. It had been this way for a month and I had no desire to move it. I pictured how the place looked before all of this and realized that if my mother somehow rose from the dead, she wouldn't recognize it.

"Jenny, I can't picture what the inside of your apartment looks like."

I now understood how this day connected to the beginning of the end on Christmas Eve, how I was standing at the terminus of that line. I could never have imagined that that night in the hospital, with her dramatic confession about my father, would culminate in this, a life without her. With this newest loss, I suddenly faced three distinct types of grieving: the loss of my father, the loss of my mother, and the loss of the two of them—the loss of parents. Each of these felt different from the others, and when one of them became too overwhelming I simply switched gears.

And what of that awful confession? The scant details she'd conveyed about the other murders my father committed were already fading, just as I wanted them to. I remembered my dream and understood with a shudder that my mother was a permanent part of my imagination now, never to be laughed with or quarreled with again. She belonged to my dreams, joining my father, who'd lived there for the last five years. From now on, if I ever needed her, I'd have to contend with her ghost.

Meanwhile, I was still living. I treated the vice president of the Redeye Grill to a letter explaining that while waitressing was a fine and noble profession, I wasn't in the most stable frame of mind to upsell lobster cobb salads to the Botoxed masses. I just couldn't stomach the possibility of waiting on families now that mine had been disbanded. I feared breaking down in tears in full view of the dining room. But I didn't spend my free time staring at the walls, either. I returned to school eleven days after her death, just as she would have wanted, and I earned honors that semester. But with only two classes to occupy my time I found myself floating through the remainder of the spring pretending that nothing major had happened. My way of feeling sorry for myself was by not feeling sorry for myself, and quickly brushing off the pity and concern of others. If I regarded myself as everyone else did—orphaned and alone—I might have gone mad.

Sarah wasn't the only one of my friends who recommended therapy to cope with my mother's death—and her surprising role as my father's accessory—but her voice was the loudest, perhaps because I told her that I'd begun popping my mother's Vicodin to brighten up my day. So in April I marched myself over to Columbia's mental health services and landed on the couch of a psychologist. Dr. Feldman was gentle, patient—and blind. He took notes anyway, and halfway through each session his computer spoke to him: "Shutting down," it would say as it went into sleep mode.

"So, Ms. Mascia," he said, "what brings you here?" The lighting was soft, the walls were draped in decorative shawls, and candles dotted the shelves. It seemed a shame to ruin the atmosphere.

"Well, Dr. Feldman, my mother died two months ago, and I've started helping myself to her Vicodin. Cancer patients get the mother lode, so my supply is holding steady at around, oh, two hundred fifty? Two seventy-five? My father died five years ago. He had lung cancer, and I'm an only child. My mother was my best friend in the world and I probably feel guilty for surviving without her. I guess our unusual closeness began the day the FBI came to arrest my dad when I was five. For years I wanted to know what he did but my mother refused to tell me. He ended up spending a year in jail for what I later learned was a parole violation. Turns out he'd served twelve years before I was born, for murder, a fact I discovered on the Internet when I was twenty-two. After that I confronted my mother and she admitted the truth: They hadn't met 'through friends,' like they'd always said, but she actually met my father while he was incarcerated—she was a teacher-slash-activist whose pet cause was prison reform and they fell in love behind the glass at Fishkill Correctional. After he was released they got married and had me. My mother counted on the redemptive power of love to straighten him out, but it didn't quite pan out that way, and when I was a few months old he was arrested for cocaine possession. He knew he'd get shipped back to jail, so my parents and I went on the lam and lived under assumed names, first in Houston, then in California, until I was five and the Feds cuffed him right in front of me. They extradited him to New York but after several months he was released, thank god, and we moved back to California, where my mother made sure we lived well beyond our means. We went bankrupt twice, and when times got really tough my father teamed up with my mother's sister in Florida to sell cocaine via FedEx, an arrangement that lasted until he snorted more than he sold and landed himself in rehab. I also suspect they had an affair in the process. We moved back to New York eleven years ago because my father's carpet cleaning business was failing. Though he was relegated to blue-collar jobs like painting Taco Bells and Exxons, things seemed to be going okay, but then my mom had a heart attack, my dad got terminal cancer and died, and my mom got cancer, had another heart attack, and died. Three weeks before I took her off life support she confessed that my father didn't just kill that one guy in the 1960s, he actually killed half a dozen guys, and she knew about it all those years but stayed married to him anyway." It was unexpectedly satisfying to finally coalesce the chaotic elements of my history into a single narrative. "So, whaddya think?"

His pen was poised over his notebook; he'd stopped taking notes about thirty seconds in. "My honest opinion?" he asked.

"Please," I said.

"I think you need to see a psychiatrist on a permanent and consistent basis."

Without peers to whom I could relate, my sole sources of comfort came from occasionally publishing my class assignments and plopping down on the couch at six o'clock with a freshly chopped salad to watch two hours' worth of *Friends* and *Seinfeld* in syndication. It was a quiet life, and just as my mother made do with a sad, solitary lamb chop after my father died, I learned that a pancake or a bowl of cereal could be dinner. I was still maneuvering around boxes, which I'd begun using as end tables, when Monika came to visit during a late spring snowstorm.

"What the hell is this?" she demanded.

"What?" I asked, reclining on my futon with a Diet Coke in one hand and a box of chocolate-covered graham crackers in the other.

"Get up!" she commanded. "No more! We are cleaning this place, *now*." We worked through the night, and three bottles of Windex later we gradually unearthed the foundations of a sophisticated, organized apartment. We placed my mother's baker's rack against the wall between the front hallway and the kitchen, where it slid perfectly into a little nook. I filled my living room bookcase with all the cookbooks she'd handpicked during her fevered bouts of conspicuous consumption. We fit her dining room table snugly against a living room wall so it didn't look so oversized and out of place, and relocated my drop-leaf table to the kitchen for use as a cooking prep table. It was all very grown up; my mother would have approved. And just so there was never any doubt that I was, at one time, part of a family, I placed framed pictures of my parents everywhere, which prompted me to nickname the place "the Museum of Grief."

With my apartment under control I focused on my body, which put on weight whenever one of my parents was diagnosed with a terminal illness. Since shin splints had ended my once-stellar running career, I joined a 24-hour gym ten blocks south of my apartment. Because it was open all the time I didn't have an excuse not to go, and I worked up to an hour of cardio a night. In six months I had slimmed down enough to fit back into the size 6 jeans I'd been wearing before cancer had come calling.

My mother didn't want to wait forever to float with my father around the Pacific Rim, so I fulfilled her wish. In April I flew to California to distribute a third of my mother's ashes from a beach in Laguna, the same place where I'd scattered my father's in 2004. When I arrived home I scattered another third of her ashes in Central Park, in a lake in full view of Bow Bridge. I decided against putting the rest of her ashes on the grave in Green-Wood because of her suspicion that my father's had been removed by his relatives (don't ask), so on what would have been their thirtieth wedding anniversary I mixed the final third of her ashes in with the final third of my father's, per her wishes, and placed the blue and white ceramic jar atop my mother's baker's rack.

But I didn't ignore Green-Wood entirely. On the fifth anniversary of my father's death I woke up before noon, bought a bunch of lilacs, and MapQuested myself to the far reaches of Brooklyn, where I stood before the nondescript plot that held four of my relatives. The fifth anniversary would have meant so much to her, so I went in her place and cried tears for both of us, because she couldn't.

And I wondered, was this what my life would become? A minefield of grim anniversaries? After my mother died, lighting the Yahrzeit candles fell to me, and I soon realized that I couldn't go more than a couple of months without tripping over one tortured milestone or another. There was January 12: Mom's death. April 10: Dad's birthday and David's death. May 6: Dad's death. October 11: Grandma Vivian's death. October 12: Mom's birthday. October 14: Vivian's birthday. November 14: Grandpa Frank's death. November 19: My parents' wedding anniversary. I kept so many tall candles around the house I began to feel like a Dominican widow. That's not including Thanksgiving, Christmas, and, most important to us three agnostics, New Year's Eve. The only promise in which we ever stored faith was that the new year would arrive.

I didn't have much time to contemplate my status as a professional widow, however, because about a week later I ran out of money. It happened right as the semester ended, and on the last day of class I hit the pavement in search of restaurant work. Even though graduate school was slowly overqualifying me for this industry, it was still the quickest way to make the most cash. Through networking I maneuvered my way into a job at Gramercy Tavern, one of the highest-rated fine-dining restaurants in New York. I was really biding my time until a news assistant position opened at *The New York Times*. I'd learned about the job during a newsroom field trip with my reporting class a year earlier, and though it was largely clerical it paid better than waitressing. And it was, after all, the Paper of Record. I'd been email-stalking the clerical supervisor for six months at my mother's urging, and continued to do so for six months after she died. After I'd been at Gramercy for a month and a half I got the call.

"So, the way it works is this," Erika and Alexis, my prospective bosses, explained. "You're hired as a floater, which means we put you wherever we need you—Metro, Foreign, Culture—until a permanent spot opens up, and if that happens, you get benefits and paid vacation and sick days."

"Um, so, does this mean I don't have to be a waitress anymore?" I asked them.

"Yes," they said, giggling good-naturedly at my naïveté. I was saved. Even though I was starting at the bottom of the food chain—I went from being the smartest person in the room to, well, not being the smartest person in the room—it was the only room I wanted to be in. If only my mother could have seen it.

I was reminded most acutely of her absence when I was offered a permanent position some months later and went to human resources to fill out paperwork. I paused when I reached "Emergency Contact." Who should I list now that my mother was gone? I settled on Sarah, the most responsible choice.

In addition to a decent medical plan, *Times* employees are also offered free life insurance. But when I got to "Beneficiaries" I had to pause again.

"Um, what do I put here?" I asked, peering up from my forms. "I don't have any beneficiaries yet."

"Oh, you can just put your parents," the HR director offered.

"I don't have parents," I said bluntly.

"Oh," she said.

What could she say to that? But instead of mourning my plight, or even crying at all, I kept going, gratefully locked in by the drudgery of routine—work, gym, sleep, repeat. Just when the predictability of my new, leaner life threatened to bore me to death, I began to think of all I *wasn't* doing: escaping into a toxic romantic relationship, or dissolving into drugs (Sarah made me flush all that Vicodin), or ditching class, my high school M.O. I had imagined that my mother dying would cripple me, but—was it possible?—it had made me stronger. I was filled with a sense of purpose, and it began in that hospital bathroom, when I glanced in the mirror and searched my face for signs of the loss that had just wrenched me in two. I wasn't bankrupt, as my parents had been; I wasn't hiding money under the carpet; I wasn't coupled with a man whose mistakes had, on more than one occasion, sent me fleeing to another state; I wasn't married to a murderer, sharing his guilt so he didn't have to shoulder it all on his own; and I wasn't hiding all of it from my kid. And, though it was bittersweet relief, I was no longer caring for two terminally ill people as they waited their turn to die.

One night after a predawn workout I walked home along Second Avenue and watched as the night sky almost imperceptibly faded into a paler shade of blue, and for the first time in years I felt hope. I followed the sunrise all the way up to my roof, and as sapphire gave way to canary I understood how lucky I was to have survived. All the mistakes my parents had made—the detours outside the law, the hand-to-mouth lifestyle honed from years living as fugitives, the guilt at having respectively committed and abetted murder, and the outsider status it had fostered in all three of us—I had somehow transcended them. It was something of a shock that I should be the last one standing; I'd always imagined that my father was the strong one, my mother his spine when his spirit sagged. But by some mix of cosmic or existential or corporeal default, I was the survivor. As the stars gave way to sun, I realized that I had outrun their past, and I was free to create my own narrative. My life—finally, blessedly—was up to me, and no one else.

. . .

CHAPTER 17

"METRO."

"Hi, my name is Stella and I am calling from New Jersey, and I called last week. I may have talked to you. Did I speak to you? It was at night."

Like all of them, she had the urgency of someone running to catch a train. "Um, I don't think so," I said, a wary eye trained on gawker.com. "What is this regarding?"

"I am calling from New Jersey, and I need to tell you what the band U2 has been doing here. They've been putting people in hospitals. I need you to come down to the state hospital and walk me out—"

Slam.

I'd been on the job only two months and already the wingnuts who called the Metro desk were the highlight of my day. Ordinarily I would have entertained her loopy logic for at least another five minutes, but today was different—I'd finally drawn up the courage to do what I'd spent the last two months thinking about. After Googling everyone I'd ever met, dated, or loathed, I did what everyone does when they work in a cathedral of information: I began to dig. I logged on to the LexisNexis newspaper and public record database, and my limited access revealed the party affiliations of all of my friends, every address I'd ever had, and which of my damaged exes had moved and where. But I was stalling, because what I was really after was the Big Prize: information about my father. It's one thing to have an oral history; it's quite another to see it in print. I dismissed the voice of my mother, which echoed in my head—"But Jenny, *why* do you want to know all these things?"—and plugged my father's name into Lexis.

His obituary popped up, but the quick one I wrote for him right after he died, not the longer, more unconventional one I called in a couple of days later. But his big crime was committed in the 1960s, and Lexis only went back so far. So I searched ProQuest, the database for historical news articles. After a few seconds, I came up with this:

The New York Times, **March 8, 1957**

TWO "WRONG" MEN FREED
Convictions Set Aside After 3d Prisoner Admits Holdup

Two Brooklyn men who had been convicted of holding up a Brooklyn gasoline station were released from jail yesterday as the victims of mistaken identity.

The men are John Gilbert, a 20-year-old trucker, of 1648 East Eighth Street, and Carmine Gotti, 22, a presser, of 2282 Dean Street, Brooklyn. A jury found them guilty Jan. 23 of robbing Henry J. Allison, 63, of $260 in his station at 9317 Third Avenue, Brooklyn, on Sept. 29.

District Attorney Edward S. Silver told Kings County judge George J. Joyce that John Mascia, 19, of 7321 Twelfth Avenue, Brooklyn, had admitted that he held up Mr. Allison with two companions. The judge then freed Mr. Gilbert and Mr. Gotti, both of whom had not yet been sentenced.

Mascia is in custody for a Brooklyn burglary.

Carmine Gotti? I wonder if his last name held any weight in 1957. (And what on earth is a presser?) My mother had told me that my father had gone to prison for stealing a car and possibly for armed robbery between Tina's and Angie's births, but I didn't know he was charged with another crime while still in jail. I couldn't find anything on the 1963 murder. But I had more than databases at my fingertips; I worked among the cream of the journalistic crop. I scanned the Metro directory for the reporter most likely to be of assistance, and landed on William Rashbaum, who worked the Brooklyn federal court beat. I gathered up my courage and jotted off an email, explaining that I was the girl who answered his calls and filed his stories, my dad had been a freelancer of sorts for the Mafia and had served time for killing someone, and could he possibly find anything on him for me? I gulped a pocket of air and hit Send.

He wrote back almost immediately, and I became a bundle of nerves as I double-clicked on his reply. He wanted details, he wrote, and after I supplied what little I knew, he called the desk.

"Hey, Jennifer, I think I found some clippings that might help you," he said. "How about we meet for a drink?"

This was it. I told one of my co-workers that Willie Rashbaum had found information about my father's crimes, and wow, isn't this exciting! He looked at me a little strangely, and I reminded myself that not everybody's father counted Sing Sing as an alma mater. I left work at nine and headed uptown. I got to the bar first and ordered a scotch and soda, which seemed like the most appropriate drink. Willie joined me ten minutes later—I believe he was wearing a trench coat, but perhaps my memory is drenched in newspaper schmaltz—and handed over what he'd dug up. The first item was a court ledger with a case number on it: 1810/63.

"Here's his name, the offense"—*Decedent shot and killed in park,* it read—"and the judge hearing his case," Willie explained. *Barshay* was scribbled next to "Judge." The ledger was handwritten, the scrawled details of one case crowding the next. Despite its dearth of details, the inclusion of a case number would be useful if I wanted to go searching for court records, Willie said. Next he handed me two photocopied newspaper clippings—before coming to the *Times* he'd had a run at the *Daily News,* and he was able to retrieve the articles from their database. The first I had seen before, in my mother's drawer, the one my grandparents had saved when my father was sentenced:

The Daily News, January 9, 1964

MASCIA GIVEN 20-TO-LIFE IN DOPE MURDER

John Mascia, 26, of Miami Beach, Fla., once a big-time dope distributor in the metropolitan area, was sentenced yesterday by Supreme

Court Justice Hyman Barshay in Brooklyn to 20 years to life in prison for the murder of a bush league dope pusher.

Last Sept. 27, Mascia interrupted his trial before Barshay on first-degree murder charges to plead guilty to murder, second degree.

Pal Changes Plea

At that time, the state was presenting evidence designed to show that Mascia and Anthony Piracci, 23, of 1593 E. 53d St., Brooklyn, shot to death Joseph (Joe Fish) Vitale, 22, in Owl's Head Park, Brooklyn, on May 25, 1963. The killing was attributed to Mascia's belief that Joe Fish held out money on drug sales and also informed for the cops.

Four days before Mascia threw in the towel, Piracci had pleaded guilty to manslaughter in the first degree.

Piracci was to have been at the sentencing yesterday also, but his counsel, Joseph Fontana, advised Barshay that Piracci wanted to withdraw his guilty plea and stand trial on the original murder indictment.

The justice instructed Fontana to present the necessary legal papers in court next Wednesday.

Detectives seeking Vitale's killers last spring found their first clue in a letter which had been torn in fragments. Patched together, the letter led to Piracci, who in turn linked Mascia with the crime.

Who the hell was Anthony Piracci? The first time I read this I didn't absorb the "news" the piece offered me: My father had help. When my mother first told me about this murder I pictured my father driving into a deserted park in the dead of night and splattering some poor guy's brains all over the windshield, and I didn't imagine he had company. Alone or not, it was a gruesome image. I reminded myself that it wasn't even his idea to kill Joe Fish in the first place—it was Robert Wyler's. My father had committed the crime out of a misplaced sense of loyalty for his former partner.

Or had he? Was it possible my mother lied to me? Would she confess the crime but not the motive? Murder is murder, it doesn't matter why.

The next clipping was some serious shit.

The Daily News, June 16, 1963

PIECING A MURDER CASE TOGETHER

A piece of paper found torn into a hundred scraps and later patiently reassembled by a detective has led, police say, to a solution of the rubout of Joseph Vitale, 24, suspected junk pusher.

Vitale was found dead in Owl's Head Park, Brooklyn. He had been shot six times, his body stomped, his right hip and left leg fractured. In his pockets were pawn tickets for $2 and $3, a billfold with $5, a hypodermic needle and syringe.

Six shells ringed the body, showing that he had been shot at the scene. The shells were from a .32 caliber automatic and a .32 caliber revolver, indicating that there were two killers.

A List of Names

Detective Stephen Crowley of Brooklyn South Homicide found the tell-tale scraps of paper. Police would only reveal that the torn bits were picked up "far from the scene of the crime." Crowley pieced them together and discovered that they gave details of a major narcotics operation.

Besides disclosing where the stuff was coming from, its price and destination, the paper yielded a number of names. Following those leads police questioned 30 to 40 characters, mostly known pushers.

Finally the pursuing cops came up with the name of Anthony Piracci, 23, of 1593 E. 53rd Street, Brooklyn. He had no record. They arrested him at his home. Under questioning, police said, Piracci admitted firing one of the six shots that caught Vitale in the head. He named a companion and said the latter fired the other five shots.

Next day in faraway Miami detectives picked up the alleged accomplice, John J. Mascia, 25, described by detectives here as "a big distributor of narcotics in the New York area."

The "Ride" Car

Miami police said Mascia was toting a .32 caliber revolver and a Luger, both fully loaded, and a pair of handcuffs. He was seized in a motel a few blocks from 960 N.E. 80th St., Miami, where he had moved his family from Brooklyn two months ago. He has a wife and two children.

Parked outside the motel was Mascia's 1963 white Pontiac, which police said was used to take Vitale from Manhattan to Owl's Head Park where he was viciously stomped and shot.

Detectives believe that Mascia suspected Vitale was a stool pigeon and, additionally, had held back money received from narcotics sales.

Vitale, who was identified by fingerprints, had been arrested eight times on drug charges. His father, Raphael, operates a luncheonette on E. Houston St. He said he put his son out of his home at 174 Grand St. some years ago because he was on junk and wouldn't work. The Grand St. address was close to police headquarters and Vitale used to run copy from the police press room.

Piracci was held without bail on homicide charges. Detectives flew to Miami and returned Mascia. He, too, was charged with homicide and held without bail.

Mascia's record dates to May 25, 1955, when he was put on a year's probation as a wayward minor for stealing an auto. On Oct. 16, 1956, he was dismissed on his own recognizance on a charge of assault and robbery. On the following Nov. 3 he was sent to Elmira Reformatory on the same charge. On March 27, 1957, he was returned to Elmira on a third similar count.

The main photo that ran with the piece was of a priest leaning over Vitale's dead, blanket-covered body and administering last rites, a melodramatic photo op if there ever was one. And I loved the stylized terms they used back then: "junk pusher," "stool pigeon," "rubout," "faraway Miami"—which must have seemed far away in 1963 if it took a plane ten hours to get there. So my father had murdered a copy boy, a job similar to the one I had now. That saddened me, as did Vitale's addiction to drugs, which obviously played a role in his death. Another photo, an old mug shot of Joseph Vitale's, depicted a handsome man with brown hair grown just past his ears, dark, penetrating eyes, and a friendly, boyish face. Someone I might be attracted to. Next to that was my father's mug shot. He had the same dominant eyebrows that I took great pains to pluck, black eyes framed by heavy eyelids, a crooked nose, and plump lips drawn so perfectly an artist could have rendered them. But where Vitale's mug shot from one of his eight arrests reveals a bit of his personality, my father's expression is totally empty—blank, defiant—and devoid of the life and the humor I so cherished thirty years later, and missed terribly today. This man was not my father; this man was John J. Mascia of 960 N.E. 80th St., Miami—a stranger.

Why would he have left those scraps of paper in the park if they contained so much information? What was he thinking? Was he phenomenally arrogant or incredibly stupid? And—ew—why did he have handcuffs? I sat there lamely, thinking that I'd just read something that my mother, in all likelihood, had never seen. Would she have stayed with him if she'd known that he stomped on someone's body after shooting him five times? Well, knowing her, probably, but my god. This was not a reluctant murder, as she'd led me to believe. It didn't sound like he had to summon the anger and courage to pull the trigger. It seemed as if there was serious rage behind his violence. It was almost as if he'd *enjoyed* it. I wondered if what my mother had described as "psyching himself up" involved cocaine.

I was also surprised to read more about his accomplice, who actually did appear to be a reluctant participant. He only fired once, probably after Joe Fish was already dead. During my shift the next night I did a LexisNexis search for Anthony Piracci and found that he was still alive, out of jail, and living in Boulder, Colorado. I also discovered that he had been busted for cocaine in 1985, along with a scion of the Kellogg family.

I now knew more than my mother ever did about my father's big crime, the one that derailed his life. Whatever he had told her about the murder was probably wrapped in the guise of a soulful midnight confession replete with scotch, sex, and tears, no doubt cushioning the blow. But to see such stark details in black-and-white might have been quite another experience for her, had she ever gotten the chance. They needed fingerprints to identify the guy!

Since this was knowledge she had discouraged me from finding, my success seemed unfair somehow, and not being able to ask her about it felt illicit. The truth might change me, harden me against my parents, and I wanted to stay just the same as when she last knew me, fearing that if I changed too much she wouldn't recognize me if she returned—a grieving person's logic. Just as when she was alive, I couldn't bear the thought of eclipsing her somehow, of having to make the choice to grow up and leave her behind.

But she'd left me first.

"Thank you," I muttered to Willie, who sipped a scotch of his own. "I can't believe you found all this for me."

"Well," he said in his wry, gravelly tenor, "it's not every day that a news clerk calls me and tells me her father was a murderer."

SUMMER STILL HELD the city in its stifling grip on the September morning I traveled to Brooklyn Supreme Court to peruse the yellowing pile of records that the chief clerk had unearthed for me. As soon as I stepped off the subway I was enveloped in a hazy soup that would have frizzed my long brown hair into oblivion had I not tied it back. When I reached the twenty-third floor of the spanking-new criminal court building on Jay Street, I was handed a pile of papers—court minutes, affidavits, motions of appeal—and given use of a conference room, "for privacy," the chief clerk explained.

"I can use this whole thing?" I asked, marveling at the view of downtown Brooklyn. "By myself?"

"Sure," he said. I sat at the conference table and prepared to learn all I could about the crime that had sent me reeling when I'd discovered it online seven years ago. The clerk hoisted a box onto the table and removed a pile of yellowing documents, which he divided into two stacks. "Here," he said, placing one of the stacks in front of me. "These are the actual court transcripts, which is what you're looking for, right?"

"Uh-huh," I said.

"And these"—he pointed to the other pile—"are appeals and various motions, but you probably won't be interested in those." I glanced at the second pile. *That's what you think.* "Well, I'll leave you to it," he said, closing the door behind him and heading to his office next door. I lunged for the high-priority pile, and as I flipped through trial transcripts typed out on delicate, nearly transparent onionskin paper, I was transported to the months before the Kennedy assassination, when a twenty-six-year-old man from Bay Ridge with several prior convictions pleaded guilty to the murder of Joseph "the Fish" Vitale.

As his mother, father, younger brother, and sister sat in the court-room, the jury heard four days of witness testimony in The People of the State of New York against John Mascia, Defendant—until Friday, September 27, 1963, when John was informed by his lawyer that his odds of acquittal weren't looking so hot. After a heated discussion in chambers, he entered a guilty plea. The judge, Hyman Barshay—who would go on to deny my father's motions of appeal for the next eleven years—asked John a dozen times whether his lawyer had explained, and if he had understood, the implications of stating his guilt. "I understand, Your Honor," he replied. When asked whether the damning witness testimony against him was true, my father responded, "Honestly, Your Honor, mostly."

"What?" Judge Barshay asked.

"Most of it was the truth," John said, sounding more like the cocky, self-assured father I'd known.

> Q: Well, the main feature is this, Mr. Mascia. Did you on this day, May 25, 1963, in Owl's Head Park, in Brooklyn, shoot Joseph Vitale?
>
> A: Yes.
>
> Q: How many times?
>
> A: I really can't recall.
>
> Q: Did you have a gun in your hand?
>
> A: Yes, sir.
>
> Q: Was it loaded?
>
> A: Yes, sir.
>
> Q: Did you empty it? The medical examiner said he found a number of bullet wounds.
>
> A: To my knowledge, it was emptied.
>
> Q: Emptied by you?
>
> A: Yes, sir.
>
> Q: Do you wish to tell me why you did it?
>
> A: Well, quite a few circumstances, Your Honor.

Whenever my father cocked his head to the side and squinted he reminded me of Robert De Niro, though when I knew him, in his for-ties and fifties, his olive features were even more refined than De

Niro's and, I think, more handsome. I pictured him this way then, as he casually answered the questions posed by the man who was charged with determining the course of his life. The line of questioning at its end, John promised to elucidate these "circumstances" to the probation department, depriving me of something I'll never obtain, though I would spend months trying: my father's version of these events, in his own words. He shared them with my mother, but never with me. It seems I was never meant to know.

Immediately following this exchange, Piracci also pleaded guilty. But unlike my father's replies, Piracci's answers were short and sweet, with no hint of personality: "Yes, Your Honor," "Yes, sir," "No, Your Honor." The state offered a lesser charge of manslaughter if John gave information regarding "other matters" in the criminal sphere, but my father was no rat. He refused. The way my mother told it, his brothers-in-crime from the neighborhood—against whom he could have helped build cases—applauded him as he swaggered through the prison gate. A romanticized version, perhaps, but he'd earned their respect by keeping his mouth shut.

During the sentencing hearing, Judge Barshay took the court on a tour of the Early Criminal Life of John Mascia, formerly of 7321 Twelfth Avenue, Brooklyn, New York. Just after his eighteenth birthday he stole a car; at nineteen he was charged with third-degree assault and discharged, only to be picked up two weeks later for assault and robbery. Two weeks after that, when my sister Tina was just a few months old, he was indicted for robbery in the second degree and spent three years at Elmira State Correctional Facility, a sentence that ran concurrently with yet another second-degree robbery charge. And then there was the early morning of May 25, 1963.

The victim was known as Joe Fish, Judge Barshay told the court, but his name was Joseph Vitale, and he was twenty-six years old. He was a known drug addict, and a police informant, and though Vitale was unaware of it, my father knew he was a rat. John's close friend and partner, Robert Wyler, was in prison, but Vitale may have had information that would have kept him there and sent John back. Robert and John sent coded messages back and forth through Robert's wife, Ann, and one of these notes, ostensibly from John, was the note that was found ripped to pieces next to Joe Fish's body in

Owl's Head Park. Pieced together by police, it read, in true *Godfather* fashion (though years ahead of its time): "Your friend went fishing, but he didn't catch the big fish"—apparently a reference to Vitale.

Vitale didn't seem to suspect his fate, evidently oblivious to the dangers of stooling to the cops. He thought he and Johnny and Tony were all pals. So when the pair showed up at Vitale's father's luncheonette on East Houston Street promising a shot of heroin, he heartily agreed. John and Tony drove Joe Fish across the Williamsburg Bridge and into Brooklyn, to Owl's Head Park at Sixty-eighth Street and Colonial Road, bordered on the northwest by the Belt Parkway. The pair was armed and their guns were loaded—John had given one of his to Piracci—and at 5:00 A.M., "in the gangland fash-

My father's portrait, taken in prison, 1970.

ion," they forged ahead into the park, Joe Fish trailing along behind them, expecting a shot of opiates. Instead, John turned and "emptied his revolver into the body of Mr. Vitale." Piracci fired a final shot, as if to make sure he was dead.

As the sun was rising in the eastern sky my father drove to Ann Wyler's house and presented both guns to her. Later that evening, presumably after a night of (restless?) sleep, he and Piracci and a woman named Louise "were together in an automobile. After Piracci departed, defendant showed her a newspaper article concerning Vitale's death and said that 'he did it.'" Then, with "a woman not his wife"—presumably Louise—he hopped into his white Pontiac and headed back down to Florida, where he had relocated with his pregnant twenty-two-year-old wife and young daughters just one month earlier. But he never saw them. When he heard that the cops had pinned Piracci to the crime he knew it was a matter of time before they crossed the Mason-Dixon to get him, so he holed himself up at the Dunes Motel so his family wouldn't have to witness his arrest. When his day of reckoning came he fought extradition, but he was brought back to New York anyway, where he cooled his heels at the Tombs for four months before his trial began.

"So he is 26 years of age, and this defendant has accumulated quite a bit of experience in the life of crime," Barshay opined from the bench. "I told him when he pleaded guilty what his sentence would be. It would be twenty years to life, as provided for by law. He deserves, and should get, more, but I am going to keep my promise, as I made it in open court to him." And with that, my father was committed to prison, where he spent the next decade of his life—first at Sing Sing, then Clinton Correctional, then Greenhaven, then Walkill, then finally Fishkill, where he met my mother.

I looked up at the clock, only mildly surprised that three hours had passed. As I gazed out the windows of the twenty-third-floor conference room and watched as big tumbleweeds of fog rolled across the sky over downtown Brooklyn, my eyes filled with tears. As a not-yet-thirty-year-old still grieving over her parents' deaths, I was offended by the cavalier manner with which my father seemed to have taken life. I also marveled at the involvement of his mistress, the aforementioned Louise, who also testified. So this was the woman my mother had told me about, the star of the photos tucked away in my father's prison scrapbook. And she took the stand—I wonder if Marie ever bumped into her in the courtroom? Did she rip Louise's oversprayed hair out by the roots? My mother would have. I thought of Rita then, and my persistent suspicions regarding her and my father, and wondered if people do, in fact, change, or whether they simply alter the circumstances slightly so they don't appear to be repeating their mistakes in perpetuity. The way my mother spoke of it, it was clear that she believed his adulterous behavior to be relegated to the past, when the truth was that she regarded my father, I now realized, with an almost willful ignorance.

I remembered my mother telling me how she and my father would clink their wineglasses and toast "to prison reform," the movement that led to his parole in 1975, as if it was the prisons that needed reforming, not a husband who had admitted to committing murder. I tried to see the romance in all this, tried to understand what my mother was attracted to, but I failed to find the seductive mystery in luring someone to a secluded park with the promise of heroin just to whip around and pump him full of bullets. And he definitely did it, despite his protestations of innocence to his parents and sister. Yet he'd sit in the Tombs, and then in his cell in Sing Sing, and pick apart every element of his multiple court proceedings, searching for the technicality that could spring him. He pointed out inconsistencies in the testimony given during his interrupted criminal trial; he even questioned the impartiality of Judge Barshay—who probably became the bane of my father's existence—by pointing out that in his days as an attorney he had once represented the father of one of the prosecution witnesses. I located each of his legal maneuvers in that seemingly unimportant second pile of papers, and they smacked of earnestness, despite his guilt.

As I read my father's words, written from behind bars, I felt the urge to run into his arms and say, "It's okay, I've found you. I'm here." The same neat, boxy lettering that adorned every birthday card he ever gave me is there, in that alien place and time, respectfully begging the court to grant his motions of appeal. Even though he shot Joe Fish at point-blank range, and probably countless others, I gazed upon his familiar cursive and missed him terribly. When he misspells words like "submittion" and "warrent," I am reminded that this John Mascia is twenty-six, three years younger than I am now, with only three years of high school behind him. He was trying so hard to get a trial; "a trial," he wrote in that first handwritten writ, "that could in any real sense be termed fair." Perhaps he felt that if he got his trial and took the stand, his charisma would cancel out the damning evidence against him. And why not? His seductive demeanor and effortless charm had carried him this far. My father could have been a movie star, he exuded so much "it."

"It" is why my mother forgave him the affair he had with that white trash waitress. "It" is how he induced my parents' friends in

California, all sophisticated yuppies, to fly to New York to testify at his parole violation hearing in 1983, and "it" is how he kept those friends after they testified, even after it was revealed in open court that he had been a murderer. "It" is how this gentle ex-convict won over the nuns at my Catholic school, who let him a barter a yearly carpet cleaning for a significant tuition discount. "It" is why his grown children never really gave up on him, even after he cast himself a permanent part in their lives only to evaporate without warning, and "it" is what keeps me from hating him now, if for nothing else than the affair I am convinced he conducted with my aunt. He had so much "it" that it's still infused in the ether around me, and even though I saw him take his last breath, saw his lips go white, "it" has kept him with me, years after I felt his graceful affability leave my dreams.

I turned my attention back to the court transcripts and imagined the guilt he must have felt—I *hope* he felt—at causing so much pain to so many people. I read about how my grandfather visited him in the Tombs twice a week, and on one particular visit Grandpa openly wept at his son's predicament, and my father wept right along with him. The thought of my grandfather breaking down as he sat opposite my father in some rancid jail cell, only to set my father off on a crying jag of his own, was almost too much to bear. It immediately brought me back to that night in 1996 when my father told me that Grandpa's prostate cancer had metastasized to the bone. He had picked me up from the Staten Island Ferry after a late night at Hunter and we drove back to New Lane in his powder-blue Ford Econoline. As we stopped for a light at the intersection of Bay Street and Victory Boulevard, he told me his father was going to die. I studied his small olive face, sorrow and helplessness and exhaustion having narrowed his eyes to slits, and started crying.

"I'm so sorry," I said, though I sensed how inadequate any comfort offered by an eighteen-year-old might be. Nevertheless, he met my eyes and burst into tears, nodding at my attempt, acknowledging his own pain. He sank dejectedly into his big puffy winter jacket and we both cried together, sentimental Italians to the end.

My father and I were close in ways we didn't talk about, simply because we sensed that we shared the same emotional DNA. I loved him and he loved me, and even though we didn't whittle away the hours gabbing and sparring the way my mother and I did, with kindred souls like us, you don't have to talk about it to know it's true.

ON THE SUBWAY RIDE back to work I flipped to the back of my Moleskine notebook and studied the Polaroids I'd been carrying around since my mother died, of my parents in the seventies, when they were either dating or first married. They were tinted blue from the water damage they suffered in the communal basement of Merle Place, lending them an ethereal quality. I'd rescued the waterlogged photo albums against my mother's wishes not long after my father died. "They're full of mildew!" she cried. "Throw them away!" I refused, removing the Polaroids and tossing the albums, and I'm so glad I did. Sometimes on the train I'd pull them out and cry. I can easily cry over my parents in public, when I'm pressed for time and privacy; it's in the luxury of my own home that I have a problem letting go.

In the first Polaroid my father has his arm around my mother and they are posing before a wood-paneled wall in my grandparents' house in Brooklyn. They look so young and beautiful, my mother's brows plucked into a perfect set of parentheses flipped 90 degrees. The second photo always makes me smile: My father, wearing a chest hair–baring brown zip-up shirt, has his arm around my mother, who is smiling in a carefree way I'd rarely witnessed during my childhood. They are both stoned, I am sure, and the picture seems to have caught my father in mid-sentence, as evidenced by the arm swung around my mother, hand open, fingers splayed, in the midst of making a point. I had forgotten how much Italians loved talking with their hands. I closely examined my father's face and noted his defined brow and dark eyes that mirrored my own, and I saw love. But for at least half a dozen other people, his face was the last thing they saw before dying, and I bet he wasn't smiling then. For them, my father's eyes held no comfort, only a whirling fury that sent them into blackness.

And I can imagine how easily he summoned that rage—I'd seen it firsthand. But killing was another thing. How did he make the decision to cross the line into such murky territory? If it was like the downward slide of addiction, what type of battle did he wage against it? How did he get to the point where the only answer to certain problems was murder? My mother said he had to "work himself up" to commit these crimes, bringing to mind a method actor prepping for Hamlet or Lear. But whose decision was it to kill Joe Fish? Did my father kill him at the urging of the incarcerated Bobby Wyler, as my mother suggested? Or should I trust the woman who testified that my father had been on the hunt for Joe Fish since the previous winter, when he swore he would "cut off his hands so he won't shoot up anymore"? According to testimony offered the first few days of the murder trial, my father explained to a friend that he killed Joe Fish because "Vitale was a rat and he had a lot on him, and he could put him away for fifteen years."

Well, he did twelve years, and it doesn't sound like he did them for Bobby Wyler.

CHAPTER 18

March 2007

. . .

"HEY, ANGIE, LONG TIME NO TALK," I PROJECTED BREATHLESSLY into the receiver. As I strolled up Third Avenue the wind was howling behind me and forming little tornadoes of leaves and plastic bags at my feet, which meant that a storm was imminent.

"Hey, Jenny," my sister Angela murmured in her signature laid-back tones. Everyone in Florida always sounded so relaxed. "When are you coming down?"

"Soon," I said. "I'm graduating in May, so I'm free after that. Listen, I need to ask you something. It's about Dad and Rita."

"Yeah," she said, sounding resigned. She must have expected it.

"You remember when Rita was up here after Mom died, and I asked her if she'd had an affair with Dad?" I asked. "And she denied it?"

"Yeah, you told me. She was so messed up that week," she said with a chuckle.

"Yeah, I know," I said. "I miss the old Rita. Remember the old Rita?"

"Yeah," she said. "We all thought she was so exotic, so beautiful."

"A life ruined by drugs," I said. "So in the car that night after the cruise, you told me that you always suspected something happened between two of them. What made you think that? I mean, you said that they seemed very 'friendly' with each other, very familiar, but was there anything else?" I suddenly wanted to be having this conversation from my bed, so I could roll over and fall asleep as soon as I hung up.

She sighed again, and her voice deepened. "I wanted to tell you the whole story that night," she said, "but you started crying."

"I started crying because you started crying!" I protested. Actually,

I couldn't remember who'd started crying first. Either way, we were both broken up.

"I also didn't want to say that I knew for sure while your mother was still alive," she said. " 'Cause I knew you'd tell her."

Oops. "Yeah, that was probably best," I agreed. "Wait—did you say 'for sure'? You're pretty sure about an affair?"

"Yeah," she said.

"How?"

Another sigh. "Because he told me."

Oh, Jesus. "He *told* you? When did he tell you?" I wanted to rip Rita's hair out, clump by bloody clump.

"Before he went to rehab," she said. "He called me up and apologized for keeping all that stuff in my house, and for running off with Rita to deal drugs. Your mom actually called me and said, 'Your father has something he wants to tell you,' and put him on the phone, and he told me he had a problem and he was going to get help. And I asked him about what happened that time with Rita, and he said, 'Yeah, we were sleepin' together.' "

How cavalier—*yeah, we were sleepin' together.* "My mother handed you the phone?" I asked breathlessly. "Did that mean she was listening to this confession?"

"I don't know," she said, "but I wondered that. It was a long conversation, I think he may have gone into another room or something. But I also thought, maybe your mom knew and kind of understood, or looked the other way, because Rita had done so much for you guys."

Rita had secured lawyers, lent us money, financed numerous vacations—but would my mother allow herself to be bought off like that? "That is disgusting," I said, visions of the du Pré sisters tormenting my brain. "I cannot believe she would just accept that, or worse, facilitate something like that."

"They just seemed so open about it, like they didn't even try to hide it," Angie said.

I immediately called Arline and told her what I'd learned.

"No!" she said, aghast.

"Yes!" I insisted.

"But how can Angie be sure?"

"Because Johnny *told* her," I said, flinching slightly at my use of my father's first name.

"He *didn't!*" she cried, in her horrified "Can you believe it?" voice.

"Yes," I said, "he did. Not only that, Angie and Tina think that Mommy *knew.*"

"No!"

"Yes!"

Pause.

"Arline, *did* Mommy know? I mean, when I asked her about this a few years ago she acted like the idea had never occurred to her. And Mommy and Rita didn't really have a falling-out, and if Mommy knew about an affair, there would have been a huge blowout over it." I caught my breath. "The only other explanation I can think of is that Mommy knew, and condoned it for some reason. Would she do that?"

"No, I can't imagine that she would," Arline said, now calm and considering the variables. "But there is something. Right after you asked her whether she thought Rita and Johnny did anything, she called me up and asked me if I thought that, too."

"No!" I said.

"Yes," Arline said.

"And what did you say?"

"Let me see if I can remember this word for word," she began. "She said, 'Jenny asked me whether anything ever happened between Rita and Johnny. Did you ever hear anything like that?' I said to her, 'No, never. I never heard anything like that.' She said, 'If I find out that *anything* ever happened between them, I don't care how old I am, I will go down to Florida myself and rip her eyes out of their sockets!'"

You go, Mom. "Did Rita ever mention an affair?"

"No, never," she said, adamant. "She never did. Of course, your mother and Rita were closer at the time than your mother and I were, but Rita never told me anything about that."

But how could my mother not have known? Of course, this was the same woman who didn't know her own sister was a drug addict when everyone around her knew, but how many trips had he taken to Florida without her? How could my mother not suspect, just a little, in her heart of hearts, that her coke-snorting husband, in Florida without her for a week or two at a time, could maybe—I don't know—trip and fall into Rita's bed? Did my mother think that because she had dropped her life to focus on my father, and loved him when he had a different name—and when he was just a carpet cleaner, and broke, and when his teeth were falling out—that he would return her loyalty and stay faithful for once in his life?

"She would have *died* for him, Jenny," Arline added. "If the FBI came to the house and started shooting, she would have put her body in front of his to take the bullets herself."

I was hardly impressed. Because how did my father reward her devotion? By shtupping her sister. But maybe that's what cocaine does. I can just imagine what the drug did for a man with my father's past. Maybe each pile of powder held a promise for him—a promise to forget. I wondered when he first tried it. Before he went to prison? Maybe while in prison? When I called Tina later that week, she told me that our father used to tip waiters with the drug, probably nestled in the crook of a folded-up dollar bill, handed off with a wink and a smile. She said that when he was high he could open up to her about all he'd done and seen. Perhaps cocaine inserted a layer between him and the rest of the world, supplying the necessary distance he needed in order to exist among everyone else who hadn't killed.

As I made the lonely trek to my apartment I began examining my child's memory through an adult's microscope, questioning every detail I'd taken for granted—like the way my father had yelled at me when I'd called Rita a selfish drug addict. My mother hadn't yet told me about all the lawyers Rita paid for, so I was baffled at my father's show of loyalty. I felt instantly ashamed, sensing I'd missed a piece of information somewhere and silently scolding myself for sounding like such a smartass punk. But if I could have relived that exchange today, this is how it might have gone:

Me: "She's nothing but a selfish drug addict."

Dad: "Don't you *ever* say anything like that about your aunt! You have *no idea* what she has done for this family!"

Me (eyebrow raised, head cocked sideways): "For this family? Or for *you*? What *has* she done for you, *Johnny*? Or, shall I say, *to* you?"

I'd be immensely satisfied at an exchange like that. After I got out of the hospital.

I had loved Rita, too, and didn't want to believe that she could betray my mother the way she had. It was Rita who *named* me; when my mother favored "Joanna"—she had insisted on a *J* name, in honor of my father—Rita gunned for "Jennifer," and won. Rita was like my third parent. During all those California visits, while Rita and my parents sat around reliving the good old days—while I eagerly hung on every word—did Rita or my father ever feel awkward because of what they had done? Did they ever lock eyes across the dinner table in secret acknowledgment of their intimacy?

If only my mother had opened her eyes! She must have been in utter denial when it came to both of them. But that was Mom— I remembered how she didn't recognize me in the stairwell at Merle Place after the doctor called with my father's cancer diagnosis. When the shit hit the fan it was like she erected a wall behind her eyes. I also remembered the vial my mother found in the pocket of my father's suit, which she blamed on Rita. My mother didn't consider for a moment that the vial, which is used to store small amounts of cocaine, could have been his. *Well, how else would you explain why there's a crack vial in the suit your father wore to his father's funeral?* But the more appropriate question was, why *wouldn't* he have had drugs at his father's funeral? I could probably look back upon every major event in my father's life and feel pretty confident that he was doing coke.

When I packed up the apartment on Merle Place I'd found the letter granting my father parole in 1988. Did he sell drugs when he was still on parole? Would he really jeopardize the rest of his life this way, possibly die an old man in prison? According to my mother, my father hooked up with Rita to sell drugs around that time, but how? I could just picture it: Rita shows up at our house in California toting her Louis Vuitton luggage, delicate gold bracelets and chains, and perfectly coiffed hair, maintained weekly by stylists. We spend a week at Le Meridien in Coronado or the Bel Age in West Hollywood and she offers to pay for another few days with one of her limitless American Express cards. Having just lost the lucrative contract at Chapman College, my father watches Rita's feats of spending with intense interest, wondering how she could possibly pay for it all. After she returns to Florida, leaving an Opium-scented cloud in her wake, my father pours a scotch on the rocks and faces a mounting pile of bills that a carpet cleaner's salary—even a tax-free one—cannot possibly conquer. He stares at the phone and remembers all the drug money he must have cleared until he got pinched. He remembers that Rita's daughter is dating a member of the Medellín cartel, who supplies Rita with all the cocaine she can spin into gold, and he wants in on the action. He's never committed a crime in California. Who would suspect a graying carpet cleaner of supplying coke to a handful of acquaintances, and more important, who would care? This was going to be small-time stuff. No body counts this time—no need. This was to be a friends-only endeavor. The more he thought about it, the longer the list of potential clients became. This was the eighties. Everyone dabbled from time to time, even in squeaky-clean Orange County. And so a gram scale appeared in our apartment and Dad began making his many trips back east.

I suddenly pined for the ignorant girl of an hour ago who didn't have to carry her mother's hurts until the end of time. Did I really want to know my parents' secrets that badly? I thought of all I'd never know, all I'd never get to the bottom of because most of the witnesses were dead—like Paul Washington, my mother's ex-boyfriend and my father's onetime cellmate. Paul had died just a month before, a fact confirmed by a *Times* researcher who did some digging for me after I made some calls and found out his last name. Or Bobby Wyler, who I discovered had indeed died of lung cancer, just as my mother presumed. I was running a race I would never win because I'd always be twenty-five years behind.

CHAPTER 19

May 2007

. . .

LIVE IN NEW YORK LONG ENOUGH AND YOU END UP RUNNING
into your past on every corner, where a memory lies in wait—
drunken nights, public breakups, crying jags in full view of ten thousand pedestrians. I wonder if it was like this for my parents when they
moved back here. Something tells me it wasn't; they had the habit of
leaving the past in the past and never looking back, probably developed during their years living as fugitives. But I especially wonder
about what it was like for my father. Did he peer down the lazy
streets of Gravesend or Bay Ridge and see a drug deal, a mistress, a
robbery? Did he ever go back to Owl's Head Park and come face-to-
face with 1963?

Where *was* Owl's Head Park, anyway? One night over penne
norcina at Al Dente I posed the question to Jeff, who was giddy over
his impending wedding to a Londoner named Paul. That's right, my
gay ex-boyfriend was getting married before I was. The union meant
Jeff would have to surrender his marketing job at Verizon and relo-
cate, as civil partnership is legal in Britain; after a few months he'd get
a green card and work authorization, which was more than the
United States was prepared to offer. I was thrilled for him, but as Jeff's
departure loomed I tried not to think about yet another loss in a lifetime already filled with so many.

"Owl's Head Park?" he asked, reading one of the *Daily News*
articles from 1963. "Are you kidding? Jen, I grew up there. I played
there as a kid. This was right by my house. My father grew up around
there, too. Your dad killed that guy there?"

I nodded. No wonder my father had liked Jeff so much. They were

from the same place, albeit separated by three and a half decades—
and half a dozen cadavers.

"I can't believe he just did it, right there in the park," Jeff marveled, reading the article. "I bet the guy deserved it, but," he added. A
true Brooklynite, Jeff always used "but" at the end of a sentence
instead of "though."

"So a junkie's life is worth less than a non-junkie's?" I asked.

"Regardless, the people your father killed were criminals, you
know what I'm sayin'?" he argued with his trademark nervous smile.

"So you're saying it's okay because he killed them for a reason?" I
asked sarcastically. "Like, he retained his humanity because he wasn't
a serial killer who preyed on random people?"

"They were dirtbags, Jen," he said. "Trust me. He did what he had
to do. It was a business."

Words that would warm my mother's heart.

I SPENT THE NEXT morning and afternoon at 111 Centre Street—after
three years of stubbornly ignoring certified letters I was forced to
succumb to jury duty, a privilege I was prepared to resist until I received
a notice threatening to cart me off to jail unless I showed up at 9:00
A.M. So it was off to SoHo to alternate between fighting sleep and
reading every newspaper published in the tristate area.

After an informative video narrated by the late Ed Bradley and
three jury pool lotteries I was called into a room with eighteen other
unlucky souls. I recognized an anchor from ESPN among the miser-
ables and realized my rehearsed excuse—"I couldn't possibly serve,
my sincere apologies, I answer phones at *The New York Times*"—
wouldn't exempt me. After we sat and raised our right hands, one of
the court officers began polling the prospective jury pool, and I was
surprised at the number of people who claimed they couldn't be
objective when weighing the burden of guilt in a slip-and-fall case on
a street corner in Washington Heights. They didn't even have to give
a reason, they just had to raise their hands! As much as I couldn't
afford to surrender my salary to spend three weeks listening to tiresome testimony, I wouldn't allow myself to go out on that note. I had
scruples! But when the officer asked whether we had either (a) sued
or been sued, (b) been accused or convicted of a crime, or (c) known

someone who had been accused or convicted of a crime, I knew I had my Get-Out-of-Jail-Free card.

"Number 13," the officer said, pointing to me, "what do you do for a living?"

"Um, I'm an editorial assistant on the Metro desk of *The New York Times*," I said, praying that my proximity to the daily news cycle was enough to grant a waiver.

"Oh, nice," he said. *Damn.* "Have you ever sued anyone before?"

"Yes, actually," I said. "I sued my former restaurant company because the owner made us share our tips with managers and never paid us overtime." That was the Redeye Grill. I'd initiated a suit right before my mother died that eventually attracted more than two hundred plaintiffs, and after two and a half years of protests and litigation we won a $3.9 million settlement. Never hire journalism students to work in your restaurant.

"I see," he said. "And do you think that would prevent you from being impartial in this case?"

"Well, I admit, I have a dim view of big corporations who take advantage of their workers, but I suppose that doesn't apply to this case." Light laughter.

"Have you ever been convicted of a crime?" he asked me.

"No," I said. *Here it comes:*

"Do you know anyone who has ever been accused or convicted of a crime?"

"Why, yes," I responded, almost a bit too cheerfully.

"And who is that?"

"My father," I said.

"And what was the charge?"

"Murder." On cue, every head in the dismally lit fluorescent room swiveled my way.

"Really. And was he convicted?"

I had to think how far I really wanted to take this. I decided that announcing unsolved murders revealed during a deathbed confession wasn't enough to build a bulletproof case. "Yes," I said. "He did twelve years." I addressed the curious eyes now trained on me. "And yes," I added, "my last name is Italian." Nervous laughter from the crowd. I didn't have to do jury duty that day, or for the next two years. Crime, it turns out, really does pay.

Later that night I decided to indulge my nostalgia, so I opened my bottom dresser drawer and began combing through the visual remainders of our past. I got a camera for Christmas when I was ten, but my own enthusiasm for snapping pictures was nothing compared to my parents'. For fugitives, they certainly weren't shy about showing our faces to the photo developers at Thrifty's. But then, my father wasn't exactly on the Ten Most Wanted List.

I paused and studied my communion picture, the one where my parents and I are standing outside the church after the ritual, and I

My first communion, May 1986.

realized I'd never examined it closely. My mother, in her $300 jumpsuit and new Vuitton bag, looks thrilled that's she's living her sunny California life; my father looks distracted and a little irritated, like he's thinking of his next score; and my eyes are closed, thanks to the blinding sunlight. We were living three different versions of the same life under that roof. Metaphorically, it's perfect.

Just then an idea occurred to me. I began searching for my father's gray phone book, the only one he ever kept, which my mother had dutifully preserved after he died. It wouldn't have held any interest for me before, but perhaps now it would.

The binding was sealed with clear packing tape, exposing the fatigue it had weathered in its quarter century of use. On the inside front cover my father had listed every one of his relatives—parents, cousins, nieces and nephews, siblings—and their birthdays. I found my letter from 1994 pressed between the back cover and the last page, the one I had written as I cruised around the hills of Laguna in the Camry, trying to find a way to say goodbye. I unfolded it and recognized my small lettering—how many nights had I stayed up as a child copying and recopying my father's neat, boxy printing? How I wanted to write like him, draw like him. The paper hadn't yellowed in thirteen years but it was difficult to read, mainly because I didn't seem to have believed in paragraphing at that tender age. I couldn't believe he'd saved it. Then again, this was a man who used my puffy-painted bookmark until the end of his life.

I reread my letter, dated May 31, 1994, and its sincerity floored me, as did my unwavering belief in him. "A girl looks up to her father and worships him like a God, and that is what you have been for me." I cringed, mindful of all I didn't know then. Calling him "courageous and admirable" for running away from his failure—and his family—struck me as heartbreakingly naïve. "It's us who have failed"? "We really didn't do our part"? I may have been a little jaded by the values in Orange County, but I didn't make their financial decisions for them. Reading my words, written nearly half my lifetime ago, I realized that you can still love someone without deifying them. I wondered why my mother never got that memo.

On the inside front cover my father had written what looked like my mother's Social Security number, except it wasn't—it was a fake, and right next to it he had written "Real #" followed by her actual Social. God, how I missed them, with their penchant for larceny. They made it seem like so much fun. On the inside back cover a dozen names and phone numbers were etched into the gray leather in pencil. I recognized the phone numbers' prefixes—Dana Point. I was, in all probability, staring at my father's client list from when he sold Rita's cocaine. It had been there all along but I hadn't known what to look for. I was disappointed that there was no Robert Wyler, no Anthony Piracci, no Tommy Palermo—no remnants of my father's former life.

But while my parents left mysteries, they also left clues, and if I walk through the rooms of my past with open eyes and ears I know just where to find them. If, for example, I want to know how my mother felt about my father—I mean *really* felt about him, not the "he turned his life around for us" line—I can travel back to 1984. It's early evening and my mother and I are snuggled together on the soft brown leather chair watching TV. A commercial for a Beatles compilation album comes on, with short melodic snippets playing behind the song titles unspooling on the screen. "Strawberry Fields," followed five seconds later by "Lucy in the Sky with Diamonds," followed by "Hey Jude." Then there's "Nowhere Man," a song I'd never heard.

My mother nudges me. "That's your father, Jenny," she says bitterly. "A real Nowhere Man. Going nowhere, doing nothing." It was a rare moment of candor. In later years she'd revert to the Johnny-Is-a-Saint routine, even after she revealed that he had sold drugs after his parole had expired and killed people without getting caught.

Did she expect more from her ex-convict husband? He had just spent nine months in prison fighting his parole violation charge, and he had returned to California to once again take tentative steps toward a legitimate life. That evening in 1984, did she really believe Johnny would come home after a long day of carpet cleaning and announce that he'd decided to take the MCAT? Her opinion of him must have brightened considerably when he and Rita started selling. That's when we began spending entire days at South Coast Plaza, prompting me to develop a lifelong aversion to department stores. My father fulfilled my mother's expectations as long as he was making money.

In lieu of answers from my actual parents, I now had their letters, which I'd recently retrieved from the basement of Merle Place. As I suspected, the box had wilted away into pancake batter, and I'd dumped its contents into the biggest garbage bag I could find and set it down in my living room, where I studied the detritus of our lives, laid bare on the floor. There were moldy books, the shoe box of letters my California friends had written to me right after I moved to New York, my baby shoes and my first pair of pointe shoes.

I turned my sights to a set of letters, the first of which was a white envelope with "Eleanor—open after I enter the hospital" written on the front in my father's script. "The hospital" meant detox, and I was pretty sure I had found this letter several years earlier, though the fact of my parents' deaths had suddenly renewed its meaning.

There were actually four separate pieces of correspondence in the envelope, three on yellow legal paper and one on wide-ruled white. I started with the white paper. It was from me. A soon as I saw what was written at the top, I felt the heat rise in my cheeks. I LOVE DADDY CASSESE MASCIA, it read in my five-year-old handwriting. Below that were two Hello Kitty stickers, and below that a crudely drawn man with enormous hands and feet standing next to a brown house with a blue door. Unlike my father, I was a terrible artist.

I cried, hyperventilating big gulps of air. *Daddy Cassese Mascia.* I was both touched and heartbroken at how a child had blended her father's alias with his actual surname without even understanding what it meant.

The next three letters were from my father to my mother, and they were angry, accusatory, recriminating—all the hallmarks of their marriage during that time.

Eleanor

It is 2:24 A.M. My bottle of scotch is almost empty and my small bottle of poison has one last toot and it is gone. I feel a sense of panic and I want to sneak upstairs and look for the packages made for Donald, but I know I won't—I can't!

Donald? My mother's friend from high school, David's best friend? He bought cocaine from my father? *Oy.* I read on.

I am in pain, and I must endure! Eighteen months ago I made the biggest mistake of my life. A bad winter left the business without funds needed to pay business bills, and to save the business and the life you and Jenny enjoyed I called Florida to buy time, hoping the business would stabilize and we would survive. I should never have called Florida! I should have let the business go under and we would have left California together as a family, for New York, Florida, or wherever.

I am crying now because I feel so lost and terribly afraid that I won't find the strength to find my way back. You were, and still remain, the only woman I ever loved, trusted, respected, and I am disgusted at all the pain I've caused you because I wanted to push you from my life and leave me free to ingest the poison I chose.

I'm sorry for making you feel inadequate, belittling you, punishing you terribly for no just cause. I resented you for being stronger than me—the strong one! I did terrible things, and I'm sorry. If I lose you I think I'll be sorry. I say I "think" because in my confused mind, and in my love for substances I can't think clearly enough to know what I feel. But I remember a friend, a wonderful girl of so long ago who gave freely of herself for me, and through my haze of liquor and drugs I now reach out to her. I am so strong, but so weak, because I fear that I can't get back! I fear I lack the strength and conviction to be a better man than I am now. I feel so totally lost and fear to be left alone after detox. I can't go through every day of my life holding your hand or Jenny's hand to give me strength.

I've seen so much, endured so much, with overpowering strength, yet today I must be convinced that this strength even existed. I'm always tense, explosive, irrational, short-tempered, cold, and just a bad guy in general. Why am I this way? How did I get here? God help me! Mom help me!

It was the first time I'd seen cocaine-induced motormouth on the page. It was impressive. I hope my mother rolled her eyes when she read this and found him as insufferable as I suddenly did. Why do all Italian men cry out for their mothers in times of crisis? And I love how he laments his drug-addled lifestyle and then claims it's a cross he must bear in order to keep me and my mother in Gucci. "The life that you and Jenny enjoyed"? We weren't exactly riding around in Beemers—we drove a car that was forever leaking coolant and we always had trouble keeping up with the rent. Concealed in my father's tight, inebriated scrawl was rare access into the mind of an addict, and I still couldn't believe this was my father. But the person who wrote these words was not my father. This was "Johnny" on his downtime, when I wasn't in the room. This was not the father who hoisted me onto his shoulders and surprised me with clandestine Twix bars. Whatever this shit was, it didn't spill over into our relationship.

Or did it? Those dozen or so times when he'd smacked my backside with the force of a car crash, was he high on coke? I never smelled alcohol on him, so it must have been coke. Was he under the influence of cocaine when he chipped away at my mother's self-esteem with his vicious insults—"*Oh, Eleanor, shut yuh fuckin' mouth!!*" She never feared him, and gave it right back when he screamed and foamed at the mouth, but after a while this must have eroded her soul.

The next letter was similar, and more accusatory than the first, blaming my mother's penchant for conspicuous consumption for what he was "forced" to do. There was a letter clipped to it, and I steeled myself for another rambling attack on my mother, thoughtless materialism, and free-market capitalism. But when I opened it I was blindsided.

It was from my mother.

Dearest Jennifer—

Someday you will read this letter, probably when I am gone.

There is truth in it, but also a drug user's self-pity and his willingness to blame everything on someone else. I became that someone else. I'm not just making excuses, although I was hurt and in pain also, especially when I read this letter.

We did not have the perfect marriage, but we loved each other— much. I sometimes think I really don't want to go on without him, but then I think of you—and also how much death scares me.

Please don't get hurt by this letter. His anger at me is justified— not his anger at you—the "life you and Jenny enjoyed."

Please don't hate either of us. We both loved you so much.

Mom

I couldn't breathe, I was crying so hard. I looked in the mirror and saw that my face and chest had broken out in splotchy pink hives, something I thought only my father's yelling could do. This was the last letter I would ever receive from my mother—there were no more hidden wills to find—and I immediately wished I hadn't read it so I could experience it for the first time all over again.

I could tell that it was written after my father died, because she writes about how she's living in a world without him, but I don't think she was sick yet. I pictured her going through his papers in the hope that seeing his familiar script would make her feel less lonely for him. I marveled at the way she blamed herself. All of his weaknesses became her fault. If he took drugs, or killed, or continued his estrangement from his kids, it was because of her, and she absorbed the fallout as well as the blame. I can't reconcile this vision of my mother as a blank page for my father's dominance because I saw her in action. But over the years and even on her deathbed, she related his sins to me without affect, as if she didn't know what to make of them and wanted to see what I thought before committing to an emotion either way. Years of living by my father's warped morals, followed by four and a half years of living on her own, had left her without a moral compass. She was in limbo, even when discussing murder.

Why was she so obsessed with defending this man's humanity? I lived with the guy—he was more Roberto Benigni than Benito Mussolini. Didn't she know by my words and actions that I could never hate him? And why did she keep these letters? She could have thrown them away and disposed of this murkiness, but she didn't. She knew I would go snooping through their papers one day, after they had gone—is it possible that she wanted me to get the full story? Maybe she didn't want to be alone with the truth. When she was diagnosed with cancer she could have taken care of the evidence, but she left it for me, her daughter, who, raised in a household of subterfuge, was always hungry for the truth, even when it hurt us all.

But there's spin there, too, paper-clipped to the historical artifacts. True to form, she always had to have the last word, and she used it to protect Johnny. To paraphrase my father, how did she get here?

CHAPTER 20

June 2007

. . .

THE FLORIDA AIR WAS WARM AND SOFT AND SURPRISINGLY FREE of humidity as it gently jostled my hair on I-95. Every time I flew down here I became seized by the same thought: Could I live here? Why not be closer to my remaining family? I was taken to New York by force, and though I have incorporated the city's rhythms into my own, it was a love born of necessity. Every night I return to my apartment and face the emptiness left by those who have gone.

But here—everything can begin again here, warm and sun-kissed and clean. Driving up and down the freeway I could feel my parents with me in a way I couldn't before. How many times during their brief stay in Florida did they drive I-95 to Fort Lauderdale, or take the Sawgrass to their house on North Commodore Drive? Back then they were only ten years older than I am now. Would we have been friends? What would an ex-con and his bad-boy-loving Jewish sophisticate wife have in common with an Ivy League grad cum journalist? These are people I probably would have covered for the paper: EX-CON FLEES BROWARD AFTER COCAINE BUST; BOUNTY HUNTERS ON THEIR TAIL. And for the ironic Day Two story: WIFE OF COCAINE CON STARTED DRUG REHAB HIGH SCHOOL IN NEW YORK. With her first husband. Who was gay. Connecting the dots from David Margulis to John Mascia began here, just off A1A in Fort Lauderdale, with Donald Halsband.

"Jennifah! Oh my gawd, you look just like Eleanor!" Donald held out his arms at the entrance to the oceanfront tower that housed his nineteenth-floor apartment. He was balder and older than I'd imagined. I had only met my mother's lifelong friend once, when I was ten, but I didn't really remember him, just as I didn't really remember David.

My mother had visited Donald during our Florida trip in 2002 after I'd branched off to see my sisters, and she'd warned me that Donald's apartment was envy-inspiring. Well, she was right. It was stunning: elegantly appointed yet comfortable, equal parts Ethan Allen and Bombay Company. The living room and eat-in kitchen faced the soft blue surf and the bedroom overlooked the low-lying city lights. If the apartment was located in Chelsea, Donald's home for most of the eighties and nineties, it would easily fetch $6,000 a month.

Before we sat down to talk he fixed me a lunch consisting of four types of organic salad from Whole Foods and sugar-free iced tea. Apparently a smorgasbord of tofu and tabbouleh awaited me in my golden years. After lunch I sat on his downy, velvety couch as he fetched a treasure from his bedroom: his senior yearbook from 1951, with a picture of my mother in her cheerleading uniform.

"My mother was a *cheerleader?*" I'd asked him on the phone a few weeks before, incredulous. Yet there she was, smack in the middle of the pack, smiling eyes peering out from a smart brown bob. She was remarkably pretty. It was as if the word was coined especially for her.

"You can have it, if you want," he said, rising to fetch a pair of scissors.

"Really?" I asked. "Are you sure?" I felt like I was defacing a library book; the Lincoln High yearbook from 1951 looked nothing like the flashy, hulking Guinness Book–type volumes handed out when I was in high school. This was a thin volume, demure. I lifted it up to my nose and inhaled dust accumulated over five decades; I relished the smell. Next he handed me an 8½-by-11 piece of construction paper covered with a collage of small photos he'd put together. In the upper left-hand corner was my mother and David's wedding photo. I'd never seen it before. David stood behind her, all dark hair and spectacles, and she smiled through a thick set of eyebrows. She was twenty-five.

"She was always so thin," I said, a little envious.

"David loved her body," he said. *Probably because she was built like a boy,* I thought. He let me keep that photograph, too. "So," he said in his effeminate Manhattan Beach drawl. "What can I tell you? I don't know about your father, but I do know about your mother and David and I growing up in Manhattan Beach."

"Well," I started, still shaking from the single hour of sleep I'd managed on the plane, "I'm trying to understand how my mother married a gay man—twice—and then went on the lam with a man who killed people."

He managed a wry chuckle. "Jenny," he said, "none of us understood how Eleanor and David could get married in the first place. But

My mother's first wedding, to
David Margulis, 1959.

twice? I mean, we were *always* gay. It was me, David, and Milton, who's dead now. We would go cruising together."

"If you guys were always gay, then why did David marry my mom?" I asked.

"In those days," he said, "David felt that if he married a woman, he'd go straight. I don't know if your mother knew during the first marriage, but I know she knew later."

"Oh, she knew," I said. "Arline, her other sister—did you ever meet her?" He shook his head. "Arline said that my mom thought she could straighten David out. Can you believe that?"

"Well, yes," he said. "In the fifties it was a lot harder than it is today to come out."

"But *you* did," I pointed out.

"Yes," he said. "But you have to understand, David was a highly disturbed guy."

"Really?" I asked, though my mother had once told me that David's mother was schizophrenic.

"Did you know David tried to kill himself twice?" Donald asked me.

"No. When was this?" I guess my mother liked her men gay, homicidal, and suicidal.

"David didn't finish with us at Lincoln High School," Donald explained. "During his senior year he was sent to the Hartford Retreat, a sanitarium in Connecticut, after sticking his head in the oven."

I shivered; shades of Sylvia Plath. "Jesus," I said.

"When David and your mother got married, we said to David, 'What are you doing?' I mean, we were gay. But he wanted to try marriage, and he really loved her. But their sex life was not great. After they got married he'd be bitterly upset over the quality of the sex, and she was frustrated, too. He had a hard time maintaining an erection. And your mother had this rape fantasy that David couldn't fulfill. That's probably why she liked your father. He was very sexual."

I was puking in my mouth. But Donald's revelation, though squirm-inducing, couldn't be discarded. My mother was married to a flaccid homosexual for twelve years, and my father had been in prison for twelve years. Their union must have resulted in sexual dynamite. But was that enough to carry a marriage? And one with so many caveats?

"I spoke with one of my mother's friends from her teaching days recently, and she told me that while my mom would wait for David to come home at night, David would be parked in some guy's car right downstairs, having sex."

"Oh, sure," Donald said. "We'd go cruising all the time. David got a job at this gay bar called Main Street, on Eighth Street in the West Village. After he got off work, we'd go cruising. He'd tell Eleanor he was somewhere else, and we'd go find guys. Look, David adored Eleanor," he said, rising to fetch two Diet Cokes from the fridge. "She called him at all hours to talk about her life, and he loved it. Just loved it. Even when I'd be over at his apartment on Horatio Street, he would be talking to her on the phone. For hours." The way he said it, I could tell it once annoyed him. But now he sounded like he had come to respect the friendship, probably relieved that my mother had married again and had a child and wouldn't be showing up at David's door for a third go-round.

"You know," I said, "I've spoken to some people who worked

at Alpha School, and I was surprised to hear that my mom never taught there. I always thought she did because of the way she talked about it. They all remember her, but said that she only helped David craft the proposal and never taught there herself." Just about everyone I'd spoken to also said it was pretty obvious to anyone with a set of eyes that David was gay. But each and every one raved about her teaching style at her previous school, from which David had poached half the staff. She really knew how to reach the kids, in a way David never even did.

"No," he said, "she never taught there. Eleanor's favorite pastime was smoking, sitting in her bathrobe and reading all day, then cooking for David when he got home. She liked staying home and David did Alpha School."

Just like when she was married to my father. "Wait," I said. "I think I have something you might find funny." I'd brought pictures to show him, too, and there was one in particular that seemed to illustrate exactly what he was describing. I shuffled through the bleached-blue Polaroids and communion and cheerleading pictures and held one up for his perusal: my bathrobe-clad mother, circa 1990, lying on the couch with a cigarette in one hand and her big round ashtray resting on a thick book. Donald knew of what he spoke.

"That's it," he said. "That's Eleanor. Wow."

"My father was always on her case about 'contributing.' I guess he didn't recognize that she was in the throes of depression," I said.

"Yeah, I guess that's what it was," he said.

"He threatened to leave her once if she didn't get a job," I admitted.

"Well, we all lent her money," he said. That didn't surprise me. I had found a letter from David bundled with my mother's papers that began, "This money is a loan, but pay it back only when you can." If my father was a part-time coke dealer and full-time carpet cleaner, why did my parents never have money?

"I remember one time," Donald continued, "I came to California when you were little, and we ate at a Chinese restaurant—"

Finally, a shared memory. "Mandarin Gourmet," I chirped. "I was ten."

"Yes, that place your parents loved," he said. "I remember she felt so guilty because she owed me money and didn't have it, so she gave me a nice gram of coke."

"*She* did?"

"Oh, yes," he said serenely.

"My *mother* gave it to you?" I'd assumed my mother's involvement in my father's drug operation consisted of tacit approval at most. But the fact that she cupped the baggie of poison in her hands, carried it with her in the car on the way to the restaurant, let it into her possession even for a minute—didn't she know better? She helped start Alpha School!

I had to ask. "Was it good? Like, pure?"

"Oh, very," he said, smiling at the memory. "I remember getting on the plane to fly home and feeling very, very happy."

At least it made someone happy. All cocaine ever did for me was perch me on the edge of anxiety and keep me there until I fell asleep. My jaw clenched at the memory. "I don't do it anymore," he added. "But I used to do it while I watched TV. I miss my coke. I miss my pot, too. I haven't smoked in five years."

Too bad. I wished he had some now. "Donald?"

"Yes?"

I repeated the question I'd first posed to him on the phone a few weeks back. "How did a woman who'd started a drug rehabilitation program for high school heroin addicts hook up with an ex-con coke dealer, go on the lam, and stay with him knowing that he'd killed people?"

Donald sighed. "I have a theory," he said. "There was an element of adventure in it, for all of us. David lived vicariously through your mother with all those phone conversations. I think it's more surprising that she married David twice than your father, to tell you the truth, because her marriage to David was stale."

I let that sit for a moment. I guess I'd gotten what I came for. I remembered then something my mother once said to me during her final year of life, during some frivolous argument: "When I die, you're just going to be sad you don't have your Mommy anymore. You're not going to really mourn me as a person."

Oh, Eleanor, how wrong you were.

"Are you hungry?" Donald asked, breaking the silence. "We should make dinner."

I couldn't believe it was already seven and I still hadn't slept. It might have been a record for me. After a dinner of steamed chicken breast, sun-dried tomatoes, and broccoli—if I ate like this every day

I'd weigh 95 pounds—we talked a little about the rest of David's life, how he left teaching in 1975 and opened an antique jewelry booth on Forty-seventh Street, following in his father's footsteps. The business became very successful and David ran it until he got sick. Donald said that both he and David were very promiscuous, and David knew who had given him AIDS: a cokehead called Snow. "He was very cute," Donald said. David didn't show symptoms until right before he died. Donald picked up the photo collage and showed me a picture of a tan, smiling David and a mustached Donald with a woman and another man. They are all laughing.

"This was the summer before he got sick, so it must have been 1987," he said. "Because he died in 1988."

"On my father's birthday," I said. His fifty-first birthday. What a day that had been. Birthday candles in his bagel, what was I thinking?

"We went to funerals all the time in those days," Donald said. "A dozen of my friends died. Why I didn't get AIDS, I don't know." Donald told me how David got angry and hostile when he became sick enough to enter the hospital, cursing his visitors, including my mother. He had developed dementia, and when my mother visited him the week before he died she slept in the hospital room with him, just as she did years later with my father.

"He cursed me for leaving him," she'd told me all those years ago, "blamed me for making him live a gay life, because that's what made him sick. I didn't take it seriously. I knew he was dying." She described wiping the feverish sweat from his forehead and then, when she left the room, asking a nurse if it was okay that she had come into contact with his bodily fluids. "It was still early," she'd said in her defense. "We weren't sure then exactly how it was transmitted, and rumors abounded." During David's lucid moments they'd tease each other and laugh, as they had on the phone for the last ten years. David was one of the few people who knew where we were when we'd gone on the lam. "He told me, 'Eleanor, I always wanted to be thin, but not like this,'" she'd recounted, smiling sadly.

"His father did not visit him at all in the hospital because he was so ashamed and embarrassed that his son had AIDS," Donald said, pulling me back into the present. "David's cousin Shari and I, we got the plug pulled." We were back on the couch now, and darkness was falling. "He was on a respirator, and there was no hope. None of the doctors wanted to pull the plug. You know, so many specialists have to be in the room for them to do it. I ran up and down the corridor looking for someone to do it, and I finally found one, a very young, cute one. I kept thinking, 'David would be so happy to know that this gorgeous young doctor was the one who pulled the plug.' The nurse overdosed him on morphine while Shari and I cradled him in our arms until he slipped away. Afterward I had to go ID him, and he was wrapped in cotton, like a mummy."

I remembered running up and down the halls of Staten Island University Hospital, searching for someone to take the machinery out of my mother's body, and being told after five hours of waiting that all of the necessary specialists couldn't be assembled until morning. My friends probably had no clue how close I'd been to rushing past the hospital administrator and yanking the tubes out myself. I knew just how Donald felt.

"He didn't even leave a will," Donald said. "He didn't think he was going to die."

If Jeff and I had been adults in the eighties, would I be mourning him now? The idea crushed me; I'd be bereft beyond words. I'd be just as my mother was in our little makeshift apartment in Marge's house a few months before we moved to New York, the stage upon which my mother's marriages to David had played out.

"David's dead," she had said, sitting on the edge of the bed and staring into space, reacting to the news as if she'd just heard it. "I can't believe David's dead." And her face crumpled, and she cried, and I held her, not even sure that I knew what grief was.

But I did now.

I slept ravenously that night, drinking in every minute, and when I awoke I could easily have slept some more.

TAMARAC IS A SLEEPY pocket of Fort Lauderdale that is primarily home to seniors and the Jamaicans who provide their services. Development after development of condominiums line the main artery, side by side with a plethora of drugstores, doctors' offices, and opticians. It took me twenty minutes to find a supermarket, and I cursed, thinking how I couldn't go two blocks in Manhattan without finding a Korean deli that sold goat cheese. But I was showing up without warning after not seeing or speaking to Rita for a year and a half and I didn't want to come empty-handed, so I gritted my teeth and found a Publix, where I bought a feast of Brie, vanilla pound cake, prosciutto, and Italian bread. My hands full of plastic bags, I rang the doorbell with my elbow. Nothing. I knocked. Nothing. I paced for a bit and considered driving away, regifting the food to Angie when I got back to West Palm. I was barking up a tree that in all likelihood even my mother would have told me to ignore. How could I be here, dredging up ancient history?

The door opened. Rita stared at me for fifteen long seconds with her face frozen, like she was trying to place who I was. Then: "Jenny?"

"Surprise!" I held up the bags. "I brought you stuff." She opened the door another crack and I slipped in. I tried not to gasp as I took in her bloated face, all but obscuring her deep, dark eyes, and her grown-in toenails, the top halves of which were painted purple, betraying the amount of time that had passed since her last pedicure. Her stomach had grown into a big, round beach ball. She didn't seem to have endured a lumpy weight gain, replete with cellulite; hers was the type of smooth, shiny overweight that happened suddenly to people who'd been thin their whole lives. She hugged me slightly reluctantly, and when she let go she remarked testily, "Why haven't you called me for a year? Where have you been?"

I wasn't prepared for her to dig right in. What could I say? "I found out that you slept with my father and lied to me about it, and I was pissed"?

"I mean," she continued, "you knew I was getting a lump removed from my breast, and you didn't even call to find out if I was okay."

I remembered that trip, two months after my mother died. I was supposed to see Rita but she called and said she had an emergency biopsy and we never rescheduled. I should have called her, but I didn't. I spent the rest of the trip dozing on the beach, still in a haze from what I'd just been through. There were others I fell out of touch with around that time, some I neglected unfairly and some I cut out of my life altogether. What can I say? Death draws a line and everything in your life falls on one side or the other.

"I asked Arline about you all the time," I started, "and I knew the lump was benign—"

"But it's not the same as asking *me*, Jenny," she said. "But I'm so surprised to see you, and I'm happy to see you! I just can't understand why you didn't call."

"I—I thought you were mad at me. For not seeing you that time." Partly true. "And you didn't call me either, and Arline said you never mention me, so I figured you were."

"Yes, but Jenny, even if we are mad at each other, we're family. You could have called me at any time."

My aunt Rita, holding me, circa 1978.

"I know," I said. "You're my favorite aunt."

"If I was your favorite aunt, then why didn't you call? Wasn't I there for you when your mother died?" Actually, I thought she had flown up because her sister had died, not for me. Arline told me that Rita didn't observe the anniversary of my mother's death, or her birthday, instead absorbed in her own problems. But now I saw why.

Rita's body looked as if it was weighing her down. She had undergone hip replacement surgery after driving into a tree, high on Percocet. She needed the other hip replaced, she was telling me, but the doctors weren't sure they could do it because she had badly broken her arm. Indeed, her left arm hung limply at her side, victim of a recent fall in her house courtesy of her bum hip. She was but a shadow of what she'd been, the gold-plated goddess of south Florida. My heart wrenched—her physical state was a stark reminder of all that I'd lost.

As she ticked off her maladies, my eyes welled with tears. I wanted to tell her the real reason I had stayed away for as long as I had, but I didn't. I felt terrible that she thought I had neglected her when she was so literally broken, when I'd actually thought of her often, though it was usually in anger. When Arline told me that Rita was depressed and nearly an invalid, I knew I had to see her. For so long we'd been a foursome, and now we two were all we had left.

I could see so much of my mother in Rita's face and mannerisms. A quick sweep of the kitchen revealed the same teakettle my mother had always owned—and exchanged when she was done with it, sometimes a year after its purchase. I spotted the same wooden block of Henckels knives that I had inherited from my mother. I saw how Rita kept her spatulas, serving spoons, and garlic press in a big round ceramic canister, just as my mother had—and as I now did. They had borrowed so much from each other, and not just Vuitton bags and St. John Knits.

"You look so much like my mother," I said, and began to cry like a baby. I felt weak and slightly paralyzed from the encounter, which I had impulsively initiated on just four hours of sleep. Rita hugged me and took me over to a painting hanging on the living room wall. Stuck in the bottom right-hand corner of the frame was a photo of my mother, with her short, smart haircut, holding her sunglasses up to her mouth and sucking on the end of the earpiece. My mother always thought Rita was the pretty one, but she was wrong. I have a feeling that Rita at seventy will not appear as milky and fragile and lovable as my mother was at that age, her final year of life.

We ambled back toward the kitchen, and while I took the food out of the bags I told Rita how I'd seen Donald a few days before, and relayed his disbelief at the fact that my mother and David had married twice. Rita said the instant their father met David he pronounced him a *fagalah*.

"You want coffee?" she suddenly asked.

"Sure," I said.

"I make it strong," she warned me.

"That's okay," I said. "I take it iced. So strong is good."

While it brewed I took our spread to the coffee table, where she had lined up her pill bottles. She had plenty of Zetia and Xanax, and a bottle of OxyContin. Well, she was visibly injured. Maybe she really was in pain. Perhaps she'd finally moved past her addictions, something my father was apparently never able to do.

The Game Show Network was playing on mute, and according to the captions, men with mullets were talking about making whoopie with Chuck Woolery. It was fitting; just the decade I wanted to discuss. But how? As if on cue, Rita said, "All I do all day is sit here and think about the past."

We had that in common. "Me, too," I said, my eyes wandering down the hall to her bedroom, where I spotted a faded oak dresser, a lamp placed on the carpet sans nightstand, and unremarkable factory-created art hanging on her wall. I glanced through the open shades to the patio, where a beaten-up baby's car seat sat on a table. The setup was a shock to anyone who had seen her spread in North Miami Beach, replete with shiny modern furnishings, a walk-in closet bursting with clothes, and a bathtub the size of a swimming pool. I thought of my mother's Henredon dining set and resplendent white velvet couch and how they hadn't made it to the end of her life, either. Very little of what they'd prized had survived.

Rita's phone rang. It was Kara. "You'll never guess who showed up at my door," Rita excitedly reported to her daughter. "Jenny. Yes, Jenny *Mascia*! I know, it's been almost two years. Well, Arline said I was mad at her, so she didn't call." I bristled when I heard Rita lay the blame on Arline, as if her comments alone had prevented me from calling Rita. I had to tell Rita the truth. I waited until she hung up.

"Rita, I have to tell you something," I began. "The real reason I stayed away for so long . . . it was because I know you had something with my father, and when I asked you about it you lied to me. It would have hurt my mother so much, and I was angry. I'm not angry anymore, I just want to know. Don't ask me how I knew, but I always sensed it, since my childhood. I mean, I saw the chemistry you two had—"

"Yes, we did," she said, and transformed before my eyes into someone calm and centered. "Jenny, I wanted to tell you when you asked me that night, but your mother had just died." She looked away for a second and cocked her head to the right, and for a moment she was the Rita of 1987. "It wasn't an affair, Jenny. It wasn't. It was a onetime thing. You have to understand, your mother and I weren't getting along very well at the time. Our relationship was . . . not so good."

And so she began. She told me everything.

———

IN THE SUMMER of 1983, my father was reluctantly extradited from New York and tried in Broward County on the five-year-old cocaine and gun possession charges. Rita hired a lawyer, a friend of one of her crooked boyfriends. Rita figured he must have had some kind of a deal with the judge, because before either of my parents could blink, my father was released.

"He should have gotten fifty years," Rita said. "Especially since your mother and I started laughing hysterically when we saw the judge. He was paralyzed. The judge was paralyzed! And he rolled up in his wheelchair, and in order to get himself situated on the bench he had to lift one leg, then the other. Oh, my god, your mother and I started laughing and couldn't stop. 'You stop, Eleanor,' I told her, and she said, 'No, *you* stop,' and we had to leave the courtroom. When we told your father later—forget it. He was hysterical, too." I imagined the two of them laughing during one of the worst crises of my mother's life, essentially mocking the man who had the power to put my father away for a long time, and I remembered what I loved most about her, and Rita—black humor in a crisis. Rita said the three of them went to dinner afterward like nothing remarkable had happened, except that my father had gotten a second chance. Again.

Kara, then sixteen, had just married Miguel, and one day Miguel asked Rita if she'd like to sell cocaine to bring in some extra cash. "I told him I didn't know what to do—who do I sell this stuff to? He said, 'Sell it to your friends, it's not hard.'" Enter my father, who knew his way around a kilo. "He took me aside and showed me what to do, how much to cut, how much to put in a bag," she said. "I didn't even do coke then; grass was my thing. So he taught me what to do." Afterward he went back to cooking eggs and pancakes at Bagels and Donuts, but not for long. "Your mother approached me and told me they were broke and asked me if I could do Johnny a favor and cut him a piece of Miguel's stash to sell."

"My *mother*? But he had just gotten out of jail!"

"Yes, your mother. I said sure, why not." But my father didn't exactly have a client base in Florida, so when we went back to California, Rita would send him the cocaine by Federal Express and he'd break it up, bag it, sell it, and send Rita her cut. "I gave him a big break, not charging him up front for the coke," she said. "I let him pay after he sold his cut, and sometimes not at all. He still owes me money, come to think of it."

"Good luck getting it," I said. So they borrowed money from Donald, Rita, David, Arline—where did all our money go? "You weren't afraid FedEx would find out what was really in those packages?"

"FedEx doesn't scan packages, unlike the postal service," Rita said. "We found a source in California, this guy I dated called Igloo. We were always giving people these names! We named him that because he kept his coke in an Igloo cooler that he carried around. Igloo found a guy who bought ounces, and we made a lot of money. A lot."

"Hey, Rita," I asked her, "is it true that Grandma was the one who gave the FedEx guy the packages of cocaine when he came to pick them up?" Arline had told me that.

Rita shrugged and grinned. "Yeah, she handed it off when the guy came."

Amazing. "Because who would suspect an eighty-five-year-old woman, right?" I said, playing along. "Did she know what it was?"

"Yeah. I mean, she knew it was coke, but didn't really know what 'coke' was. You know, I only sold it to my friends, I only had four or five people I knew who came to get it from my house, and Grandma would say, 'Why do these people like this stuff? They're always buying so much!'" I pictured Grandma Vivian, shuffling around in her floral housedress and Coke-bottle eyeglasses with a package of cocaine in her leathery, manicured hand, wondering why all the kids these days were doing it.

"Did my mother know? About Grandma?" I asked, giggling at her unlikely role as in-house drug mule.

"Of course," Rita said, laughing now, too. "She thought it was funny. What? It's funny!" It *was* funny. What's funnier was that family participation in drug deals didn't seem all that strange to me. I remembered volunteering to sell my mother's Vicodin for her when she had cancer, just as she and my father had sold his OxyContin. In the end she refused to let me sell the pills to some willing friends, but I didn't think it was illegal—I thought I was helping her. God, I needed therapy.

"What did you cut it with, just out of curiosity? I've always wanted to know."

"Oh, I don't know," she said, "it was cut by the time I got it. Mostly vitamin B, maybe baby laxative, that sort of thing."

Curiosity satisfied. "Did Kara know you guys were selling her husband's coke?" I asked.

"Of course," Rita said. "She wanted me to make money."

That explained the BMW, not possible on a diner manager's salary, and the manicures, the hairstylists . . . "So what happened when they broke up?" I asked.

"Well, Kara started dating Miguel's best friend, Juan," she said, "and Juan, who was also a dealer, sold to us."

"So Dad gets out of jail, and you guys are mailing coke and money back and forth?"

"Yes." That was longer than I thought: five years—from 1984 to 1989—as opposed to the two or three I'd presumed.

"And it stopped when he went to rehab?" I asked.

"Not exactly," she said. My father started doing the drugs he was supposed to be selling, just like my mother had told me. Doing the drugs made him crazy, Rita said, and one day Igloo called to say that the package my father had sent him showed up empty. It was supposed to have contained ten ounces of cocaine. "Johnny kept saying he was going to kill him," she said. "I begged him not to. It was the coke, the coke made him crazy." I remembered a line from one of his coked-up letters to my mother: *So, here I sit in a one-room apartment in Dana Point being reckless with phone calls and traffic.* This must have been what he meant.

"Did he do it?" I asked.

"No, and I know because I ran into Igloo at an airport just after that, randomly. And he said, 'Your brother-in-law has some temper. I'm going to fix him.' So here he's going to kill your father, and your father's saying he's going to kill him. It was a mess. Meanwhile, neither of them did anything."

"Are you sure?" I asked.

She looked at me with wide eyes. "But I saw him at the airport."

"But did you see him *after* that?" I asked. Her eyes got wider, until I said, "It's okay. I don't think he killed anyone in California. Don't worry." I considered what that sentence might sound like to an outsider and decided that no one else would ever really understand.

"But he did crystal meth, so he was going crazy," she said.

"When he couldn't get coke," I said. "Yeah, my mother told me. But before he went into rehab he called Angie to apologize for bringing coke and packing materials into the house where her two-year-old daughter was living, and he also confessed to her that he had slept with you."

She closed her eyes briefly. "Oh, why did he tell her that?"

"Maybe he was in a confessional mood," I said. "She said she suspected for a long time, and so did Tina, because of the way you two acted together. You had great chemistry," I admitted, praying my mother couldn't hear this concession.

"We did," she said. "I loved him. Like family, like a brother. He was my brother, practically. Jenny, your father and I sat behind locked doors cutting coke for years, and nothing ever happened between us. Nothing. Then you and your father came to visit this one time."

"In 1989," I reminded her. "Yeah, I remember."

"Yeah, whatever," Rita said. "I'm terrible with years, you have such a good memory. He was with Carmine the whole time he was there, doing business with him, selling him coke."

"Carmine?" I asked.

"You know, Big Vinny's son."

"Carmine Cassese?" The same Carmine my father once advised to rat out his Mafia buddies, who was now a full-fledged member of the Bonanno crime family, I'd recently learned. According to my mother, he also knew about the hit on Tommy Palermo, the only one of my father's victims besides Joe Fish whose name I knew. Since he was currently sitting in federal detention, I had a feeling I'd have to pay Celie a visit as well.

"Yeah, he was down here with his girlfriend," she said. "Johnny was trying to help him get into the business, you know, teach him. So we went out to dinner one night, and Johnny went to the bar and Carmine's girlfriend was in the bathroom, so Carmine said to me, 'Johnny told me about you, that you're real nice. I'm going to be down here for a while after Johnny leaves, if you'd like to hang out. He'll never know, so don't worry.' I thought, is he making a pass at me?

"So when Johnny and I got back to the apartment," she continued, "of course, he was high. I wasn't, but I'd been drinking and I'd smoked some grass. And he sat down on my bed, just plopped down. And I said, 'You know, I think Carmine made a pass at me,' and I told him what he said, that Johnny didn't have to know if we were together. And the look on your father's face—it was rage, just incredible madness, then jealousy, all at the same time. Then he seemed to calm down, and he said, 'Well, why not. If I wasn't married, well, you know.'"

"'Married to your *sister*' is what he should have said," I spat. I couldn't believe I was hearing this. I was finally behind a door that had always been closed to me.

"But he'd been asking me for so long. I—"

"Asking for so long? How long, Rita?"

"A while, but I always took it as a joke," she said. "You know, he'd smack my ass and run away, that kind of shit." He used to do that with my mother, too. I cracked my knuckles to relieve the tension. "But all of a sudden he wasn't joking," she went on. "It's because he was high, I know it, because he never said these things to me when he wasn't high. When he wasn't high, we were just like brother and sister. The way I got along with Eleanor was the way I got along with him. But Eleanor and I, at this time . . . we weren't getting along. I'm not saying it's an excuse, but we weren't."

"You weren't?" I asked, genuinely surprised. I couldn't remember a time when they weren't gabbing on the phone, and even more so after David's death.

"No," she said. "I was busting out my credit cards, and I gave her one of mine to use."

"We were busting them out, too," I said.

"I know," she said. "We did it at the same time. And when she was done with hers, I gave her one of mine, because she wanted to buy more. And I called her one day and asked her to buy me a purse I wanted, since by then my cards were maxed out. And she said no. I couldn't understand it—I had given her my credit card to use, and she said no."

"She said no?" That seemed a little harsh. Why would she say no? "She loved shopping," I reasoned. "She couldn't stop spending money. That was her addiction, I guess."

"Mine, too," Rita said. I remembered our weekends at South Coast Plaza, and I couldn't reconcile that person—the person she became around money—with the person she'd been toward the end of her life, who no longer cared about Vuitton purses, who would beg me in a panic to recount the mere thousands my father had left her, afraid a tide would come and wash it all away.

"And we borrowed so much money from you," I said. "Where did it all go?"

"From everyone," Rita said, echoing Donald. "Eleanor borrowed from everyone. And there's something else. Before you came to Florida with your father to visit me, many months before, Johnny was doing coke and your mother was spending his money and it was breaking up their marriage. So she asked me to talk to him, you know, straighten him out. We spent hours on the phone, and he'd tell me about his problems."

"Mom knew?"

"She knew, of course she knew, she asked me to do it," she said. "I think she enlisted me to do her dirty work. So when Johnny came to Florida after we'd spent all those months on the phone, maybe he expected something.

"So he sat on the bed that night and got angry that Carmine had maybe made a pass at me, but then he changed. He said, 'Well, why wouldn't he want you? If I wasn't married, maybe we would, you know, we would have something. We'd be together.' And I said, 'But we'd be hurting people, so many people.' And he said, 'Who would know? I wouldn't tell anyone.' And I said, 'But Johnny, *I'd* know. What will I do when I see Eleanor again? When I talk to her? She's my sister.' And he said, 'Do you want to know about your sister? You have no idea what she really says about you,' and he told me all this shit Eleanor had said about me. And I said, 'She said *what*?' And he reminded me how she took the credit card and didn't let me buy anything with it, she just spent it up herself, and he told me everything else she'd said about me. And that's how he got me. He steamed me up."

What an asshole. How could he do that to my mother, first betraying her confidence and then talking shit about her?

"And the next morning," she continued, "I woke up and he was snoring. And I opened the door and you were there, just standing in the hallway, and I looked into your eyes and, I swear to god, Jenny, you just *knew*. You looked at me with these wide eyes, like you knew what had happened. And after that I told him, never again."

Now I knew she was telling the truth—it was the same snoring that had kept me awake on the plane ride over. But I didn't remember the exact moment she described, as much as I longed to. I must have blocked it out.

"You mean to tell me that when you came to California the year before that and stayed with me and Dad when Mom was in New York because David was dying of AIDS, nothing happened?"

"Nothing," she said, shaking her head. "Not a thing. He was at work most of the time, and I came there to watch you. I don't even remember where I slept. So that morning," she continued, "when I saw your eyes, I told him, 'Never again. She knows, I think Jenny knows.'"

"Oh, my god. What did he say?"

"He said, 'Don't be silly, she doesn't know anything.'"

How dare he underestimate me! "Yeah, he always told my mother that I didn't remember him getting arrested in front of me," I said. "But I did."

"He probably wanted to believe you didn't," Rita said. "He tried to convince me that we could continue, you know, start an affair. He said, 'I'll make up reasons to come here, I'll say it's because of our business.' And I said, no, it can never happen again."

"Did it?"

"No, it was just that once. But we did it all night." Opiates made her honest. She'd already popped at least three Percocet since I'd walked in, and it reflected in her slurred speech.

"Well, cokeheads can go forever, right?" I asked her.

"I've been with cokeheads before, but this . . . every time I'd tell him we couldn't do it again and try to go to sleep, he'd start up again—"

"So how was it when you saw each other after that?" I interrupted, not especially eager to hear more about my father's sexual prowess. I'd already heard about my mother's rape fantasies, and all of this intimate knowledge was enough to make me never want to have sex again.

"Very bad. We stopped talking on the phone, our relationship was over. Eleanor would ask why, and I told her it was because the coke was making him crazy. It was that, but also this. And the one time I did come back to visit, he was insane. Crazy. Your mother and I were downstairs, and he was upstairs, and he was yelling that he was going to kill us both."

"You know he wouldn't have," I said. "He never hit my mother, ever."

"I know," she said. "But he'd had a whole bottle of liquor, and he was grinding the deering, looking for coke. Do you know what a deering is?" I shook my head. "It's one of those things you use to grind coke. And he was grinding it up, insane, but he didn't have any more coke in there, so he was frantically looking for any residue he'd left behind. And Eleanor and I walk in, and he's up there talking to himself, and he screams at us to shut the fuck up. I went up there to try to talk to him, but he was just . . . there was just no talking to him. After I left, Johnny and I didn't speak for years. Except when I came to dry out, you know, kick the coke habit—"

"When he had cancer," I said, remembering the Jell-O stain, the massages, the OxyContin.

"Yeah. He and your mother were so good to me, they did everything they could, they were so wonderful. And there was a point when your father and I went out on the balcony to talk, and it was just like before. We talked like brother and sister again."

"Well, it was eleven years later," I reminded her. "It was long enough to start over."

"Yeah, and we did. I put it out of my mind, and so did he. And when he dropped me off at the airport, we hugged goodbye, and he went to kiss me goodbye, and I turned and gave him my cheek, and he kind of did the same thing. It was like, there was nothing there between us anymore, you know?"

"Hey, Rita," I said, remembering something, "during that visit, did you—and you can tell me, it really doesn't matter, I won't be mad—but were you by any chance doing coke or smoking crack and stuck the pipe or glass coke container into the pocket of one of my father's suits?"

"What?" Her expression told me that the possibility was preposterous, and as I found myself explaining it I began to agree with her.

"Mom was going through his clothes after he died and found one of those glass bullets, you know, the kind that holds coke so you can do it on the go."

"No way, Jenny," she said. "How would I get it? Bring it on the plane?" She started laughing. "I certainly didn't know any dealers in New York, and I know your father was clean then—he had cancer!"

"Yeah, I know," I said. "It sounds so silly, but my mother thought it was yours."

"Mine? She did?" I almost felt bad that Rita hadn't gotten the chance to correct that impression, but then again, maybe it was better my mother didn't know—about the coke, or any of it.

"She thought you were doing coke in her bedroom and someone was about to catch you red-handed so you reached for whatever you could find to hide it in," I explained. "Because he hadn't worn that suit since Grandpa's funeral in 1996."

"Well, there you go," she said. "He probably did coke that day." The more I discovered about my father, the harder I had to look for redeeming qualities. If it was anyone other than my dad, just some random coke dealer/adulterer/murderer, I'd have given up on him already. I never expected my love to be tested this vigorously, and so long after his death.

"Look, Jenny, please don't hate him," Rita implored. "He was a good man, so good to you, and he really loved your mother. He loved me, too, but like a sister. He really, really loved Eleanor."

"I know. He was her soul mate," I said, remembering what she'd told me before I slammed the car door on her confession. "And she knew what he was, how he had a mistress during his first marriage, that he killed people."

"I didn't know about the killing," she said; she'd claimed the same when I first asked her about it in the week following my mother's death. "But the waitress—he took her everywhere. For six months! I think he was definitely fucked up on drugs. I mean, he'd have to be to take up with her, right? And then he fell off the ladder when he was painting and broke his arm and the waitress came to see him. He told her he was leaving your mother for her."

Now this was news. My mother told me my father had had an affair while on the road, but she never said that he promised the woman anything, or that he took her everywhere. A real mistress, just like the old days.

"Your father confessed everything to your mother one day," Rita explained, "you know, 'I was stupid, I was lonely, it means nothing,' and then the buzzer goes off downstairs. And the waitress is there! She was there to confront him about leaving your mother. And he said, 'I'll deal with this,' and raced downstairs, and I don't know why your mother didn't go after him, but she said she saw the little skank from the balcony and she was a mess, real trashy-looking."

I was shocked. Our bedrooms were separated by a single wall and I never knew. They really did a good job of hiding things from me. At that point my mother was sixty-two years old. I couldn't imagine her having to mark her territory at that age, doing battle with a twenty-five-year-old at the tail end of her marriage.

"Why did Mommy stay with him?" I asked Rita. "Why, when he did all this? It's like she blinded herself when it came to him."

"She didn't want to see," Rita said.

"So you really did help him out a lot in his life—you paid for a lawyer when he needed one, and gave him a part of your, um, business," I remarked. I told her how, right after she had visited to "dry out," my father admonished me for calling Rita a drug addict, telling me how much she had done for us but not telling me what.

"Really? He said that?" She thought for a moment. "Well, I did. When you were going to go to Houston, after the arrest, I bought you a car to leave with."

"Wow," I said. How had my parents accepted all this from her? Her financial aid was like a Band-Aid for a much more deeply rooted problem that they never cared to solve. "You know, ever since I was a kid," I said, "all I wanted was to be your age so I could be a part of your gang. You all seemed to be having so much fun."

"Oh, we were," she said. "We did."

Unfortunately that era was lost to time. I glanced at the clock: It was almost five. I would be late for my plane if I stayed another minute. I stood up and gathered my things and Rita limped out with me.

"Hey," I said, "she never knew, you know."

"I thought she did, once," she said.

"No way," I said, remembering how Arline told me that my mother said she'd mutilate Rita if she found out about an affair. "She didn't know, trust me." Why was I comforting her? Maybe because my mother should have known better than to trust my father.

"Please don't hate him," Rita said again as I got into the car. Why was everyone so concerned that I might hate this man? It said a lot about Rita, though, that she seemed more concerned that I'd end up hating my father than her. And here I had gone to Tamarac expecting to loathe her.

"I don't hate him," I assured her. "Don't worry." I started the engine of my rented Trailblazer and rolled down the window. Since Rita wasn't one for proper goodbyes, she left me with, "I hope his penis shrivels up and falls off."

I hit the brakes. "Rita," I said, "he's dead."

"Ghosts can have sex," she deadpanned.

"RITA DID THE right thing," Jeff said over spinach and artichoke dip at Houston's the next evening. "She cut it off. I forgive her."

"So do I," I said. "She fucked up, but she wasn't the backstabbing slut I thought she was. And I believe her. When she was talking to me, there wasn't that lag time between the truth and the lie, you know, when someone is trying to think up a story. She was high on Percocet, though, but other than that she sounded truthful. This affair they had, it changed her relationship with my mother, with all of us."

"Did it, but?"

"Yeah. The facts back it up—she hardly ever came to visit us after that. I only saw her once when I was in high school."

"It almost makes me change my opinion of your father, but," he said. "It doesn't, in the end, but almost. You know?"

"Believe me, I know. It's like it's another person we're talking about. I think it's because he's dead. I can't question him about this, so for me, he'll always be the person I thought he was." I could barely eat. My wine was untouched, and it was my favorite, a Sauvignon Blanc from New Zealand. "What kills me the most," I continued, "was how materialistic they were. Jeff, I had no idea how much of this was about money and greed. I *never* want to live my life like they did."

"I know, Jen. But at the end of the day, they were good to you. They were just a little bit selfish."

"How did they find the time to be good parents? It was almost like they were good parents in spite of themselves." I picked at my salad, separating the romaine from the chicken. I couldn't register taste or texture. It was all just matter to me.

"They gave you whatever you wanted," Jeff said. "They put you through private school."

"Yeah, with drug money," I pointed out.

"Believe me, you wouldn't be the first," he said.

"True. Especially in Southern California," I conceded. "But, my god, those years? From 1995 to 1998, before my father got cancer, when I was dating you, remember?"

"Yeah," he said, picking at his rice.

"I always considered them the best years of my life," I said, "because we were finally together, after being separated and on welfare. But I think I only thought that because of what came after—heart attack, lung cancer, more lung cancer, another heart attack . . . In reality, we were broke, fighting, and not six months into our new lives in New York my father finds a mistress who he proceeds to drag across the country. I'm living in the same house and I don't even know all of this is going on. I just wish," I said, my forehead crumpling, "I just wish that the ten percent I knew of them, the good, legitimate part, could compensate for the rest. I wish they could have been the people I thought they were on a full-time basis." I put my hand over my eyes. I thought I might come close to crying but didn't expect to actually do it. Jeff put his hand on my arm.

"Hey," he said, "let it out. You *need* to cry over this."

I was really too wired to cry, but I choked out a sob or two before quickly recovering. "Now that I know what my mother went through, I wish so much that I could sit across this table from her and look her in the eye and tell her that I finally understand all she had to deal with." Just like I wanted to do in the hospital, to tell her all I went through trying to keep her alive, and how I survived her death. There was so much I wanted to tell her, but this suddenly popped to the top of the list.

"She was a smart woman," he said. "At the end of the day, she wanted to keep her family together. She stayed with your father, and every time he dabbled in the coke she spent his money shopping. She wasn't stupid. It was her way of acting out."

"Maybe," I said.

"Well, why do *you* think she stayed with him? You knew her best."

"Well, she—" I said, and stopped. I could answer the right way—that she was older and didn't want to be alone. But while that may have been the truth, my mother didn't see it like that. "If you asked her, she would say it was because she loved him. She loved him so much, Jeff, and he loved her. I've read all the letters he wrote her, and the cards. All the affairs, they didn't change how much he loved her."

"I bet he had a *lot* of affairs, too," he said. "A lot. But nothing substantial."

"Oh, I'm sure." In fact, I was growing more certain of it by the hour. "I mean, she knew the deal. She knew what she was getting into. I guess when you know somebody's deepest secrets it binds you together. Jeff, nobody else knew about the murders."

"Really?" he asked, his face scrunched in disbelief. "No!"

"Yes. She didn't tell Rita, she didn't tell Arline. She only told me."

"She wanted you to know who they really were," he said. "You had a real mother-daughter friendship. Very deep."

"It's not just that, though. Maybe she didn't want to be alone with it anymore. And I never would have known any of it if I hadn't seen the FBI arrest my dad. If it had happened when I was two, it would have been off my radar. And I wouldn't have known the rest if I hadn't searched the Internet and found his record. That's when I became her confidante. People seem offended when I tell them that she told me so much, like she broke some unspoken child-rearing rule. 'Don't tell your children where the bodies are buried.'"

"It isn't strange to me," Jeff said. "We're just different, I guess."

"New Yorkers," I said, smiling. My mind was a jumble of questions and emotions, of disbelief. Jeff must have sensed the synapses firing.

"I can't imagine what's going on in your head," he said. "How you must feel."

"I can't believe it: My father was a cocaine addict. He did it, off and on, his whole life. And I see why. How do you continue to live your life when you've killed people? I might turn to drugs, too. And the only way he could open up and talk about anything substantial was when he was high."

"He had a hard life, you know?" he said.

"But he did it when he was on the road, painting buildings," I said.

"My god, he was an old man then, no?"

"He was sixty," I said.

"He was doing such hard work at that age, he needed an escape, you know?" Jeff was starting to make excuses for him, just like every-one did. I knew he said it to make me feel better, so I let it slide. "A man goes from twenty to sixty and he doesn't change," he continued. "He's the same person. People don't change."

"You thought you were straight when you were twenty," I objected.

"Ha *ha*," he said.

Ah, the age-old debate: Can people really change? My father did change, in a way, because of my mother. He became more tolerant, more cultured, better read, a better judge of cuisine. He lost his big-otry and became a better father. But in some ways he remained the same man who dated all of Marie's teenaged friends when she left for summer camp.

"My mother looked me in the eyes and told me that my father changed his life for us," I said. "But he didn't, Jeff. He never changed. The scary part is that I think she convinced herself that he did, even when the evidence said otherwise."

"But didn't he?" Jeff asked.

"No," I said. "Just for the five years we were fugitives. He had to keep his nose clean, so to speak, because he knew they would come for him one day. Jeff, *those* were the best years of my life."

"Wait, tell me when that was again?"

"1978 to 1983," I said. "I only remember a couple years of it, of course, but he was a carpet cleaner, he wasn't doing anything illegal. He stayed legit because he was building a résumé, so when he went to court one day—because he must have known that day would come—he could say, 'Look, I'm a law-abiding citizen now, I've given up the criminal life.' And it worked—he was released. But after that he went right back into doing coke and dealing it, and the only thing that finally ended all of it was cancer." I thought for a moment. "You know some-thing?" I said wistfully. "The FBI finding him was probably the worst thing that could have happened to him." I thought about the life he could have had as Frank Cassese, always looking over his shoulder, yes, but always keeping his nose clean, literally. Of course, he'd still be dead.

"You're finding more out about them," Jeff said, "but you'll never know for sure, because you weren't there. You're skimming the sur-face of it, but who knows what's really inside? Who knows why they did what they did?"

"That's the hardest part," I said. "I'll never know it all." Our plates were cleared and our waiter dropped the check. "You know what he'd say if he knew I was doing this, researching his life? He would tell me to mind my own fucking business."

"No, he wouldn't," Jeff said.

"Oh yes he would."

"No, they would both be proud," he said. "They'd want to be able to tell their side, but they'd ultimately stand back and let you do your thing." I knew he was wrong, but at least someone believed it. It made me feel better. "You were his pride and joy, you know that, Jen," he added.

"Yes, but I always sensed that there was a distance between us," I said. "I mean, we were close, but we could just as easily have been estranged, like he was with his other children, if he'd gotten arrested for dealing. And what was my mother thinking, getting my father into dealing coke when he was still on parole?"

"She turned a blind eye to it," he said.

"Which reminds me of someone else," I said. "How many blind eyes did I turn when it came to men—to Kareem, to you? I've been with liars ever since I started dating. I thought the only way to break the pattern was to find out where it came from."

"And you have," he said.

"We'll see," I said. I laughed.

"What?" he asked.

"Of all the things I could have been, John and Eleanor Mascia's daughter had to be a journalist. Of all things."

Jeff laughed. He paid the bill.

I DRAGGED MYSELF home and dropped like a sack of potatoes on my leather futon. I was ready to fall asleep right there when I spotted the contents of the cardboard box I'd rescued from my mother's basement, which was still spread out on my living room floor. I decided I could either torture myself by picking through its remnants or watch *The Daily Show* and *Colbert*. I made it halfway to my bedroom before I turned around and headed back toward the living room, where I sat on the floor and flipped through the day planner I'd used in high school. My mother's Mobil card was still inside, as was my first learner's permit, a white piece of paper with just my vital information typed on it and no photo. I glanced at my high school diploma, various term papers, and all the other files I felt deserved preservation. What on earth would I ever need them for? After a few minutes my fingertips turned brown from the dust. I got up to wash my hands and spotted a VHS tape out of the corner of my eye. I knew what it was before I even picked it up and saw "Eleanor's Childhood Movies" on the label in my father's cursive. It was now or never. I tiptoed to my bedroom and slid the tape into my VCR, which I never used anymore, and there she was.

Pigtailed, bespectacled, freckled—I could see them dotting her nose and cheeks through the grainy black-and-white haze—she waves to the camera from her spot on the grass before she returns to the magazine in her lap, which she studies contentedly as Arline dances for the camera behind her. "CAMP" had ignited the blackness before the movie began, and when I saw Vivian enter the frame I assumed that it was visiting day in the Catskills, circa 1940. My future grandmother is blond and perfectly coiffed, wearing dark lipstick even in the heat of summer, her enviable waist defined by high-waisted riding pants and her sparkling eyes concealed by Harold Lloyd–style sunglasses. She looks like a cross between Ginger Rogers and Gillian Anderson, and she is never without a thousand-watt smile. Strains of big-band music, added years later, accompany the silent action, and some scenes are so dark they hurt my eyes, almost as if they were filmed during a solar eclipse. When the camera pans to my grandfather Sam, he waves vigorously and smiles broadly. His torso is egg-shaped and his pants are halfway up to his armpits, but he has a certain rugged appeal, with his five o'clock shadow and dark brown hair. This must have been before he started drinking, because my mother was twelve when Vivian had her breakdown and she looks to be about six here. My great-grandmother Fanny, who my mother had dubbed "the Pit Bull," lurks in the background in her full-length black schmatte, her stubby arms folded across her thick waist. Fanny really did look like a pit bull, with her straggly gray hair and scrunched-up face. She never bothered with her grandchildren, though she is seen sharing a giggle with a woman her own age.

As boats full of little girls and their counselors make their way across the lake behind them, my mother runs up to Vivian, who pulls her closer so she can plant kisses all over her face. A jump-cut later, my mother and Arline are dancing in their matching white sailor outfits, their heads topped with white sailor hats. After they swing each other around, my mother plops down on the grass and reads aloud from a magazine or comic book, her mouth chewing each and every consonant and vowel. After that loses its excitement, she conducts an invisible orchestra while her mother looks on adoringly. Then suddenly my mother is swimming, her straight brown hair obscured by her bathing cap, and she waves excitedly from the water. She looks—dare I say it?—*happy*. She's certainly giddy and hyperactive, as I was at that age, dipping in and out of the water in a state of undisturbed bliss. A moment later, as she climbs out of the lake, she becomes animated and lectures someone off-camera, straining with her whole body to punctuate her point. When she sees that she's not getting her point across she waves her arm dismissively and abruptly turns away, and in that single moment I recognized my mother. She was a little know-it-all! I knew it! My arms and legs melted as I watched her happy face dancing before the lens, and as she blended with a gaggle of her nearly identical fellow campers I felt pride at always being able to pick her out of the crowd. There is something regal about her as she prances about in her blouse and skirt and saddle shoes—she was a princess of privilege, but a goofy, charming one.

As the seasons fly by—winter flashes to summer, black-and-white to color, the years zigzagging back and forth through time because of the uneven editing—she sulks, she pouts, she dismisses, she glowers, and she becomes quite pleased with herself, all in the space of a minute. As an instrumental version of "You'd Be So Nice to Come Home To" plays, the entire extended family—few of whom I recognize—gathers before the lens and waves, giving the impression that primitive movie cameras were used as little more than an extension of still photography. Arline is the only one who appreciates the medium's potential, grasping every opportunity to exhibit her considerable dance moves, whereas my mother is only vaguely aware of the camera's presence, preferring the company of a book or her mother's arms. As she plants one peck after another on her mother's lips in rapid succession, I saw a closeness I didn't expect to find, an intimacy that seemed more like what she and I had. "We had anything and everything we wanted—except affection," Arline had told me over the phone one night. But that must have come later, because here even her father seems warm, tossing my mother up to the sky the way my father tossed me and then pulling her in for a kiss. By the look on my mother's face, I could tell that this was a little girl very much in love with her parents. Where was the unhappy family I'd heard so much about? Half a dozen years in the future, a time period I glimpsed when the tape skipped ahead to Rita's infancy. Vivian looks tired as she holds her newest addition up to the camera, but in a flash Rita is three or four and attended to by Clotie, who looks to be about twenty. Clotie loads Rita onto a homemade toboggan and pushes her into a snowbank that put the Blizzard of '96 to shame. A jump-cut later we've entered drier months, and my teenaged mother appears behind Rita, grabs her tiny hands, and swings them up and down.

Watching how my mother doted on her baby sister, I got mad all over again at Rita's betrayal. How could they do that to her? My mother, who put both my father and Rita to shame in every way—she was more intelligent, more cultured, more sophisticated than the both of them put together. For the first time I faced the hard fact that my mother might have been too good for my father. Did my mother ever imagine that the adorable little pudgepie bouncing around their home movies would grow up to sleep with her husband? But then, did my mother ever imagine as she was running around the Coney Island boardwalk or the grounds of the Arcadia Lake Hotel or Loch Sheldrake that her daughter would one day grow up to watch her after she'd gone, that this battered videocassette would be the only place left to find her? Did she ever imagine I'd be crying as hard as I was? Because I burst into tears as soon as I caught sight of her carefree pigtails. She is the child I could only hope to have, everything I imagined when I imagined being a mother. How I'd love to raise a charismatic, self-possessed yet sensitive bookworm. Seeing my mother as a child, in the shoes I was so used to inhabiting, turned my brain upside down. I cried until my face throbbed, and I slid quickly into bed so the pain didn't migrate to my head.

As I mercifully drifted into sleep my mind journeyed back to a day seven years before, during my final summer with my parents on Merle Place, when I was enjoying the last few minutes of a pre-dinner nap. The sun had set for the most part, and the last rays of light lingered in the blackening sky with all their stubborn futility. Laughter from the Albanian children playing catch in the sun-baked parking lot floated its way up to my ears, competing with the clash of pots and pans and my parents' conversation in the kitchen. In those last moments before I groggily joined them at the dinner table, I'd felt a lightness, and some peace: Life was moving, the world was turning, and even though my father had less than a year to live, it was the last time I can remember when death was far enough away for me to be able to breathe.

I was jarred back to my bed on 103rd Street by a truck clanging its way down Second Avenue. My reverie had been so real that leaving it unleashed another round of tears. It was the first time in months that I had given in to the ache. I might not have felt it every day, but the love was still there—so much love, rising to the surface, as though my parents were in the next room waiting to receive it. I hadn't expected to feel that again. It was a nice surprise.

CHAPTER 21

August 2007

. . .

"SO, DR. B., WHAT I WANT IS TO UNDERSTAND THE MIND-SET OF someone for whom killing has become an option," I began. I was sitting in the Court Street office of a forensic psychologist, asking him to posthumously shrink my father. Dr. B., who runs his own neuropsychology center in addition to his graduate teaching position at John Jay College, had granted me a full hour, and I intended to use every minute.

He listened as I described my father—convicted murderer and fugitive, but charismatic, loving man—and my mother, the woman who willingly lived with a murderer and kept his secrets until the last moments of her life. He nodded, listening intently. As I spoke I noticed that he kept a pager clipped to the top of his shirt, which I later called him on. "I like having the option of calling people back," he explained.

I had come here on the recommendation of a mob reporter I knew named Jerry Capeci, who penned an online column called *Gang Land News*. "If you want to understand the criminal mind, this guy's the best," Jerry told me.

"It sounds to me like a large part of your father's personality would have to be antisocial," Dr. B. said when I finished. "Even if you don't picture him as sadistic or mean, part of his personality is psychopathic, permitting him to do things people wouldn't normally do."

Did he just say that my father was a psychopath? "Like, he compartmentalized what he did?" I ventured. "Compartmentalized" was the word my mother had trotted out to counter the perception that my father could be a monster. How else could he have coexisted as a loving father and a killer?

"For him to take this on as a job," Dr. B. said, "part of him had to rationalize it. And all these guys—like Sammy the Bull, for example—they use the rationale 'You gotta do what you gotta do,' or even 'Well, everyone's crooked on *some* level.'" I remembered that scene from *The Godfather* when Kay says to Michael, "Senators and presidents don't have men killed!" To which Michael responds, "Oh, who's being naïve, Kay?"

"Yeah, my mother always said that killing was part of my father's job," I said. "It was like she absorbed his rationale and adopted it as her own, like, 'It was unavoidable, so how can you question it?'"

"Part of what makes these guys so dangerous is that psychopathic aspect, that they can take life so easily," he said. "Usually these guys are beaten as a kid, their fathers are rough on them, that's not uncommon. Something early on compromised the sanity of his household. Maybe his father was addicted to something? Knocked him around?"

I tried to remember the little my father had shared about his early life: a domineering mother and a good-natured but slightly absent-minded father who gambled and drank too much until his wife put her foot down and seized control of the family finances. All I could recall was a story my father once told me about stealing his father's car while he was in the barbershop and later persuading him that he'd walked to his haircut appointment. His father smiled, nodded, and gobbled it up. I remembered Grandpa's hapless wheeze, his thicket of white hair. There may have been a few instances when he chased my father around the house with his belt, but it was my grandmother Helen who had the real control.

"As far as hitting him," I said, "I don't think my father was beaten or anything, other than a few spankings here and there. But I did talk to someone, his first wife's brother, who said that my grandfather's gambling addiction became so bad that he was running numbers to support his habit until his wife put a stop to it."

"Sure, sure," Dr. B. said. "The wins made him high, and the losing could make him angry, and it could have had everyone in the house walking on eggshells. If he was terrorized as a kid, he developed a psychopathic invulnerability. Which means he adopted a sense of bravado and became, like, a 'tough guy,' a stance which was reinforced by his social and cultural environment."

Like, maybe, a community in which men of power and perpetrators of crime were revered. "My mother told me a story about how my father was this nice, shy kid who always got teased for reading books during recess," I recounted, "until one day he'd had enough and brought a baseball bat to school and threatened to knock his bullies' teeth out." That image had always made me sad: my father, sitting under a tree, all innocent eyes and fine sandy hair, with his nose in a book, just like my mother at that age. Except instead of going to college—or even finishing high school—he veered violently off course. "Wasted talent," as my mother would say, quoting that line from *A Bronx Tale*.

"Any element of unpredictability can upset the household," Dr. B. explained, "and your father found a way of exerting power by using violence. He grew a thick skin and developed a desire to punish other people. You don't really just become a guy who does hits. It doesn't happen overnight, it's not magical. Your father then developed his own compulsive behaviors, like alcohol and drug addiction, as a way of identifying with his oppressor, in this case his father. People tend to identify with the behavior of their oppressors."

Was my grandfather really a monster? How bad was his gambling addiction? I reached into the far corners of my memory and pulled out a hazy anecdote, something about Grandpa Frank gambling all their money away, much to my grandmother's chagrin. My father laughed as he told it. He didn't seem angry about it; his chuckle didn't reveal any underlying pain about having an addict as a father and having to cower in the face of unforgiving mood swings. But then, maybe he was simply minimizing the impact of his father's weaknesses, the way my mother had with my father. Or maybe my grandmother was the true oppressor. I had no way of finding out—my father's siblings were dead.

"Maybe, if your father had been raised in a WASP family," Dr. B. continued, "he might have become a ruthless man of business. If he'd been weaker than he was, he might have just been a drug addict, mired in depression. But because of his temperament, he became this. Then he uses the 'It's just business' excuse as a way to funnel these negative experiences, and as a way to funnel the rage, the anger."

"It's interesting, what you say about rage," I said. "His first murder—well, the one he did time for—was supposed to be this simple hit on a guy who was informing on him to the cops. But he lured the guy into a secluded park with the promise of heroin, shot him five times, and stomped on his body. My mother always contended that his killings were 'just business,' but this sounds like a very angry act, don't you think?"

"Yes," Dr. B. agreed. "This crime tells you a lot about his level of rage. And once you let the genie out of the bottle, it's hard to put it back in. Once he succumbed to that rage, those impulses, it's very hard to rein them in again. I'm sure he calmed down afterward, though—maybe got high or drank, that probably helped—because he wasn't psychotic; he could control it."

Like when he'd fly into a rage after I'd somehow provoked him only to calm down and forgive me hours later, granting me permission to run free, ungrounded. "You know, that way of insulting the body," Dr. B. added, "like when your father stomped on his victim *after* he died—that's something serial killers do. They insult the body after death. Look, if it really was 'just a job,' as your mother would probably say in his defense, he would have shot the guy once in the back of the head. But he didn't. He shot the guy five times and stomped on him. I see a lot of anger there."

"And then he bought the afternoon edition of the *Daily News,* which featured the murder on the cover, and showed it to his mistress and said, 'Look, I did this.' Like he was proud or something."

"You see, that's the hallmark of the psychopath," Dr. B. said. There was that word again. "They have no conscience, no empathy. There's paranoia mixed in there, too, because their own lives are so unstable, and it becomes difficult for them to regulate their emotions after that."

"When he first started out he used to rob houses on his own block," I revealed.

"Well, sure," he said, "a lot of criminals start out robbing their neighbor's houses because they know when they're not home. Stuff like that is dyed-in-the-wool antisocial behavior. He had contempt for the weakness of his victims, so he exploited it. Did he ever abuse you or your mother?"

"No, he never laid a hand on my mother," I said. "Me, he got out the belt once or twice—well, maybe more than once or twice—but you know, that's typical old-school parenting. I did see his rage, though—he'd get so angry so fast but calm down later, just like you described. But my mother," I continued, even though I saw Dr. B.

opening his mouth to interject, "she always stood up to him. She was never scared of him, and this was a man she knew was capable of murder. She stood up to her own father in the same way. He was this dreadful alcoholic who would push her away when she wanted a hug and chip at her self-esteem by telling her she was stupid, but after a while she told him to shut up." Another tidbit I'd gleaned from Arline. "She was the only one of her sisters to do that. She was the only one who wasn't scared of him." I was so proud of her for that.

"Often these Italian guys put 'family' on a pedestal, even though they're capable of such violent acts," Dr. B. said. "Your father probably idolized his own mother, which was his way of overcompensating for treating others so badly."

"He definitely idolized his mama," I said, groaning slightly. "All Italians do. So then," I said, shifting gears, "he spends twelve years in prison, and that certainly didn't help him change his ways, I bet."

"I'm sure in prison he was surrounded by mob guys who shared his values," Dr. B. said. "But by twenty-six, your personality is solidified. You're already pretty much who you're gonna be."

"And what does it say about my mother, that she stayed married to a killer?" I asked.

"She met him in prison, right?" he asked. I nodded. "So she already knew the deal with him. She got off on it, the excitement." *There was an element of adventure in it, for all of us.* "Something in her background predisposed her to a man like this."

"Her father," I said.

"And she found in *your* father the penis she didn't have," he said. I laughed out loud. "No, really," he iterated. "This was her way of giving the world the ass-kicking she wanted to, but was too weak to do herself. She lived vicariously through him and his tendency toward violence. And in return she justified his antisocial behavior."

"Did she ever," I said. "When I came to her with my father's prison record, which I'd found on the Internet, her chief concern was not that her daughter had discovered the truth, but that my father had no privacy, that anyone with a modem could find out about him." I remembered that day in the car and, for the first time, felt how inappropriate her reaction had been. Time away from her had exposed how out of tune it was with civilized society.

"Oh, sure, some of the sex offenders I see are angry about the national sex offender registry," he replied. "And I feel for them, but, you know, I see the other side of it, too."

"So what would you say about a woman who keeps all of her homicidal husband's secrets and takes her infant child and goes on the lam at the age of forty-three?" I asked.

"The fact that he told her so much, that's rare," Dr. B. said.

"He never told his first wife as much as he told my mother," I said. "That was how he pulled her in—he made her feel needed."

"More than that," he said, "it's pathological." My blood curdled. "Look, she wasn't eighteen when she went on the run, she knew better. Most women, when they find out something like that, they leave, especially with an infant." *But I loved him*, she would say. *But it was different—it was your father.*

"Wait, I just want to back up a second," I said, my mind finally catching up to my pen, which was furiously taking all of this down. "Are you telling me that my father was a psychopath?"

"Yes," he said. "He had many of the characteristics of a psychopath: He displayed antisocial behavior, he acted without conscience or remorse"—*he had nightmares about it, you know*—"he was given to bouts of rage, poor impulse control—I bet he lied rather easily." *And that's how he got me. He steamed me up.*

"My mother told me this story about how she had to talk him down from killing someone," I said. "And this was when they were only dating. She had to actually dissuade him from doing it—they were on their way to the guy's house with a gun. And she didn't leave then, and that was before they had a kid together. But, you see, he was so charming, so charismatic—everyone in my mother's family immediately accepted him, and his charm practically erased everything bad he had done. Everyone always made excuses for him." His wives, his parents, his children—even me. *My father transcended his mistakes with a grace and elegance unmatched in the most moral of citizens*, I'd said at his memorial service. What a load of garbage.

"Antisocials are also very charming and seductive," he said. "Serial killers can wander into a bar and pick out their prey just by reading physical cues. They can identify which women will accept rides from them because they're good at reading people. And you hear people who knew these guys say, 'But he was so charming, so nice.'"

"Like Ted Bundy," I offered.

"Yeah. They have girlfriends, they're good-looking," he said. "But they can tell who will be receptive to them and who won't."

"So if my mother was absorbed in this pathological relationship," I said, trying it on for size, "and my father was a psychopath, what does that say about the child from this union?"

"You mean, how much did they mess you up?" he asked. I shrugged. "Well, if you'd been a son, maybe he would have been more aggressive toward you and showed you a more violent way of dealing with things. If he'd been coked up, then maybe you would have seen that side of him, but he compartmentalized, and made sure you never saw him that way. He hid a lot from you, which was good."

"I was the only one of his kids who didn't know what he had done, what he was capable of," I said. "He was still innocent in my eyes, and I think he liked that. Listen, Dr. B., on a scale of one to ten, just how damaged were they?"

"Your father, definitely a nine or ten," he said without hesitation. "Your mother, maybe a little less, like an eight."

"Really?" I asked. Hearing it from someone else was like a stranger describing a dream I'd had, one that I could barely remember upon waking. I could feel the details were true, but hearing them from the lips of an outsider was like having my mind read. It was also vindicating, in a way; a suspicion confirmed. Because, let's face it, I always knew.

"Your mother wasn't a killer," he conceded, "but she *was* an enabler."

"Some might even call her an accessory," I said.

"Yes, she was," he said. "Like I said, she enjoyed the excitement, probably."

"Her first husband, whom she was married to for twelve years before my father, was a homosexual," I said. "Then she met my father and, needless to say, he was very different."

"I would say your mother probably chose a husband who couldn't deeply engage her," he said. "Maybe she feared men. A lot of women do, because, you know, we can be scary. But after twelve years of rejection, she became pathologically involved with your father." I shuddered again at the suggestion that my parents' relationship had been sick. Even though I always felt that it might be, I'd never heard it characterized that way.

"Let me ask you something," I said. "Would she change her mind about him if she had seen the court transcripts and the newspaper clippings with her own eyes?"

"Probably not," Dr. B. said. "She made her decision not to question it a long time ago. She made a decision not to challenge it right at the beginning."

My mother was warped. She had been my best friend, I trusted her implicitly, but she was warped; her moral compass was fucked. And I grew up with her—she raised me! But I didn't think like her—*I* was here, *I* was questioning it, which she never did. And I didn't like what I had found, and I was not afraid to tell everyone close to me about it, or about how, though I loved them, I rejected this part of them. *I* was different.

"Would you be surprised if I told you I've had relationships with damaged men—addicts, rageaholics, closet homosexuals?" I asked him, supplying the basic facts of my ill-advised affairs.

"It doesn't surprise me," he said. "There's an uncanny ability for people with this vulnerability to attract damaged people."

"Like a homing device," I said. I learned long ago that there was something about me that attracted darkness, a quality exuded on such a subliminal level that I couldn't perceive it. Even for men who hid their darkness in shadowy corners, one conversation with me seemed to draw it out.

"Exactly, like a homing device," he said. "People subconsciously mimic their parents. It's instinctual, it's a vibe. It's a very primitive thing."

"Does it make sense that despite all this, there was a lot of love in my house?" I asked. "Is it possible that being on the lam fused us together, in a way?"

"When you have to lie to the outside world, when you have to conspire to keep a secret, the atmosphere inside the household can become like a cult," he said. "It's like a witness protection mentality."

"But I was never brainwashed like my mother was—like she allowed herself to be," I pointed out, cringing as I said it. "I like to believe my life is different than theirs. My mother was never without a man in her life, and here I'm single, and I've lived on my own for eight years. I don't act out or lose my temper with people, like my father did."

"You are not your mother or your father," he said. It was reassuring, but it also depressed me. Their way of life was truly over for me, and there was some sadness in that. "But you're also not immune to the choices that affected their lifestyle," he continued. "Your skepticism is indicative of your own temperament and intellect. Look, the life you live now—you have your master's degree, you work at *The New York Times,* you appear to have your life in order." I wanted to tell him how lousy I was with my finances, but I let it go. That one was easy—I'd learned by example, and I needed to grow up and craft a fucking budget. End of story.

"What does that mean for me?" I asked. "Obviously I have this pattern with men, which I am trying to break, but other than that . . . What I'm trying to ask is, did they fuck me for life here?"

He laughed. "Look, you can stop any behavior known to mankind. But, honestly, I would advise that you shouldn't ever really drink or do drugs, because you know where that led your father. I would also suggest that you have some therapy intermittently throughout your life, to recognize the patterns and stop them before they have a chance to take root."

I nodded, thanked Dr. B., let myself out of his office, and almost walked into a wall on my way to the waiting room. I hit the street, which was steamy with the humidity that signaled a coming storm. I was tired, drained, and changed. I had never realized just how much I had going against me until I sat down on Dr. B.'s black leather couch. I knew it was going to sink in on the train ride back to Manhattan, and I had a decision to make: cry now, or save it for when I got home.

My tears made the decision for me. I wiped away eyeliner-tinted sobs as I sat hunched over on the 4 train, listening to my iPod. It was her I couldn't stop thinking about, how she'd put herself in lockstep with a killer and stayed there, never questioning him or his crimes, even in the privacy of her own head. Just as easily as she'd told her father to "fuck off" as he terrorized and rejected her, so she effortlessly slipped into my father's orbit, and together the two of them taught me that love meant saving damaged men from their own self-destructive tendencies.

My father always existed on the margins of society, in a little lawless niche he had carved out for himself, but he was no Ted Bundy—he wasn't even Sammy the Bull. I knew him not to be someone who was indifferent to the pain of others, because I saw how the death of his parents had moved him, and how he'd shed tears when I ran and hid in the parking garage for four hours, or after my mother's heart attack. I'd seen him moved by the plight of others. Perhaps he started out indifferent, but he didn't stay that way. Maybe before he killed Joe Vitale he did "see people as obstacles to be eliminated," in the words of Robert Hare, a Canadian psychologist whose studies I researched online, but he didn't treat my mother that way, and he didn't treat me that way. At one time murder was an option for settling disputes, but over time his tempestuous reactions became muted. I remembered the way he was with me, and there was love there. We were attached to each other, even if we often had little to say to each other. The tears he shed the day I left home, the way he gave himself over to his sobs, that was real. I believe my father had a heart and a conscience when it came to his family.

But I couldn't deny the fact that at one time in his life, he treated outsiders with less regard, including sometimes his own children. They never understood the way he could disappear and reappear with little explanation, and he never shared his anguish with us over the decisions he made—or simply didn't make—regarding his older children. "I just don't understand," my mother would admit to me, baffled, when I brought it up, like the time I found Angie's letter. She didn't get it either, and when she mentioned it to my father—delicately, gingerly, so as not to piss him off—he would say, "Eleanor, mind your own fucking business. They are my blood, and you are not my blood." In fact, he'd use this refrain often whenever he deflected one of her arguments. "You are not my blood. My daughter is my blood"—here he'd gesture to me, dying of embarrassment over my plate of chicken wings—"but you aren't." It was very antiquated, this obsession with blood, this paranoia regarding outside interference.

"Jen, don't let the opinion of one expert negate the relationship you had with your parents," Ji Young said after I dialed her number with shaking fingers. "There was a lot of love there. I remember your dad! He was so sweet, and he loved you guys so much."

"Maybe he softened with age," I said, testing out this new theory. "He was older when you knew him."

"Maybe," she said. "But psychologists like to put people in categories, and people are way more complex than that."

"I know," I said wearily, "but what he said about my father—it's all true. Sure, there's more to the story, but he did kill people. He did manipulate my aunt into sleeping with him. He did foster a cultlike atmosphere, making my mother his only confidante and trying to hide everything from me and expecting I wouldn't tell. I know there was love there, but there was also this."

"But that's not the whole story," she insisted. "I don't want you to get upset and regret your whole childhood." She was right. Because that was exactly what I was doing. Like when I had come home from my appointment with Dr. B. ready to climb into bed and take a nap before work, but instead found myself surrounded by pictures of them—the happy couple—and of the three of us together: sick, sicker, and sickest. I couldn't escape the photographs, and they were everywhere: on my living room windowsill, the baker's rack, nailed to my walls. My Museum of Grief, which I'd proudly erected to mourn my lost love, had suddenly become confining. Maybe it was time to dismantle it. I certainly felt like smashing the framed photos as soon as I entered my humid apartment, where the air never moves, even when it's 20 degrees outside. Jesus, I carried pictures of them with me; it was her wedding ring I had chosen to wear around my neck, the symbol of their union. Their sick, "pathological" union, or so said Dr. B.

I finally truly understood how my twisted relationships were a direct outgrowth of my life with my parents. Of course, "Shut the fuck up, Eleanor" and "Oh, Johnny, go fuck yourself" were practically the theme music to my childhood, but it ran deeper than that. My household had been pervaded by sickness—no, conceived in it. I knew what they'd say to me as I cried openly on the 4 train that day, for once not caring who saw me: "What are you crying for? Our relationship is none of your goddamn business." But I recognized the limits of that argument, and I saw that I had surpassed them. And for the first time, I actually believed it.

CHAPTER 22

August 2007

. . .

THE SUN WAS HIGH IN THE SKY AS I SAILED DOWN THE SOUTHERN State Parkway. As I fiddled with the radio I floated back to that first summer at Cecilia Cassese's house and remembered how it felt to be perched between one life and another, with no clue how it would all turn out. From where I stood now, I was pleased with the results— excepting the obvious—but it made me more aware of the fact that at seventeen, when I was pinned by my own summer sweat to Celie's couch, I was just floating in the ether, directionless. That earlier version of myself very much interested me as I pulled onto Celie's street with tears in my eyes; that person was still a relic of her parents' world, a world I'd fooled myself into thinking I'd left behind. I might live in "the city," and I might have my master's degree, but that girl was still alive inside me, and it took returning to Lockwood Avenue to figure that out.

I cradled my shopping bag—which contained a bottle of red, a bottle of white, and rugelach for dessert—climbed up the darkened staircase that ran along the side of the house, and knocked on Celie's door.

"Come in," came her muffled reply. She'd been expecting me. I opened the door and within seconds Celie was in my arms, and we were both crying.

"Oh, Celie," I said.

"Jenny, Jenny, Jenny," she said, sniffling. I pulled away and beheld a plumper Celie with a pin-straight bob, a bit more Angie Dickinson than Ellen Barkin now. But her blue eyes still shone with the same openhearted tenderness. As she took my bag and walked over to the counter I studied her apartment, which was more homey than it had been thirteen years ago: Her TV rested in an oak entertainment center filled with wineglasses and champagne flutes; a white hand-painted sign that read NANA'S HOUSE hung over the small dining room table; she'd installed carpeting.

"Oh, my God," she said, examining my face. "You look so much like your father from here down," she said, tracing a line in the air from my nose to my chin, "and your mother from here up."

"A perfect hybrid," I said. "And, just like Dad, I have some grays," I said, pointing to the front of my head, where doll-like white strands had sprouted. I needed to get my roots done, badly. "Celie, I am so thankful you agreed to talk to me. I mean, this isn't something we're supposed to talk about. I'm surprised, actually."

"Oh, I don't mind, but like I said, I just hope I remember everything," she said as she made her way to the kitchen. "Listen, I have chicken and I have pasta because I wasn't sure which you'd prefer."

"Oh, pasta's fine," I said, even though I was far from hungry. "How is Carmine doing?"

"Oh, Jenny, he's doing okay," she said. "Like I said on the phone, it's so hard having this cloud hanging over my head. I just wish he'd be sentenced already."

"Is it true he's a made guy, Celie?" I'd rehearsed this line in my head many times, but saying it was easier than I'd expected.

"Jennifer, I couldn't even tell you," she said as she fiddled with the pilot light on the stove. "You know, I told Carmine, you wanna live this life, fine." She returned to her seat at the table. "But you have a child now. This is no life for a child." Tears sprang to her eyes.

"I can relate to that," I said.

"But your father, he was always a gentleman," she said, pausing after "always" for emphasis. "So respectful, so dapper."

"He really was," I said. It was true: To my father, everyone was "dear" or "sweetheart," even strangers, and not in a pervy way.

"I was on the stoop downstairs waiting for you before, and my brother-in-law came out and said, 'They stopped making men like her father.' Your father went away for something where he could have gotten off, all he had to do was talk, but instead he did over thirteen years!"

"They wanted him to talk, but he refused," I said.

"Of *course* he refused," she said passionately. "It never would have *occurred* to him." Her words wrapped around me like a blanket. I couldn't tell if it was her familiar accent or the syllables that could have just as easily come from my father's mouth, but Celie felt like home.

"And I hate to say it," she continued, "but I said to Carmine, 'You can't have two families. You've got to protect the one that you're in, this one'"—meaning the mob—"'or you have to protect your own family. You have a child.' It's a very hard decision. For him. Not for me. I think he's made the *wrong* decision," she said, and choked up again.

"Aw, god, Celie," I said. She was such a kindhearted woman, always. My heart leapt across the table toward her.

Celie cleared her throat. "I'm a little tired of it, so if I sound a little bitter . . ."

"No, I understand," I said. She began eating her salad, so I followed suit, picking at the fresh romaine.

"It's only because today, in this day and age, I don't even talk to anybody who's affiliated like that, or who's 'in the mob.' I can't even look at them."

I nodded. "What did you think about the fact that my mother, of all people, got mixed up with my father?" I asked.

"We were all shocked!" she said. "We used to laugh about it—your father, me, and my husband. She would laugh about it, too. I think she liked the . . . oh, what word am I looking for?"

"The excitement?" I ventured.

"The excitement," Celie said. "Trying to outsmart them. You know, like, us against them. In those days it wasn't so cutthroat."

"She told me how they met, too," I said.

Celie emitted a brief chuckle. "You see, I only met your dad when my husband went away."

"Sing Sing?"

"Sing Sing," she replied. "That's how Vinny and Johnny met. They were only together a few months there. I think your dad got in touch with my husband when he came home, and your father and my husband decided to sell pot together. And, of course, they weren't selling a pound, they were selling *tons*."

"Really?" I asked.

"Oh, they had *boats* coming in," she said with a knowing look.

"I'm glad it was pot and not, like, heroin," I said.

"Nope, it was pot," she said, toying with her penne. "They had someone in Miami that they knew and they used to make these arrangements for the pot to come in, and I can't tell you how many times the rudder on the boat was broken," she said, drawing a circle in the air with her finger, "or the boat was going around in circles, all that." I could just imagine these New York guys, never been camping in their lives, fancying themselves masters of the high seas, all in the name of marijuana. *The Good Ship Lollipot.*

"How long did they do that for?" I asked. "Couple years?"

"Oh, they had quite a run," she said. "They really did. They had a good run."

"Where did it come in?" I asked. "One of the piers in Chelsea or something?"

"No," she said through a mouthful of pasta. "It came in from Miami."

"Oh," I said, realizing that this was what my mother had described, the bales of marijuana floating in the Intracoastal.

"And then they would send cars to get it," she said. "They started out small at first, each shipment was, like, barrel-sized. Your mother had it in her closet."

"My mother?" I asked, laughing.

Celie nodded and started laughing. "In her apartment. They started having problems with the smell, and the people downstairs started to complain. So they had to move it."

"And my mother just went along with this?" I asked, still mildly surprised despite all I'd learned.

"Yeah. So they moved it to my place. And again, the odor," she said, rolling her eyes. I had to laugh. My father and mother running a "grassroots" marijuana operation? It was official: I was pot royalty. I'd never feel guilty about smoking the stuff again.

"When your father got arrested that time," she said, "my husband told your mother, 'You go to court tomorrow and go to the bail bondsman and you *cry*," she said. "You be an actress and you *cry*."

"She brought me in, I was in my stroller," I said.

"She did," Celie said. "And she got him out," we said in sync.

" 'Cause they shouldn't have," Celie said. "They got him out before the warrant fell. And that's when yous took off."

"It was a week later, right?"

"A couple days later," she corrected. "And your father went to North Carolina, and your mother had to fly back up here to get some extra money. I think I had to give her money and she was gonna give me this pot. I guess we were more involved than I ever remembered," she said with a shrug. "I had to meet your mother in Manhattan, and she called me, I think she was at the Ritz, and she'd ordered oysters Rockefeller . . ." Celie's laughter ate up the rest of her words.

"Typical," I said.

"That's what I thought! I said, 'You're *where*?'" Celie said.

"She always did have expensive taste," I said. "Hey, when we were living in Texas, my father was kind of straight, though, right? What was our name then? Was it Angelo? Because I found that name in the FBI record, and I was, like, what's Angelo? *Another* alias? I know we used your name." My father's FBI record, which I'd obtained through a Freedom of Information request—thanks, Bush administration!— also informed me that we had bounty hunters on our tail for years. And there was this nugget, from a report issued right as they were closing in on us: "Subject and wife have a child, JENNIFER NICOLE MAS-CIA, white female, approximately 3–4 years old. Subject is reportedly most attentive towards this child." As soon as I read that I began hyperventilating tears again—our closeness was so obvious that the Department of Justice couldn't help but notice it.

"I think that's when he started to use 'Frank Cassese,'" Celie said. "Frank after his father, along with our last name." We ate pasta and filled in the blanks for each other, since we knew different halves of the same history. She said she never saw my father use drugs, and hadn't pegged him for an addict, but she had heard that he occasion-ally used, thanks to her other son, who'd served on the same paint crew. She was also shocked that my mother didn't know Rita used drugs—"I knew Rita used," she said—and when we got to her affair with my father, Celie was adamant.

"Oh, Jenny, I *know* he loved your mother," Celie said apologeti-cally. "But when I heard about Rita, I was shocked. That's a horrible, horrible thing Rita did. And your dad was wrong for doing that, too. Very, very wrong. You don't come between sisters like that. And then, as a sister, you don't betray your sister."

It was like the voice of reason washing over me. Celie, who sprang from the same milieu as my father, was advocating for my mother, acknowledging her betrayal. I wish my mother could have heard her words. "But I always felt like Rita wanted what your mother had," she went on, "and your mother wanted what Rita had. She loved the way Rita dressed, she thought Rita was the most stylish, the funniest—she just loved Rita's whole life. She wanted to be her."

"She thought Rita was the pretty one, but my mother was so beautiful," I said.

"She was," Celie agreed, and I saw the sadness in the situation: My mother had chosen the wrong person to emulate. Her values were lopsided. My mother putting Rita on a pedestal was like Meryl Streep emulating Shannon Tweed.

"Listen, can I ask you about something?" I said, deciding to go full throttle.

"Sure," she said, clearing the table. "Go ahead, whatever you wanna ask."

"Right after that mini-stroke, my mother told me that before we went on the lam, when my father was in Florida dealing drugs, in the course of his work, you know, he, uh, he killed some guys," I said, dropping an octave. "People who had double-crossed him, or whatever. She told me that one of them was a hit ordered by some mob guys that was carried out in order to save Vinny's life."

"My *husband's* life?" she asked.

"Yeah. And she said the only person who knew about it was your son Carmine."

"I have no idea," she said, searching her memory. "I never heard that."

"Vinny didn't even know about it," I said.

"Then I wouldn't have heard about it," she said. "And I have no idea how Carmine would have—"

"She told me the name of the guy he killed," I revealed.

"Who was it?" she asked.

"It was Vinny's partner at the time, a guy named Tommy Palermo."

Her face was expressionless. "Tommy? I knew Tommy Palermo. But he was your dad's partner, too."

"Huh?"

"Tommy Palermo took money from a lot of people—" she started.

"My father killed him, Celie," I said again, and this time it seemed to penetrate. She'd been wiping the table down with a sponge but stopped and sat back down at the table.

"I identified the body," she said quietly, instinctively lowering her voice as she invoked the dead.

"The body was found?"

"After he was missing for about three months," she said.

"Where was he found?"

"In a car trunk, out by the airport," she said.

"In the trunk of a car? Was it JFK?" I asked, rapid-fire.

"Mmm-hm," she said, nodding solemnly.

"Lemme guess, we were living in Florida at the time," I said.

"I'm not sure where yous were," she said. "They needed some-body to identify his body, and I couldn't get ahold of his wife, and the cops were there, at Tommy's mother's house, she was an old lady. And his son was there, and he was only, like, sixteen or seventeen years old at the time, little Tommy, and they insisted on taking him to the morgue, so I said, 'Listen, let him stay, I'll go.' And they said, 'No, we need a family member,' so I said, 'Fine, let me go with him.' I didn't want to send the kid by himself. So that's how I got to be there to see the body."

"Where was he shot?"

"I don't know," she said.

"Did you see his face?" I asked. "Was there any blood on his face?"

"You know, I took a peek, but what he looked like was a dried-up prune, he was all black and dusty," she said. "If they didn't tell me it was Tommy, I never would have known. I just identified the clothes. The officer said, 'Don't even look at him.'"

My father's handiwork. Great. I'll take the check and a lifetime of therapy, please. "Who would Tommy have stolen from?" I asked. "Any made guys?"

"I don't remember who they were involved with at the time. I really don't. I'd be lying to you if I said I did."

"Of course, no, I believe you," I said.

"I can't say for sure, but I know he was supposed to go to—god, *Tommy*," she said, suppressing a giggle. "He'd just come home from prison. But when he was away he really lost his mind. He felt like everybody owed him something. He did a lot of time—he did time for other people, too. He and some guys ripped off, um, a savings and loan place? And they got away with it, but Tommy got picked up for it. And Tommy brokered a deal where he'd do less time if he gave it all back, and they wouldn't investigate anybody else. He had to do a certain length of time—eight years, I think—and a lot of other people walked away. But when Tommy came home, he felt like they all owed him. So he just went around and got money from everybody, and said he was gonna go over to Cuba, he had friends, he was gonna go over here and do this, he was gonna go do that—and meanwhile, he called up and said, 'Ha ha, I lost it all.'"

"Apparently one of the guys he stole from was a made guy," I said, "who thought Vinny had something to do with it, and Dad got wind that they were going to kill the both of them, and he drove up to New York and talked to the made guy and said, 'Vinny Cassese had *nothing* to do with this.'"

"He didn't," Celie interrupted, "because Tommy stole money from Vinny, too."

"Really?" I asked, and vaguely remembered my mother telling me something similar. "The made guy told my father that if he was so sure Vinny was innocent, then *he* could kill Tommy Palermo. So he did."

"I could see that, because Tommy would get into a car with your father in a minute," she said.

God, how many times in my father's life had he gone from friend to executioner in the space of a few minutes? "Are you surprised that Dad did that for Vinny?" I asked.

"No," she said immediately. "Because you know why? Tommy was wrong, what he did. But I don't know if Vinny ever knew."

"But Carmine found out," I said. "Maybe my father told him later, maybe after Vinny died."

"Maybe," she said. "Although I don't see your father saying anything."

"So Vinny was more affiliated with this Tommy Palermo guy at the time?" I asked, wondering why my father wasn't also implicated in this Vinny-Tommy-made-guy mess.

"At the time, yeah," Celie said. "Because when your father left prison, he left Vinny and Tommy there together."

"Oh, wow," I said. "Dad knew Tommy from prison?" This gang was growing by the minute. I could probably identify half the guys in that prison football team photo now.

"Yeah," she said. "Then Vinny left, but Tommy was still there."

"I wonder which family ordered the hit," I said.

"I have no idea," she said.

"It's an unsolved murder," I said. Was I supposed to call someone now? The Queens Cold Case Squad?

"Yeah," she said.

"Solved now," I said. "The perpetrator's dead, that's it. No one goes to jail."

"Nope."

"You know, when my father told my mother that he'd killed other people, she didn't tell *anyone,*" I said. "Her sisters didn't know. That's why she told me that night, I think—I think it was weighing on her, that she knew about this. Because she didn't grow up with this element, she didn't grow up in this life, it must have registered deep down somewhere that it was wrong, but she did whatever she could to protect her family. There was no way she would let him go back to jail. I think it weighed on her after a while."

"Yeah," Celie said. "It does. When you know something like that, it does."

"Did Vinny ever kill anyone, that you know of?" I asked.

"No," she said, "But I suspect. And that does weigh on my mind, too."

"Did you ever wonder who killed Tommy Palermo?"

"I always thought it was somebody that was connected," she said. "Because I knew he took money from them. I think they were people from Brooklyn."

"You rip off the wrong people . . ." I said.

"I don't think it was just the person he ripped off, either, I think it was the way he did it. You don't do it like that. I don't even think he was out of prison a year."

And my father killed him. This poor hapless jackass. "You know, when I found out Dad killed someone, I was shocked. But it's funny, I used to ask my mom if he ever raped anyone. To me, that was a worse crime. I didn't even consider the fact that he could have killed someone."

"Your father would never have raped anyone," she said quietly.

"I know. So when I found out he killed someone, it sounds crazy, but a part of me was relieved that it wasn't rape."

"If your father had to kill a rapist, how would you feel?" Celie asked me pointedly.

"Fine," I said. "*I'd* kill a rapist."

"Well, don't you see?" Celie said. "Your father felt that these people that he killed were just as bad as rapists. He didn't kill for joy, he didn't kill for money. Never. He killed to protect the people that . . . and I don't want to say 'family,' but in a way, it was their family on the outside. See, in their minds they were protecting a good guy from being taken away from his family because of something he did, and maybe this other person did also. But the other person didn't have enough balls to do what he was supposed to. I mean, how do you do that? How do you dare do that? So to them, it was like rape. And they never, never hurt anybody for money."

She told me this, but instead of feeling anger, I felt love—for Celie, for my father, for my parents. Where was my sense of moral outrage? He killed, but it was to protect his "family." Never for money, never for joy. Was there honor in murder? Whatever the answer, I had forgotten that these were my roots. I'd spent a year alternately hating and pitying and cursing and crying over my father, but when Celie spoke of his elegance and grace, I couldn't gather up the strength for even an imaginary rebuke. I just missed him, and my mother, no matter what they did or covered up. And no matter where I journeyed in my life, a part of me would always belong to this world, to our past, and I was relieved. I didn't really want to spend the rest of my life denying it.

"Mom said he was haunted by what he did," I told Celie. "He had nightmares. She said he had to work himself up to do it—which, I now understand, meant he probably had to get high. He didn't like it."

"Um, yeah, who *likes* to do something like that? Unless you're a psychopath. And he wasn't."

"Actually, I went to a forensic psychologist because I thought it would be useful to get an expert opinion," I said, "and he said that anyone who believes that murder is an option has psychopathic qualities."

"I guess you have to be a little psychopathic to be able to do something like that and then go on living," Celie conceded.

"And pretend to fit in among the rest of the world, among us," I said.

"But you have to remember that it was justified in their minds. They were protecting their people, their 'family.' Was it right? Of course not. But that was *their* life."

We sat in silence for a moment. I glanced out the window, where glimmers of pale twilight still clung to the sky. "You don't know how depressed I got to find out that your mom had passed," Celie finally said, rubbing her eyes.

"I'm so sorry," I said.

"No, it's okay," she said. "It's part of life, you know."

"We were very close," I said. "She was my best friend. I'm sorry she won't be able to see my kids."

"She'll see them," Celie said. "I truly believe that." I nodded politely. "Where are her ashes?" she asked me.

I recited the various locations of the various piles of ashes that had once been my parents. "It's very complicated with the thirds, but they're together now, on my mother's baker's rack, surrounded by framed photos of the three of us." I suddenly thought of something Jeff said when he'd come over for dinner the previous week: He'd paused at the blue-and-white ceramic pot of my parents' ashes on the baker's rack, gestured with one of his spindly arms, and said, "When are you gonna get rid of those?"

I'd looked at him, appalled. "Never. What do you mean, when am I going to get rid of those?"

"You're not going to spread them somewhere?" he asked.

"No!" I said. "I've spread enough of them. Those are the last of my parents. I can't part with them."

"Oh," he said, shrugging. "Okay."

"Am I *supposed* to get rid of them?" I'd asked.

Celie must have read my mind, because she leaned forward and looked into my eyes. "You know you have to move on," she said. I nodded. "It's hard," she continued. "It's still early. And you lost the two of them like that, and you were just the three of you, such a tight-knit group. It's gonna take time."

"Yeah," I said. "It will."

THE FOLLOWING AFTERNOON I ran in to work with enough adrenaline to power an army. I searched the *Times* database and found a brief item from August 15, 1980, about Thomas Palermo, gun dealer. "According to law enforcement sources," it read, "Mr. Palermo is the son of Thomas Palermo, Sr., a convicted jewel thief who was the victim of a 'gangland style' murder. The slain man's body was found in 1977 in the trunk of a car at Kennedy International Airport."

I sat back in my chair. Now it was real. I jumped up and ran over to Willie Rashbaum and asked him to call up a spreadsheet he kept of unsolved Mafia hits from the seventies and eighties. Thomas J. Palermo popped up immediately; his body was found March 23, 1977, and while there was no perpetrator listed, it was credited to the Genovese family. "Yep. That's him," I said. Willie also dug up an article from the *Daily News* archive, MURDER VICTIM LINKED TO $4M ROBBERY IN QUEENS, which shed some light on the rather significant haul Celie had mentioned: "Palermo was one of several robbers who escaped with the jewels from the Provident Loan Society in Queens on February 17, 1969."

> Police said that Palermo, whose hands and feet were bound with wire, had been shot several times in the head. . . . Identification was made through papers found in the clothing of the victim. The discovery was made by an Avis Rent-A-Car employee, who checked out the car after it had been abandoned in the parking lot Jan. 17. It is believed Palermo was killed on or about that date.

January 17 was mere weeks after my parents moved to Florida, and just before I was conceived. I tried to imagine my father binding someone's appendages with wire, but decided against it.

"This may make a difference, it may not," Willie said when he approached my desk a little while later and handed me a memorandum from the Queens district attorney's office. It trumpeted a tip from an informant who claimed that Palermo was killed by someone named John W. Quinn in retaliation for another murder. "But I know my father did it," I called to Willie as he started back toward his desk.

Did someone else get killed for murdering Tommy Palermo, when my father was the real perpetrator? Or did my father have nothing to do with it—did my mother make it all up? "Is it possible that this informant was trying to shorten his sentence by offering a bogus tip?" I asked. Willie shrugged.

I ran back to my desk and filled out a FOIA request for the homicide file of Thomas Palermo, but even as I skimmed over the familiar fields—address, phone number, subject, purpose—exhaustion washed over me. If I opened this door, it could open several others, and several others after that. How far did I really want to take this? Didn't I already know plenty? For the first time I felt I'd learned enough about my father's criminal life. Unless he was responsible for the Lufthansa heist or some other sensational caper, what more did I really need to know?

Before he left that night, Willie handed me another *Daily News* clip from 1980. It was a column by the late newspaper great Jack Anderson entitled ANOTHER OUTBREAK OF .22-CALIBER FEVER IN MAFIALAND? It went on to describe a "series of nearly 30 mob-style executions across the country." He singled out four in particular, all slain on contract for the Genovese family and all performed with the same gun, according to "a secret ATF analysis of the killings in the New York and New Jersey area." Thomas Palermo was one of them.

"Maybe it wasn't your father's gun?" Jeff offered when I called him in a panic. "Other people could have used that gun."

"Like if he sold it?" I said. "Or maybe whichever family he performed the rubout for, maybe they gave him the gun and he gave it back right after."

"Maybe if they are kept by trusted people they can be passed on?" Jeff theorized. I didn't have a better answer. I didn't know how any of this stuff worked.

"But killing informants was his M.O.," I argued. "It's why he went to jail in 'sixty-three." I shuddered—could Jack Anderson have been describing my father? "Either way, it gives a face to the murders my mother only told me about."

"Jen, you can't dwell on the past; it was what it was," he said. "And you can't ever fully understand what he was."

I spent the rest of my shift sulking, though an email from my mob reporter friend Jerry Capeci lightened me somewhat. "To paraphrase one federal judge who has sentenced a lot of wiseguys," he wrote, "there's good and bad in every man, and once in a while, his offspring is proof positive." I smiled at my computer.

The next morning Jerry wrote again: "I would assume that Palermo was really killed by your old man, not John Quinn. Quinn was killed because he was a car thief who they thought might go bad."

So it was official. Now I could stop.

I never did figure out who ordered the hit on Tommy Palermo, and I never wrote Carmine Cassese in jail to ask him what he knew about it. Sometimes I fantasize that my father's deadly deeds were only in my head, and my mother's confession was merely a dream from which I'll wake. In a way, it was—it didn't seem I was going to crack any cold cases. But one look at his record, still available on the Department of Corrections website, disabuses me of that notion. He had committed murders, even if I didn't know every single detail about them. Maybe some things are best left in the dark.

CHAPTER 23

December 31, 2007

. . .

IF I WAS GOING TO BE STUCK AT WORK ON NEW YEAR'S EVE I decided I was going to make full use of my location. A few days before the ball drop I began scouting possible routes to the forbidden fifty-second-floor rooftop of the six-month-old Times building, construction of which was not yet completed. A security guard had been nice enough to take me up there two days before, and after a jerky trip on the freight elevator I found spread before me a knee-knocking 360-degree panorama of New Jersey, Queens, the Statue of Liberty, and the George Washington Bridge. "You won't be able to see the ball from here, you know," the guard informed me. "Maybe from the old building, but the Reuters building is just too high." The Reuters building was relatively new and rose behind the spot where the ball traditionally dropped—starting exactly one hundred years ago, in fact. But from Fifty-two I couldn't even tell what I was looking at, so I had no choice but to nod and thank him for the tour.

But as darkness fell on the thirty-first I decided I was going up there anyway, and I was taking Jeff with me. We'd just spent Christmas together at his parents' house in Staten Island and I wanted to return the favor on this, his final New Year's Eve as a New Yorker. To my surprise I discovered that after thirty-five years of living here, he'd never once been in Times Square on December 31.

"I have a plan," I said. "I think I can access the roofbound elevators undetected from the twenty-eighth floor. But, you know, it's iffy, so I can't promise anything. Just be here by eleven."

Jeff showed up with a bottle of cava, lemon hummus, garlic parmesan pita crisps, and two bunches of fat red grapes. "You're supposed to eat twelve grapes," he instructed, "and make twelve wishes."

"What? Why?"

"It's a Cuban thing," he explained. "You make a prayer for each grape." I stuck one in my mouth. It had seeds. "Eat!" he said. "More! All of them!"

I laughed and prayed he knew the Heimlich in case a grape lodged itself in my throat. In exactly two months and seven days, Jeff would be waving goodbye to me from the doorway of his parents' house in Staten Island. This man, who had been a boy when we met, was the closest thing I had to a brother. My first friend in New York, he'd known me at eighteen, when I thought I knew everything but had seen nothing. He'd known my parents, played Tucker Carlson to my mother's James Carville more than once, and most important, he'd been consigned with me to suburban hell in Staten Island, the forgotten borough, where the biggest attractions were a halfway decent mall and a garbage dump. On that night in March I'd also be saying goodbye to that place, as my only reason for returning would be flying off to London. I'd whip down Hylan Boulevard one final time and pass the turnoff to Staten Island University Hospital, reminding me of a week I'd like to put away forever. Then I'd hit the Verrazano and roll back the sunroof and turn up the radio and raise my hands into the wind and yell, "Goodbye, shithole!"—forever free of the place that had taken my parents.

One by one I ate my dozen grapes and remembered all those nights I'd begged Jeff to drive me into "the city," walking the Village and eating at the Around the Clock diner, finally returning home at dawn. My mother would rage because I had class that morning and she feared I was putting my education on the back burner. But Jeff *was* my education: He'd brought me out of my claustrophobic world each night and introduced me to Manhattan, a place I would go on to call my home. I might still live on Staten Island if it hadn't been for him. He told me years later that I saved his life by forcing him to drive over the Verrazano and down the BQE and across the Brooklyn Bridge every night—the 3:00 A.M. ride home took us twelve minutes without traffic, we timed it—but the truth is that we saved each other. Now he had to follow his love across the Atlantic to a more progressive place than even New York, where two men who love each other can marry. And our lives would progress separately, joined only by phone calls and occasional transatlantic jumps, and, barring a legislative miracle, we'd never live on the same trajectory again.

"When you say you have no family," he'd tell me by phone from Newark Airport ten minutes before he boarded his plane, "just remember that I'm your brother."

But he hadn't left for England yet, and here he was, standing beside me in the newsroom of the Paper of Record, demanding I fill my mouth with grapes.

"Did you make your wishes?" he asked.

I nodded, but I was fibbing. I didn't believe in wishes.

At twenty minutes to midnight, I gathered a motley crew of copy editors, page designers, web producers, and a stray news assistant, and we blazed a trail to the fifty-second floor. We could barely see where we were at first, as the lighting wasn't yet installed, and the octagons that made up the floor were jagged, and stray bits lay scattered among the concrete. I followed the lights of Times Square, situated far below us. It was a hazy night but luckily it was just above freezing. I led the group to the northeast corner of the building and got as close to the railing as I could without throwing up.

"Where's the ball?" asked a voice behind me.

"We can't see it from here," I reported again; it was the same lecture I'd given in the elevator.

"Then what's that?" Jeff asked, gesturing toward a hot pink dot in the distance below us. After a moment the dot turned blue, then blinding white. The ball was right in front of us.

"Oh, my god!" I yelled. "I can't believe it! It's right there!" We had the best view in the city, and better yet, we didn't have to contend with the drunks. At 11:59:50, the ball began to drop, and the crowd began to roar. Even from the fifty-second floor, and with all the wind that howled between us and the street, we could hear wave after wave of voices counting down. It was exciting and also reassuring. It sounded like life, messy and loud.

JEFF AND I WAITED until 2:00 A.M. to venture into Times Square, knowing full well what awaited us when we got there. "Just think," he said as we walked north on Broadway, "how different our lives were ten years ago."

I didn't even have to think. I knew exactly where I was ten years ago: standing on the seventh-floor balcony of the apartment on New Lane and gazing upon lower Manhattan, glittering and intact. "You weren't out of the closet," I said, reminding him, "It'll be ten years in March."

"You didn't work at the *Times,*" he said.

"I didn't work at all then, did I?" I asked.

"Nope," he said. "And I was at Starbucks. God, if I'd stayed I'd probably be corporate vice president by now."

"But you'd be in Seattle," I pointed out, "and you wouldn't have met Paul."

"True," he said. "And our friendship wouldn't have survived."

"Probably not," I said. "Ten years ago I had parents."

"Just think how proud they would be to see where you are now," he said. It was a sentiment that often inserted itself into our conversations. What would they think of my life now? I wasn't inching along on training wheels anymore; this was it. No more practice—for better or worse, my life now was pretty much what it would be.

"If it was ten years ago," I said as we deftly dodged drunken tourists and multicolored clumps of confetti on Forty-seventh Street, "we'd be driving back to Staten Island."

"Yep," he said. It had been my dream to live in Manhattan. I thought of the list of goals I'd made at Celie's house that summer. I had achieved them, but I hadn't been able to take my parents with me.

By 2:30 we'd reached Central Park South with the intention of catching a cab. Rather, Jeff held out hope for a cab; I knew better. "Don't you know New Year's Eve is notorious for its unavailability of cabs?" I asked him as couples stumbled around us. "Fuck you!" a girl slumped on the sidewalk yelled at someone sitting in a car on Fifty-ninth Street. Her friend knelt down to tend to her as I turned to Jeff and smiled. "Remember the end of *When Harry Met Sally?*" I asked. "When Harry wants to get to the ball in time to see Sally but there are no cabs, so he has to sprint there?"

He shook his head and shot me a goofy smile. "I don't remember that part," he said.

"No?" I asked incredulously. It was one of my favorite films. "Well, this is it. I'm headed that way," I said, pointing east.

"Safe home," he said as he started up Central Park West. After a few seconds he called out, "Text me when you get home!"

"Will do!" I called back, but I wasn't going home. I had an appointment with the water on this, the last and first night of the year, and after a half hour of brisk walking I was back at Carl Schurz Park. I realized that only a crazy person would venture into a desolate park to sit beside black water topped by thin sheets of fish-flavored ice. But I'd come here—to the little pier on Eighty-first Street where I felt most at peace—to tell my mother and father what I'd wanted to tell them in all the dreams I'd been dreaming since they left me.

"I've heard you guys. I know you're here."

I traced the waterfront with my footfalls and thought about the last several months. Behind each answer, another question had lain in wait. Even if the two of them had been standing before me right then I don't know that I'd have gotten a straight answer. I certainly learned which mistakes of theirs I cared not to repeat. I want my children to know their witty, intelligent, flawed grandparents, even if it's second-hand. But I also want them to know stability. I don't want to keep anyone's secrets. I don't want to nurse anyone's hangovers. I don't want to go bankrupt. I don't want my children's father to be arrested in front of them. I can't promise a perfect childhood for my children, but I can shoot for sanity, sobriety, and calm.

But as my hair whipped in the wind, I couldn't help but wonder if marriage and children would ever happen for me. I thought about my apartment and its single bedroom, and my nocturnal existence, and I wondered how long I could keep it up. I'd been living my life in my own bubble, parallel to everyone else, and I'd been doing it while most of the world was asleep. I preferred it to the alternative—fading into the grind with eight million others—but after all these years I can hear my mother's voice, etched on my brain: "Jenny, why do you insist on living like a vampire?"

While I may not rise at dawn, I have come to terms with the fact that the life I'm living is happier than hers was—than both of theirs. I am independent and relatively stable, and for that I can't help but feel proud. But living on my own terms has its price: Every broken relationship is a reminder that I have that much further to go to be part of a family again. But I don't want to sacrifice my identity for a man, either. My mother was my father's emotional accomplice, if not his actual accomplice. Johnny provided her sense of self, in the same way that David had. She had followed David into teaching, even helped him build a school in which she never taught. No wonder she made such a smooth transition from college graduate to humanitarian to married man's mistress to gun moll—she merged with these men. They gave her direction. And once she changed direction, she never looked back, especially after becoming the wife of a fugitive. Her time on the lam taught her to devalue the past, and never to leave her heart in 1978, or 1981, because accountability might be lurking there, hidden in the folds of time. But she must have sensed my appreciation for the past, my need to hold on to what had been,

My parents, May 1986.

because she told me everything—the good, the bad, and the gory. Thank god for my mother's big mouth.

Would they have sat me down, maybe one day when their hair was white, and explained it all? Would they have answered my questions? Would the passage of time have neutralized the gory details, producing a confession that we would sift through and learn from, cry over and eventually accept? I'd like to think so. Because that would have meant they were finally at peace with all this. My father ran from his crimes, physically and mentally; my mother ultimately confessed, but it didn't come from a place of peace. And even her confessions were seasoned with mendacity: My father did *not* turn his life around for us, not completely. After his parole hearing, he carried on in California as he had in Florida and New York. But I know why she lied to me about this thing, this most important thing: She didn't want me to hate him. She was so concerned I would grow up and learn the truth and develop a hard heart toward my dad, like she had toward hers, when Sam Sacks disappointed his family by morphing into a vicious drunk. She used to envy my relationship with my father, but in a good-natured way, genuinely happy that I had a dad who loved me to bits. So she lied to me, and tried to defuse my natural curiosity about him and his crimes, and prayed I would forget the times I'd visited him in jail because she wanted me to keep him in my heart, perhaps because she sensed very few people in his life kept him in theirs.

And this is where I get a little angry. She should have trusted me a little bit more, a little bit sooner, and never should have told me that lie—that he changed his life for us—or the half-truths about his prison sentence, which I was forced go outside the family to correct. I know she omitted the whole truth to protect me, but protection, if never corrected, looks a lot like a lie. If she had been honest with me, she would have appreciated what I am feeling right now, after I've dug up nearly every secret they tried to bury: I could never hate my father. Each time I read his testimony, or whenever I imagine him isolated in the Tombs, painstakingly crafting writs of *coram nobis,* I love him even more. Whenever I imagine him nourishing his weaknesses with cocaine or scotch or extramarital affairs, my heart swells and I want to run into his arms—not yell and judge and slam a door. When I imagine him at his lowest is when I feel for him the most. I know he killed people, yes, but that doesn't stop me from wishing I could meet him in the kitchen for our traditional 2:00 A.M. bowl of Frosted Flakes. If my mother had trusted me from the beginning with the whole truth, she would have been pleasantly surprised to learn that I am capable of loving my father while also understanding that he was capable of bad things.

But she also lied because she was ashamed. Loving a reformed criminal provided enough cover for her to be accepted, even admired for her courage. But remaining married to a man she knew had killed after he was supposedly rehabilitated was just too much to ask anyone to swallow. One hasty mistake carried out in the ferocity of youth in a dark park at the foot of the Belt Parkway could be forgiven, but five more? Six? She knew her sisters, even her loyal ex-husband and her handful of lifelong friends, would be horrified, just as I was. I remembered those years after my father died, how it seemed that my belief in her was the only thing keeping her afloat, and I realized it had been. She didn't want me to stop believing in her. Even though she shielded him, somewhere deep down she knew it was wrong.

I sat on the steps of the grand staircase at Eighty-first Street and remembered how, after my father died, I'd perform arias to an audience of rippling currents, my voice soaked with grief. I was glad not to be back in that place, so lost after the horror of that first death. It was my mother who pulled me through, patiently letting me cry all night and question the justice of such a tragedy. I smiled bitterly at the thought. There are people who might think his death was just, and while I cried, "Horror! Tragedy!" my one confidante knew it, too. She was the person I loved the most and she lied to me. I suppose she cut me the deepest of anyone I've known, and yet, when I call up her betrayal, I feel nothing. And then I think: What was she *supposed* to tell a child? Bedtime stories starring kilos of cocaine and a .22? How could she have explained that the monster who lived in my closet was the very one who let me dip a finger in his scotch?

A jogger whizzed past me down the steps. I stood up and leaned over the railing of the pier and closed my eyes, then opened them, fixating on the two or three visible stars over the Triborough. I briefly considered staying a few more hours so I could watch the sunrise, but decided that my vampire days needed to end sometime. I remembered calling my parents from a cab as I passed this very park in 2001 to wish them a happy New Year, my father's last. I'd made sure to call precisely at midnight, and when they both picked up an extension I cried because I knew we should have all been together. I wished for that moment again, wished for it on the Fifty-ninth Street Bridge, knowing that any wish I make for them now will never be made with my whole heart because the odds are permanently stacked against its ever coming true.

I reached into my bag and my fingers skimmed the Ziploc bag of Polaroids I kept with me. But I hadn't come here to look at pictures. Before I left for work that afternoon I'd slipped the jar holding what was left of my parents ashes into my bag, praying all night that the top wouldn't come off.

And it hadn't. I pulled it out and studied the pattern on the ceramic. "Crabtree & Evelyn, London" was printed underneath. For so long this jar had stayed in my mother's linen closet. She didn't put my father's ashes on top of her baker's rack like a trophy, so why should I? Letting them go wasn't tantamount to losing them. I had them, forever: in my mother's breathless laugh, now mine; in my father's silver hair, now sprouting virally along my scalp. My parents were my first memory—standing in my crib, I had watched as their slumbering figures rose and fell with each breath under their blue velour blanket. They could never be erased from my heart. I thought of all the places we'd lived, the life spent in each apartment, each house, the echoes that had bounced off the walls, now forever silenced. All that couldn't be lost—how could it? I didn't need their ashes now—I could carry our history with me. I studied my hands, which resembled my mother's more every day, and understood that I was a part of them. I had been made from their flesh—*I* could be their memorial.

I had to let them go.

"I'll never forget you," I whispered to the river as I reached back and threw the whole jar into the black carpet of water. I did it this way so the wind couldn't blow whatever remained of my parents onto someone's windshield as they drove along the FDR below—a new kind of New York nightmare. It hurt, sure, but only for a second. I hadn't lost them—I was releasing them. The tears ran silently down my face, and I didn't try to stop them. I thought of what my father told me and my mother when he was diagnosed: "I'm not scared of dying. I just want to see my parents again." If I knew that my parents were awaiting me when this life was through, maybe I wouldn't be so scared of death.

It's funny—I thought I'd be much angrier at Johnny and Eleanor: for their crimes, for their denials, for the veneer of deceit they'd laid over my life. When I talk about it with the people closest to me now, they each have a different take. Ji Young still thinks my parents were the coolest pair to come down the pike, and still thinks my father is hot, no matter what he did. Jeff believes that my father had to feed his family one way or another, and even if his income had a body count attached he should be lauded as a working-class hero. Sarah shakes her head and wonders how I don't have a needle sticking out of my arm.

But if you ask me, the biggest tragedy here is not that my father killed people, or that he had an affair with my aunt, or that my mother shed her career, family, and friends to try to save an ex-convict with a dark past that always beckoned him back. For me, the most tragic part of this complex tale is that they died. No arrest record or eyewitness or unearthed letter or dusty, yellowing court transcript can change this for me. Because I know why they did what they did, at least as far as I was concerned. Impulsive and misguided as it may seem to the logical mind, my mother risked everything for love. Maybe it was sick, maybe it was pathological, but it was a love that only the two of them could understand. She loved my father in such a passionate, abiding way that she lost herself in it. And he clung to her, suspended perilously between violence and peace. Out of this union, I was created—their hope for a normal life, their one shot at absolution for my father's ugly sins, for harboring secrets that woke them in the night. Though they yelled and cursed each other, and though their love ebbed and flowed dramatically through the years, they had the real thing, the kind of love we all wish we could find: inconvenient, risky, unconditional. It cut through all the adultery, the bankruptcies and the addictions, all the crap that doesn't really change what people mean to each other. And my love for them is precisely the same: It never wavers. And if we could choose our parents, I still would have chosen them. They were a lot of work, but shit, what a ride.

I started the lonely walk back to my apartment, and the blustery air hitting my face reminded me that I was still crying. I wiped my tears on my sleeve and reminded myself that I should be grateful for my mother's lies—they'd enabled me to have a blissfully ignorant childhood. I laughed out loud as I considered the parallel lives we'd been living under the same roof: I had Play-Doh, my father had cocaine, and my mother had a shopping addiction, and a secret. Maybe the illusion of a placid childhood was my mother's final, enduring gift. It was a generous one, considering the turbulent childhood she'd had, infused with sorrow and disappointment. Could I blame her, then, that she fought like hell to keep her husband and child together, even if he was a killer? Even if he was a drug addict? Even if he told her to shut up and yelled and screamed and cheated? I had a childhood filled with love, so now I can give my children the same thing. Maybe that can be my final gift to her.

Standing on East End Avenue and facing a future yet to be written, I finally understood what she must have felt all those years ago when my father gave her a choice to be a family or watch him leave. For Eleanor, there was no choice to be made: She packed up her house and infant child under cover of night and seized the opportunity to begin again. She never looked back and she never apologized for her choice, because more than anything in this world she wanted a family—a real one that sat down to dinner together and explored and traveled together and showed each other real love. She thought she deserved a second chance, and I know exactly how she felt.

I'm ready for mine.

ACKNOWLEDGMENTS

Nancy Sharkey—without you, there would simply be no book. (Thanks also to Joe.)

Dan Jones, a truly great editor, for pulling this story out of me for the column.

Trip Gabriel, for taking a chance with such unconventional subject matter.

Alice Martell, for your constant nurturing and support, and for taking on a news clerk who'd never written a book before.

Joe Siano, for the perfect title.

William Rashbaum, for offering himself as an invaluable resource.

James Imperatrice.

Mark Johnson and Carole Weaver at the New York State Division of Parole.

Joseph Green and Michael Zeppieri at the Department of Justice Bureau of Alcohol, Tobacco, Firearms and Explosives.

Carolyn Wilder, for all those Accurint searches.

Jill Abramson, because I don't actually expect to be the first woman executive editor of *The New York Times*.

Alexis Rehrmann, Margaux Laskey, and Steven McElroy, for juggling my schedule so I could fly to one interview after another.

Jennifer 8. Lee, for being so generous with your time, and for your invaluable guidance.

Peter Khoury, Karin Roberts, and Denise Fuhs, for pretending not to notice as I wrote my book every night on company time.

Jackson McPeters and Bill Gorman at the New York State Archives.

Roja Heydarpour and Magdalena Sharpe, for being among my first readers.

Christine Kelly.

Angela Rimi, for returning to some dark places and divulging so much.

Tina Haines, the family historian, for prizing the past as much as I do.

Donald Halsband, for your frankness and humor.

Rita Stier.

Barry Addison, "Mr. B," for accurately remembering my mother as a "hottie."

Arthur Johnson, Mark Gruss, Benita Kaimowitz, Gabe Kaimowitz, and Willa Williams—if only you all knew how much you meant to my mother. I was so glad to have found you all again.

Robert Gangi.

Jerry Capeci, my erstwhile partner in crime, and www.ganglandnews.com.

Dr. N. G. Berrill, for telling me what I needed to hear, even though it hurt.

David M. Hardy at the Department of Justice.

Doree Shafrir.

Lynn Buckley, for your dedication, and your truly unique cover design.

Emily DeHuff and Beth Pearson, for their thoughtful and thorough copyediting.

Stephanie Smith, for shrewdly advising me to write down everything that happened that week in the hospital.

Dr. Diane Meier, for being our angel in the night all those years ago.

Natalie Aitkens Auger, for reminding me that my life didn't peak in high school.

Erin and Nash Padula.

Carol Levithan, for always listening.

Jack Levithan, for sharing his grief and wisdom.

Grace Cassese.

Angela Macropoulos, for being among the first to believe in me, even when she barely knew me.

Arline Russo, for loving my mother as much as I do, and mourning her as intensely as I do.

Monika Hryszkiewicz, for waking me up from my grief-induced stupor and forcing me to clean my apartment.

Bruce Tracy, for setting this project in motion.

Jill Schwartzman and Lea Beresford, for your invaluable editing skills. We did it!

Raymond T. Colleran, my Lester Bangs. For your inexhaustible patience, you have my eternal gratitude.

Ji Young Park, for seeing the potential of this story very early on, and for your continued support throughout this process.

Jeffrey Matthew Mulligan, the brother I never had and always wanted.

Sarah Levithan, for filling the gaps in my memory, and for being the first to suggest that this should be a book. And for reading and advising and reading some more.

Bruce Springboard, a.k.a. John Angelo, a.k.a. Frank Cassese, a.k.a. Nicholas Angelo, a.k.a. John Mascia, for giving me the freedom to be my own person. You always knew just what to say when I was down and you will always have my respect. I miss you terribly.

And Eleanor Teodora Sacks Margulis Mascia, who told me so much more than a mother should ever tell a daughter. Whenever you thought I wasn't paying attention, I was, and I remembered everything. I have never had a friend like you, nor will I ever again. You are my heart; you are the best. *No wasted talent, Ma.*

Some names have been changed to protect the good, the not so good, and those who may run for public office.

To all those contained within these pages: I tried to recollect these episodes as accurately as I could. If my recollection differs from yours, it was not intentional. Sometimes impression weighs more than fact. I tried my best.

ABOUT THE AUTHOR

Born in Miami in 1977 to Brooklyn-reared parents, JENNIFER MASCIA was raised in Southern California and New York City. She graduated from CUNY Hunter College in 2001, and in 2007 received an M.S. from Columbia University's Graduate School of Journalism. She has spent the past three years as the nightside news assistant on the Metro desk of *The New York Times*. She lives in Manhattan.

ABOUT THE TYPE

This book was set in Monotype Dante, a typeface designed by Giovanni Mardersteig (1892–1977). Conceived as a private type for the Officina Bodoni in Verona, Italy, Dante was originally cut only for hand composition by Charles Malin, the famous Parisian punch cutter, between 1946 and 1952. Its first use was in an edition of Boccaccio's *Trattatello in laude di Dante* that appeared in 1954. The Monotype Corporation's version of Dante followed in 1957. Though modeled on the Aldine type used for Pietro Cardinal Bembo's treatise *De Aetna* in 1495, Dante is a thoroughly modern interpretation of that venerable face.